A DYNASTY OF WESTERN OUTLAWS

To

BLISS ISELY

with gratitude for his unfailing friendship toward me
throughout all these years

A DYNASTY OF WESTERN OUTLAWS

PAUL I. WELLMAN

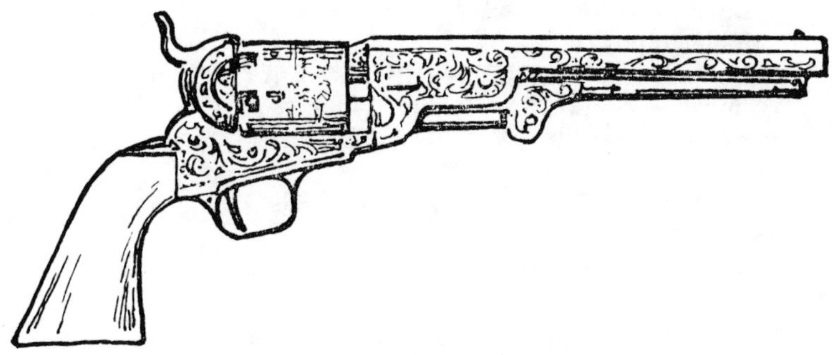

Foreword by Richard Maxwell Brown

University of Nebraska Press
Lincoln and London

Manufactured in the United States of America

First Bison Book printing: 1986
Most recent printing indicated by the first digit below:
5 6 7 8 9 10

Library of Congress Cataloging-in-Publication Data
Wellman, Paul Iselin, 1898–1966.
A dynasty of western outlaws.
Reprint. Originally published: Garden City, N.Y.: Doubleday, 1961.
Bibliography: p.
1. Outlaws—West (U.S.)—History. 2. Crime and criminals—West (U.S.)—History—19th century. 3. Frontier and pioneer life—West (U.S.) 4. West (U.S.)—History. I. Title.
F591.W415 1986 978'.02 85-28899
ISBN 0-8032-4736-2
ISBN 0-8032-9709-2 (pbk.)

Reprinted by arrangement with Paul I. Wellman, Jr.
Originally published in 1961 by Doubleday & Company, Inc.

CONTENTS

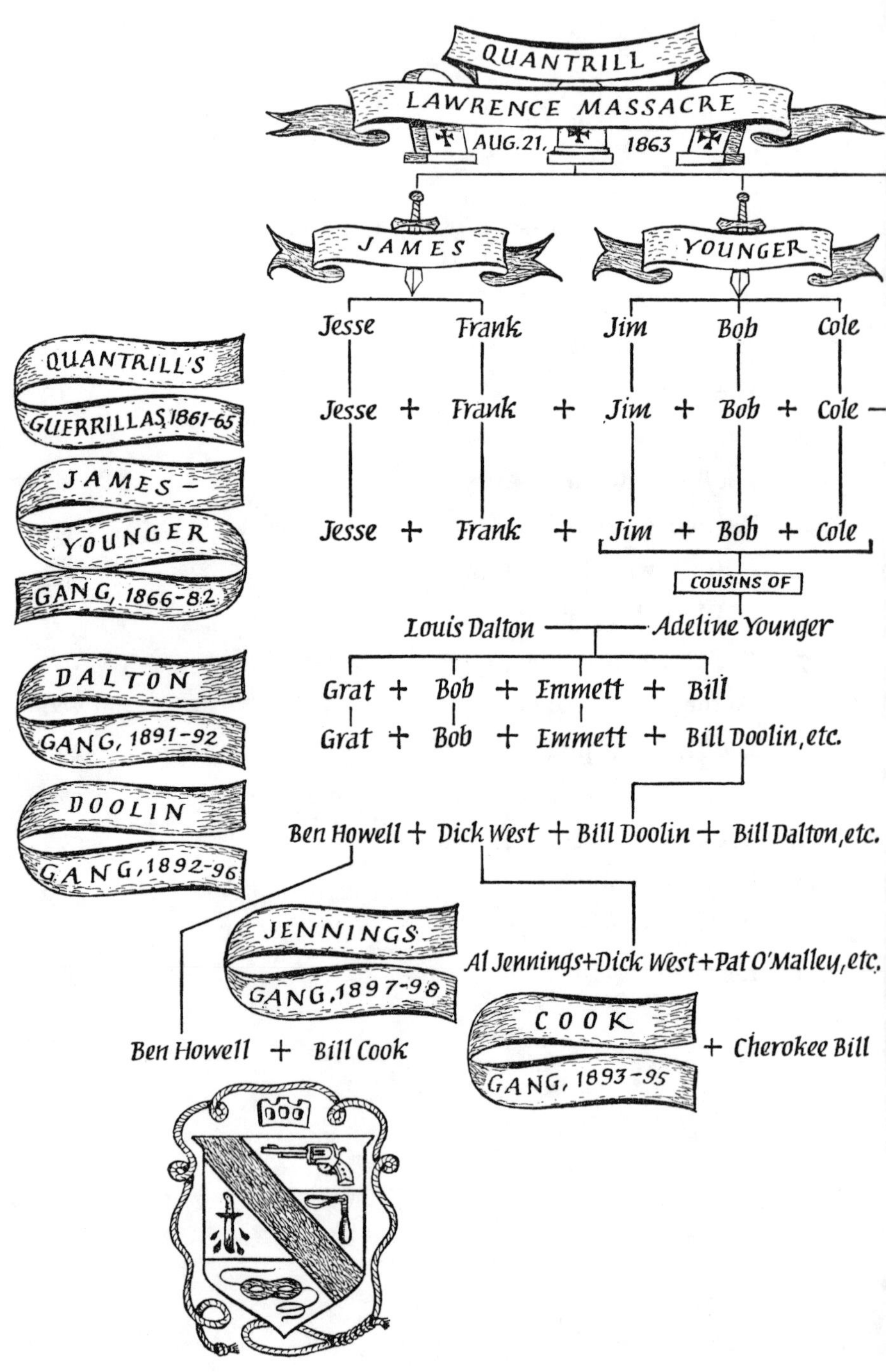
QUANTRILL
LAWRENCE MASSACRE
AUG. 21, 1863
JAMES
YOUNGER
Jesse
Frank
Jim
Bob
Cole
QUANTRILL'S GUERRILLAS, 1861-65
Jesse + Frank + Jim + Bob + Cole
JAMES–YOUNGER GANG, 1866-82
Jesse + Frank + Jim + Bob + Cole
COUSINS OF
Louis Dalton
Adeline Younger
DALTON GANG, 1891-92
Grat + Bob + Emmett + Bill
Grat + Bob + Emmett + Bill Doolin, etc.
DOOLIN GANG, 1892-96
Ben Howell + Dick West + Bill Doolin + Bill Dalton, etc.
JENNINGS GANG, 1897-98
Al Jennings + Dick West + Pat O'Malley, etc.
COOK GANG, 1893-95
Ben Howell + Bill Cook
+ Cherokee Bill

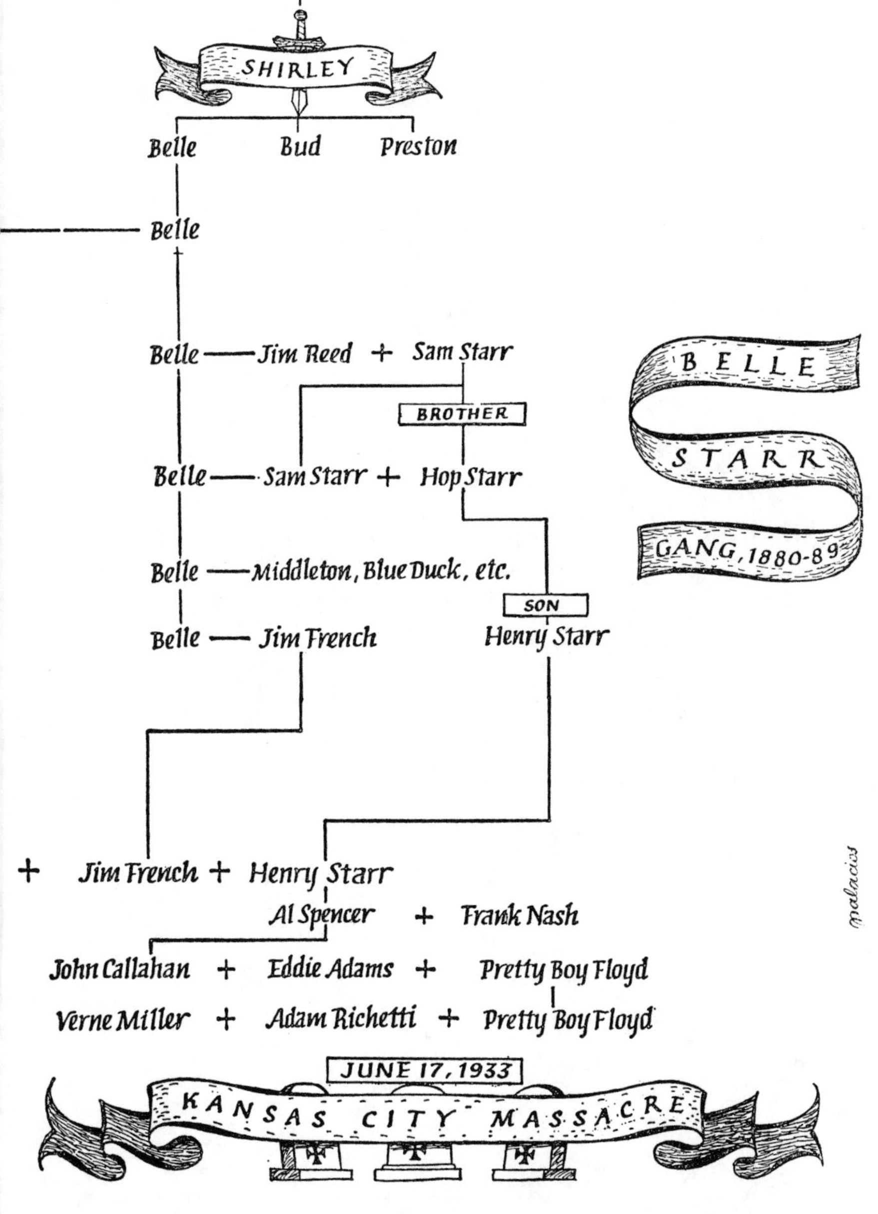
SHIRLEY
Belle
Bud
Preston
Belle
Belle — Jim Reed + Sam Starr
BROTHER
Belle — Sam Starr + Hop Starr
Belle — Middleton, Blue Duck, etc.
SON
Belle — Jim French
Henry Starr
BELLE STARR GANG, 1880-89
+ Jim French + Henry Starr
Al Spencer + Frank Nash
John Callahan + Eddie Adams + Pretty Boy Floyd
Verne Miller + Adam Richetti + Pretty Boy Floyd
JUNE 17, 1933
KANSAS CITY MASSACRE

IOWA
Council Bluffs
Murray
Corydon
Gallatin
St. Joseph
Kearney
Liberty
Richmond
Lawrence
Kansas City
MISSISSIPPI R.
MISSOURI R.
KANSAS
Paola
Otterville
MISSOURI
Spearville
ARKANSAS R.
Wichita
Roscoe
Ste. Genevieve
OHIO R.
Bloomfield
KENTUCKY
Columbia
OZARK
PLATEAU
Coffeyville
Carthage
Gads Hill
Mammoth Cave
Russellville
Woodward
Bartlesville
Lenapah
Eureka
Springs
Perry
Nowata
Nashville
Ingalls
Kingfisher
HX Bar Ranch
Tahlequah
Harrison
TENNESSEE
Guthrie
Stroud
Fort Smith
Cromwell
Younger's Bend
ARKANSAS
OKLAHOMA
Lawton
Hot Springs
Malvern
TEXAS
Dallas
MISSISSIPPI R.

Foreword
By Richard Maxwell Brown

THE AUTHOR: PAUL I. WELLMAN

Paul Iselin Wellman was born in Oklahoma Territory, grew up close to the frontier in Utah and western Kansas, and spent twenty-five years as a journalist in America's heartland of Kansas and Missouri. Out of this background came his eighteen histories and novels about the American frontier and West—an intellectual and artistic effort inspired, he said, by "an almost spiritual reverence" for the history of America, "its varied peoples, and its uniquely magnificent characteristics."[1]

Wellman was born on October 14, 1898, in the boom town of Enid in country where the desperadoes that he would write about in *A Dynasty of Western Outlaws* (1961) were then riding high. Paul's father, Dr. Frederick C. Wellman, came from a long line of pioneers who had followed the westward movement across Virginia, Kentucky, and Missouri until, soon after their marriage, the physician and his wife, Lydia, moved into Oklahoma's newly opened Cherokee Strip. Within a year after Paul's birth, the Wellmans were on the move again—not farther west but from America to Angola in southwest Africa. This surprising journey was motivated partly by Mrs. Wellman's deep religious faith, which led her to do missionary work among the Bantu natives while her husband became an expert in tropical medicine. Meanwhile, Paul learned to speak the native tongue, Umbundu, before he learned to speak English. These first ten years of his life spent in Africa remained vivid in Paul's memories, but he made little use of them as an author—perhaps, he wrote, because "emotional trouble" growing out of the incompatibility of his parents, who were divorced when he was fourteen, caused him to block Africa out of his writings.[2]

As the marriage of his father and mother crumbled in Africa, Paul was sent back to America for schooling—first for three years in Utah, where he lived for a time with an aunt in Vernal, a town deep in the country of outlaw Butch Cassidy and his "Wild Bunch" and one just then emerging from the pioneer era. From Utah, Paul was sent to Washington, D.C., to be with his father, who was then associated with the Smithsonian Institution, but after a year it was back to the frontier West—this time to live with his mother, two younger brothers, and sister in Cimarron, a village in western Kansas making the transition from the ranching to the farming era. Here, before going to college, the youth worked on farms and cattle ranches and got to know some of the veterans of the Indian-fighting and trail-driving days of the West. The strong impressions gained in this period were the genesis of a number of Wellman's books: *Death on the Prairie* (1934) and *Death in the Desert* (1935) on white–Indian warfare; *The Trampling Herd* (1939) on the history of the range-cattle industry; *Glory, God, and Gold* (1954) on Europeans and Americans in the Southwest; and three novels—*Broncho Apache* (1936), *Jubal Troop* (1939), and *Ride the Red Earth* (1958).[3]

Graduating from the University of Wichita in the midst of World War I, Wellman served in the U.S. Army in 1918–19 and attained the rank of sergeant in the Signal Corps. He spent the next twenty-five years as a newspaperman: as reporter and city editor for the *Wichita Beacon* (1920–30) and as Sunday editor and news editor for the *Wichita Eagle* (1930–35). In 1935 he settled into a nine-year stretch as a writer of features and editorials for the region's leading newspaper, the *Kansas City Star*. While busily occupied as a full-time journalist Wellman wrote and published the first seven of his books. Newspaper work by day and intense work on his books at night brought on a physical breakdown and caused him to give up journalism. With his wife, Laura Mae, whom he had married in 1923, and their son, Paul I. Wellman, Jr., he moved to Los Angeles in 1944. The senior Wellman spent his first two years in Southern California as a screen writer, and then he happily settled down to the steady production of historical works and novels until his death at the age of sixty-seven on September 16, 1966. In the last year of his life Wellman received the recognition of a great university, the University of California at Los Angeles, which awarded him an honorary doctorate of humane letters at its June, 1966, commencement.[4]

Schooled in the journalistic routine of daily deadlines, Wellman was a disciplined, prolific author who worked seven days a week from morning until after luncheon. His wife was of great help to him, especially in the characterization of women in his many novels. A photograph of Wellman in middle age reveals a man whose steady gaze falls just short of being stern. In religion Wellman was an Episcopalian, and in politics he was a liberal and a Democrat. For relief from his regimen of hard work as a writer, he read extensively, went fishing, and soaked up the life of a cattle ranch in Oregon of which he was co-owner.[5]

Wellman's long career as a journalist was crucial for him. As a young reporter and editor in Wichita he gained material for his fictional tetrology—*The Bowl of Brass* (1942), *The Walls of Jericho* (1947), *The Chain* (1949), and *Jericho's Daughters* (1956)—dealing with the imaginary western Kansas community of Jericho, which made the transition from a village like Wellman's home town of Cimarron to a growing city reminiscent of Wichita in his newspaper days. While he was acquiring the raw material for the Jericho novels in Wichita, Wellman, as a fledgling reporter, was also putting in time on the police beat. As early as 1920 he became seriously interested in the outlaw tradition of the region, and his journalistic work kept the interest alive, for Wichita was situated on a corridor of crime that stretched to Kansas City, St. Paul, Chicago, and Detroit. During the 1920s Wellman got to know a key member of the Wichita underworld, John Callahan. Callahan, Wellman learned, had extensive connections with some of the deadliest criminals of the time, including Al Spencer (whose early-twentieth-century apprenticeship under Oklahoma outlaw Henry Starr, Wellman found, led back through a series of personal links to Jesse James) and Charles A. "Pretty Boy" Floyd. In 1933—only two years before Wellman went to work for the *Kansas City Star*—Pretty Boy Floyd perpetrated one of the most savage acts in the annals of American crime, the massacre of five men at the Kansas City Union Station. With such exposure to the criminal history of Kansas, Oklahoma, and Missouri, Paul Wellman knew by 1940 that he wanted to write a book on the subject.[6]

THE BOOK: A DYNASTY OF WESTERN OUTLAWS

The most original of Wellman's historical works, *A Dynasty of Western Outlaws* has for its subject some of the best-known badmen in American history. Wellman's innovation was to connect those criminals in a personal chain one to another from the 1860s to the 1930s. With pardonable license Wellman used the inclusive word *Western* in his title, but he actually focused on his own home region of Kansas, Missouri, Oklahoma, and Arkansas, in whose bounds he treated, among others, the exploits of the Confederate guerrillas of William Clarke Quantrill; the bank and train robberies of Jesse and Frank James and the Younger brothers; the Dalton, Doolin, Jennings, and Cook gangs; Belle and Henry Starr; and such gangsters of the 1920s and 1930s as Al Spencer, Frank Nash, Eddie Adams, and Pretty Boy Floyd. In writing of the likes of Jesse James, the Youngers, and the Daltons, Wellman dealt with outlaws upon whose real lives a mass of legend and mythology had fastened like barnacles on a hulk. Wellman sought to cut through the "fakelore" of the subject to its reality, and in so doing he offered one of the most provocative interpretations in the historiography of American crime: what might be called his "succession thesis"—that Pretty Boy Floyd, who died in 1934, "was the lineal successor of that other arch-criminal, William Clarke Quantrill; not by blood, but by a long and crooked train of unbroken personal connections, and a continuing criminal heritage and tradition handed down from generation to generation" to link Quantrill and Floyd "as closely as blood lines could have done" (p. 20). In support of his succession thesis, Wellman contended that guerrilla leader Quantrill had in only four years (1861–65) established "a pattern of outlawry that continued long after him: hard riding, hard shooting, a network of hideouts, loot as the great objective, and murder without compunction" (p. 64).

Aside from his innovative thesis, Wellman's *Dynasty of Western Outlaws* vividly presents the sweep and feel of the outlaw history and tradition as for us they fade farther into the past. With the skills of a veteran writer of history and fiction who came out of a journalistic background in the region of which he wrote, Wellman brought his subject to life with a fast-paced narrative of criminal daredevilry and aggressive legal retaliation. He gave his readers the stories not only of Jesse James, Belle Starr, the Daltons, Bill Doolin, Henry Starr, Pretty Boy Floyd, and other famous outlaws, but also of the officials who pursued and punished them: Bill Tilghman, Chris Madsen, and Heck Thomas as well as the notorious "hanging judge," Isaac C. Parker, and his baleful executioner, George Maledon. The Lawrence, Kansas, massacre of 1863, so well described in the first chapter, is the prototype for a sequence of murderous events in which citizens and lawmen resisted quick-firing outlaws. Some of these episodes were epic battles as the bandits and their opponents fought it out on the streets of Northfield, Minnesota (1876), Coffeyville, Kansas (1892), and Ingalls, Oklahoma (1893). Other violent confrontations featured posse vs. gang or the drama of man against man, as in the case of the capture of Bill Doolin by Bill Tilghman. Finally, as weaponry escalated and the submachine gun was added to the arsenal of the latter-day outlaw, there was the hail of gunfire on June 17, 1933, at the parking plaza of the Kansas City Union Station in which Pretty Boy Floyd and two others claimed five lives.

Steeped in the lore of the region through youth and manhood, Wellman gleaned stories and insights from the many oldsters whom he questioned over a twenty-year period. In addition to the well-known accounts, he collected and pored over rare books and pamphlets, and he rustled the pages of many an old newspaper. To this endeavor Wellman brought the critical, skeptical intelligence of one who had been a hard-boiled reporter and editor in Kansas and Missouri. In a nutshell, his approach "in reconstructing so disputatious" a subject as that of the legend-shrouded outlaws was to "weigh the available evidence in moot cases, and hew to the line of greatest logic and probability" (p. 16). For the most part, Wellman's stance served him well, but *A Dynasty of Western Outlaws* is not flawless, and there are times when Wellman stumbles into error in matters of detail. He was well aware that the accumulation of myth, special pleading, and controversy had created a historiographic mine field for the researcher and writer. Yet he strode ahead, knowing that some might disagree with his "version of an instance here or an episode there in the long and complicated series of events" (p. 16) he explored in *A Dynasty of Western Outlaws.* A leading authority on the "Oklahombres" of the late nineteenth and early twentieth centuries, Glenn Shirley, has cited mistakes by Wellman (and others) on Belle Starr and Bill Tilghman, but Wellman's treatment of two foundation stones of his narrative has been largely confirmed by the principal experts: Richard S. Brownlee and Don R. Bowen in regard to Quantrill and his guerrillas and William A. Settle, Jr., on the James-Younger gang.[7]

Wellman kept his pledge to the reader not to glorify criminals, but he took note, too, of the wide popular sympathy for the Jameses and the Youngers and of the detestation that so many felt for the Pinkerton detectives who pursued them. Wellman also emphasized the Robin Hood image associated with Jesse James in the decade before his death. In all of this Wellman anticipated an interpretation of European and American outlaw history that has been popular among scholars in recent years: the concept of the social bandit—the notable breaker of the law who has, paradoxically, widespread approval among the law-abiding members of society. Initially advanced by British historian E. J. Hobsbawm, the social-bandit concept has been applied to the James-Younger, Dalton, and Doolin gangs by a young scholar, Richard White, in a way that Wellman would probably have applauded. In his study White portrays the three gangs as social bandits in that they gained the admiration of law-abiding farmers for robbing the banks and railroads, who many of these farmers believed were robbing them, in effect, with onerous mortgages and larcenous freight rates.[8]

Despite his obvious disapproval of violent crime, there is in *A Dynasty of Western Outlaws* a strong tone of admiration for the courage and daring of the Jameses, Youngers, Daltons, Bill Doolin, and many of the other outlaws Wellman treats. This, too, reflected an admiration of such qualities that was common among the contemporaries of the outlaws. In his research on the conditions that prevailed in the localities where the James-Younger, Dalton, and Doolin gangs operated, Richard White found that the lines between outlaws, vigilantes, and enforcers of the law were often blurred by local feuding and power struggles. In such chaotic conditions, White shows masculine strength was at the core of the popular mystique of these middle-border social bandits whom citizens saw to be "brave, daring, free, shrewd, and tough" but also "loyal, gentle, generous, and polite"—attributes that were seen to differentiate them from "common criminals." "Strong men who protected themselves and aided their friends could gain local respect," White observes, and "this respect for strong men who could protect and revenge themselves" was crucial to the appeal of these outlaws as social bandits. Similarly, Wellman wrote that these outlaws were "by the very nature of their upbringing . . . restless spirits, far-ranging and daring"; "to many of them, perhaps to most, the desire for adventure, for excitement, was a force possibly as motivating as the actual loot obtained—which, after all, never was enough to make any of them prosperous beyond the spending limits of a short spree or two" (p. 14). In the end, however, Paul Wellman's fascination with the outlaw lineage turned into revulsion as he dealt with the last in the succession, Pretty Boy Floyd, in whom he found not the knight-errantry of a social bandit but the brutality and blood-lust of a compulsive machine-gun killer.[9]

A major commercial publisher, Doubleday & Company of Garden City, New York, issued *A Dynasty of Western Outlaws* in early 1961, and soon the reviews began appearing. Wellman must have been pleased by them. Richard H. Dillon, a respected writer on western U.S. history, liked the book. His review in the *New York Times* let Wellman know that he had succeeded in all of his principal objectives, for Dillon noted that Wellman was as "accurate, interesting and readable" as ever in a "balanced account" that lent authority to his interpretation of a "ruffian's family tree." Applauding the tone of the book, Dillon commended Wellman for not belaboring his distaste for crime and murder. Equally appreciative was a top expert on the violent history of the Southwest, Wayne Gard of Dallas, Texas, who informed readers of the *New York Herald Tribune* that *A Dynasty of Western Outlaws* was "of historical value in a field that too long has been left to legend and folklore." Among other favorable reviews were those in the *Chicago Tribune* and *San Francisco Chronicle* and a prepublication notice in the *Kirkus Review*. With a sheaf of laudatory notices to his credit, Wellman had the additional satisfaction of seeing *A Dynasty of Western Outlaws* published in England in 1962 and reprinted twice in America.[10]

NOTES

1. "Wellman, Paul Iselin," in *Twentieth Century Authors: First Supplement,* eds. Stanley J. Kunitz and Vineta Colby (New York: H. W. Wilson, 1955), pp. 1061–62. The entry was written by Wellman. A complete list of Wellman's books was compiled by David Morton Holman for "Wellman, Paul I[selin]," in *Twentieth-Century Western Writers,* eds. James Vinson and D. L. Kirkpatrick (Detroit: Gale Research Co., 1982), pp. 790–92. See also, "Wellman, Paul I[selin]," in *Encyclopedia of Frontier and Western Fiction,* eds. Jon Tuska and Vicki Piekarski (New York: McGraw-Hill, 1983), pp. 350–51.
2. *Twentieth Century Authors.*
3. Ibid.
4. *Twentieth Century Authors; Twentieth-Century Western Writers.*
5. *Twentieth Century Authors.*
6. *Twentieth-Century Western Writers*; Paul I. Wellman, *A Dynasty of Western Outlaws* (Garden City, N. Y.: Doubleday & Co., 1961), passim.
7. Glenn Shirley, *Belle Starr and Her Times: The Literature, the Facts, and the Legends* (Norman: University of Oklahoma Press, 1982); *West of Hell's Fringe: Crime, Criminals, and the Federal Peace Officer in Oklahoma Territory, 1889–1907* (Norman: University of Oklahoma Press, 1978), pp. 266–70 and passim; Richard S. Brownlee, *Gray Ghosts of the Confederacy: Guerrilla War in the West* (Baton Rouge: Louisiana State University Press, 1958); Don R. Bowen, "Guerrilla War in Western Missouri, 1862–1865: Historical Extensions of the Relative Deprivation Hypothesis," *Compara-*

OUTLAW COUNTRY

PAOLA, KANSAS. Here William Clarke Quantrill narrowly escaped lynching, April 3, 1861.

LAWRENCE, KANSAS. Here Quantrill and his guerrillas massacred 142 citizens and burned the town, Aug. 21, 1863.

BLOOMFIELD, KENTUCKY. Near here Quantrill received his death wound, May 10, 1865, dying from it June 6, at Louisville.

LIBERTY, MISSOURI. Here Jesse James "invented" bank robbery, and killed George Wymore, a student, Feb. 14, 1866.

RICHMOND, MISSOURI. Here, for the first time, the James-Younger bandits met citizen resistance, and in a street battle killed Mayor Shaw, Jailer B. G. Griffin, and his son, May 23, 1867. Later three of the outlaws were captured at various places and lynched.

RUSSELLVILLE, KENTUCKY. Here the James-Younger bandits robbed a bank, May 20, 1868.

GALLATIN, MISSOURI. Here Jesse James murdered Capt. John W. Sheets while robbing the bank, Dec. 7, 1869.

Near here, at Winston, Mo., the James gang held up a train and killed Conductor William Westfall and a passenger, Frank McMillan, July 15, 1881.

CORYDON, IOWA. Here Jesse James, as a joke, addressed a political gathering after robbing a bank, June 3, 1871.

COLUMBIA, KENTUCKY. Here the James gang robbed a bank and killed R. A. C. Martin, the cashier, April 29, 1872.

STE. GENEVIEVE, MISSOURI. Here the James-Younger gang robbed a bank, May 23, 1873. They robbed banks also in Kentucky and West Virginia in this period.

COUNCIL BLUFFS, IOWA. Fifty miles east of here the James-Younger gang staged its first train robbery, wrecking the train and causing the death of Engineer John Rafferty, July 21, 1873.

KEARNEY, MISSOURI. Near here was the Samuel home, where the James brothers were brought up.

Near here, also, Detective John W. Whicher was trapped by Jesse James and murdered the night of March 16, 1874. The Samuel home was attacked, and an explosion caused by Pinkerton detectives killed the James brothers' half brother, tore off the arm of their mother, Mrs. Zerelda Samuel, and seriously injured their stepfather, Dr. Reuben Samuel, the night of Jan. 5, 1875.

Soon after, Jesse James shot and killed Daniel H. Askew, a neighboring farmer, for harboring a Pinkerton detective, April 12, 1875.

ROSCOE, MISSOURI. Near here John Younger and Detectives Louis J. Lull and E. B. Daniels were killed in a gun fight, March 16, 1874.

MAMMOTH CAVE, KENTUCKY. The James gang was charged with holding up a stage near here.

MALVERN, ARKANSAS. Here the James-Younger gang robbed a stagecoach, Jan. 15, 1874.

Gads Hill, Missouri. Here the James-Younger gang robbed a train, Jan. 31, 1874.

Otterville, Missouri. Near here the James-Younger gang robbed a train, July 7, 1876, on their way north to Northfield, Minn., where they were practically wiped out in a street battle, Sept. 7, 1876.

Nashville, Tennessee. Here the James brothers had a favorite hiding place and rendezvous, especially in their later years.

St. Joseph, Missouri. Here Jesse James was assassinated by Robert Ford, April 3, 1882.

Carthage, Missouri. Here Myra Belle Shirley (Belle Starr) spent her childhood.

Dallas, Texas. Here (Sycene neighborhood) the Shirleys made their home after leaving Carthage, Mo., in 1863.

Here Cole Younger had a love affair with Belle, and begot a daughter in her, later named Pearl Younger, in 1866.

From her home here Belle was carried away by Jim Reed and had a son by him, named Ed Reed.

Here John Younger killed Captain S. W. Nichols, Feb. 16, 1871.

Younger's Bend, Oklahoma. Here Belle, after "marrying" Sam Starr, a Cherokee Indian, and taking the name she forever after carried, Belle Starr, established her home in 1880 and named it after her first lover, Cole Younger, father of her daughter.

Here outlaws gathered for years, Jesse James sometimes staying there.

Here Belle Starr was murdered, Feb. 3, 1889.

Fort Smith, Arkansas. Here Judge Isaac C. Parker conducted his famous "hanging court" for twenty years.

Here George Maledon personally executed 60 men.

Here Cherokee Bill murdered Lawrence Keating, a prison guard, July 26, 1895, and himself died on the gallows, March 17, 1896.

Kingfisher, Oklahoma. Near here the Dalton family took up claims and lived from 1889 on.

Perry, Oklahoma. Here, after Grat and Emmett Dalton escaped from California following their murder of George Radliff in a train holdup that failed, the Dalton gang staged its first successful train robbery, May 9, 1891.

Coffeyville, Kansas. Here the Dalton gang was wiped out, four of them killed and one wounded and captured, while four citizens were killed and three wounded, in the street battle which took place Oct. 5, 1892.

Location of Halsell's HX Bar Ranch, from which came many of the Oklahoma outlaws.

Spearville, Kansas. Here the Doolin gang robbed its first bank, in Nov. 1892, losing one member, Ol Yountis, who was killed by pursuing officers

Ingalls, Oklahoma. Here the Doolin gang repelled officers, killing Tom Houston, Lafe Shadley, and Dick Speed, Sept. 1, 1893.

HOT SPRINGS, ARKANSAS. Here Frank Nash was captured by FBI officers, June 16, 1933, leading to the Kansas City Union Station Massacre next day.

LAWTON, OKLAHOMA. Near here Bill Doolin was killed by Deputy Marshal Heck Thomas, Aug. 25, 1896.

LENAPAH, OKLAHOMA. Here Cherokee Bill killed Ernest Melton, Nov. 9, 1894.

Here Henry Starr committed his first robberies.

Near here Al Spencer was born and brought up.

NOWATA, OKLAHOMA. Here Henry Starr killed Deputy Floyd Wilson, Dec. 13, 1892.

Near here Cherokee Bill was captured through the treachery of his "friend," Ike Rogers, Jan. 30, 1895.

TAHLEQUAH, OKLAHOMA. Near here, while the Cherokee money distribution was being made, Cherokee Bill killed Deputy Sequoyah Houston, June 6, 1894.

WOODWARD, OKLAHOMA. Here Temple Houston killed Ed Jennings in a saloon gun fight, given by Al and Frank Jennings as their "reason" for becoming outlaws.

GUTHRIE, OKLAHOMA. Near here, the capital of the Oklahoma Territory, Little Dick West was killed by Bill Tilghman and Heck Thomas, April 7, 1898.

STROUD, OKLAHOMA. Here Henry Starr, trying to rob two banks at once, was wounded and captured, March 27, 1915.

HARRISON, ARKANSAS. Here Starr was killed by William J. Myers, as he tried to rob a bank, Feb. 18, 1921.

CROMWELL, OKLAHOMA. Here Bill Tilghman was killed by Wylie Lynn, Nov. 1, 1924.

BARTLESVILLE, OKLAHOMA. Near here, at Okesa, Al Spencer staged his only train robbery, Aug. 20, 1923.

Ten miles northwest of here, Spencer was killed, Sept. 15, 1923.

MURRAY, IOWA. Here Eddie Adams killed C. W. Jones, and with his gang wounded three others of a posse, in escaping after a bank robbery at Osceola, a few miles east, Oct. 19, 1921.

WICHITA, KANSAS. Here Eddie Adams was killed after a reign of terror in which he caused the deaths of at least six persons, Nov. 23, 1921.

Here John Callahan operated his combination "fence" for disposing of stolen goods, liquor-running organization, and criminal-training establishment.

Here Pretty Boy Floyd took his first lessons in crime.

KANSAS CITY, MISSOURI. Here occurred the Union Station Massacre, led by Pretty Boy Floyd, in which Raymond J. Caffrey, W. J. Grooms, Frank Hermanson, Otto Reed, all officers, and Frank Nash, their prisoner, were killed June 17, 1933. Floyd later was killed by FBI men near East Liverpool, O., Nov. 22, 1934.

Here Jesse James was nursed back to health by Zerelda Mimms, after being wounded, in 1865.

Here the James gang took the cashbox from the Kansas City Fair Grounds, Sept. 26, 1872.

Here Jesse James married Zerelda Mimms, in 1874.

Here Eddie Adams killed a gambler and escaped a life sentence in the penitentiary by leaping from a moving train in 1920.

A WORD TO THE READER

Wars breed crime and criminals; and the American Civil War did not differ from others in this respect. Out of the dislocations of that conflict grew a wave of lawlessness that transcended all expectations in the length of time it lasted, and in the number of successive generations in which it perpetuated itself as a noteworthy dynasty of outlawry.

From the first essays into crime by William Clarke Quantrill to the death of Pretty Boy Floyd before the guns of the FBI, three quarters of a century was spanned. In all that time there never was an hour when some connection, evident or latent, did not exist between one set of outlaws and the next, which would succeed it in the Quantrill legacy of crime. Only in the comparatively recent past did the FBI, with its national jurisdiction, and the mightily improved local and state police methods, equipment, and personnel provide an answer to it.

Some of the men in those Western outlaw gangs might very well have lived orderly lives had they not come under the influence, in one way or another, of others who were criminals. The majority of them, however, possessed inherent lawless tendencies rather easily channeled, and it is a matter of interest to follow the chain of succession, sometimes direct, sometimes indirect, but always present and picking up new recruits, in this branching line of outlaws.

Let it be noted that the names of the men in these pages are, with a few exceptions, not "foreign" names. Quantrill, James, Younger, Dalton, Doolin, Cook, Callahan, Adams, Spencer, Nash, Floyd—they are "American" names, that is, names of families of the old American stock.

These men were no products of congested cities, where the foreign-born were segregated in slums. They were, in most cases, the product of farms, frontier towns, or the cattle range. Poverty, lack of opportunity, and discontent—the great breeders of crime—were, to be sure, present; but by the very nature of their upbringing these men were restless spirits, far-ranging and daring.

To many of them, perhaps to most, the desire for adventure, for excitement, was a force possibly as motivating as the actual loot obtained—which, after all, never was enough to make any of them prosperous beyond the spending limits of a short spree or two.

That very fact lifts them out of the class of the urban criminals of today. Crime, to the city gangster, is a business, a cold-blooded, cruel, cowardly, inhuman business—in which, for example, the operations of "dope pushers" creating new narcotics addicts among adolescents with the endless misery that follows, merely to widen the market for illegally smuggled heroin, is only a single phase, but a typical one. I have no desire to glorify any criminal, but the outlaw of the West was less despicable than the city "hood" of the present. He at least took his risks, and he did not prey on children and the helpless.

I have made no attempt to encompass all outlawry or outlaws in the United States during the period studied. There were other bandits, some very notorious, each with a story. But here I have contented myself with the persons who succeeded each other in a single unbroken chain, because they illustrate a pertinent fact—the contagious nature of crime—and form a vivid page in our national history.

In the more than forty years I have been interested in this phase of the American scene, and especially in the twenty years since I first thought of putting it into book form, I have traveled much, visited most of the important places where the events I have described took place, and interviewed many persons for information, besides studying all available records and writings. The result was a veritable mountain of labor, of selection, of sometimes difficult tracings of movements, of weighing divergent accounts, one against the other.

Legends are durable things and are not without their value as part of the folklore of a people. Nevertheless, I have endeavored to separate legend from truth and present fact rather than fable in this book. On the other hand, I do not subscribe to the school of professional so-called "debunkers." The truth, yes. But what is the truth? It is as easy to twist the significance of facts one way as the other, and if the purpose of the writer is to display his own cleverness by such methods, the uses of truth are by no means always served. He may please himself, and even a certain class of his readers, who will derive from his "cutting down to size" this or that storied figure of the past, a secret feeling of comfort in their own mediocrity. But in the end the legend itself may come nearer the actual truth than the "debunker" who writes from the dim distance of decades.

As for the direct testimony, one of the interesting, sometimes amusing, characteristics of the "old-timers" was the positive manner in which they "remembered" events, and their often cantankerous insistence that their versions, and theirs only, were true, however they might differ from the versions of others who witnessed or took part in the same events at the same time. I have interviewed scores of old-timers, and sometimes found their stories wildly contradictory. It can be no matter for surprise that these disagreements go over into the writings also.

There are, for example, at least three different accounts of the death of the outlaw Bill Doolin; three or more of the capture of Blackface Charley Bryant and his duel with Deputy Marshal Ed Short; numerous books and writings, all disagreeing radically, on the life, career, and character of Quantrill; perhaps even more, and as divergent, on Jesse James; almost as many versions of the bristling street battles at Northfield, Coffeyville, and Ingalls as there were participants; and so on.

In reconstructing so disputatious a period, one can only weigh the available evidence in moot cases, and hew to the line of greatest logic and probability. Some may disagree with my version of an instance here or an episode there in the long and complicated series of events this book surveys. That is their privilege, and I freely accord it. Fortunately, the questions arise in most cases over subordinate details rather than the major events.

I must acknowledge especial thanks to Bliss Isely, of El Dorado, Kansas, who gave me the benefit of his rich recollections, based on personal knowledge of happenings at the time they occurred, in the era of transition from the horse to the automobile in outlawry; and who also did much research and contributed important information from the records.

I owe also very much to the late Captain W. O. Lyle, of the Wichita, Kansas, police force, who out of sheer interest and with no thought of compensation made for me many vital inquiries which were of great value to this book.

Many others made contributions, including the late John Patrick Gilday, of Kansas City, Missouri, on the era of Missouri banditry; Ralph S. Hinman, Jr., of Wichita, Kansas, on the Adams-Callahan Midwest brigands; Gene Campbell, of Oklahoma City, Oklahoma, on the later Oklahoma bandits; Kirke Mechem, of the Kansas State Historical Society, who over the years has made available to me the vast records and publications of that fine organization; and not the least, Betty Wood Vedder, who proofread and typed the manuscript with care and intelligence and made some suggestions of importance in improving it technically. To all of them, my thanks.

PAUL I. WELLMAN
Los Angeles, California
June 1960

1. *The Bloody Chain*

The cocks are crowing at dawn of August 21, 1863, and the Civil War is just entering its last and bitterest stage, when a pale-eyed killer leads a horde of bearded horsemen, bristling with weapons, down upon the sleeping town of Lawrence, Kansas.

An eyewitness[1] later describes them: "Low-crowned, broad-brimmed hats—nearly all alike—unshaven—stoop-shouldered—all without coats, nearly all [in] red flannel shirts, much begrimed with camp grease and dirt."

These are Quantrill's dreaded guerrillas.

At their head rides: "A spare man making a fine figure on horseback . . . magnificently mounted . . . a soft black hat with a yellow or gold cord around it for a band, cavalry boots . . . a shirt ornamented with fine needlework."

That is William Clarke Quantrill himself. Always the dandy,

[1] Joseph Savage, a farmer who witnessed the guerrilla cavalcade ride past his house, about two miles out of Lawrence on their way to sack the town, furnished these vivid word pictures.

his personal vanity causes him to keep himself neat and clean-shaved, however unkempt his followers. Yet, though he likes fine clothes, his mind is as cold as death itself.

Suddenly the peace of the slumbering town is broken by a hideous din of gunshots and yells, and the people of Lawrence awake to a nightmare of horror. Terrified women scream, men are shot down and groan as they die. Galloping squads of fierce riders seek victims in homes, gardens, ravines, even fields of growing corn. Through the town roars a holocaust of flames, kindled by the raiders, "consuming sometimes the living—often the dead." When Quantrill and his wild retinue ride out of Lawrence hours later they leave it looted and burned, and in its streets, its ruined houses, and its environs lie 142 murdered citizens.

This, the celebrated Lawrence Massacre, unlike sackings of some other cities during the Civil War, has had no real military purpose, strategic or otherwise. It has been an orgy of blood and destruction inspired, led, and carried out because of vindictive hatreds, and because of a hunger amounting to an avarice, for notoriety on the part of one man—Quantrill.

Turn now history's pages forward to the year 1933. Three quarters of a century has passed, during which those pages have been studded almost constantly with outlawry, robbery, and murder in the West.

It is morning again—seven o'clock, June 17—and into the Union Station at Kansas City, Missouri, only forty miles from Lawrence, pulls a train. Among the passengers who get off are four men: one, a manacled prisoner, the others, his three grim-faced guards. The prisoner is Frank (Jelly) Nash, bank robber and outlaw, who is being returned to the federal prison at Leavenworth, from which he is an escapee. The officers are Otto Reed, chief of police of McAlester, Oklahoma, and two members of the Federal Bureau of Investigation, F. J. Lackey and Frank Smith.

At the station the group is met by four other officers, Raymond J. Caffrey and Reed E. Vetterli, of the FBI, and W. J. Grooms and Frank Hermanson, detectives on the Kansas City police force.

Immediately the party walks out from the station to the parking plaza, where cars await them.

"Get into the front seat," Caffrey orders the prisoner. Nash obeys. Chief Reed and two FBI men climb into the back seat while Caffrey walks around the car to take the wheel. The two city detectives and the remaining FBI agent, who are to follow in another automobile, stand beside the car in which the prisoner and his guards are seated.

At this moment, while they are all grouped together, a voice cries sharply, "*Up, up!*"

As if from nowhere three men have appeared, covering the party, two with submachine guns, the third with a pair of automatic pistols.

Grooms, the detective, whips out his revolver and fires, wounding the leader of the trio in the left shoulder. With a snarl the wounded man says, "Let 'em have it!"

At once he begins to spray the officers with bullets from his machine gun. His two companions join him in a murderous burst of fire.

"Don't shoot me!" despairingly cries out Nash, the prisoner.

But as the machine guns, with their staccato bursts of shots, grimly traverse the party, he wilts down in his seat, killed by a bullet in the head. Four others lie dead on the pavement or in the car: Chief Reed, of McAlester; Grooms and Hermanson, of the Kansas City police force; and Caffrey, of the FBI. Two FBI men, Vetterli and Lackey, are badly hit. The other FBI man, Smith, by some miracle is not wounded.

The machine gunners leap into a car and whirl away out of sight. The crime which is known as the Kansas City Union Station Massacre has been committed.

Between those two massacres exist some strange and sinister parallels. The motives and execution of the later crime were of the same cold-blooded ferocity as the first. Its leader was another dandy who was vain of his looks, a merciless killer, and greedy for publicity—Charles (Pretty Boy) Floyd.

But more important, there is a weird sort of historical connection between the two crimes so far removed from each other in time, though so near in distance. Bizarre as it may seem, Pretty Boy Floyd was the lineal successor of that other arch-criminal, William Clarke Quantrill; not by blood, but by a long and crooked train of unbroken personal connections, and a continuing criminal heritage and tradition handed down from generation to generation, linking the two as closely as blood lines could have done.

The succession in what is, for every practical purpose, a veritable dynasty of outlaws in the West is important both to sociology and history. To trace it we must begin with Quantrill.

One approaches with caution any comment on the rights and wrongs of the Kansas-Missouri border warfare, which began years before the Civil War, continued with mounting savagery during that conflict, and did not entirely cease for some time after the fighting and killing elsewhere ended. There were grievous wrongs on both sides, and hatreds became so intense that many men who in later years proved to be good citizens rode and robbed or murdered in the sincere belief that they were helping the Confederacy (if they happened to be Missouri guerrillas) or the Union (if they were Kansas Jayhawkers).

Yet though most of the irregulars on both sides were perhaps basically honorable and upright, however they behaved during the war, some among them assuredly were outright thieves and cutthroats. Of these Quantrill—largely because of the Lawrence Massacre—was certainly the most celebrated, and also the most execrated.

And this in spite of the fact that, bad as he was, others on the border equaled, perhaps exceeded him as terrorists. Even Kansas had its ferocious Charles Jennison and half-mad Jim Lane, bloody leaders of the Kansas Red Legs and Jayhawkers.[2]

[2] The names are interesting. One Pat Devlin, a Kansas raider, gave the word "Jayhawk" currency in connection with private plundering across the border into Missouri, in 1856, though a party of Forty-niners used it earlier on their way to California. Devlin, an Irish immigrant, explained that in Ireland "we have a bird we call the Jayhawk, which makes its living off other birds." The late John Patrick Gilday, a pleasant and seasoned student of all things both Western and Irish, told me that in some parts of Ireland the name was applied to the shrike, or butcherbird, which has some of the qualities of both the jay and the hawk. I wrote the Library of Dublin but could get no confirmation,

Yet Quantrill received the overwhelming brunt of the condemnation, and little is said even today of the excesses of his opposite numbers in Kansas. This is partly due to the fact that Kansas, with a heavy infusion in its population of New England lawyers, fanatical Abolitionist editors, and pulpit-pounding Puritan preachers, was far more articulate than Missouri, which was peopled largely by planters and farmers. Kansas also had much the better publicity outlets—the Eastern press—so that Kansas excesses in Missouri usually were glossed over, while Missouri excesses were if anything exaggerated. Finally, Kansas was on the winning side. The losers had few historians who could command an audience for the then unpopular cause immediately after the Civil War.

As an example: While there can be no palliation of the Lawrence Massacre, in which 142 Kansas men lost their lives, almost nothing has been said of the fact brought forward by Major John N. Edwards, Quantrill's chief apologist, and conceded by William Elsey Connelley, Quantrill's bitterest chronicler, that in the fifteen days preceding the Lawrence raid more than two hundred men were killed by Unionists in Missouri. Commenting on this, Connelley justifies it in his book *Quantrill and the Border Wars*, by speculating that "those men who were killed must have been disloyal." Perhaps they were Confederates at heart, but only on the Kansas border was that an accepted reason for murder.

Under such bitternesses, one must, in attempting to assay Quantrill's character, take into account the prejudices, whether in his favor or against him, of those who described him.

Major Edwards, no guerrilla himself but an officer in the Con-

---

although the librarian said the name might exist in an isolated community. Perhaps I should have tried the Library of Belfast in Northern Ireland. At any rate, the term "Jayhawker" has become associated with Kansas and has assumed a fabulous design as the patron fowl (imaginary) of the state university. In the 1860s it was an epithet anything but complimentary. The Red Legs were so called after a raid by Jennison on a boot factory in Independence, Missouri, when a job lot of red sheepskins used for boot tops was captured. The men used the red sheepskins as leggings, and these red leggings later became a sort of article of uniform for Jennison's raiders. "Red Leg" was by no means a term of endearment in Missouri then, nor is it today.

federate Army, and a celebrated newspaper editor in Missouri after the war, wrote in the Kansas City *Times*, May 12, 1872:

> Quantrell[3] might be likened to a blond Apollo of the prairies. His eyes were very blue, soft and winning. Looking at his face, one might say there is the face of a student . . . If there is a race born without fear, Quantrell belonged to it . . . In his war-life which was one long, long merciless crusade, he exhibited all the qualities of cunning, skill, nerve, daring, physical endurance, remorseless cruelty, abounding humor, insatiable revenge, a courage that was sometimes cautious to excess and sometimes desperate to temerity.

The passage illustrates the curious deification of figures in the border outlawry—extending later to the James and Younger bandits—by persons who were still bitter over the unhappy events of the Civil War. To Major Edwards, Quantrill was a romantic hero, but his phrase "eyes very blue, soft and winning" hardly accords with the impressions others had.

Mrs. Roxey Troxel Roberts, who knew Quantrill, said: "Large, light-blue eyes, a Roman nose, light complexion, light hair . . . *peculiar* eyes, like no other eyes I ever saw—upper lids heavy . . . dressed neatly, secretive and peculiar . . . no one knew how to take him." To which Connelley added: "The upper lids [of the eyes] fell too low, imparting a peculiar expression which became very marked when he was in a rage."

Connelley never saw Quantrill, and he based his observations on what others told him. Nevertheless, allowing for individual prejudices, there was something about the man, decidedly, which impressed those who did see him. Over and over reference is made to his care in dress and appearance; his secretive habits, at least in his early years; and those eyes of his, with their drooping upper lids, perhaps giving a look of hidden speculation or cruelty at times.

Even Major Edwards speaks of his "remorseless cruelty." Connelley goes further. He states (on imperfect and highly prejudiced testimony) that as a boy Quantrill enjoyed maiming and torturing animals, and adds that as a man he directed this sadism

[3] "Quantrell"—a frequent misspelling of the name Quantrill.

against human beings. Yet not even Connelley can adduce one single instance where the guerrilla leader tortured or tormented a man or woman. On the other hand, the record shows that Quantrill sometimes intervened to save the lives of prisoners when his men wanted to kill them.

He was a killer, as the Lawrence Massacre showed. There can be no question that Quantrill was evil. But he probably was neither as evil as Connelley paints him nor as good as Major Edwards describes him. Bitter and vengeful he was, but far less cruel than some of the other guerrilla leaders, notably Bill Anderson, who boasted of his killings and, according to Connelley, "when he was killed he had, so it is said, the scalps of two women on the headstall of his bridle."

In passing, note that phrase "so it is said." Over and over it appears in Connelley's biography, *Quantrill and the Border Wars*, to buttress statements for which he has no real evidence.[4] Whatever their faults, murdering or subjecting women to violence was not a guerrilla practice, and I doubt the story of the women's scalps, although some scalping of *men* was done by both sides in the border warfare.

Wrote Connelley himself:

> Quantrill, inhuman as he was and fond of fallen women as he is known to have been, made it a law in his band that the violation of chastity would be punished by death, and it is said this penalty was inflicted more than once.

Again that phrase "it is said." There is no record of any man's being executed by Quantrill for rape. Perhaps there was no need for such an execution. Without any question Quantrill was bad, but it does not require the animus of a Connelley to prove it. Not only was he bad but he infected others with the virus of his badness.

[4] Connelley inherited the Lawrence bitterness and frequently is not specific in his evidence, relying on that phrase "it is said," or variations of it, in his desire to portray the guerrilla chief as a super demon. In some particulars he discredits himself by his evident bitterness, his extreme statements, and his denunciations of all who disagree with him. Some of his material must be accepted with caution. Nevertheless, *Quantrill and the Border Wars* is the best researched of all the Quantrill books, and though completely prejudiced it furnishes some of the best source material.

He robbed and looted and murdered, but even Quantrill's detractors agree on his courage and address in moments of peril.

One of the most signal proofs of this quality was given on July 11, 1862, less than three months after he and his band were outlawed, in a fight near Pleasant Hill, Missouri, when the Union forces, with every advantage of numbers and the element of surprise in their favor, had their one best chance to annihilate him and his followers. As an example of Quantrill at his fighting best, it is worth briefly reviewing.

Major James O. Gower, with two hundred and sixty-five officers and men, had trailed Quantrill, who had with him only sixty-five riders at the time. The guerrillas did not know they were being pursued, and since it had rained heavily the night before, they were busy drying their blankets and clothing on the fences of a farmhouse.

Shouts and shots from the picket outpost were the first hint that the enemy was upon them. Quantrill, realizing at once that he was in a desperate situation, ordered the horses saddled and hitched in a ravine, and placed his men along the bush-grown fence of a horse lot. In the savage battle that followed, he was in full control all of the time, a figure that seems shadowy and gigantic, seen moving in a mist of powder smoke. . . .

Gower's advance, sixty men under Captain M. Kehoe, which had first drawn the warning shots from the picket outpost, charged the camp hoping to catch it disorganized and off guard. But as the charge thundered toward the silent fence with its concealing bushes, a surprise volley belched out flame and smoke, and emptied fifteen saddles. Kehoe retreated.

Calmly, Quantrill had his men round up the horses of the fallen enemy and secure all arms and ammunition. Of the fifteen who were dropped when Kehoe was repelled, nine were dead.

For a few minutes there was a long-range exchange of fire, in which each side lost a man or two. But Quantrill could see his foe being heavily reinforced. He sent away his wounded and led his men to the only possible position in which a numerically inferior force could defend itself—down into a ravine, which was surrounded and filled with dense thickets of rough brush.

The Union forces dismounted, then charged the hidden guerrillas. The first volley left gaps in their ranks, but running forward with considerable bravery, the blue soldiers reached the brush-choked ravine, and in a moment scrambled down into it to engage Quantrill's fighters hand to hand.

Heavy foliage made it impossible to see ten feet in any direction. Sometimes men, groping through the brush, in which the visibility was even more reduced by powder smoke, found themselves glaring into an enemy's face, less than a foot separating them. The grapple followed at once, with the flash of flame or steel. Everywhere individual little battles, for life or death, raged in the general melee.

Hoarse yells of the combatants, the constant crashing of carbines and revolvers at close quarters, officers shouting orders which nobody could well obey in the confusion, the clash as saber strokes were parried by clubbed guns, outcries of the wounded, who were often trampled underfoot as the fight reeled back and forth, and the powder smoke which hung like a heavy pall in the ravine, marked this as one of the fiercest little conflicts during the entire war.

Quantrill was at bay, but fierce as a wolf. His men, pressed by overwhelming numbers, were forced up out of the ravine, only to run into a volley from a detachment placed there by Major Gower to intercept them.

It was a dilemma which might have brought despair to a commander less cool and resolute than Quantrill. He had no thought of surrender—indeed, had he given up his arms, he and his men would have been executed on the spot. Instead, he executed one of the boldest and most difficult of maneuvers.

In the face of enemy fire, he turned his men so that the enemy was blasting volleys at their backs, and led them wildly charging down through the ravine again. His attack was irresistible. The very force that lately pressed him back was cut in two by his charge and he was able to draw his men into a different branch of the ravine.

There for an hour and a half he held back repeated assaults by a force that outnumbered him four to one. Toward the end his men, having exhausted their ammunition, resorted to throwing stones at their foes. They suffered heavy losses, and Quantrill himself was wounded in the thigh.

Yet, incredibly, at the end of that time he was able to draw off the survivors of his band, twenty-one of the wounded mounted, and the rest, including himself, on foot, leaving his weary foe behind. It was a brilliant little battle. Though heavily outnumbered he had killed or disabled a fifth of his enemy, and while half his own men were casualties, he had saved his dark command as an entity for further actions and depredations.

William Clarke Quantrill was a strange product of his disordered times. He was born at Canal Dover, Ohio, July 31, 1837, the oldest of several children of Thomas Henry and Caroline Clarke Quantrill. The father was at times a sort of author, at times a tinsmith, and had difficulty over some school funds, but at his death, in 1854, was the principal of the school at Canal Dover. Connelley says, "He was a good teacher and was much beloved by his pupils."

But a little further on, as if regretting this temporary lenience, Connelley goes to the opposite extreme concerning the couple which brought William Clarke Quantrill into the world:

> The union of this couple produced him that shed blood like water, a fiend wasteful and reckless of human life. They endowed him with depravity, bestowed upon him the portion of degeneracy. In cruelty and a thirst for blood he towered above the men of his time. Somewhere of old his ancestors ate the sour grapes which set his teeth on edge. In him was exemplified the terrible and immutable law of heredity. He grew into a gory monster whose baleful shadow falls upon all who share the kindred blood. He made his name a Cain's mark and a curse to those condemned to bear it.

That is pretty good invective, even for Connelley. And it is true that by the time Quantrill went to Kansas in 1857, when he was about twenty, he had learned to be many things to many men. For the times he was well read and wrote a clear, legible hand, and on occasion he played the role of a respectable schoolteacher. On other occasions, however, he was a cook for a wagon freighting outfit across the plains, a crooked gambler in the Rocky Mountain gold camps, and a thief suspected of at least two murders by the time he reached his majority.

In the bitter sectional troubles arising on the Kansas-Missouri border before the Civil War, Quantrill for a time played both sides against the middle, posing as an Abolitionist in Lawrence, Kansas, under the name of Charley Hart, and at the same time secretly consorting with pro-slavery people in Missouri. This enabled him to prey on both sides, stealing horses in Missouri to sell in Kansas and kidnaping free Negroes in Kansas to sell into slavery in Missouri.

By 1860 Quantrill had become a confirmed bandit, thief, and murderer, yet as a criminal he might have remained relatively obscure—ending, perhaps, as "guest of honor" at a lynching party —had not the dislocations of the Civil War enabled him to capitalize on the inflamed emotions of the period and win his page in history—deserved or not—as the arch-ogre of the border.

Sometime in December 1860, Quantrill accompanied a stealthy party of Kansas Jayhawkers across the line into Jackson County, Missouri, to plunder the home of Morgan Walker, near Blue Springs. Walker was a prosperous and highly respected planter, owning nearly two thousand acres of fine land, a large house with numerous outbuildings, more than one hundred horses and mules, and about thirty slaves. He also had, at this date, about two thousand dollars in money in his house. Some report of this, perhaps, had a strong bearing on the decision of the raiders to descend on him, since there were other slaveholders more easily available and nearer the Kansas border than he.

As was the case with most such raids, the laudable declared purpose was to carry off Negro slaves to Kansas and free them; but the less laudable and undeclared purpose was to overlook no opportunity of picking up any movable and valuable property which could conveniently be "liberated" at the same time.

Leader of the party was Charles Ball. Others, besides Quantrill, were Edwin Morrison, Albert Southwick, Chalkley Lipsey, and John Dean. All of these, except perhaps Quantrill, were eager to free slaves, but all were just as eager to engage in a little profitable horse larceny and gold robbery, as the sequel will show.

The defect in their scheme was in Quantrill himself. He was

interested in Morgan Walker's daughter, Anne (or Nannie or Nancy), who was living at her father's house at the time.

Anne Walker was described as a "fine-looking" young woman, and she had been married to Dr. Riley Slaughter, a neighboring planter. She had, however, a wayward nature, and her husband one night caught her in bed with another doctor (unnamed). Dr. Slaughter would have killed his wife's lover, but the amorous and anonymous physician, with a celerity that might have put to shame a panic-stricken antelope, escaped. Dr. Slaughter thereupon obtained a divorce from Anne.

It was after this that Quantrill met her. He visited her father's house several times, conducted a secret love affair with her, and had no difficulty, it appears, in making her his mistress.

His interest in the winsome and willing Anne, it seems reasonable to believe, was what caused Quantrill, when the raiders camped in the woods near the Walker place, to go by night to Andrew Walker, Anne's brother and Morgan Walker's son, who lived near by, and reveal the presence of the party and its plan.

Connelley, of course, would have it otherwise:

> It was said that Quantrill had planned to assassinate a number of his associates at Lawrence, then flee to Missouri. Failing in this, he planned to take them to Missouri on a predatory foray and there have them killed.

Again that "it was said," the good old Connelley substitute for provable fact. He was unable to show any proof of this deep-laid scheme on Quantrill's part. It may have been that Quantrill did not know until too late that his inamorata's house was to be attacked, and that his warning was a last-minute decision.

In any case, an ambush resulted, set by the younger Morgan at his father's house. When, in the darkness of night, the Kansas raiders, led by Ball, approached the place, Morgan Walker, who had only just returned home from a business trip that day, met them at the door. Standing on the porch of the house with his men, Ball coolly informed the planter that "they had come to take his slaves to Kansas; that they would also take his horses and mules; that they would take what money there was in the house."

The Jayhawkers were all armed, and Walker was not. He consented to their taking any Negroes who were willing to go, asking, however, that those who did not want to go be allowed to remain. He also mildly protested against their robbing him of his money and stealing his horses and mules.

At this point Quantrill, who had been standing on the porch with the others, stepped into the house. The rest of the party was left on the porch with both Morgan Walker and Quantrill inside.

It seemed to be a signal. From a harness room at the end of the porch burst a sheet of flame and the sudden, shocking crash of a volley. Within that harness room were hidden Andrew Walker and some of the neighbors—including, interestingly, Dr. Slaughter, the ex-husband of Anne Walker. They had fired almost as one man at the raiders.

Morrison, of the Jayhawkers, was killed instantly. Southwick, Dean, and Lipsey were wounded, the latter severely. Southwick and Dean in spite of their wounds ran and managed to escape back to Lawrence in a wagon they commandeered. Ball was braver. Though unwounded, he carried away the helpless Lipsey. A day or two later the two were found together, hiding in the woods, where Ball was trying to attend to his comrade's wounds. Both were killed by a Missouri posse led by Andrew Walker and Quantrill.

Any further connection between Quantrill and Kansas was effectively severed by the Walker incident. At Lawrence cries of "treachery" and "murder" were raised. The Walkers, and other Missourians, on the other hand, considered the action a friendly warning against "an attack by Kansas desperadoes"—which indeed it was, from their standpoint. In gratitude Andrew Walker gave Quantrill a very fast mare, called Black Bess.

Quantrill was perfunctorily arrested and quickly released. Meantime he appears to have invented a story to explain his presence among the Kansans—a point on which the Missourians were decidedly edgy. He told them that some years previously a band of Jayhawkers under James Montgomery had killed his elder brother and left Quantrill himself for dead with severe wounds. Recovering, he went to live in Lawrence under the name Charley

Hart, killing one after another his brother's murderers in vengeance.

Actually he had no older brother, being himself the eldest of his family, but the Missourians had no way of knowing that, the story was plausible, and it was accepted. He was safe in Missouri.

But Quantrill was restless. Several times he crossed the state line to visit friends around the settlement of Stanton. There, March 26, 1861, he was captured by a posse of Lawrence men under Captain Ely Snyder, who "desired to kill him for his treachery at Morgan Walker's, but he wished to kill him under some color of justification."

Snyder hoped Quantrill would obligingly resist arrest and be shot. To his chagrin his quarry surrendered peaceably. Balked of the excuse of the *ley de fuego,* he tried to shoot the prisoner anyway, but his gun was knocked aside. Another man, John S. Jones, thrust his rifle against Quantrill's side and pulled the trigger, but the weapon missed fire. The devil appeared to be taking care of his own.

Failing in these expeditious methods of disposing of their prisoner, the men of the posse next decided to take Quantrill to Lawrence and "hang him to the nearest tree," for the edification of that city, where most of them resided. Unfortunately for this plan, word of the arrest reached Paola, then a Kansas pro-slavery settlement, as were Fort Scott and Leavenworth. The sheriff arrived from Paola with a larger posse and papers giving him custody of Quantrill.

Over protests from the Lawrence contingent, the prisoner was lodged in the Paola jail—a somewhat safer habitation for him than the bastille at Lawrence—where he remained for a few days, while his friends were working to obtain his release on a writ of habeas corpus.

But the Lawrence people were busy, too. Captain Snyder, the implacable, obtained a writ from the court there, and with a group of eager followers, rode hard for Paola to get Quantrill and complete the interrupted project of festooning a tree with him. This program, however excellent it might have been, was not carried out. Quantrill was released by Judge Thomas Hodges of the

Paola court, just as the Lawrence posse reached the outskirts of the town.

It was touch and go, but Quantrill's friends were ready. His mare was already saddled and waiting when he stepped out of the courthouse. As he mounted, the first of the yelling and vengeful Lawrence party appeared up the street galloping toward him.

But Black Bess could show her heels to most other steeds in the country around. Wrote Connelley:

> Quantrill put his thumb to his nose and made a defiant gesture, and then, leaning forward in his saddle, patting himself in a still more defiant, vulgar, and insulting gesture, put spurs to his beast and bade a final farewell to Kansas. This was the third day of April, 1861, and he never returned again except as a spy, murderer, or assassin under the cloak of a soldier of the Rebellion.

One sympathizes with the rage and frustration of the panting citizens of Lawrence who arrived only in time to see their hated quarry slip away with "defiant, vulgar, and insulting" gestures. To say the least for it, all this was decidedly inconsiderate of Mr. Quantrill.

Mark that date—April 3, 1861. Nine days later, April 12, the Confederate batteries at Charleston, South Carolina, began the bombardment of Fort Sumter, which surrendered the following day. The four-year horror of the Civil War was on.

To Quantrill the war represented unparalleled opportunity. He spent a little time with Cherokee irregulars in the Indian Territory, and served "as a nondescript" briefly with the Confederate Army, taking part, apparently bravely, in the battles of Wilson's Creek and Lexington, Missouri. But when General Sterling Price retreated with his rebel army toward the south, Quantrill instead rode north—back to Jackson County.

There he joined a band of about eleven men, organized by his old friend Andrew Walker, and helped rout a group of Kansas Jayhawkers who were robbing and burning houses in the neighborhood. One of the raiders was killed and two mortally wounded. When the Union provost marshal charged two members of Walker's band with the murders, Quantrill coolly went before a justice of peace, swore to an affidavit that they had nothing to do with the slaying, he himself had killed all of the men, and then, knowing the defendants would be freed by the affidavit, just as coolly rode away.

The fight and the affidavit made Quantrill the ruling spirit of the band. Walker went back to his farm. Only eight of the original eleven men remained to follow Quantrill, but from this nucleus developed his guerrilla band.

His first act as leader was to capture George Searcy, a deserter from Price's Confederate army, who was robbing and intimidating *Union* families in the country. Searcy was given a drumhead trial and hanged. Seventy-five head of horses he had collected, together with a number of deeds to lands, mortgages, and private accounts, were returned to their owners—Union sympathizers.

Thus far there was not much to criticize in Quantrill's behavior, considering the exigencies of the times. He treated Confederate and Union families alike, seeming to desire to redress wrongs committed against either.

But times rapidly changed, bitterness grew corrosive, and the lines became sharply drawn. Union cavalry began to scout for the guerrillas, and a change came over Quantrill. Gone was the "quiet, secretive" man. Overnight he showed that he was a born leader, with a magnetic personality that drew men to him. "In the midst of a band who knew no law but the revolver, his slightest wish was anticipated and obeyed . . . his power to command was unquestioned." The band grew in numbers, and now Quantrill instituted a course of training which had a far-reaching effect.

Connelley describes one phase of it:

> The arms of the guerrillas consisted principally of Colt's navy revolvers of forty-four caliber. Some of them carried cavalry carbines which they had captured, a few had Sharps rifles, and there were even shotguns and old muskets among them. The main reliance of the guerrilla, however, was upon the revolver. And the guerrilla was usually a dead-shot, either afoot or on horseback. Quantrill became very expert with the revolver. There has been much said about his teaching his men to shoot by drilling them and insisting upon compliance with some certain formula or routine of action. He did nothing of the kind. He urged constant practice

> at first, but each man could shoot as he liked if he shot well. Quantrill required results in pistol firing, and the guerrilla understood this art much better than any other soldier. The powder charge of the Union soldier was made up for him and these charges were uniform in size. The guerrilla made up his own charge. He was compelled to be economical of his ammunition. He discovered that a small powder charge enabled him to shoot more accurately than he could with a heavy charge. His pistol did not "bounce" when fired, and the aim was not spoiled. And the ball ranged as far and penetrated as deeply as did that fired with a heavy charge. Every guerrilla carried two revolvers, most of them carried four, and many carried six, some even eight. They could fire from a revolver in each hand at the same time. The aim was never by sighting along the pistol barrel, but by intuition, apparently without care, at random. But the ball rarely missed the mark—the center. Many a guerrilla could hit a mark to both the right and left with shots fired at the same instant from each hand.

Connelley was no firearms expert, and some of this can be discounted, such as the penetration of a bullet with a light charge being equal to that with a heavier charge; and particularly that about shooting with both hands at the same time at different marks, and hitting both. It is simply not within human capabilities to do that, except by sheer accident. Nevertheless, the important matter was dependence on the revolver as the chief weapon, and a highly developed dexterity with it. It proved so successful that it carried on as a tradition in the West long after the Civil War.

There is neither space nor occasion in this book to describe the varied and bloody activities of the guerrillas, and their enemies the Jayhawkers and Red Legs, in the carnival of death and terror that followed. Quantrill in Missouri was matched by Jim Lane and Charles Jennison in Kansas.

Of the former, his own men sang a verse to an old hymn tune, quoted by William Allen White:

Am I a soldier of the boss,
A follower of Jim Lane,
And would I fear to steal a hoss,
Or blush to ride the same?

He was over six feet tall, very lean and cadaverous, with deep-sunk eyes and a half-maniacal lust for power. Elected to the Senate, he frequently harangued that body with a voice that at times "thundered denunciation of his enemies," and at others "rose to a shrill scream like that of an angry vixen."

Gathering about him a force of irregulars, he was responsible for many of the outrages committed in Missouri, which he invaded often and as quickly retreated to the safety of Kansas.

Governor Charles Robinson, governor of Kansas in the early years of the war, denounced him in unmeasured terms as "a bloodthirsty maniac clothed with authority from Washington," and charged him with atrocities in Missouri as causing "the retaliatory raids, including the massacre . . . of Lawrence by Quantrell [*sic*]." He added that Quantrill was "more considerate than Lane had been, as he told one of the prisoners taken at the Eldridge House [during the Lawrence raid] that he should spare the women from outrage, which Lane in his raids in Missouri did not do."

There are numerous records of protests by Union officers, as well as Confederate officers, against Lane and Jennison, contained in *The Official Records of the Rebellion,* a compilation by congressional authority of orders and reports from both sides during the Civil War. One of these is sufficient to give their general tenor. In July 1861, General H. W. Halleck wrote to General George B. McClellan officially protesting the actions of those two Jayhawking leaders, using the following words:

> The conduct of the forces under Lane and Jennison has done more for the enemy in this state [Missouri] than could have been accomplished by twenty thousand of his own army. I receive almost daily complaints of outrages committed by these men in the name of the United States, and the evidence is so conclusive as to leave no doubt of their correctness.

Concerning Jennison, whose bloodthirsty career in Missouri later was officially condemned and who was relieved of his rank and command, it is only necessary to recall the fact that well into the present century, old folks living in Jackson, Clay, and Cass counties of Missouri still called a skeleton chimney, standing where a house had been burned down, a "Jennison Monument."

I lived and wrote in Kansas City, Missouri, for some years and knew that country well. That interesting phrase, handed down from the days of the border wars, was first called to my attention by the late Joseph B. Shannon, then a member of Congress. I later heard it used by others on several occasions.

Some of Quantrill's followers actually outdid him in murderous activity. But the Quantrill name caught on—chiefly, I believe, because of the notoriety of his leadership in the Lawrence Massacre—and he was credited with all the deviltries the guerrillas performed.

Let me hasten to say that he did not object to this sort of fame. Rather he seems to have gloried in it. And whatever others did, he was the real genius, the leader who taught them the tactics of strike and scatter until another blow was planned; who developed an intelligence system that kept him informed of his enemies' movements; who trained his men in their own peculiar tactics and use of arms; who searched out, or had his scouts search out, every kind of a hideout, including remote and well-grassed valleys, caves in which the country abounds, and houses of persons who were sympathetic and daring enough to give the guerrillas hospitality.

It was Quantrill, and Quantrill alone, who devised the means whereby the guerrillas of Missouri, in spite of overwhelming numbers of enemies who hunted them, were able to live and operate for years in a country occupied by Union forces, in which every town of any size was garrisoned; and thus carry on their activities, most of the time when the nearest Confederate lines were hundreds of miles away.

On April 21, 1862, Quantrill and his men were declared outlaws officially in Special Order No. 47, issued by General James Totten, then commanding in Missouri, which said in part:

> All those found in arms and open opposition to the laws and legitimate authorities. . . . will be shot down by the military upon the spot where they are found perpetrating their foul acts.

No quarter! Quantrill first heard of the order when it was published in a newspaper which was brought to him while he and his men were camped about the Little Blue Baptist Church, twelve miles south of Independence. He read it and, climbing on a bench, called his men about him. At the time the guerrillas had a prisoner, Lieutenant Reuben A. Randlett, Fifth Kansas Cavalry, whom Quantrill had saved from being killed when he was captured. Randlett later recounted what followed.

The guerrilla chief read the order aloud to his men, and then carefully explained to them that by its provisions they were deprived of all benefits of civil or military laws, but would be hanged or shot wherever found. As the men scowled, muttered, or cursed, he turned to Randlett.

"What do you think of that, Lieutenant?" he asked.

Randlett was a brave man. "I could not blame you for shooting me now," he said.

But Quantrill laughed. "Not a hair of your head shall be harmed," he said.

Randlett later was released as promised, and returned to his regiment.

As a reply to General Totten's order declaring the guerrillas outlaws, Quantrill "raised the black flag," which meant that he, too, would give no quarter.

Surprisingly, and a signal proof of his power as a leader, the outlawing of his band not only made his men more desperate and ferocious but actually increased their numbers. That Special Order No. 47 perhaps had a direct bearing on Quantrill's chief act of infamy—the sack of Lawrence.

Lawrence was not entirely the innocent victim as is sometimes represented. It had some sins of its own to answer for.

From the beginning it had been the main headquarters of the Jayhawkers, from which many of their forays were made. It was the home of Jim Lane; and Jennison and Montgomery, those notorious Red Leggers, also operated out of it at times. The guerrillas hated the town, and many had vengeful motives against it growing out of raids emanating from it.

An episode not directly connected with Lawrence, but one which infuriated all Confederate sympathizers in the area, was the arrest and imprisonment of a number of young women and girls who were relatives of men known or believed to be with

Quantrill. General Thomas Ewing, who ordered them taken into custody, did so on the ground that they might be carrying information to the guerrillas, in which he perhaps was correct. Three of the girls imprisoned were Josephine, Mary, and Jennie Anderson, sisters of Bill Anderson of bloody fame.

Altogether, seventeen women and girls were arrested, and twelve of them were placed in a ruinous brick building in Kansas City. During a heavy windstorm the walls of the structure collapsed, killing some of the girls and injuring others.

At once the Confederate sympathizers furiously charged that the walls had been deliberately undermined to cause the building to fall upon its unfortunate inmates. Union people countered by saying the girls were trying to burrow their way out, which weakened the foundations, bringing about their own destruction.

Most likely neither of these assertions was true. The disaster in all probability was due to natural causes—a heavy wind and crumbling walls. The blame was on those who put the feminine prisoners in such a position of jeopardy.

At this time Quantrill was having trouble with some of his leaders, notably Anderson and Todd, who were jealous of his power. The deaths of the girls in Kansas City silenced any insubordination, for the time being at least.

Now, Quantrill felt, was the propitious time to strike a deadly blow, and he had a stronger motive than mere resentment for leading the attack on Lawrence. And here is where General Totten's "outlaw order" perhaps enters in.

Late in 1862, after he was outlawed, Quantrill traveled by devious routes through enemy country and then across Confederate-held territory, all the way to Richmond, Virginia, the capital of the Confederacy, to ask for a colonel's commission in the Confederate Army. Perhaps he thought an authorized commission would lift the outlaw brand from him and his followers. More probably, when his nature is considered, he simply desired the rank and the pride it would carry with it.

When, however, he interviewed James A. Seddon, Confederate Secretary of War, he startled that gentleman by suggesting that the whole Confederacy ought to "raise the black flag" and no longer give quarter to its enemies. The Secretary must have gasped, but he suggested rather mildly that "even war had its amenities and its refinements, and that in the Nineteenth Century it was simple barbarism to talk of the black flag."

General Louis T. Wigfall, C.S.A., who was present at the interview, quoted Quantrill's reply, in part, as follows:

"Barbarism! Barbarism, Mr. Secretary, means war and war means barbarism! For twenty years this cloud has been gathering. The cloud has burst. Do not condemn the thunderbolt!"

It sounds pretty high-flown, but it must be remembered that in the 1860s conversations and actions were inclined to be florid. The flourish, in speech or gesture, was much admired.

Seddon was not, however, changed in his convictions. He answered the guerrilla chief coldly, and the commission was not granted, although Quantrill sometimes signed himself later as "Colonel" Quantrill.

Very much dashed, he returned by the same crooked trail to Missouri, arriving there early in 1863.

Back in his old retreats he brooded, those heavy-lidded eyes slitted in speculation, in anger, in bitterness.

Ambition burned at him, and he began to feel that some spectacular act, some great deed of derring-do, might force the Confederate government to grant the commission he so desired. At last came his great idea: to smash Lawrence—self-righteous, sanctimonious, hypocritical Lawrence—Lawrence the focus of everything he and his followers hated.

Early in July 1863 he called his men together. The scene must have been a spirited one that day the guerrillas gathered. All of the fiercest of their leaders were there: Bloody Bill Anderson, chewing his ragged mustache in craving for blood vengeance for his sister, dead in the collapse of the Kansas City building; George Todd, cold-blooded and growing more murderous as the war progressed, even now a rival of Quantrill's for leadership; Bill Gregg, John Jarette, Dick Maddox, George Shepherd, Cole Younger. With them were their fierce bearded riders.

Quantrill's men listened as their chief spoke, outlining his plan, not failing to take note of the dangers involved, but using every bit of his magnetic persuasive ability to carry them with him.

One sentence was remembered: "All the plunder—or at least the bulk of it—stolen from Missouri will be found stored away in Lawrence. We can get more revenge and more money there than anywhere else in Kansas."

And, like the born gambler he was, he ended on this final note: "I know the hazards this enterprise bears, but if you never risk, you never gain!"

His personality was irresistible. Completely, he won them over, especially by that cunning suggestion of plunder and loot. The men gave a great yell of approval, the officers forgot petty jealousies and joined with them. So Lawrence was decided upon and a general rendezvous set.

On August 18, with 448 men and officers by official count, Quantrill began his fateful march. He gloried in that column—an army of lank, bearded killers with murder on their minds. He stalked their ancient foe, Lawrence, and they, like a pack of wolves, stalked with him. He noted their array: every man armed and double armed, every man mounted on as fine a horse as expert larceny could provide.

In that long column rode Thomas Coleman (Cole) Younger, and a long-faced taciturn youth named Frank James. They were to win notoriety later, in the postwar years, as bandits and outlaws, along with others of this hard-riding troop. Frank James had a younger brother, Jesse Woodson James, who was not on the raid that day. He was considered too young as yet to be a guerrilla, but he soon after joined Quantrill's men, became of them all one of the most reckless and ruthless, and before his end won greater fame than any other outlaw in American history.

Night, August 20. Quantrill's men had been on the march almost without a rest for two days and were showing signs of weariness. The moon, in its first quarter, threw shadow patterns like sorcery, and then, about ten o'clock, went down. From then until dawn there was only starlight.

Through this darkness the column of horsemen twisted along crooked roads like a great snake, in silence save for the trampling of hoofs, creaking of saddle leathers, and a few words spoken now and then in lowest, gruffest tones. Tension filled every mind, for these men knew they were deep in enemy territory, without support of any kind.

Their presence here must be known, for their outriders had encountered Union vedettes—who fled. They did not know that these scouts had notified their commanders, and their commanders promptly made themselves very scarce, one of them marching all the way to Paola—for what reason, no one knows to this day, unless prudence was the overriding consideration.

Quantrill was worried. On him rested all responsibility. He knew the way better than most of his followers, but he took no chances. From a farmhouse along the road the owner was routed out to guide the raiders across the maze of creeks and gullies of eastern Kansas. Presently it was discovered that the guide was a former Missourian—therefore, presumably, a traitor. He was shot. Other guides also were shot as the march continued, if they were suspected of leading the wrong way, or even did not know the road.

As the column neared Lawrence, gunshots were banned. A Missouri refugee, Joseph Stone, was captured. He could not be shot, and no rope was available to hang him, so the ferocious Todd beat his brains out with an antiquated musket someone picked up.

After that, Quantrill needed no more guides, for he was on familiar ground. As day began to break he put his column into a trot. Well might his men be described by Savage as stoop-shouldered and unshaved. They had been continuously on the road for so long that many of them had to strap themselves in the saddle to keep from falling off their horses.

But as the order to trot rang back and forth, the men sat straighter, looked to their weapons, pulled their slouch hats lower over their eyes, and glanced at one another, ready for what was to come. From the top of a rolling elevation the guerrillas presently looked down on the streets of the city.

A pistol shot for a signal! Down into Lawrence galloped Quantrill, followed by the avalanche of his whooping men. The slaughter and the looting and burning began.

It lasted for four terrible hours. Some of the guerrillas carried in their pockets lists of men they wanted to kill. The leaders had death lists also, men marked for murder because of their activities against Missourians. Quantrill had one he supremely wanted—Jim Lane.

But once the killing started, many men died who were on none of those lists, who had committed no offenses against Missouri, shot down in the crazed orgy of blood lust. Everywhere the outlaw guerrillas robbed. Money, jewelry, anything of value which was easily portable was seized by some of the men, and what could not be carried in most cases was consigned to the flames.

Women were spared. There was not one case of rape, or one instance of physical injury to a woman, except insofar as "sometimes they were rudely flung aside with savage threats to save them injury from the bullet that bereaved them" of the husband, son, or brother they were clinging to in an effort to shield. They were, of course, robbed, and saw their homes destroyed, and experienced the anguish of witnessing the murders of their men in "the pent wrath and mad fury nursed for years by border-ruffians against Lawrence."

Some terrible things occurred during that awful day, as guerrillas broke open the liquor stores, became drunk, and in not a few cases got completely out of hand. There is a story of two men being thrown into a burning building to die. Husbands were slaughtered before the eyes of their families, sometimes while their wives clung to them pleading for mercy. Everywhere lay the dead.

But it should be stated that many persons were saved, and others not molested or harmed, *at the special orders of Quantrill himself.*

Wrote Governor Robinson, who was in Lawrence during the massacre:

> He [Quantrill] said, as Robinson, while governor, did what he could to preserve peace on the border, he should not molest him or his property. Of this intention Robinson had no knowledge, but both his person and his property were spared, although the raiders were within a short distance of him, and in full view, and could have destroyed him and his property without trouble. Had the raid not been for retaliation for similar raids in Missouri, there is no reason why Robinson's property should not have shared the fate of Lane's, nor why he should not have been killed as were others when completely in the power of the raiders.

To his vast disappointment, Quantrill was cheated of the man he most desired—Jim Lane. The guerrillas intended to capture that lank fanatic, and take him to Missouri, to be publicly hanged in Jackson County. But Lane did not have those long legs for nothing. At the first alarm, when the raiders charged the town, he leaped out of bed, wrenched the plate (with his name) off the front door, and then, clad only in his nightshirt, bolted like a jack rabbit for a field of corn, into which he plunged, abandoning his wife in the house to face the raiders.

Through the field he crept, while the sounds of the massacre and destruction of Lawrence roared behind him, crossed a ravine, and came to a farmhouse, where he borrowed a pair of trousers from the farmer—who was a short, fat man, whereas Lane was tall and gaunt. He got also a battered straw hat and a pair of old shoes. In this ridiculous garb, with his nightshirt tucked inside the wide-girthed pants, which were buckled about his skinny waist with their bottoms halfway up to his knees, he mounted a plow horse with a blinder bridle and safely escaped.

His wife remained and confronted the guerrillas. They did not harm her, though they burned Jim Lane's house down. They even tried to save her piano, at her request, but could not carry it out and abandoned it to the flames.

Other men, marked by the guerrillas, escaped in various ways, by hiding, fleeing in time, in some cases buying off the men who were ready to kill them, even by disguising themselves as women.[5]

At last, disappointed by his failure to catch Lane, but with his men weary of killing and the town thoroughly gutted—the damage

[5] One of the more whimsical stories of escape is that of two printers, who were sleeping in the Lawrence *Tribune* office when the raid occurred. They were M. M. Murdock and another man, and they probably were aware that members of the staff of that Abolitionist newspaper were proscribed. They acted promptly, if somewhat startlingly. To quote Connelley: "Murdock and his companion ran into an adjoining building, in the cellar of which was a deep pit for drainage purposes. In this pit they hid and escaped death." What the blushing Connelley fails to make clear is that the "adjoining building" was the office privy, and it was under the seat in the noisome "pit for drainage" that the two printers waited until the coast was clear. M. M. Murdock later founded the Wichita *Eagle*, one of the great newspapers of Kansas, and was a considerable figure in the history of his state.

in property looted or destroyed was estimated at $2,000,000—Quantrill withdrew, leaving 142 dead Kansans and one dead guerrilla behind him. The name of the sole guerrilla casualty was Larkin Skaggs. He was killed, and also scalped, by White Turkey, a Delaware Indian, who seems not to have been caught up in the general panic of the people of Lawrence.

There was a feeble pursuit, but the Union forces took care not to come too close, and Quantrill soon was safe in Missouri. Aside from the terrible onus of the massacre, he had displayed considerable daring and skill in leading his men so deep into enemy territory, accomplishing his purpose, and returning to his own base with scarcely any loss.

2. "Order No. 11" and the Aftermath

Quantrill may have believed that his adroit leadership in the sacking of Lawrence would be recognized and rewarded by the Confederate government, but if so he was bitterly disappointed. Far from gaining him favor, that butchery was viewed with horror by the South and repudiated by it. Whatever chance he had for recognition as a legitimate officer of the Confederacy was destroyed. More than ever he was on his own, despised by blue and gray alike.

Two days after the massacre came a thunderclap. General Thomas Ewing, commanding Union forces on the Missouri border, issued the now famous—or infamous—"Order No. 11." By it the Missouri counties of Jackson, Cass, Bates, and part of Vernon were depopulated, save for small areas in the immediate environs of garrisoned towns. Families, without regard to right or justice, or even loyalty to the Union cause, were forced by the military to leave their homes with what little they could carry, and go to seek shelter of some sort in whatever direction they might flee, while their belongings left behind were looted and their houses and grain fields burned.

This Order No. 11, and its effects, deserves to be examined because of its direct bearing on the outlawry that followed the war.

For issuing it, as one writer put it, "Quantrill himself did not receive such condemnation . . . as General Ewing had to sustain for the rest of his life."

Yet the order was not Ewing's idea, and he issued it with reluctance. It had been discussed before, but he expressed himself as greatly opposed to the measure, which he considered too cruel and drastic. The impetus that caused the order to be issued came from Kansas, and from Jim Lane, the archenemy of the Missourians, in particular.

Still smarting from his narrow and humiliating escape, Lane met General Ewing on the day after the raid at the De Soto crossing of the Kaw River, and berated him for "his milk-and-water administration." Lane was not only a partisan leader but a United States senator, elected in 1861, with the admission of Kansas as a state. He was a violent man. He murdered Gaius Jenkins in 1857 in a quarrel over some land, using his powerful position to get himself exonerated. And he proposed in 1858, when he was a quasi officer in command of Kansas irregular forces, a march on Lecompton, then the center of pro-slavery interests in Kansas, to stage a general massacre there exactly like the one Quantrill had just engineered at Lawrence. His proposal was rejected by other leaders of the Free State element. Since the beginning of the Civil War he had divided his time between making raids across the border and visits to Washington in his capacity as senator, where he seems to have had a strange influence in high places. Wrote L. W. Springer, in his book *Kansas:*

> Lane's singular influence over Mr. Lincoln and the Secretary of War, Mr. Stanton, is one of the most inexplicable and disastrous facts that concerned Kansas in 1861–65. It was the source of the heaviest calamities that visited the commonwealth during that period, because it put him in a position to gratify mischievous ambitions, to pursue personal feuds, to assume duties that belonged to others, to popularize the corruptest political methods, and to organize semi-predatory military expeditions. . . . In 1864, Mr.

> Lincoln, remarking upon Lane's extraordinary career in Washington to Governor Carney, offered no better explanation of it than this: "He knocks at my door every morning. You know he is a very persistent fellow, and hard to put off. I don't see you very often, and have to pay attention to him."

Now, confronting General Ewing, he stormily told the officer that as soon as he got back to Washington he would have him removed.

Lieutenant William Mowdry, a military aide, was present at the start of the interview and was authority for the statement that "Ewing begged hard for his official head."

Lane then said he would make no complaint "if Ewing would issue the order, which had been contemplated for some time, depopulating some of the border counties of Missouri."

This Ewing agreed to do, whereupon he and Lane retired into a cabin beside the river and drew up Order No. 11, probably at Lane's dictation. When they came out of the cabin Mowdry heard Lane say: "You're a dead dog if you fail to issue that order as agreed between us."

Ewing promulgated the order the following day. Its terms were ferocious. The unfortunate families living in the proscribed counties were ordered within fifteen days to leave their homes and go out of the state, except such as could "establish their loyalty to the satisfaction of the commanding officer nearest," and these could move to one of the garrisoned towns. All hay and grain in the field or under shelter was to be confiscated or destroyed. Officers were directed to see that the order was "promptly obeyed" —method of enforcement not specified.

Order No. 11 was the signal for unparalleled destruction and misery. Families could only take along what they could carry, and they could not even sell property they left behind. Furniture, personal effects, and livestock were confiscated or looted. Homes, barns, and other edifices were in most cases burned down.

A fourteen-year-old boy named William Wallace, forced to leave with his family, later left his impressions of that terrible occasion.

"The Union forces had full possession of all the towns, and were, except as to the trouble given them by the guerrillas, in absolute control of the country. There was nothing to do but obey the Order.

It was a tragic hour. All of our horses broke to work, except two, had been taken. We had three or four yoke of oxen. Many of our neighbors had no conveyance of any kind . . .

"No other night has painted upon my memory such a scene of silent horror . . . Houses were on fire in the distance . . . I gazed at the stars as they came out. Though I knew I could see them when I reached my destination, it seemed that I was telling my boyhood stars goodbye forever. It was August, and the balmy air was not stirring a leaf; the hush was intense.

"After awhile the silence was broken. A dog left behind at a neighboring house began to howl piteously. The dogs throughout the neighborhood took it up. Their howls rang out upon the stilly air, some of them seeming miles away. They missed their masters and the children with whom they had played, and their doleful voices continued throughout the night. Thus was the awful reign of 'Order No. 11' howled in."

That boy, though he came from a family of Confederate sympathizers, after the war became eminent in the Missouri bar, was the chief spearhead in breaking up the outlaw gangs, prosecuted Frank James, and became Judge William H. Wallace, one of the most eminent jurists the state has produced.

Order No. 11 reduced the population of Cass County from 10,000 to 600; and there were even fewer left in Bates County. The area was ruthlessly laid waste by the Red Legs. When, after the war, the exiles were permitted to return to their former homes they found the roads and fields overgrown with weeds and only charred remains of their homes. The term "Burnt District" was for many years applied to the counties of Bates, Cass, and part of Jackson. Missourians suffered far more in damage to property and loss of goods in this action than had Kansans in the Lawrence raid, although the loss of life was relatively small when the proscribed families were cleared out.

Order No. 11 was Lane's means of revenging himself on the Missouri people. As a military measure it was expected to drive out the guerrillas because they could no longer subsist on the country. In this respect it was only partly successful. After the war General John M. Schofield tried to aid Ewing by saying he authorized the order, but the records show that the superior officer was notified of the action *after* it was taken, by a telegram in which Ewing apologized for acting without authority and offered to submit to a military court of inquiry if Schofield thought it necessary. Schofield backed his subordinate up, but visited the proscribed areas officially and rescinded the order as to burning crops—too late, for nearly all of them had been burned.

What Order No. 11 was completely successful in doing was to create bitterness that for a generation was not entirely healed. Even families with Union sympathies were in many cases alienated.

And this should be underlined: The amazing ability of Jesse James and his band of outlaws to operate for fifteen years after the war out of this very area which had been so terribly stricken, was due to the resentments still burning. People who had suffered from Order No. 11 were slow to inform against former guerrillas who had become bandits, out of sheer antagonism toward the authority that had ruined them.

The subsequent fate of the two men most involved in promulgating the order is interesting. General Ewing, a foster brother of General William Tecumseh Sherman, was a politician from Ohio. He was pursued by execrations, even though he was forced to issue his decree by Lane's threats. After the war he returned to politics and ran for governor in Ohio in 1872.

George Caleb Bingham, an artist of considerable renown and an officer in the Union Army, was so infuriated by the order and the events following it that he painted his famous picture, "Order No. 11," depicting a band of Red Legs looting and burning a house, murdering one member of the family, and threatening and abusing others. Seated on a horse, looking on with cold unconcern was a Union officer, his face the likeness of General Ewing. Near him was another, with the countenance of Jim Lane.

That picture, and Bingham, followed Ewing into Ohio, and the story of Order No. 11 defeated him. Ewing succeeded in reaching Congress, and his friends started a movement to nominate him for Vice-President and even President. But though Bingham had died meantime, his ghost haunted Ewing. He failed to gain the goal of his ambitions and retired into political obscurity.

At a reunion of Union veterans in Kansas City, in 1890, he told his audience that he held no bitterness against his artist enemy, and added, significantly:

"I remember when I came here, that on my trip to Independence along a road where I had once seen beautiful farmhouses so thickly located as to make it almost seem a great long street, I saw, with but one exception, only the monuments which Jennison left—blackened chimneys."

He had picked up a local phrase there—"Jennison's Monuments."

Ewing was killed in a traffic accident in New York in 1896.

Jim Lane's career was shorter.

Frustrated in his political ambitions, and facing probable exposure for corrupt practices in the Senate in 1866, the man, half or wholly crazed—as indeed he seemed to be much of the time during his period of power—in an hour of black depression, committed suicide by shooting himself with a pistol.

Whatever the effects of Order No. 11 in general, it was not that decree but the massacre of Lawrence that caused Quantrill's power to wane. Perhaps, also, a new romance to which he succumbed had something to do with it, and it shows his progressive degeneration, and growing lack of responsibility.

Sometime in the summer of 1863 he induced a girl to run away with him from her home in Jackson County. His enemies said he carried her off by force, but Fletch Taylor, a guerrilla leader who after the war became a much respected member of the Missouri state legislature, unequivocally denied that.

"She went willingly," he said, "and he [Quantrill] borrowed my gray mare for her to ride on, to a place some five miles from camp."

To this, of course, Connelley added his own postscript:

> Others say [the good old Connelley trademark] he kidnaped this girl and it took her some time to become reconciled to the life to which he had doomed her, but that she became infatuated with him, even wearing a man's clothing and riding in the ranks to be near him.

Not much is known of this girl. Her name was Kate King, but she took the name Kate Clarke after running off with her guerrilla lover, and whatever Connelley's surmises, she appears neither to have felt "doomed" by being Quantrill's mistress nor to have required any time to become "reconciled" to it. She entered into it right blithely. Clarke was Quantrill's middle name, which he sometimes used as an alias, and she occasionally said she was married to him, but no record of a wedding or marriage contract of any kind has ever been found.

"From that time on," said Fletch Taylor, "he never did much fighting. He kept her [Kate] that summer and winter. We went south and he left her. The next summer he went back and got her, and stayed in the brush until he started to Kentucky, where he was killed."

We went south. It is Quantrill's expedition down into Texas after he wiped out a Union detachment of 98 men at Baxter Springs, Kansas, October 6, 1863. The Texas episode marks the final decline of the guerrilla leader from any pretense of being a soldier, into his true character as a bandit and murderer.

Already, by the time he made his first camp at Mineral Creek, Texas, the old dissensions had arisen to new proportions in the command. Todd was beginning to gain ascendancy, and so was Anderson. There were bickerings over division of spoils in various raids.

In Texas the guerrillas began to rob and kill citizens who were unquestionably Confederate in sympathy. A Colonel Alexander, a Major Butts, and a man named Froman, all Confederate soldiers, were murdered and robbed.

In Sherman, Texas, on Christmas Day, most of the guerrillas got drunk and terrorized the town. "They shot the steeples of the churches full of holes and they shot the lock off the door of the post office. . . . They rode their horses into Ben Christian's hotel and shot away the tassels and other ornaments on the cap worn by Mrs. Butts, widow of the murdered man [Major Butts] and mother-in-law of the proprietor."

But Texas did not tamely submit to such activities. At Bonham the commanding officer was General Henry McCulloch. He was a brother of the famous General Ben McCulloch, who commanded the artillery at San Jacinto and who was killed at Pea Ridge. Like his brother, Henry had been a captain in the Texas Rangers, when that organization was one of the most redoubtable fighting units in the world. He had ideas of law and loyalty somewhat at divergence with Quantrill.

On March 31, 1864, he summoned Quantrill to his headquarters, and ordered him under arrest. Yet he listened to Quantrill's explanations, and finally told him that his parole would be accepted and he would not be imprisoned before his trial. He even invited the guerrilla to go to dinner with him.

But Quantrill was furious. "No, sir," he said. "I will not go to dinner. By God, I don't care a damn if I never taste another mouthful on this earth!"

McCulloch made no reply. He simply went to dinner by himself, leaving Quantrill in his office, guarded by two armed soldiers.

The guerrilla chief glared about him like a trapped wild animal. He dreaded anything like imprisonment, and particularly any kind of stern military investigation of his record. But above all, the humiliation of this arrest must have been like a corrosive in him.

He—*he*, William Clarke Quantrill—the terror of the border—in a guardhouse like any ordinary man? His vanity simply could not accept it.

McCulloch's office had a bed at one end of the room, and on this the guerrilla's revolvers had been rather carelessly laid. Toward them edged Quantrill as the soldiers lounged carelessly by the door.

Nearer—nearer—and then suddenly, with a cougar's feral instinct, he leaped!

The revolvers were in his hands, ready, before the open-mouthed guards could so much as move.

"Lay down those guns!" he ordered.

They felt constrained to obey—and quickly—with the menacing black bores of the Colts staring, it seemed, at the pits of their stomachs.

Backing them away from their weapons, Quantrill buckled on his belt and holsters, picked up the guns, and taking them with him, unlocked the door and stepped out, locking the two men inside and pocketing the key.

Down a stairway he went quickly, almost jauntily. Two more sentries stood at the foot, and they also found the revolvers covering them.

"Drop your guns and step into the street!" said the guerrilla.

At his voice they "obeyed with alacrity," and Quantrill followed them outside.

A few of his men had ridden with him into Bonham when he was summoned by McCulloch. He leaped into the saddle of his horse and gave a shout to them:

"Mount and get out of Bonham. We're all prisoners here!"

In a wild clatter of hoofs the guerrillas were gone, leaving McCulloch perhaps a little chapfallen, perhaps a little relieved, starting up from his dinner at the news.

Pursuit was organized. And here came the first great defection. Bill Anderson and his contingent of guerrillas, including Fletch Taylor's command, *joined the pursuit.*

But a courier on a very fast horse had warned Todd, in the camp at Mineral Creek, to get his men to horse immediately and meet Quantrill at Colbert's Ferry over the Red River.

Todd obeyed. As he and his men joined Quantrill, where the roads joined five miles east of Sherman, Anderson and a detachment of cavalry appeared riding hard after Quantrill.

Forming a line in the timber of a creek, Todd's men waited until the pursuit was within gunshot, and carbines began to speak. It was not much of a skirmish, one man being slightly wounded on each side, but it marked a mighty turning point. *Guerrilla was hunting guerrilla . . . guerrilla was shooting at guerrilla.*

From that moment Quantrill's command broke up, his men dropped away from him, his leadership was lost.

Anderson already had taken one contingent, and Fletch Taylor another. George Todd, who once was afraid of Quantrill, now faced him down in his own camp after they crossed the Red River, into the Indian Territory, where McCulloch had no jurisdiction, and marched off with a good third of what was left.

There were smaller bands who took their independent ways, and new faces were appearing among the dissident leaders. One of them was a youth with steel-blue eyes, so reckless and deadly that even his companions, all much older than he, stood in awe of him. His name was Jesse Woodson James and he owed allegiance to no man. Another was Cole Younger, big, with a good-humored face, and quite murderous.

They were to be heard from later, when they were much together, and it is time we took a look at them.

The parents of Jesse James, the Rev. Robert James, a preacher-farmer, and Zerelda Cole James, his wife, arrived in Missouri from Kentucky late in 1842. They had kin living on the border, but their decision to change residence seems to have been quite sudden, for it interrupted the seminary course of the young minister. On January 10, 1843, Zerelda gave birth to a son, whom they named Alexander Franklin James, but who became known to history as Frank James.

Jesse Woodson James was born September 5, 1847. He never really knew his father, for the Rev. Robert James had an adventurous streak and joined in the gold rush after the strike in California was announced, going probably across the plains with the Forty-niner caravans. He died, however, within a short time after his arrival in the gold fields, and was buried at the mining camp of Marysville, California.

His widow, only twenty-five at the time, was perhaps quite comely, and besides women were scarce on the frontiers. In 1851 she married again, her new husband being a farmer named Simms. This marriage lasted only a short time and ended apparently in divorce. For a third time Zerelda was espoused, this time by Dr. Reuben Samuel, who was also a Kentuckian, with a medical training in Cincinnati. This marriage lasted. Throughout the long troublous period that followed, Dr. Samuel remained faithful to his wife and her boys.

The family was strongly pro-Confederate, and when the Civil War began, Frank James, though only sixteen, enlisted in the Confederate Army and fought in the bloody battle of Wilson's Creek. When he returned home on a furlough, he was arrested by Federal officers, and released on parole. The parole meant nothing to him. Shortly after, he joined Quantrill's band, was one of its first recruits in fact, and rode with his leader until the final fatal days.

Jesse did not ride in the Lawrence raid. He was considered too young, and stayed on the Samuel place helping to work the farm. He was not too young, however, to be mistreated by a band of Union "militia" who came to the place in June 1862. For his too outspoken sentiments Dr. Samuel was hanged from a black-jack tree and left dangling. He was saved by his wife, a woman of great resolution, who "followed stealthily, and the moment the militia had departed she rushed to the rescue of her husband, whom she hastily cut down and by patient nursing saved his life."

The soldiers went on and found Jesse in a field plowing. They gave him a flogging between the corn rows and told him if he paid any more visits to the guerrilla camp they would hang him, too.[1]

In that June of 1862 Jesse was only fourteen years old. He did not at once follow Frank to the guerrillas. His mother and half sister, Susie, were arrested and held in custody for a time in 1863. I do not know if they were among the seventeen women and girls

[1] This episode has been scouted by some modern writers on the ground that it was "probably" an invention to erect a "revenge" motive for Jesse James' career of crime.

For example, James D. Horan, whom I respect, in his book *Desperate Men*, comments: "Though the incident may be true, there is nothing to support it but the repeated retelling."

But it *was* repeatedly retold, and by the Missouri neighbors of the Samuel-James family, who presumably knew of it. None of them, so far as I know, ever refuted it. Quite naturally the militia would make no official report of such an atrocity.

J. W. Buel, in his book *The Border Outlaws*, published in 1882, recites the story as an accepted fact. Buel was a newspaper reporter on the Kansas City *Journal* much of the time the outlaws were operating, and personally covered some of their crimes for his paper, and had correspondence with Cole Younger and Frank James. He was no partisan of the James brothers, but he was rather close to the sources, his book being published in 1882, shortly after Jesse James' death.

I believe the incident may be accepted as truth, especially since other families in the district received treatment as severe, and it is a standard tradition of the neighborhood and district, told from father to son for generations.

Jesse did not need a revenge motive for his later robberies, but he certainly carried some fierce resentments with him into his guerrilla activities during the war.

imprisoned on orders of General Ewing, some of whom later were injured in the collapse of the building in Kansas City, but it seems probable. They were later released and joined Dr. Samuel, who presumably had preceded them in the forced exodus when Order No. 11 was issued. The family made its home at Rulo, on the Missouri River in the extreme southeast corner of what was then the Nebraska Territory.

It was at this time that Jesse, by now nearly sixteen, obtained a horse somewhere and rode off to join his brother and Quantrill.

As of that period he was described as having "a face smooth and innocent as the face of a school girl. The eyes, very clear and penetrating, were never at rest."

The last sentence may refer to Jesse's habit of blinking his eyes. James D. Horan brings out this peculiarity in his *Desperate Men*, a recital of the operations of the Pinkerton National Detective Agency, for which he had access to the Pinkerton records, and in which he has added some valuable data to the story of the outlaws.[2]

Frank James was "four years older and somewhat taller than Jesse. Jesse's face was something of an oval; Frank's was long, wide about the forehead, square and massive about the jaw and chin, and set always in a look of fixed repose. Jesse laughed at many things; Frank laughed not at all."

These descriptions were given by Harrison Trow, who rode with Quantrill and the James boys and styled himself "Captain."

Brothers who did not look alike, whose personalities were almost opposite—were they really full brothers? Remember the somewhat sudden move of the Rev. Robert James and Zerelda to Missouri, and the birth of Frank so soon after. These matters will be examined more closely later.

When Jesse went into the war he was derisively called "Dingus," because of his youth and smooth, girlish face. On one occasion

[2] *Desperate Men* is a fine and thoroughly studied work, although unfortunately for its thesis it fails to show that the Pinkertons were anything but bunglers in their efforts to combat the James gang. Horan is too good a historian to twist the facts, even though he writes entirely from the viewpoint of the operatives whose activities he describes most sympathetically.

he was actually dressed up like a girl and used as a lure to bring several would-be amorous Federal soldiers to their deaths. But when Jesse came out of the war he had two or three battle wounds, and a list of personal killings so impressive that nobody called him "Dingus" any more—or anything else derisive or disrespectful.

We have a picture of him as he was then, about seventeen or eighteen years old, hair rather long and pushed back of his ears, low-crowned hat cocked up at the sides, a revolver in one hand and two in his belt. He is beardless, but the once boyish mouth is thin as a knife slit, without one softening curve, and his level eyes are icy cold.

Those eyes had seen more of death than could have been good for a youngster his age. This was the Jesse James who slew eight men in one bloody day at Centralia, and nobody knows how many more in his reckless, deadly career as a guerrilla. This was the Jesse James who came out of the war leading a guerrilla band, all men older than himself. This was the Jesse James who had come to place no value on human life as the result of his brutal schooling in the years that are most formative. He could kill a man with no more qualms than he would feel in crushing a bug under his boot.

Cole Younger, who led his own little band, also had a grievance. He and his brothers were first cousins to the James boys, and two of them—Cole and Jim—were graduates of the Quantrill "school." John and Robert Younger were never guerrillas, being even more youthful than Jesse. Cole followed Quantrill almost from the first of the war, but Jim joined the black flag in 1864.

Their father, Colonel Henry Washington Younger, owned two farms, a fine home, a stable of valuable horses, some cattle, and at times considerable cash money. His title appears to have been honorary. It is still customary to call every auctioneer "Colonel" in the Midwest, and perhaps he did some auctioneering in connection with his livestock business.

He was murdered and robbed while driving alone in a buggy between Independence and Harrisonville, Missouri, July 20, 1862. Buel wrote:

It was reported that the assassins were Jennison's Red Legs, but of this there is no proof, though Cole harbored suspicions, and he never rested until the last person whom he suspected of complicity in this crime was dead, and his vengeful hand murdered not a few.

Whatever Buel surmised, the Younger family had very definite ideas as to who did the killing, even to the name of the leader of the Red Legs, a Captain Walley. The countryside was thoroughly interested in the murder, and information was sought and handed on rapidly. Even though Walley and his merry men—quite naturally—made no report of the episode, persons in Independence, where they were stationed, would have ways of knowing their identities and passing them on.

But Cole Younger did not murder Walley. While in prison he wrote Buel:

In relation to Walley I will say: if I were what the world paints me, there could be no excuse except cowardice for my neglect to kill him. During the war I did everything in my power to get hold of him, but failed. . . . When I returned home from the war . . . I could have killed Walley nearly any time, but only by assassination—slipping up to his house and shooting him through a window. Some people might have perpetrated such a deed, but I could not pollute my soul with such a crime. . . . I could not shoot him like a dog, especially when I knew he had a wife and children.

Cole, who was born in Jackson County, Missouri, January 15, 1844, and was therefore not yet nineteen years old when his father was killed, was away with Quantrill at the time. Colonel Younger was found dead "with his pockets turned inside out, about $400 having been taken. The assassins, however, failed to find a larger sum, several thousand dollars, which Mr. Younger had placed in a belt he wore around his body beneath his underclothes."

Queries Burton Rascoe, in his book *Belle Starr*, "How could they know that $400 was taken from Younger's body?"

The answer seems to me quite simple. Younger had sold a herd of cattle the previous day in Independence—at wartime prices. His receipts would be of record, and the deficit between what was paid him and what he still had on his body could easily be determined by the family.

The following February the Younger home was burned to the ground by the Red Legs. Incidents such as these might embitter even long-suffering people. The Youngers were not long-suffering.[3]

Quantrill led what was left of his men back to Missouri, where he speedily found the hue and cry so persistent that it was too dangerous to remain there, however tempting his dalliance, which he resumed, with the charming Kate. He therefore sent the girl to St. Louis, and in November 1864 headed with a handful of his guerrillas for Kentucky, hoping to maintain himself in the mountain country. This was when Jesse James and Cole Younger parted from him, somewhere in Arkansas, and turned toward the Indian Territory, where they operated for a time in the Cherokee country.

Frank James and Jim Younger, however, stayed with Quantrill. Altogether, perhaps twenty men followed the leader, a long, long fall for him from that day when he led a column of 448 hickory-hard horsemen toward Lawrence.

As a matter of fact, time was running out for William Clarke Quantrill, and he must have known it. His band fought some skirmishes with pursuing Federal forces, did some looting, and had narrow escapes—on one occasion Quantrill himself raced barefoot through the snow to save his life when his camp was surprised.

There were a few pleasant interludes. Near Wakefield, Kentucky, he stopped at the home of a farmer named Dawson, whose daughter, Nannie, asked the guerrilla leader to write in her album. Years before, at great labor, he had composed for another Nannie—Anne, the daughter of Morgan Walker—some

[3] Nothing can excuse the later outlawry of the James and Younger clans, but it is bad history to discount parts of the whole story merely to buttress an author's thesis that these men lacked any grievances. They did have grievances. So did many others. I lived for years in the Missouri border country and have talked with many of the old-timers about the war years. The significant point, to my way of thinking, is that of the thousands who were robbed, burned out, and sometimes saw members of their families murdered, only a scattering few took to crime. And these did so, not because of their grievances, but because they had wild and lawless tendencies, exaggerated by guerrilla warfare. The greater portion of the people in the Burnt District quietly worked after the war at rebuilding their homes and trying to restore their shattered prosperity, obedient to the laws of the state and nation.

verses in which he borrowed rather liberally from Byron. Remembering what he could of them, he wrote for this later Nannie:

My horse is at the door
And the enemy I soon may see
But before I go Miss Nannie
Here's a double health to thee.

Here's a sign to those who love me
And a smile to those who hate
And, whatever sky's above me,
Here's a heart for every fate.

Though cannons roar around me
Yet it still shall bear me on,
Though dark clouds are above me
It hath springs that may be won.

In this verse as with the wine
The libation I will pour
Should be peace with thine and mine
And a health to thee and all in door.

Very respectfully, your friend,
Feb. 26, 1865 W.C.Q.

The meter limps and the sense is at times a little hard to follow, but Quantrill did not claim to be a bard. The poem, such as it is, is still preserved.

When, on April 16, word came that Lincoln had been assassinated, the guerrillas were at the home of Judge Jonathan Davis, a strong Confederate sympathizer. They held a drunken celebration, for which Quantrill apologized politely to the ladies. One of the men proposed a toast:

"Here's to the death of Abe Lincoln, hoping that his bones may serve in hell as a gridiron to fry Yankees on."

To this macabre and unseemly sentiment the guerrillas drank with inebriated enthusiasm.

But Quantrill's luck had turned bad.

On May 10, he divided his band, sending part of the men toward one farm to quarter themselves, while he stopped with his immediate party at the farm of James H. Wakefield, near Bloomfield, about thirty miles southeast of Louisville. Both Frank James and Jim Younger were quartered at the other place.

With Quantrill at the time were, apparently, only eleven guerrillas: John Ross, William Hulse, Payne Jones, Clark Hockensmith, Isaac Hall, Dick Glasscock, Bob Hall, Bud Spence, Allen Parmer, Dave Helton, and Lee McMurtry.

A heavy rain was falling, and Quantrill was napping in the hayloft of the barn. Wakefield, the farmer, stood idly talking with Dick Glasscock, sheltered by the wide eaves of the stable, while others of the men held a sham battle inside, choosing up sides and using corncobs for ammunition.

Suddenly Glasscock uttered a wild yell:

"Here they come!"

He saw, galloping over the rise through the pelting downpour, a body of horsemen in blue uniforms.

The surprise was complete. Quantrill had not dreamed that an enemy was within twenty-five miles of him.

Shots began thudding out. Some of the guerrillas scrambled for their horses and rode away, others plunged into a nearby pond and hid under the bushes on its border.

Quantrill slid down from the loft and tried to mount his horse, but the animal, frightened by the shooting, yelling, and confusion, became unmanageable, reared, and broke away from him.

In that moment, alone in the barnyard with the blue cavalry roaring toward him, all the strangeness and terror of his life must have passed before him. Where now was that column of lean, terrible hunters he once led? Dead, many of them. Following other leaders, most of the rest.

Horseless, he turned and sprinted from the barnyard for the woods, but the oncomers were close now, shooting at him.

Then Glasscock, seeing his peril, bravely turned back to rescue him. His horse was hit by a bullet and began to rear and plunge, making it impossible for Quantrill to mount behind. A moment later Glasscock was knocked out of his saddle by a lead slug, dead.

Quantrill whirled as if to fire at the charging foe, but at that instant Clark Hockensmith came galloping back. Quantrill did not shoot, but tried to get up behind his man.

A level sheet of flame seemed to blaze from the blue line, ranged behind the farmyard fence. Hockensmith was stretched dead by the volley. And Quantrill was down, struck by a ball in the back, his spine shattered so that he was paralyzed below the shoulders, while another bullet took off a finger of his right hand.

There, on the wet ground, with the rain pelting his face, Quantrill lay near the bodies of the two men who had given their lives for him, fully knowing that his wound was mortal. Blue-clad soldiers gathered about him.

"Are you Quantrill?" he was asked.

"No," answered the pallid lips. "I'm Captain Clarke, Fourth Colorado Cavalry, U. S. Volunteers."

There was no such regiment.

Someone took off his boots, and a blanket was fetched, in which he was carried to the house. He asked that Hockensmith and Glasscock be given soldier's burials. Then, knowing there was no use longer to deny it, he admitted his identity. By that time the rest of his band had made good their escape.

Ironically, Quantrill suffered his death stroke at the hands of "Federal" guerrillas no better than himself. The leader of the company called himself Captain Edwin Terrill. He was a deserter from the Confederate Army, who became a guerrilla and announced his "loyalty" to the Union cause when he saw the way the tide of war was turning.[4]

Quantrill was left at the Wakefield house that night. He was helpless, able only to move his arms and head. In the dark hours some of his men, including Frank James, came to the house and begged him to let them carry him away. He refused. He told them

[4] The summer after the Quantrill fight, Terrill was jailed for the brutal murder of a Union soldier. He escaped, but a little later got drunk, tried to "shoot up" Shelbyville, Kentucky, and killed an old man. A posse very properly shot him to death.

Wrote R. T. Owen, who knew him: "His [Terrill's] reputation was the worst imaginable and his fighting qualities were only developed when under the influence of whiskey; and his death was a great relief to his family, his friends, and his enemies."

That feeling of relief came to a considerable category, to say the least.

he knew he was going to die and had pledged his word to stay. Furthermore, if he broke his parole and allowed them to take him with them, Wakefield's house would be burned down in reprisal. The guerrillas stole away and left him.

Next day Terrill returned and took Quantrill to Louisville in a farm wagon filled with straw to ease the jolting. He was placed in a military hospital, where he lingered in pain until June 6, when he died.

Quantrill was a Catholic. Before his death he was visited by two old priests, and to one of them he made a complete confession of his life's sins. It must have curled the hair of the aged clergyman to listen to that lengthy and unexpurgated catalogue. But in the end Quantrill received the Church's blessing.

As one of the last acts of his life, he entrusted two thousand dollars in gold to the priest who confessed him, asking him to deliver it to Kate Clarke, whose address in St. Louis he gave. The good father later faithfully carried out the errand, but he must have been taken aback somewhat by the use she made of the money.

She established what the times euphemistically called a "fancy house," and for years was a well-known figure in the red-light district of St. Louis.[5]

There is one especially unpleasant aftermath of the Quantrill story.

He was buried in a Catholic cemetery in Louisville. His mother, Mrs. Caroline Clarke Quantrill, living in a strongly pro-Union community at Canal Dover, Ohio, had throughout the war expressed great surprise and horrified disapproval whenever she heard of her son's deeds. After the war, however, when feeling had somewhat cooled, she began to profess grief and affection for the memory of Quantrill, and eventually induced W. W. Scott, a neighbor at Canal Dover, to try and find his grave. This was in 1887. Scott succeeded in his mission, and Mrs. Quantrill then visited the place with him.

[5] Kate Clarke, incidentally, was the second of Quantrill's mistresses to embark on the oldest profession. Her predecessor, Anne Walker, for years ran a similar palace of sinful pleasure at Baxter Springs, Kansas.

Next she requested that the dead man's bones be exhumed, so that she could take them "to the family burial ground in Ohio." Scott at first refused, but she pleaded so strongly that at length he did as she asked.

With the connivance of the custodian of the cemetery and an employee, to both of whom Scott gave a few dollars, Quantrill's bones were disinterred, placed in a box, and turned over to Mrs. Quantrill.

Scott's written account of the episode ends with these words: "Mrs. Q. [Quantrill] afterwards had the lot sold and received the money."

Quantrill was no good. But the ghoulish mother, who sold her son's bones as curios, could hardly have been much better.

3. *The Wild Riders of Missouri*

Quantrill was dead, but the evil that he did lived after him, as no less an authority than William Shakespeare said of such matters.

When he first became leader of the guerrillas he was twenty-four years old. When he led the raid on Lawrence he had just passed his twenty-sixth birthday. At his death in Kentucky he was not yet twenty-eight. Yet in so brief a span of time he established a pattern of outlawry that continued long after him: hard riding, hard shooting, a network of hideouts, loot as the great objective, and murder without compunction.

His men who drifted back to their homes in Missouri after the war found it difficult to resume their normal lives—if, indeed, they ever had normal lives. Most of them were young. They had known nothing in adulthood but adventure, excitement, war. It is a habit-forming drug that is hard to shake off when one has tasted it and finds himself returned suddenly to a humdrum workaday existence.

What made it even harder was that hatreds still flamed in

Missouri. People in the Burnt District could not forget or forgive what was done to them by Order No. 11 and the Red Legs. Some elements of the victorious Union party were vengeful and vindictive. Men who had served with or sympathized with the "Secesh" were not infrequently called to their doors at night and shot down by masked gangs of men who called themselves "Regulators."

Ex-guerrillas were particular targets of hatred. The general amnesty given Confederate soldiers after the war did not extend to Quantrill's men, who had been officially declared outlaws. Wrote August C. Appler, editor of the Osceola, Missouri, *Democrat*, in 1875:

> There was abundant reason why these men should not surrender unless the guarantee of protection was given . . . Many of Quantrill's men had to flee the country; many were hung or shot in other places. For months after hostilities ceased, predatory and bloodthirsty bands, under the guise of vigilance committees, swept over the border counties, making quick work of Confederate guerrillas wherever found.

With such blood feuds flaring and everything so unsettled, conditions were ripe for the creation of a special brand of outlawry: bitter resentments, an entire population of men as deadly with weapons and indifferent to death as any this country has seen, and the restlessness and craving for action and excitement that seem inevitably to affect many veterans of any war.

Only a week more than seven months after Quantrill's death, his aptest pupils began their careers as bandits: Jesse and Frank James, and their first cousins, the Younger brothers.

At the war's very end young Jesse had one more thing to remember. On April 15, 1865, he led six guerrillas, all that was left of his immediate band, toward Lexington, Missouri, to surrender. Riding in the lead, he carried a white handkerchief, tied to a stick, as a flag of truce.

On the way in they suddenly encountered a squad of eight Union cavalrymen, the advance party of a column of thirty Johnson County (Kansas) militia, and thirty of the Second Wisconsin Cavalry.

The men of the advance—"drunk" according to Trow—did not

see the flag of truce, or disregarded it. At once they opened fire.

Jesse got a bullet through his right lung, and his horse was killed. About this time the main body of cavalry came up and went off in pursuit of the five remaining guerrillas, who put spurs to their horses and eventually escaped.

Five, however, remained behind to pursue Jesse, who, in spite of his severe wound, rose from his fallen horse and ran for the woods. He reached cover, with the enemy coming up fast. Weak from loss of blood, he could hardly lift his revolver, but, taking both hands, he managed to raise it and killed the leading horseman. Another of the five was wounded by the savage, desperate boy, and the others drew off.

For two days Jesse lay hiding in the woods beside a small creek, delirious and suffering from wound pneumonia. On the third day he was found by a farmer, who took him to his house and notified his friends.

Four days later, more dead than alive, he was conveyed in a wagon to Lexington. The provost marshal there, Major J. B. Rogers, was "a liberal officer of the old regime, who understood in its fullest and broadest sense that the war was over, and that however cruel or desperate certain organizations or certain bodies of men had been in the past, all proscription of them ceased with their surrender."[1]

Rogers examined the wounded boy, decided he was sure to die, and did not even take the trouble to exact from him a parole. He gave the youth a pass and allowed him to go, with the help of some of his friends, to Rulo, Nebraska Territory, where his mother and stepfather still lived.

Even a bullet hole through a lung complicated by pneumonia could not quell the whipcord vitality of young Jesse. He managed to reach Rulo, helped by some of the ex-guerrillas; and Dr. Samuel, who appears to have been a pretty fair country physician, managed to pull him through.

The following August the family returned by steamboat to

[1] Trow's words. But Rogers must have known the guerrillas were still outlaws. Actually, he seems to have been a kindly man, genuinely sorry for the boy, who appeared certain to die soon, and willing to stretch a point out of mercy.

Missouri, stopping for a time at the home of John Mimms, near Kansas City. Mimms had married a sister of Jesse's father, and was therefore his uncle. So haggard and emaciated was the youth, and still so weak from his wound, which took long in healing, that it was decided that he ought to remain at the Mimms home while Dr. Samuel and his wife went on to their farm in Clay County, to see what was left of it.

The period of convalescence must have been pleasant for Jesse. A pretty girl about his own age cared for him part of the time, perhaps read to him, and otherwise played the classic role of the charming ministering angel at the bed of pain. She was John Mimms' daughter, Jesse's own cousin, Zerelda Mimms—named, indeed, after his mother. It is hardly surprising that he fell in love with her, and she seems to have responded to him, for though it was nine years before he was able to marry her, and a number of suitors sought her in that time, the girl would have no other man than Jesse James for her husband.

Meantime Jesse's mother, now about forty, and her husband, somewhat older, a grave, fatherly man, who acceded then and always to his strong-minded wife's wishes, found that their house, a plain log edifice, had escaped the general burnings that destroyed so many finer homes. Perhaps it was not considered worth setting afire. After some repairing it was habitable, and the land was still there; so Dr. Samuel and Zerelda set up housekeeping, prepared to resume farming and medical practice, and in due time conveyed Jesse to their home.

He was still very thin, but his wound had healed and his strength began to return. In those weeks he began to form the plans which were to make him an incredibly successful outlaw and bandit. Former comrades rode over to visit him at the Samuel place. Among these his kinsmen were most important. Cole Younger and his brother Jim had two more members of the family coming along, John and Robert, neither of whom had been in the war. There were others of the family blood—Wood and Clarence Hite, who were cousins and had ridden as guerrillas and could be counted on for action; and such "kinfolks" as the Mimms family of Kansas City, and the Daltons, a branch of whom later made outlaw history of its own, though these in Missouri were never outlaws. Besides, there were many close friends in the Burnt District who took no active part in outlaw acts, but out of common hatred and clannishness at times hid the bandits, at times furnished them with alibis, and at times gave them warnings and timely information.

In this blood-relative combination Jesse James, though junior both to his cousin Cole Younger and his brother Frank, who soon joined him, became the unquestioned leader.

Sometimes in those formative months, as Jesse improved in health, he would ride over to Liberty, the county seat, and have a few drinks with his ex-guerrilla friends. Occasionally they would "hurrah" the town—riding up and down the street with their shrill yells, firing their revolvers in the air. People did not particularly resent this exuberance, but they learned to stay indoors when the wild riders were on the loose.

But was this an indication of mere exuberance? Might it not have been a matter of settled and well-planned policy? Jesse James, the ablest pupil of Quantrill's "school for crime," had ideas and schemes, and it may have been that he instituted the practice of "hurrahing" Liberty in order to get the citizens trained to conform to a certain pattern, for a project he already had in mind.

In his secret conferences with friends of his guerrilla days, he had little trouble convincing them that there was more excitement and profit in what he had in mind than they could find any other way. Already the young men were tiring of a peaceful life, and longing for the old days of continual intensive action, risk, adventure. Following a plow behind a team of mules, or husking corn from early dawn to dark, seemed very dull compared to whooping cavalry raids and the ambushing of enemy columns in a rattle of revolvers, with the sharp tang of powder smoke in the air. The substitute offered by the thin youth with the blinking blue eyes seemed pretty good to their restless minds.

We know the names of some of his associates in those days, former guerrillas all: Frank James; Cole and Jim Younger; Ed and Clell Miller; Wood and Clarence Hite; George and Ol (Oliver)

Shepherd; Bill Ryan, Charlie Pitts, Jim Cummins, Tom Little, Payton (Payne) Jones, Arch Clements, and probably Dick Burns and Andy McGuire. They were an unfragrant crew of tough characters, who had seen war at its worst and bloodiest, killers and robbers to a man. And to a man they acceded to Jesse James in the leadership of the gang.

Jesse was a criminal with imagination. He "invented" bank robbery, and he "perfected" train robbery—although the first train holdup was committed by another gang of bandits in Indiana, in 1866.

Throughout his career he and his followers asserted and continued to assert that they were "persecuted" into outlawry. Judge William H. Wallace, a Burnt District man himself, who later probably had as much to do with breaking up the outlaw ring as anyone else, made an interesting observation on this point in his memoirs:

> The usual defense of the outlaws, namely, that their robberies and homicides were committed in just revenge upon Northern men for mistreatment received by them or their relatives during the Civil War, or afterwards, is overwhelmed by the evidence. Every bank robbed by them during the fifteen years of their career with possibly two exceptions, belonged to Southern men, and most of these banks were located in Missouri, some of them in Kentucky and Virginia. The truth is, too, that the persons killed in these bank robberies were Southerners. We had as well admit the truth—they robbed for money, not for revenge.

Money, and the lawless craving for excitement which their restless natures demanded, impelled them—and Jesse James was there to show them the way.

The dubious honor of being the first bank held up in American history was bestowed by Jesse on a local institution, the Clay County Savings and Loan Association, of Liberty, only about a dozen miles from his home. This was not because of any civic pride. It was because for his first effort in the brand-new field, he wanted a town he knew, a bank he knew—and perhaps people who were habituated to getting off the streets when his yelling, shooting crew went through.

The morning of February 14, 1866, dawned cold and blustery, with a blizzard threatening. On the streets of Liberty few were moving. Shopkeepers were sweeping their floors and keeping roaring fires going in their iron stoves for the scattering of early customers to huddle around. A few students hurried toward William Jewell College, hoping to reach their classrooms before the tardy bell rang.

Just as eight o'clock struck, the frosty air was split by a volley of shrill whoops, and down the main street of the town tore ten horsemen, all superbly mounted, all bundled against the cold in long blue overcoats and mufflers, all wearing revolvers in holsters conspicuously strapped about their waists.

Now for the first time the formula of the new technique of bank robbery was put into execution. It consisted simply of an adaptation of the old Quantrill guerrilla tactics, tailored by Jesse James to fit the new situation.

A band of whooping riders would sweep into a town and "hurrah" it, terrorizing the citizens into shutting themselves in their houses or stores by yells and threats and shots. By this furious display the robbers counted on numbing the town, until the bank could be looted and they were gone. For Liberty, which had seen enough of the drunken riders to stay indoors when they were on a spree, such a display was sufficient. That was why Jesse James chose it for his first coup.

But for future robberies—and mark this—the bandits must have *a known reputation for deadliness*, to make their threats effectively fearsome.

On this icy morning the cavalcade came to a jolting stop before the bank. Four men quickly dismounted, leaving their horses to be held by two others, who remained in their saddles, and half-ran into the bank. Out in the street the horsemen who were not holding mounts for their accomplices careered about at a gallop, glancing here and there, revolvers in hand. Persons who saw them quickly dodged into shelter behind closed doors.

Greenup Bird, cashier of the bank, and his son, William Bird, his assistant, were just opening up for business. When the four men tramped in, they looked up, saw revolvers covering them, and dazedly obeyed an order to hold up their hands. With businesslike briskness the bandits herded them into the open vault, the shelves of which they swept bare of gold and silver coin, as well as greenbacks and some bonds, all of which they dumped into an ordinary grain sack.

The leader smiled grimly at the cashier and made a bad pun as he pointed to the vault. "Stay in there," he said. "Don't you know all Birds should be caged?"

Then, leaving the father and son shut in the vault, the four dashed outside, tied the heavy sack of money to a saddle horn, mounted, and whooping shrilly, the whole band galloped out of town.

At this moment George Wymore (or Wynmore) a nineteen-year-old student at the college, was hastening to his class. When the horsemen came thundering down the street toward him he ran to get into a house.

One of the riders wheeled his horse, drew a revolver, and fired four times.

The youth tripped, stumbled to his knees, then fell prostrate on the frozen ground. When he was picked up later, quite dead, it was found that every one of the four shots had taken effect, and any one of them would have been fatal.

Out from their hiding places the citizens of Liberty crept to see what had happened. The outlaws were gone. The dead boy was carried into a house. Such a murder was blood-chilling. But something else, for a curious psychological reason, seemed even more stunning to the people.

Greenup Bird and his son had succeeded in getting out of the vault and were telling their story.

The bank had been robbed!

In that day banks possessed, to the public mind, a sort of sacrosanct character. Common folks regarded them with awe. The banker was the town's big man, and his institution was a somewhat mystic symbol of wealth, power, and security. That a bank should be robbed—and in broad daylight—was so unheard of and even unimagined that it took people's breath away.

Belatedly a posse was formed to pursue the bandits, who had taken the road toward the resort town of Excelsior Springs. But by that time the outlaws were well out of sight. They not only had the finest mounts available but could outride any ordinary man in the country. Furthermore, the posse probably did not feel an overwhelming urge to catch up with them. After all, there were ten in the gang, and every one of them probably knew only too well how to shoot—and was only too ready to do it!

Presently the pursuit slackened. That night the threatened blizzard swept over Missouri, obliterating any trail that might have been left. The bandits had scattered and disappeared.

No very serious effort was made to catch the perpetrators of the first of all bank holdups. Yet some people must have known pretty well who they were. For example, Greenup Bird, the cashier, was addressed by name by the bandit who made the bad pun. If the outlaw knew him, it follows that he knew the outlaw, who was not masked. None of the bandits wore masks, and all of them had been in Liberty many times on nighttime sprees. Yet after the excitement abated both the Birds said they could not identify any of the men, and none of the other citizens came forward to name them.

A man living near Blue Mills ferry had sold two sacks of meal to some horsemen before the robbery. He told neighbors he recognized the James boys and Bud Pearce. Later he became frightened and told the sheriff he was mistaken—he knew nobody in the crowd.

This brings up two points that had a large bearing on the career of the outlaws. By some people they were regarded with a sort of hero worship because the guerrillas had been the only resistance group in the bitter days of the war—a sort of underground, like the French Maquis. But even those who had no such feeling toward them considered it unhealthy to inform against ex-guerrillas in the Burnt District. An incident to illustrate was told by Judge H. P. White of Jackson County, after a later bank holdup:

"A man who knew the perpetrators was summoned before the grand jury. He gave them all the facts and names. When being excused, he said, 'Gentlemen, I have told the truth. I will never swear to a lie.' And drawing a pistol, he said, 'The notches on this pistol give the number of men I have killed. My life is now in danger and I desire to say that if anybody is indicted, each man on this grand jury can dig his grave.' No one was indicted."

In later years it was pretty well established that the ten who rode into Liberty that morning of February 14 included Jesse and Frank James, Bud Pearce, Arch Clements, George Shepherd, Bill Ryan, Payne Jones, Andy McGuire, and two of the Younger brothers, probably Cole and Jim. Jesse James was the leader—he of the grim smile and the bad pun.

And who killed George Wymore?

The slayer fired four times, from the back of a prancing horse, at a running target. Every one of the shots took deadly effect.

Jesse James, even among men who were experts with the revolver, was celebrated for his skill with the weapon.

Jesse, in his guerrilla career, had lost all moral sense of the value of human life.

The slayer's identity never was officially established, but if it was not Jesse, someone else in that crowd had uncanny marksmanship.

One factor points directly at Jesse. Although he would have needed no reason for killing—he might merely have tried his hand at shooting, as a man would use a scuttling rabbit for a target—in this case he would have had a definite motive.

Jesse was the leader, the planner. He wanted to establish a pattern, *a precedent of deadliness*, so that future towns when he raided them would know that he and his gang would kill on the slightest excuse or without excuse. It is more than likely that Jesse James cold-bloodedly made poor young George Wymore serve as an example and a warning to the country at large.

Jesse James, at the time of the murder, was not yet nineteen years old—not quite as old as the inoffensive student who was shot down.

The first bank robbery was an astounding success, but it left the outlaws with a problem. They got about $15,000 in gold coin, some silver and greenbacks, and $45,000 in bonds.

The bonds were worthless to them, since they were nonnegotiable, and were thrown away. The gold was not much more valuable because people used little gold in ordinary transactions, and anyone who began spending gold pieces freely would be certain to attract to himself undesired attention.

There was, however, a way to dispose of it. In San Antonio, Texas, lived a man named Gonzales. Presumably the outlaws became acquainted with him during the war, when they campaigned in Texas. Gonzales was willing to change any amount of gold into silver or greenbacks—for a "cut" of 40 per cent. Some of the outlaws, certainly Cole Younger and one or more of his brothers, and probably Jesse James, rode south to make this exchange, and out of that ride came a highly interesting—and important—set of circumstances in the tangled skein of outlaw succession.

One of the families of Confederate sympathizers which left Missouri during the Civil War was that of John Shirley, an innkeeper at Carthage, in the southwestern corner of the state. Shirley knew Quantrill's guerrillas and probably gave them hospitality. His second son, Ed (better known as Bud), was one of them, and was killed in a skirmish with Federal irregulars near Sarcoxie, Missouri, in June 1863.

Shirley's eldest son, Preston, had gone to Texas early and was not involved in the war, although he was destined to die in a saloon shooting scrape. Perhaps Preston helped persuade his father to leave war-harried Carthage for the comparatively minor risks of life in Texas. At any rate, John Shirley in the latter part of 1863 traveled to Sycene, then about ten miles east of Dallas, where he bought a farm.

With him went his wife, and a daughter, Myra Belle. It is with this girl that we are chiefly concerned, since it is she, who became known to history as Belle Starr, who is important to this narrative.

Myra Belle was fifteen years old, ripening into maidenhood, when she rode in one of her father's wagons, loaded with household goods, from racked and tortured Missouri in 1863. By the spring of 1866 she was eighteen, not exactly beautiful, but possessing a fine figure, seductive ways, and ready susceptibility to masculine attentions. She could play the piano and was a magnificent horsewoman, riding a sidesaddle in a riding habit with a bravely flaring skirt after the fashion of the times, a laughing vision of youth and vivacity.

Sometime that spring the Younger brothers and Jesse James—

who must have gone along to supervise the money exchange in San Antonio—stopped at her father's farm, to visit their old friend and break the journey to the mysterious money-changer, Gonzales. They were made welcome and seem to have spent some little period there.

Cole Younger, eldest of the brothers—he was now twenty-four years old—was also the handsomest. Even among the guerrillas he had a mighty reputation as a rider and killer, which may have given him an aura of glamour in the eyes of the girl whose brother had been a guerrilla, and who therefore was a partisan of all guerrillas. As for Cole, he seems to have been far from insensible to feminine charms, and the two found an immediate attraction in each other.

How or when it happened is not recorded, but romance blossomed into something more ardent. Before Cole Younger rode on, he had made the Shirley girl his mistress to such good effect that after he departed she bore him a daughter. At least it is the general belief that Cole Younger was the father; and this is given pretty circumstantial confirmation by the fact that Myra Belle named her child Pearl Younger.

Furthermore, Belle later indicated that she and Younger were married. But Cole Younger, while in prison, said he never was married in his life. It was, undoubtedly, a warm summer love affair, in which hot blood and headlong desire overcame discretion and fear of consequences. Belle was not married to Cole. In fact, Belle never was married, in the legal and conventional sense, to any of her numerous male consorts in her later life.

As to the child, Pearl Younger, she grew up to have an illegitimate offspring of her own, eventually became a "daughter of joy" in a bawdy house, and finally madam of one in her own right. But of this, more later.

By the trip to Gonzales the bandits succeeded in turning their gold into negotiable currency, but allowing for the 40 per cent discount demanded by the money-changer, their $15,000 netted them only $9000. If split up equally, the ten who took part in the Liberty holdup each received less than $1000—not counting the silver and greenbacks, which were divided beforehand and promptly spent.

That does not sound like a very great reward. Yet $1000 was considerable money in those days. Common wages were a dollar a day or less, and a man could work hard all year for a third of what the looters each netted on one raid. Nevertheless, "easy come, easy go," the bandits spent their money rapidly, and it became necessary to look around for some other place to obtain cash without toil.

They made it look easy, holding up the banking house of Alexander Mitchell & Company, at Lexington, Missouri, October 30, 1866, and getting away with $2000. People began to consider the insecurity of country banks.

The following spring, on March 2, 1867, the bandits struck again, but neither the James brothers nor the Youngers were with them. Five ex-guerrillas, J. F. Edmunson, Jim White, Bill Chiles, Bud McDaniels, and Sam Pope, rode into Savannah, Missouri. But this time they ran into difficulties. Judge William McLain, owner of the private banking house they entered, refused to submit tamely.

Instead, when five masked men appeared in his place of business, he seized a revolver which lay on the bank counter and opened fire. One of the bandits shot him in the chest, but he chased them out of the building. They leaped on their horses and fled empty-handed. The doughty judge later recovered from his wound.

It was the first resistance the outlaws had encountered. Judge McLain had shown the way, and from that time on the bandits were to find the robbery of banks increasingly risky.

The failure at Savannah left the gang's funds still low. Probably feeling that the five who attempted that job bungled it, Jesse James took personal charge in the next attempt, and used the methods that had succeeded before—the grand swoop and the "hurrah" of the town.

With fearsome guerrilla yells and revolvers popping, fourteen men raced into Richmond, Missouri, May 23. In a cloud of dust they milled about before the Hughes & Mason Bank, while six of their number went in and took $4000 in gold.

Now, however, the citizens fought back. Led by Mayor Shaw,

men with guns began to shoot at the raiders from behind trees and fences and from the upper stories of buildings. The mayor exposed himself too much and fell dying with four bullets in his body.

With complete scorn of this civilian defense, the robbers, carrying their meal sack of money, rode to the jail and attempted to free some prisoners held there, who were said to be friendly to the ex-guerrillas.

But B. G. Griffin, the jailer, was not cowed, and neither was his fifteen-year-old son. The father opened fire from the jailhouse and the boy emptied a revolver at the swooping horsemen from behind a tree.

The outlaws were too expert. Down went the boy, dead, and Griffin, half crazed with grief, ran out and stood over his son, fighting in frenzy until he, too, went down lifeless, with seven bullets in him.

With that, the outlaws galloped yelling out of the town. Strangely, not a single one of them was wounded by the shooting of the citizens, although the battle lasted several minutes.

By this time the whole state of Missouri was aroused. In Richmond some of the outlaws had been recognized. Business was suspended for three days, and the wealthier citizens made up a "pot" of money to spur pursuit.

Warrants were issued for Jim and John White, Payne Jones, Dick Burns, Ike Flannery, Andy McGuire, and Allen Parmer. The last-named was the Jameses' brother-in-law, having married Jesse's stepsister, Susan Samuel. But he proved an alibi—the outlaws had begun to use that device, although in this case it was genuine.

Not so genuine were some other alibis. Neither of the James brothers, nor any of the Youngers, were named in warrants, although responsible citizens said positively that some of them, especially Jesse, had been there. Perhaps it was because they provided themselves with a novelty—"alibi cards" furnished them by friends—which were distributed rather widely over the country, "proving conclusively" that the innocent sons of Mrs. Zerelda Samuel were engaged in laudable, even pious pursuits—such as attending church meetings—on the day the robbery and street fight occurred.

Others in the Richmond affair were not so lucky. A posse located Payne Jones near Independence. As it closed in on the farmhouse in a night made black by a heavy rain, he leaped out into the yard with a shotgun. The moment his feet hit the ground he discharged both barrels and the buckshot instantly killed B. H. Wilson of the posse and fatally wounded a little girl, daughter of a Dr. Noland, who had guided the posse to the spot. Jones escaped into the woods, aided by the wet inky blackness. For the time being he was free, though he was killed in a gun fight two years later.

Dick Burns, found sleeping in a farmhouse near Richmond itself, was aroused by a party of ten men and unceremoniously strung up to a tree. Andy McGuire eluded pursuit for a few days, but a posse caught him near Warrensburg and used him to decorate an oak with fatal effects. Tom Little, making his way from cave to cave in the limestone hills, at last was captured at St. Louis. He was returned to Warrensburg, where a mob one night took him from the jail and "left his body oscillating from a large tree, as an example to law breakers."

None of these persons was legally tried, let alone convicted, of the Richmond raid. The public feeling, evidently, was that if they weren't guilty of this crime, they had it coming to them for something else they had done somewhere along the line. Lynching parties were not choosy. So long as they had a good subject for their attentions, they were usually quite willing to overlook legalistic trifles, and "git the hangin' under way."

Three men had been "neck-stretched" to pay for the three who were killed at Richmond. It was the last real cleanup of the bandits until Northfield.

Now a new factor entered the game. Four bank robberies, three of them successful, and three men, a boy, and a little girl killed, with others wounded, stirred the financial houses to the point where they pooled funds to try to cope with the bandits. They chose for this purpose the Pinkerton National Detective Agency, the largest and best known in the nation. It was headed by Allan Pinkerton, the man who was Lincoln's personal security officer in the early years of the Civil War and later headed the Union Army secret service.

Already the Pinkertons had broken up one bandit gang. In 1866 four brothers, John, Frank, Slim, and Bill Reno, staged the first of all train holdups and followed it with several other acts of robbery. The Pinkertons hunted them down, arrested them, placed them in jail, and gathered evidence to convict them. Before their cases came to trial, however, Frank, Slim, and Bill Reno were taken from the jail and efficiently lynched by a party of vigilantes. John Reno, eldest of the brothers, and the man whose imagination and daring conceived the whole idea of the train robbery in the first place, escaped lynching but served a long term in the Missouri penitentiary.

To the Pinkerton organization, fearsome because of its reputation for wily and dogged pursuit of criminals, the bankers turned. In combating the James outlaws, however, the agency soon discovered it was dealing with a more slippery and deadly foe than the Renos. The stubborn fact emerges in the history of their operations that the Pinkertons, unfortunately, were more active than effective against the bandits. It was aroused citizens, not professional thief catchers, who eventually brought about the gang's downfall.

The first robbery the Pinkertons were called upon to solve was that of the Long & Norton Bank, at Russellville, Kentucky, May 20, 1868. On that day a man who called himself "Mr. Colburn"—really Cole Younger—and a younger man with "blinking blue eyes" —unquestionably Jesse James—entered the bank and offered a fifty-dollar bill, asking for change.

"I'm sorry, this bill is counterfeit," said Nimrod Long, the cashier.

"I reckon it is," said "Mr. Colburn" with a grin. "But this isn't."

He was aiming a cocked revolver at Long.

"Open up the vault" was the next command.

But the cashier did not obey. Instead he ran for the rear entrance of the bank. The second outlaw fired at him, cutting a flesh wound in his scalp at the side of his head, then battered him to the floor with a heavy blow from his six-shooter.

Long was desperate. In some manner he threw his assailant off him and reached the door, leaping outside and slamming it shut behind him. Down the street he ran, shouting for help. Two other horsemen, sitting their mounts outside the bank, fired at him with rifles but both failed to hit him.

Meantime, Younger and James, inside the bank, had cowed a clerk and a customer who were in the building, and loaded their traditional grain sack with $14,000 in gold, silver, and greenbacks. As they stepped outside, a man named Owens began firing at them with a pistol. He was shot and wounded, but not fatally.

Other citizens now began blazing away up the street. But the bandits mounted and the whole group raced away. Wrote Buel:

> Ten minutes later, some forty citizens, mounted on such animals as they could collect from buggies, wagons, and hitching posts, started in hot pursuit. All the advantage, except in point of numbers, was with the robbers. They rode splendid horses, and were as completely armed and equipped as the most daring and accomplished highwayman could desire. Five miles from Russellville the trail was lost in the woods.

Jesse James and his friends were always particular about their horseflesh. Being able to run away from pursuit was one of the most important factors of their trade.

At this point the Pinkerton Agency, in the person of A. B. (Yankee) Bligh, took up the trail. Bligh found that the chief suspects had the usual alibis. But he managed to trace down George Shepherd, an old guerrilla, at the home of the widow of Dick Maddox, also a former guerrilla. Mrs. Maddox, whose husband was killed by a Cherokee Indian after the war, needed consolation; and big George Shepherd was just the man to console her. He lived with her most of the time—without benefit of clergy—until one night some weeks after the Russellville affair, when he was surrounded at her home by a posse led by Bligh.

Shepherd put up an all-night battle, one against many, but at dawn he tried to make a break, jumping out of a window, and was brought down with a bullet in one leg. He was sent to the Kentucky penitentiary for a two-year term, but refused to tell who were with him at Russellville, or even admit that he knew any of the others. The secrets of the James gang were still safe.

After Russellville, Jesse and his men allowed things to quiet down for more than eighteen months. In that period Cole Younger and Frank James—possibly Jesse also—made a trip to California and spent some time in Texas. Their ruse was successful. As Buel wrote:

> Their deeds were so far forgotten as to be remembered only in the tradition of what were called "stirring times." The country banks had relaxed their vigilance, and detectives, anxious to pluck honors by bringing noted criminals to justice, looked no longer toward the border bandits.

Then the bandits struck again—with suddenness and deadliness that shook the whole country.

On December 7, 1869, three men—Jesse and Frank James and Cole Younger—quietly rode into Gallatin, Missouri. They dismounted before the Daviess County Savings Bank, and while Frank remained outside, holding the horses and keeping a lookout, Jesse and Cole entered the building.

Captain John W. Sheets, a former Union officer, was cashier. He was talking with a young farmer named McDowell, who had just made a deposit, when Jesse James tossed a hundred-dollar bill on the counter and asked for change. Sheets went back to the safe and returned with a handful of money. As he did so he was startled to find Cole's pistol covering him, while at the same moment Jesse drew his gun on the frightened McDowell.

Cole went behind the counter and plundered the safe and money till, getting only about $700. As he returned to the front, according to McDowell's story, Jesse whispered to him and glanced at Sheets.

Then the shocking thing happened. With a swift movement, Jesse fired at the cashier. The bullet entered the victim's right eye and passed out at the back of the head. Sheets was instantly dead, his body thudding to the floor almost before the heavy report of the revolver had ceased.

The shot was heard, and citizens began looking for guns. Frank James, outside the bank, cried a warning, and Cole and Jesse emerged.

Already the horses, spirited animals, were prancing and surging for flight. Shouts and the first guns that began to speak further alarmed them, and as Jesse started to mount, his horse plunged aside.

With his foot caught in the stirrup, the outlaw made one more effort to mount, then his horse shied away, throwing him to the ground.

It was a moment of deadly peril. He might have been dragged to death had he not disengaged his boot. Fortunately for him, the citizens, seeing the rider fall, for a moment held up their shooting.

Jesse regained his feet, and Frank, whirling his horse, galloped back to his brother. In an instant Jesse vaulted up behind him and they were gone in a cloud of dust.

A posse pursued within ten minutes, but the brigands relieved a man named Dan Smoot of the fine horse he was riding toward town, and escaped. Later, when they "induced" a Methodist minister, Reverend Helm, to guide them around the town of Kidder, Jesse made the remark that he was a brother of "Bloody Bill" Anderson, and "I've killed S. P. Cox, if I haven't mistaken the man."

Lieutenant S. P. Cox, a Union officer, was believed by the guerrillas to have commanded the contingent that ambushed and killed Anderson in the later stages of the Civil War, and beheaded him, placing the head on a post.

Was it a case of mistaken identity? Horan believes it was only an "alibi for a cold-blooded murder." But remember that Cole Younger and Jesse James whispered together and looked at Sheets before the fatal shot was fired. They must have discussed something—perhaps asked each other that very question: "Is that man Cox?"

I am inclined to think that Sheets resembled the hated Cox, and the shot was fired on revengeful impulse by Jesse, who in his first guerrilla days rode in Anderson's company. The truth, of course, will never be known. And whatever the excuse, there was no justification of any kind in the murder. Sheets was not resisting. He did everything the bandits asked, only to meet his death at their hands.

Of some importance was the fact that the horse which broke away and threw Jesse was captured. In its issue of December 16, 1869, the Kansas City *Times* had this bit of illumination:

> The horse, held by the sheriff of Daviess County, has been fully identified as the property of a young man named James, whose mother and stepfather live about four miles from Centreville,[2] Clay County, near the Cameron branch of the Hannibal & St. Joe Railroad.

As a result of this disclosure, Deputy Sheriff Tomlinson, with his son and two men from Gallatin, went to the Samuel place. When they approached, the James brothers burst out of the barn already mounted, and fled, the shots that were fired after them taking no effect. Tomlinson, who had the only horse in the posse that could "take a fence," leaped the barrier and pursued. He was back some time later, without his horse. It had been killed by the brothers. Tomlinson returned to Liberty on a horse borrowed from the Samuel stable.

About this time John Younger, who had killed a deputy sheriff, Captain S. W. Nichols, a former Missourian and a Confederate officer, in or near Dallas, Texas, joined his brothers Cole and Jim —and therefore the James boys—in Missouri.

An odd trait was beginning to manifest itself in Jesse—the desire to do the spectacular, to catch the public eye. One of the more amusing evidences of this occurred at Corydon, Iowa, on June 3, 1871. The Hon. Henry Clay Dean, an orator of some repute in that area, was "spellbinding" at an outdoor political meeting, and only the cashier was in the Ocobock Brothers Bank, which made it easy for the gang to loot it of some $45,000.

As they rode away, the outlaws passed the crowd which was listening to the inspired flights of the orator. Jesse could not resist his little gesture. A colloquy occurred, quoted by one source as follows:

"Mr. Dean," said Jesse, interrupting a highly ornamental passage, "I rise to a point of order, sir."

"What is it, friend and fellow citizen?" inquired the great Dean magniloquently. "If it is anything of paramount importance, I yield to the gentleman on horseback."

"Well," said Jesse, "I reckon it's important enough. The fact is, Mr. Dean, some fellows have been over to the bank, robbed it of

[2] The old name of Kearney, Missouri.

every dollar in the till, and tied up the cashier. If you all aren't too busy you might go over and untie him. I've got to be going. Thank you all for your kind attention."

When he finished he and his six companions "set up a wild yell, lifted their hats, and sped away southward."

They got away, of course. Clell Miller later was arrested on suspicion, but nobody could identify him, and he was released.

Back in Chicago, Horan relates, Robert Pinkerton told his father and brother:

"We must smash this gang if it is the last thing we do. They are cold-blooded murderers and brigands and I pray God that I live to see the day that they are put behind bars for the rest of their natural lives."

The Pinkertons were preparing to launch a new attack, which unhappily would be most tragic—for the Pinkertons.

Other robberies followed. At Columbia, Kentucky, April 29, 1872, R. A. C. Martin, cashier of a bank, was killed for refusing to deliver the keys of the safe to the robbers. Only $200 was netted by the five men—three Youngers and two James brothers—due to the bravery of Martin.

Five months later, September 26, 1872, three horsemen snatched a tin box from the hands of a young man who was just leaving the Kansas City Fair Grounds a little after four o'clock in the afternoon to deposit the contents—said to be a little under $10,000—in the First National Bank of Kansas City.[3]

[3] This robbery is questioned by some modern writers. Horan suggests that the money would be in small change and therefore too heavy to be "seized by a rider on a horse." Rascoe asks, "What sort of a bank would it be that would be open after 4 p.m.; and what sort of treasurer would entrust $10,000 in cash in a tin box to a messenger boy in a crowd in a rough town, even if the boy could carry it?"

But J. W. Buel, at the time a reporter for the Kansas City *Journal*, was covering the fair that day, with its horse races. He was right on the spot within a few minutes of the robbery and questioned Hall, the Fair Association treasurer, and other witnesses who were milling about.

Here are the answers to the questions of Horan and Rascoe, written for the newspaper the day of the crime—not more than eighty years later:

"Although it was after banking hours, arrangements had been made to make the deposit"—which accounts for the 4 P.M. hour.

Actual participants in the holdup at the Fair Grounds were believed to be Frank and Jesse James and Bob Younger. Bob Younger, only twenty years old, had just recently joined the gang, and this must have been his first robbery. During its career the James gang made a practice of replacing members it lost with new recruits, and the later additions in most cases were not former guerrillas.

The Kansas City incident caused plenty of talk and much journalistic fervor, but already Jesse was looking for wider fields —something even bigger and more flashy to do. He led another successful raid on a bank at Ste. Genevieve, Missouri, May 23, 1873, but bank robbery was becoming an old story to him.

Horan speculates, I think plausibly, that some member of his gang served time in the Missouri prison with John Reno, the Indiana bandit, and learned how he robbed a train, later communicating this to Jesse.

If so, however, Jesse James did not follow the Reno technique when he held up his first train. What he did, the night of July 21, 1873, was to wreck a Rock Island express about fifty miles east of Council Bluffs, Iowa, by pulling a rail loose—an atrocious act, be-

---

The money was handed by Hall "to one of his assistants to take it to the First National Bank"—not to a "messenger boy."

One of the bandits, "leaping to the ground, snatched the box and handed it to his mounted companion"—no "rider on a horse" seized the box.

As to the "weight of the box," who knows what it weighed? And why should it contain "small change"? More likely it was money of larger denominations, chiefly currency, the small change being kept in a safe at the Fair Grounds for the next day's business.

"More than a dozen persons" saw the robbery. One of them, a young girl about ten years old, was knocked over and injured by one of the bandits' horses. Since several pistol shots were fired, it was at first thought she was wounded by a bullet, but this was not so, the shots evidently being fired in the air to cow the onlookers.

The robbery was accepted as actual at the time. Hall and his assistants, as well as other witnesses, were questioned by police, and their accounts agreed as to the events and the estimate of the money involved. It is hardly likely that writers taking a telescopic view of events eighty years later would have a better set of facts on which to base conclusions than those who were actually involved.

Finally, when Dick Liddil later made his confession of the gang's activities to Prosecutor W. H. Wallace, he positively listed the "Kansas City Fair robbery" as one of the outlaw coups.

cause the engine, thrown off the track, turned on its side, the boiler burst, and John Rafferty, the engineer, was horribly scalded to death. The fireman was severely burned also, and several passengers were injured in the wreck.

Jesse had heard that a large shipment of gold was being sent on this train, but he was twelve hours too early. It came on a later train. He and his seven companions took what money was in the express safe and everything of value from the passengers, but they netted only about $7000.

Now the railroads added their money and pressure to the pursuit of the outlaws, and the Pinkertons redoubled their activities. In spite of this, the robbers stopped a stagecoach on January 15, 1874, near the small town of Malvern, Arkansas, looting the passengers; and a little more than two weeks later, January 31, "captured" the village of Gads Hill, Missouri, holding the citizens and station agent under their guns while the Iron Mountain express was flagged down.

Again the "take" was disappointing—only about $2000—but the robbery revealed once more that Jesse James was becoming enamored of his widely spreading fame. Like most major outlaws, he had a flair for showmanship and a weakness for notoriety. On this occasion he gave the engineer of the Iron Mountain express his own handwritten press release, with instructions, "Give this to the newspaper. We like to do things in style."

The press release even had a headline: *The Most Daring Train Robbery on Record!*

It contained a brief but quite accurate account of the holdup, omitting the amount of loot taken (it had not yet been counted), and ended with this sentence: *"There a hell of an excitement in this part of the country."*

Jesse might sometimes forget his verbs, but he was pretty good at making plain his meaning.

Jesse James was now twenty-seven years old, not ill-looking, with a crisp brown beard, which he kept well trimmed, eyes of intense blue, and "particular about his dress."

Having achieved what he probably considered the peak of success in his chosen "profession," he did something he had wanted to do for eight years: he married Zerelda Mimms.

Frank James married also, that year of 1874, but he eloped with his bride, Annie Ralston.

Jesse did nothing so gauche. Dressed in black broadcloth, with his riding boots shined until the sun fairly flashed back from them, the outlaw rode into Kansas City alone and in broad daylight, and said his vows with the girl who had waited for him all this time. The wedding was performed by a relative who was a minister.

During the years when their outlaw husbands were "on the dodge," these two devoted women followed them whenever possible, living sometimes in cabins, perhaps even caves, and sometimes in towns where they did not see their men for weeks at a time, enduring fear and exile from contact with society by force of their circumstances. Jesse's wife and her two children were in the house when her husband was murdered in St. Joseph, Missouri, and endured the long tragedy of being subjected to the curiosity of the morbid afterward. Frank James' wife, however, lived to see her husband return to a lawful existence.[4]

This much may be added concerning the marriages of both Jesse and Frank: they were true to their wives throughout their married lives. Their sense of clan loyalty was so highly developed that faithfulness to their women was a requisite of the strange code under which they lived.

Meantime, the Pinkerton detectives still were trying to smell out the trail of the outlaws. It was a difficult task, but it would have been far more difficult had conditions really existed such as

[4] Frank James and his wife were parents of a son, Robert, whom I knew and talked with more than once, when he was conducting a sort of museum at the old Samuel place, where he had gathered many relics and photographs concerning his family and their outlaw career. Robert James served in the United States Army during the Spanish-American War and was well regarded as a citizen and farmer.

Jesse James' wife bore him two children, a boy and a girl. She reared them well in spite of their father's outlawry, and both lived normal lives with many friends. The son, Jesse, Jr., studied law and became a member of the bar at Kansas City, Missouri.

have since been alleged. The statement was made and repeated that the ex-Confederates all over Missouri sympathized with and sheltered the bandits, while the pro-Unionists valiantly (and vainly) tried to bring them to justice. The Republican party in Missouri even attempted to make a campaign issue of the James gang, charging that the Democratic party's policies were responsible for the wave of outlawry. It was a political gesture purely, but it caught the headlines. Judge Wallace, the nemesis of the James gang, set forth the following facts in his memoirs:

> I desire . . . to notice most specifically the charge made hundreds of times that the Southern people of Missouri endorsed the depredations of these outlaws and were opposed to their being overthrown. This is absolutely untrue. Especially has it been charged that the ex-Confederates of Missouri . . . endorsed the conduct of the James Boys. Precisely the opposite is true . . . The ex-guerrillas in Jackson, Cass, Clay, Johnson and Lafayette [counties] were as a rule intensely in sympathy with the outlaws, but the ex-Confederates throughout the state outnumbered them probably one hundred to one, and were earnestly opposed to outlawry.
>
> Another plain truth never before told . . . should be emphasized here. The charge was so long and so persistently made that the Southern men of Missouri were protecting train robbery and murder that they seemed to think that it was their special duty to suppress these crimes, and they arose and destroyed the outlaw band . . .
>
> I wish to say that I am not charging the Northern men of Missouri with defaming the state, for, as a rule, they never did so. The defamation of Missouri has been confined almost exclusively to the metropolitan press, both inside and outside of the state. Nor am I complaining of Northern men that they did not overthrow the James Boys . . . Under all the circumstances they seemed to think that the Southern men of Missouri ought to destroy the outlaw band, and these Southern men seemed to think so themselves.

Judge Wallace named, as some of the most prominent figures in the long battle, the following: General John S. Marmaduke, Major James F. Mister, Colonel Hiram Bledsoe, Captain M. M. Langhorne, Major E. A. Hickman, Colonel J. E. Payne, Judge R. E. Cowan, Judge John O. Wofford, and Judge James B. Gantt, all veterans of the gray armies. He should also have named himself, for he was a Southern man and was foremost in the fight against the outlaws.

Nevertheless, the James brothers were for a time a political issue, and Missouri came perilously close to being permanently nicknamed "the Robber State," as she is now called "the Show Me State."

The Pinkertons had plenty of help from the people when they began to probe into Missouri. Their first plan was to locate the hideouts of the bandits and try to run them to earth there. It was not a very practical scheme—the hideouts were too numerous and too far-scattered.

Nevertheless, in pursuit of this idea two of the agency's detectives, Louis J. Lull and James Wright, started for Missouri when they received a tip that the Youngers sometimes forgathered at Monegaw Springs, St. Clair County, clear across the state from Gads Hill, where the last train holdup took place.

It was Ozark Mountain country, heavily wooded, cut up by valleys and streams, and scantily populated save for the county seat, Osceola, and a few tiny crossroads villages. Into this backwoods district, in March 1874, rode the two Pinkerton men, with a former peace officer, E. B. Daniels, as a special agent to guide them. They were posing as stock buyers, looking for cattle and horses—a device often used by the outlaws themselves in scouting a place before a robbery.

At best it was a touchy business. The people of the Ozarks were suspicious of strangers, and when they appeared word went out in every direction, warning other folks to be on the lookout for some possible "skulduggery." Since the Youngers were accepted as neighbors and friends in the strange clannish way of the hill people, it would be little less than a miracle if the movements of the intruders were not made known to them.

Now and then Lull, Wright, and Daniels stopped to look around and inquire the way. On the afternoon of March 16, they halted at the farm of Theodore Snuffer, said to be a relative of the Youngers, at least their friend.

Snuffer met them at the door and asked their business. But he did not invite them into the house. After a little conversation they asked the way to "Widow Simms." Snuffer gave them directions in a rather gruff manner, and watched them mount and ride off.

The hair would have raised on the heads of the three officers had they known that while they talked with the farmer, there brooded over them, listening to every word from a window just above their heads, two of the terrible men they were seeking, Jim and John Younger. When the visitors were gone, the brothers argued fiercely with each other. Jim appears to have tried to restrain his younger brother, but John, swearing that the "cattle buyers" were in reality detectives on their trail, seized a shotgun, and ran down the stairs. At that Jim caught up his weapons and followed.

In a moment the two had leaped on horses and set off after the officers.

Lull left an affidavit of what happened. Over the years we can almost see it.

It was midafternoon, a warm March day, and the hills were turning beautiful with new green foliage in the trees.

Behind them the detectives suddenly heard the pounding of horses' hoofs at the dead run, and glanced back. Two savage-looking men were spurring wildly after them, "one . . . armed with a double-barreled shotgun and the other with revolvers."

The outlaw with the shotgun was John Younger. He cocked his weapon and shouted for the men to halt.

There were three detectives to two pursuers, yet a kind of mystic terror seemed to embrace the very thought of the Youngers. The officers did not even think of fighting at first.

Lull and Daniels pulled up by the side of the road. Wright, drawing his pistol, put spurs to his horse and fled. A bullet took off his hat, but he was not hit and made his somewhat craven escape.

Pale and fearful of what was going to happen, the other two detectives were confronted by the glaring outlaws.

"Drop your guns on the ground!" ordered Jim Younger.

Daniels threw down his revolver, and Lull dropped two. He retained, however, a third pistol concealed in his clothes.

Swinging out of his saddle, Jim Younger picked up the weapons.

"These are damn fine pistols," he said with a hard grin. "You must make us a present of them."

John, still mounted, asked a sharp question: "What are you doing here?"

"Just rambling around," said Lull.

But the outlaws seemed to know all about them.

"You've been at the Springs," said one.

And the other added with a bitter scowl, "Detectives have been hunting for us, and we're going to put a stop to it."

At this Daniels, knowing he was in their power, lost his nerve and began to plead.

"I'm no detective!" he said in a trembling voice. "I can show you who I am and where I'm going!"

But Lull read death in their eyes.

Suddenly he drew his hidden pistol and fired point-blank at John Younger.

The bullet was fatal, but in the moment of death John managed to press the trigger of the shotgun he carried, tearing a gaping hole in Lull's neck. Then he fell from his horse, dead.

At the shots, Lull's horse bolted into the brush. The wounded detective was swept out of his saddle by a low-hanging tree limb and hurled to the ground beside the road.

Jim Younger, wild with grief and rage, killed Daniels with a revolver shot, then, mounting his horse, rode like a raging devil past Lull, who was crawling in a sick effort to find a hiding place in the brush, and pumped two more bullets into his body. Lull lay still.

Younger halted and glared about him, "half demented" by his brother's death. Wright was gone, out of reach. The other two officers lay motionless in the contorted positions in which they were stricken.

After a moment he dismounted, lifted the body of his brother John, slung it across the back of his horse, and slowly rode back to the Snuffers'. There he buried the dead man in the orchard.

Back on the road Daniels was dead, but Lull, though terribly wounded, was still living. When the outlaw was gone, he rose and managed to stagger for some distance, bleeding and only half aware of what he was doing, until he collapsed again. There he was found by some persons traveling along that road and taken to the little village of Roscoe, where, after making his affidavit concerning the events, he died six weeks later.

It is to be noted that Lull, the Pinkerton man, fired the first shot. Did he lose his head? Or was it an act of desperation by a man cornered and facing what he considered sure death? What if he had not fired? Perhaps he and Daniels might have been sent on, without weapons, but with a warning to get out of the country. Perhaps not. In any case, his shot was his own death warrant, as well as that of Daniels, and Jim Younger could always say he killed in self-defense.

Another Pinkerton man's fate, on almost the same day, inclines one to the belief that Lull and Daniels would have been slain no matter what happened. The victim was John W. Whicher, and his murder was one of the most brutal and cold-blooded committed by the outlaws. Jesse James engineered it.

About the same time that Lull and Wright went down into the Ozark country looking for the Youngers, Whicher, a Pinkerton operative with a fine record, left Chicago with the intention of entering Clay County, the very stronghold of the Jameses, and tracking them down. He was warned of his danger by Allan Pinkerton before he left Chicago, but he persisted.

When he reached Missouri he was warned again, by a horrified banker at Liberty, with whom he left his credentials and valuables; and by Colonel P. P. Moss, former sheriff of the county, an ex-Confederate officer but an avowed foe of the Jameses.

Whicher, however, was a very brave or a very stubborn man. His plan was to go dressed as a farm hand, looking for work. Unfortunately, there was an important flaw in this impersonation: Whicher was a city man "with a tender complexion and hands like a city fellow's."

He left Liberty on March 15 and arrived at Kearney late that afternoon. How could he know that Jesse James, through his perfect intelligence system, knew all about him?

It was only four miles from Kearney to the Samuel place, and without even spending the night in the town, Whicher started to walk toward the farm. Perhaps he had covered half the distance when from behind a pile of dead brush stepped a man with blue flint eyes, and a revolver, cocked and aimed.

Whicher was taken completely by surprise. It was Jesse James himself who confronted him, and there was no chance to reach for his own gun.

"Where are you going?" asked the outlaw.

"I'm looking for work," said Whicher.

"What kind of work?"

"I'm used to farm labor—I hope to find something to do on some farm hereabouts."

"You don't look like a farm hand. Tell the truth. Just what are you doing in this country?"

Whicher must have known his fate then. The outlaw was playing a cruel cat-and-mouse game with him.

"I'm nothing but a poor man, without a dollar in my pocket, and I've told you the truth——"

As he was speaking Frank James and Clell Miller, grim-faced, stepped from concealment. And then poor Whicher, with his face blanching and the cold sweat beading his forehead, heard his own movements described to him by Jesse in that hard, deadly voice:

"I think you're from Chicago. When you arrived in Liberty a few days ago you wore much better clothes than you have on now. Seems that you and Moss [the ex-sheriff] had some kind of business together. Didn't you set out to locate the James Boys . . . and found them quicker than you thought?"

It was like a cold sentence of death. Too late, Whicher tried to reach for his pistol. The bandits sprang on him, disarmed him, and tied him tightly with small cords Frank produced.

The pistol they took from him was evidence damning enough; but when the outlaws examined his hands, they were soft and uncallused. Whicher's story of being a farm hand was palpably false.

It was enough. That night the doomed detective, bound, gagged, and tied on a horse, was taken over into Jackson County. Next day—March 16—the very day that Lull and Daniels were shot down farther south in Missouri—his body was found. A rope was around the neck and the corpse was full of bullet holes. Hogs had eaten off part of the face.

William H. Wallace, then a reporter on the Independence *Sentinel*—earning money for his law studies—identified him. "I pulled up the blue flannel shirt above his wrist and saw 'J.W.W.' in indigo ink on his arm."

Years later, as prosecuting attorney, Wallace was to consider trying Frank James for the Whicher murder, before turning to the murder of Frank McMillen, in a train robbery, as a better case for conviction.

Much later it was learned, through accounts of the outlaws themselves, how Whicher was trapped, the conversation between him and Jesse James, and the manner in which he was put to death. He was first cruelly abused, pricked with the points of bowie knives and choked, in an effort to get him to divulge the plans of the Pinkertons against the outlaws. When he refused to give any information, he was killed. Jesse and Frank murdered him, one shooting him through the heart and the other through the brain. The members of the murder party were Jesse and Frank James, Clell Miller, and James Latche, "a hanger-on of the gang," who was Jesse's spy and who conveyed to the outlaw chief all the details of the detective's movements from the time he reached Liberty.

4. *Northfield—and "The Dirty Little Coward"*

As far as the Pinkerton National Detective Agency was concerned, the score now stood: One outlaw, dead; three Pinkerton men, ditto.

At the Chicago headquarters there was fury, quite understandably. Three operatives killed all at once provided a score that must somehow be evened.

Allan Pinkerton and his son opened secret headquarters in Kansas City and took personal charge of the case. They found another operative, Jack Ladd, who had the guts to try to get into Clay County. Ladd was luckier than Whicher. He managed to get a job on the farm of Dan Askew, near the Samuel place. Askew did not dream of his new hand's true identity, and Ladd worked so hard that nobody suspected him. Meantime he gathered information.

On January 5, 1875, he got word to his chief in Kansas City that the James brothers were paying a visit to their mother. The Pinkertons had been awaiting just that information, and had their plans all set, their arrangements made.

That night a special train took the Pinkerton men and other officers into the outlaw country. Perhaps Conductor William Westfall (or Westphal) was the only one of the train crew who had an inkling of the real purpose of the "excursion." It was his duty to halt the train, let off the party aboard, and signal the engineer up ahead to pull away, so that no word of a mounted detachment riding through the country could reach the bandits.

The night was clear, with a bright moon, and bitter cold, the thermometer dropping to near zero. In silence the armed detectives and special deputies surrounded the log farmhouse on three sides, at about ten o'clock at night.

What followed was a ghastly farce that for a time swung public opinion clear over to the side of the outlaws. The house was dark, except for the glowing embers of the fireplace.[1] Within it were Dr. and Mrs. Samuel, their two youngest children, Fannie and Archie, and an old Negro servant woman.

Stealthily one of the Pinkerton men managed to open a window on the west side of the house. A moment later an explosive missile was hurled into the place.

What was it? Trow, and members of the family, described it as "a lighted hand grenade, wrapped about with flannel saturated in turpentine." The Pinkertons said it was a round iron flare, of the type used about excavations, weighted at the bottom so it would always come upright, and filled with some inflammable fluid. Its purpose, according to the Pinkerton version, was to light up the interior and let the men outside get a clear view of the inmates.[2]

Whatever the intention, the infernal thing exploded.

Stories are confused. Trow says, "The lurid light from this in-

[1] One story is that Mrs. Samuel heard the prowling steps of the men about the house and caused the lights to be extinguished. More probably, since this was about two hours before midnight, the family had gone to bed. Indeed, Harrison Trow, who knew all of the Samuel people well, said, "The family was wrapped in profound slumber."

[2] I have examined the bursted shell of the "bomb." It could be an old-fashioned iron grenade of the round type used in the Civil War. It could also be the round bottom of an iron flare. I believe it is the latter, because I simply do not think that responsible and law-respecting people would knowingly throw a grenade into a room when they were not even sure who was there. But the grenade story still persists in Missouri.

flammable fluid awakened the Negro woman and she in turn awakened the sleeping whites. They rushed to subdue the flames and save their property. The children were gathered together in the kitchen, little things, helpless and terrified. All of a sudden there was a terrible explosion."

The Pinkerton version was that Dr. Samuel used his cane to thrust the cylinder into the fireplace, causing it to blast.

However it happened, the explosion wreaked bloody havoc. Mrs. Samuel's right arm was torn off at the elbow. Archie Samuel, a bright little boy eight years old, was disemboweled and died that night. Dr. Samuel was severely cut and burned, and the old Negro woman received serious injuries.

Then came a disclosure that made the whole bloody affair more deplorable: neither Jesse nor Frank James was in the house!

Operative Jack Ladd, the phony "farm hand," who from the neighboring place of Daniel H. Askew wrongly reported the outlaws' presence at the Samuel home, departed at once, leaving his employer, who did not even know he was a Pinkerton man, to face the consequences.

A little more than three months later, April 12, Dan Askew was shot down near his own house. Shortly after, Jesse and Frank James and Clell Miller stopped at another farm and told the owner, Henry Sears, with bitter irony:

"We've just killed Dan Askew. If any of his friends want to know who did it, tell them the detectives did it."

The implication was that the detectives, by their acts, had caused the death of the farmer.

Jesse later stalked Allan Pinkerton in Chicago. He did not kill him, although he had opportunities to do so. His reason: "I want him to know who did it."

That blast in the Samuel home ended the usefulness of the Pinkertons. Public opinion swung violently against them. Newspapers, not only in Missouri but in other states, denounced the "night of blood" and the men who caused it with furious editorial invective. A bill to give amnesty to the outlaws was introduced into the Missouri legislature and actually carried, but was declared out of order and did not become a law.

The Pinkerton Agency still remained on the railroad and bank association payrolls, and kept men going to every new point where a robbery was reported, but where before they had received public co-operation, they now found it difficult to get. Everyday citizens, not the Pinkertons, ended the outlaw reign.

After the tragedy at the Samuel house the outlaw gang lay quiet for most of the year. Then, on December 13, there came another train robbery. Once again the Gads Hill tactics were employed—the bandits took over the entire little town of Muncie, Kansas, herded the small population into the depot, and kept it there under guard.

When the train stopped, the outlaws took charge, uncoupled the express car, forced the engineer to pull it up the track, slugged the messenger, Frank Webster, into insensibility, and looted the safe. The pockets of the passengers were gone through also, and the gang rode away with money and valuables worth at least $60,000, even though they left behind them, as too heavy to carry, a shipment of silver bars.

A little later Bud McDaniels got drunk in Kansas City and was arrested. He had on him about a thousand dollars—too much for one of his talents and habits of industry—and under examination confessed to a part in the Muncie robbery. Sentenced in a Kansas court to the Kansas penitentiary, he escaped, but was trailed by officers and killed a week later.

The rest of the gang disappeared. Later it was known that the Younger brothers rode down to Dallas, Texas. Was Belle Shirley the magnet? Perhaps. At least Burton Rascoe thinks so, and I am inclined to agree with him.

By this time—late 1875 or early 1876—Belle had been "married" to a former member of the James gang, Jim Reed, and "widowed" by a straight-shooting deputy sheriff. She was living in Dallas with her daughter, Pearl.

It might be that Cole Younger had some lingering paternal interest in his offspring, now eight years old.[3] Or perhaps he only

[3] Pearl was definitely named as Cole Younger's daughter in a Fort Smith, Arkansas, newspaper years later, after her mother's death. She was described at that time as "a beautiful girl, possessing her mother's fire and her father's reckless criminality."

wanted the company of his former mistress, now a somewhat gaudy but striking woman in her middle twenties. In any case, the head of the Younger clan chose Dallas as his hideaway.

I find no record of Belle and Cole being seen together during this time. The Youngers, in fact, behaved like model citizens in Dallas. Available accounts say they attended church, even sang in the choir, and at times helped the sheriff as deputies, to round up "desperate characters" who needed a little jail pallor to temper their sunburned tan.

Next spring the James brothers joined them in Texas, and on May 12, 1876, they robbed a stage between San Antonio and Austin. With the $3000 thus garnered, the two sets of brothers journeyed back to Missouri.

One more train holdup—the Missouri Pacific at Otterville, Missouri—July 7, in which $15,000 was taken—and the gang was ready for a coup that would astound the world, but hardly in the way they planned. Having robbed a stagecoach deep in Texas in May, and a train in Missouri in July, they proposed to complete a triple tour de force, spanning the nation south to north, by robbing a bank in Minnesota in September—all in the same year.

Bill Chadwell, a horse thief and refugee from the regulators in Minnesota, was the man who persuaded the outlaws to make a raid in that state. Chadwell was not an ex-guerrilla. He joined the gang in Missouri, and probably aided in the Otterville train robbery. In talking with the James and Younger brothers, he waxed enthusiastic in extolling the wealth of the state he recently had quitted (under some pressure), described the heavy deposits carried by some of the banks, and assured his fellow bandits that he "knew every road and hog path, cave and swamp," in the country where he proposed to lead them.

The James brothers, Clell Miller, and Jim and Bob Younger took fire at the scheme. Cole Younger at first was reluctant, but accepted the wishes of the majority.

They were all old hands, and knew all the tricks, or thought they did. Well dressed and prosperous-looking, they made the first part of their journey north by train, visiting several cities in Minnesota, including St. Paul, Minneapolis, and Mankato.

Presently they bought horses—excellent and well-selected steeds, for which they paid good prices in the coin of the realm (acquired in the Otterville robbery). Now, mounted, they proceeded on their leisurely way, stopping at the best hotels, dining luxuriously, smoking the finest cigars, and spending money freely, though not ostentatiously.

Sometimes they politely introduced themselves as cattle buyers, obviously well heeled, and looking for choice stock. On other occasions, especially when they wanted to scout a certain area, they would pose as surveyors. It was more like an outing, a sort of picnic, than a grim foray. If the truth be told, they were somewhat overconfident; and who, really, could blame them, after ten years of almost uninterrupted success?

So they rode along, usually in twos or threes somewhat widely spaced along the road so as not to attract undue attention: eight bold, athletic young men, superb horsemen, skylarking at times in sheer exuberance.

Jesse James, to judge by a photograph taken about that time, wore a close-clipped beard and mustache, his steel-blue eyes alert under his level brows. His brother Frank was the least handsome of the group, with his long, sly nose and moody face, and a long mustache, slightly drooping at the ends. All the Youngers were fine-looking men. Both Cole and Jim wore short beards and mustaches, but Bob was clean-shaved except for a narrow, well-groomed mustache on his lip. Clell Miller, probably the handsomest man of the crowd, with a direct wide gaze in his blue eyes and good forehead and features, was clean-shaved, as was Bill Chadwell. Charlie Pitts, the eighth member of the gang, wore a close-cut beard and mustache like the older Youngers. All of them were recklessly brave. All were in the very prime of manhood.

On September 3, they were in Mankato. There an untoward event took place. Jesse James was "recognized by an old acquaintance, but the recognition was not returned, Jesse claiming that the speaker was a stranger." Nevertheless, the man warned the sheriff, and Mankato was alerted for a possible raid. The bandits sensed the stir, and Jesse quickly led his men out of the town.

Mankato was not the real objective, anyway. Northfield, a properous little city of two thousand people, north and east of

Mankato, was a better prospect. It had only one bank, the First National, but in that single depository the entire country around kept its money. Bill Chadwell told his friends that this was the richest country bank in the state.

Taking it easy, the outlaws headed in that direction. They wore over their clothes long linen ulsterettes, which not only protected them from the dust of the road, or rain if it fell, but concealed the weapons they carried. With these linen overgarments, their wide-brimmed hats, and their boots, the gang had almost the appearance of wearing a sort of uniform.

And Northfield? Northfield, September 7, 1876, drowsed in the early autumn sun, never dreaming of the strange violent fame that would belong to it by nightfall of that day. A small stream, the Cannon River, ran burbling through it, spanned by a neat iron bridge. Upstream from the bridge was a millrace and the flour mill owned by Ames & Company, where Minnesota wheat was stone-ground into flour. On the bluff overlooking the town stood the buildings of Carleton College, with the residences of prosperous citizens about it, and a tall-spired church. Below lay the business section: Bridge Square; Division Street, which was the main business thoroughfare; the Scriver Block, a stone building two stories high with a dormered roof, part of which was occupied by the bank; and other commercial and office structures.

Just before noon that day three men in long linen dusters rode into the town and dined at Jeft's Restaurant, near the iron bridge. They were Jesse James, Charlie Pitts, and Bob Younger, the three chosen to make the actual entrance and robbery of the bank. As they ate heartily they seemed pleasant enough, and while picking their teeth after the meal, complimented the restaurant man on his menu and talked politics with him. One offered to bet him one hundred dollars that the state would go Democratic at the next election. Jeft did not take the bet.

Outside the town, Jesse had sent his other five men, incomparable riders, killers, and robbers, to their posts; for the old tactics of swoop and "hurrah," proved effective so many times, were to be employed here, and they waited to ride yelling into town at the agreed signal.

Jesse and the others were relaxed, supremely confident. Why

should they not be confident, in preparing to loot the bank of a community of "hayseeds," who probably would be too slow of wit to know what to do, and too awkward and unskillful to be able to act if they did know? They had always succeeded. They were men who believed in luck. They had intelligence, skill, and audacity to carry out their bold designs—and luck had always been with them.

How could they dream that this day, so abruptly, fate was to exact from them a terrible and long overdue payment?

The three men in Jeft's Restaurant finished their cigars, paid their bill, and went out. They mounted their fine horses, and rode over the bridge, at a leisurely walk, to the intersection where stood the Scriver Block.

The building stood on the southwest corner of the intersection. Its front was occupied by the Lee & Hitchcock store and the H. Scriver store. An outside stairway of iron ran up the east side of the building to the second floor above, which was occupied by offices. At the very rear of the building, its entrance facing east, was the First National Bank. A back door from the bank opened into a narrow alley on the west side, which separated the Scriver Block from two hardware stores belonging to J. A. Allen and A. E. Manning, both of which faced on the street.

Across that street from the Scriver Block and the hardware stores was a row of mercantile buildings, including the Wheeler & Blackman Drugstore, and a small hotel called the Dampier House.

Almost nobody could be seen. The town appeared asleep. The three outlaws tied their horses in front of the Scriver Block and for a few minutes stood on the corner, calmly talking. They were awaiting the signal that would send them into action.

All at once it came—wild yells and shots, followed by the hammering of horses' hoofs as three men charged into the business square. Almost at the same moment two others rode in from another direction, at the same headlong gallop and with the same whoops and pistol poppings.

The "hurrahing" method was in full swing. Northfield, at first, was stunned by an experience such as it had never known before. "For a few minutes the slamming of front doors almost drowned the noise of the firing." It appeared that the outlaws had cowed the town into fearful submission.

As their outriders appeared in the square in a tumult of dust, smoke, and noise, the three bandits standing at the corner walked rapidly to the bank, entered it, and vaulted athletically over the counter.

Within were only three men: J. L. Heywood, the cashier, and Frank Wilcox and A. E. Bunker, tellers. No customers were in the place at the moment.

To the startled three came a yell which struck terror. "We're robbing the bank! Open up the safe!"

Revolvers were looking their way, and the bank employees lifted their hands. But Heywood, knowing these men would kill at the slightest excuse, yet had the courage to refuse their command.

The bandit leader, Jesse James, seeing that the outer door of the vault stood ajar, stepped into it to try the inner door. If he had reached it, he could have opened the safe with a pull, for it was not locked.

But before he reached it Heywood, a slender man with a soft brown beard, but with unlimited courage, jumped forward to slam the vault door and lock the outlaw in. Charlie Pitts saw the movement and, stepping forward, struck the cashier a crashing blow over the head with his pistol barrel, knocking him down with blood running from a bad cut in his scalp.

Disconcerted, Jesse stepped out of the vault without trying the inner door. On the floor Pitts was kneeling, with a bowie knife held at Heywood's neck.

"Open that safe, or I'll cut your throat!" he snarled. To make his threat more vivid he inflicted a slight wound on his victim's gullet.

Not one instant did Heywood quail. Expecting instant death, propped up against the vault door, he looked the glaring bandit squarely in the eyes and still refused.

At this moment Bunker, one of the tellers, made a desperate break for the rear door of the bank. Pitts fired at him and missed. Fairly hurling himself at the door in his terrified desperation, Bunker burst it open, tumbled down the concrete steps into the alley, then scrambled up, running for life.

At the door appeared the scowling visage of Bob Younger. He fired—once—and his bullet, tearing through the teller's shoulder, almost threw him. But though he stumbled, Bunker recovered his feet and an instant later dodged into the doorway of a building.

Outside the bank, in the street, shots were clattering at a mounting tempo, and it began to sound as if others besides the outlaws were shooting. Younger glanced into the bank. He saw his comrades scoop up what small change and bills were in sight, and joined them as they made for the door.

Last to leave the bank, Jesse glanced around just in time to see Heywood reach into a drawer, as if for a gun. The outlaw's shot was instant and the heroic cashier fell dead with a bullet through his head.

Wilcox alone of the three bank employees had remained perfectly still and was not harmed.

Meantime, matters had been going badly for the bandits in the street and rapidly were becoming worse. The Minnesotans did not cow as easily as had at first appeared. They lived in deer country, and most of the men were deer hunters. Many of them also were veterans of the Civil War, and others had fought the Sioux in Little Crow's bloody uprising of 1862. They were not gun-shy, as the outlaws had thought. But it remained for a youth to show them the way.

When the wild outlaws charged into town, Henry M. Wheeler, a nineteen-year-old medical student, home on vacation, was standing in front of the Wheeler & Blackman Drugstore, of which his father was one of the owners, across from the Scriver Block. He heard the yells and a cry that the bank was being robbed, and a bullet whizzed past his head. Back he tumbled, into the store.

The youth was a hunter himself. His rifle was at home, but he remembered that almost next door, in the Dampier House, was a breech-loading carbine (probably a Sharps 50-70 caliber used by the Union cavalry in the Civil War).

A quick dash and he reached the Dampier House. In a moment he had secured the carbine and some ammunition, and bounded upstairs, two steps at a time, to where he could look across the street from the window of Room No. 8, on the second floor.

He saw Nicholas Gustavson, a Norwegian who did not understand English enough to obey the orders of the shouting bandits, try to run across the street. The running man seemed to stumble, then fell crumpled up, a bullet through his head.

Just at this time the three outlaws who had murdered Heywood came bursting out of the bank. At the two hardware stores, J. A. Allen and A. E. Manning, the proprietors, were busy loading every gun in their respective shops, and yelling for men to come and get them. Rifles began to reply to the bandit fire.

Caught in the street, without cover, powder smoke hanging hazy, while bullets went *spang* as they ricocheted, and the racket of the guns was increased by the crash of shattering glass, the raiders knew it was high time to get out of there.

One of them had blood streaming from his face, the result of a charge of small shot fired from a window of the Scriver Block. But he was not disabled, and if anything more ready to kill than before, with the pain of his wound. He swung into his saddle, revolver in hand.

As he did so, young Wheeler, cool as a veteran, caught him in his sights and pulled the trigger of the carbine. Death-stricken, the brigand plunged from his saddle into the dust. Later he was identified as Clell Miller.

By now a number of men had joined the battle. Elias Stacey, seizing the first gun he could get hold of, ran up to the second floor of the Scriver Block. His weapon proved to be a shotgun, the loads bird shot. Nevertheless, he began firing, and it was his shot that brought the blood spurting from Miller's face.

He continued to shoot. Bill Chadwell got a dose of the stinging little pellets. It did not kill him, but he swayed in his saddle. Other shots sprayed the street from Stacey's window. Almost every one of the bandits carried a birdshot "souvenir" before the battle was over.

One of Wheeler's bullets clipped Cole Younger's hat off, and the bandit, like a wild man, careered up the street with the bullets kicking up the dirt about his horse's hoofs. Manning, the hardware man, stepped out into the street and fearlessly exchanged shots with him. A bullet from Manning's breech-loading rifle punctured Cole's shoulder, and the outlaw whirled his horse around and retreated.

One of the horses—Bob Younger's—was down, killed at the hitch rack. The outlaw sprinted to the foot of the iron stairs leading up to the second floor of the Scriver Block, where some drygoods boxes were piled.

Shooting from there he almost got Manning. The hardware man jumped around the corner of a building, and at the same moment a slug from Wheeler's carbine smashed Bob Younger's right elbow. He gamely shifted his revolver to his left hand, but he was not nearly as good with his left as with his right.

Down the street Bill Chadwell, half blinded by the bird shot from Stacey's gun, was riding slowly. Manning aimed carefully and brought the outlaw down, shot squarely through the heart.

The outlaws had enough—more than enough. Those who could, mounted their horses and charged down the street, guns blazing, in a break to escape. From beneath the Scriver stairs, Bob Younger cried out:

"My God, boys, you're not deserting me? I'm shot!"

Cole Younger, though wounded himself, heard it. He wheeled his horse and came careering back. With bullets spattering about him, he took his wounded brother up behind him and followed the others westward out of town.

The Northfield fight was over. Every one of the bandits had a wound of some kind, and two of them lay dead back in the town. Of the citizens who rallied so unexpectedly and furiously, Heywood and Gustavson were dead; Bunker had a serious wound in the shoulder, from which, however, he recovered; and a man named Bates exhibited a furrow on one cheek from a bandit bullet.[4]

Northfield was a terrible defeat for Jesse James and his men, but the aftermath was worse than the fight itself.

A short way out of town the survivors stopped, bathed their

[4] In after years young Wheeler became something of a celebrity. When he received his medical degree he opened practice at Northfield and was highly successful as a physician. Sometimes, in his later years, when Dr. Wheeler felt inclined to do so, he would take a chosen guest and show him a skeleton, carefully articulated, which he kept in a closet in his office. It was the skeleton of Clell Miller, the bandit, whom he shot in front of the bank that bloody September day, long before.

wounds, and bandaged them. Some of them were badly hurt. Jim Younger had a disabling bullet through one shoulder and half his upper jaw carried away by a Minié ball. Bob Younger's right elbow was so shattered that he had to hold it with his left hand while one of the other men led his horse—the animal killed in town was replaced by one the bandits took from a farmer named Empey, whom they held up on the road.

Cole Younger was wounded in the shoulder, Frank James had a bandage around his leg outside his trousers, and Charlie Pitts was bleeding. Jesse, perhaps, had some of Stacey's bird shot in him, but he was the least seriously hurt.

The hemorrhage from Jim Younger's shattered mouth was so serious that the bandits stopped at a farmhouse, got water, and tried, by tearing his linen duster into strips, to stanch the flow of blood. They were not entirely successful, and in the succeeding days as they tried to retreat, hampered by their wounds and traveling through swamps and woods to avoid the roads, Jim grew continually weaker, retarding them and making their situation ever more dangerous. Toward the last Cole had to ride double with him, holding him on his horse.

Each hour the situation grew more desperate. Every town in Minnesota had been alerted by telegraph, and the whole state rose against the raiders. Posses seemed to be searching everywhere. Over the wires came offers of rewards to spur the search—$1000 for each of the outlaws, dead or alive, by the state; $700 by the Northfield bank; $500 by the Winona & St. Peter Railroad.

Long ago, what had started out as a sort of holiday outing had become a nightmare of pain and terror to the fugitives. The six men, all wounded, were crazed with anxiety to get away, fearing the posse's bullets and the lyncher's noose, if they were caught, perhaps more than the legal hangman's gallows.

Yet it was impossible to make any speed. To show how slow was their progress, a posse of fourteen men "jumped" them the night of September 11, in a ravine near a hamlet called Shieldsville. This was four days after the robbery, yet they were less than fifteen miles from Northfield. Perhaps they had been hiding all day and moving very cautiously and painfully at night. Or they may have been lying over somewhere for most of the intervening time to ease their wounds.

In the brief skirmish near Shieldsville one of the bandits' horses was killed, but the dismounted man was taken up behind one of the others and all of them disappeared into the timber around Elysian Lake.

Within a very short time four hundred men had gathered about the area, combing the woods. By the next day the number of armed searchers had increased to an estimated one thousand. Yet somehow the raiders managed to slip away from this net.

Toward evening of September 13, two days later, they were located in a stand of heavy timber near Mankato. All bridges, fords, and roads were put under guard at once, so it was thought they could not escape.

The outlaws, in their little camp of dirt and misery, knowing their pursuers were all around them, that night had a council of war and decided to split up to make the chase more difficult for their enemies.

Buel says, on the authority of "an ex-guerrilla who has maintained relations, for many years, with the James and Younger boys" (perhaps George Shepherd), that Jesse James, the pitiless and practical, that night said substantially this to Cole Younger:

"Cole, we're in a bad fix, and there's only one way out, it appears to me. Our trail is so plain a blind man could follow it. If we're caught it means death to us all. It's a terrible thought, but the circumstances are terrible: Jim can't live, he's almost dead now, and we can't continue our retreat with him, because it would only end in death for every one of us. We wouldn't want him to fall into the hands of the men hunting us. I think it would be right to dispose of him; end his sufferings, which will only end in his death anyway. We could then travel faster and, I think, escape."

The cold-blooded suggestion was rejected by both of Jim's brothers, and Cole is said to have addressed Jesse James in terms nobody else ever did, and survived. Clan loyalty would not let the Youngers leave Jim, much less kill him.

In the end the matter was left to a vote. Those who wished to go with Jesse James could do so. The same privilege (if it was a privilege) was extended to those who wished to stay with the Youngers.

Frank James chose to go with his brother. Charlie Pitts wavered, then decided to stay with the Youngers.

Though it may be apocryphal, this story is given some plausibility by the evident enmity of Cole Younger for Jesse James in later years when he was in prison. In any case, the split was decided upon, and it was as wise a decision as could be made under the circumstances, whatever the method by which it was reached.

At two o'clock next morning the Youngers and Pitts—one of them holding Jim on his horse—charged the guard at the Blue Earth River bridge. The guard, caught by surprise, scattered at the whooping, shooting rush, and the outlaws thundered over the bridge and beyond, leaving a regiment of pursuers behind.

Jesse and Frank James remained hiding in the forest. Nobody reached them during the day, and the next night, riding double on a single horse, they burst through the picket line near Lake Crystal.

Richard Roberts, one of the possemen, fired at them blind in the dark. His shot was very lucky. It brought down their horse, and the bullet plowed through Frank James' right leg near the knee and imbedded itself in Jesse's right thigh—nasty wounds in both cases.

But though they were limping badly, the brothers took to a corn field. It must have been sheer torture to run, one with a bullet hole through his leg, the other with a bullet lodged in his thigh, and the blood dripping from their wounds. But the night favored them. Nobody in the posse was anxious to go hunting through those corn rows for men who were armed and deadly dangerous. Better wait until morning, they decided.

In the morning Jesse and Frank were gone. They had hobbled right on through the corn field, stolen two gray horses from a farmer named Rockwell, and continued their flight. From there they headed west.

Two men on gray horses? It was a telltale mark. The description of the two animals was broadcast, and posses began to watch for gray horses.

The brothers guessed this. At another farm along the road they stopped, and forced the farmer not only to swap horses with them but to give them a meal. Later the farmer told how the outlaws were "so bad hurt and so stiff that . . . they had the greatest difficulty in climbing up a fence to get on the horses' backs."

When the outlaws crossed the line into Dakota Territory, September 17, there was another brief exchange of shots with a posse, but one of the pursuers was wounded, the others grew cautious, and once more the brothers got away.

Farther on, near Sioux Falls, they met a Dr. Mosher, forced him to dress their wounds and extract the bullet from Jesse's festering thigh, and then made him exchange clothes with Jesse, to make identification more difficult. They did not harm him, other than taking his clothes, nor did they injure any of the other persons they met, except for the posseman they wounded in the skirmish at the Dakota border.

From the time they left Dr. Mosher their getaway was clean. It was an almost unparalleled escape, considering the numbers hunting them. They were both sorely wounded, living most of the time on green corn and whatever else they could pick up in brief halts along the road, and forced to travel most of the time by night, hiding wherever daylight found them.

Not for three years were they heard from again.

Far less fortunate was the Younger party. West of Mankato, after the wild charge across the Blue Earth River bridge, they robbed a chicken house to get something to eat. Jim Younger later said, "We felt real mean when we were robbing that hen roost." For men who had made their reputations as bank and train robbers, chicken stealing was a terrible comedown.

What made it more unhappy, they did not even get to eat the hens for breakfast, because a posse interrupted them as they were preparing to cook the fowls in the woods. The chickens were found, already plucked but not yet roasted on the fire.

Never for one moment was the chase relaxed. Hundreds of farmers, townsmen, and officers, all armed, scoured the country. But the outlaws displayed such consummate woodcraft that although they had with them men with extremely severe wounds, and Jim in particular, had grown so weak it was difficult to move him, for several days their pursuers lost all track of them.

Their camp sites were found, however, and at each were bloody bandages the fugitives had left behind. Judging from the footprints, one of the men appeared to be barefoot.[5]

Hunger finally tipped the balance against them. The fugitives had some money, but for days they had found very little to eat. On the morning of September 21, one of them ventured to a farmhouse near Madelia, about one hundred and fifty miles southwest of Northfield, to try and buy bread and eggs for the famished group. He walked so stiffly that an inquisitive boy, Oscar Suborn, paid particular attention to him. He noticed a bulge under the man's coat and deduced that he carried revolvers. Following him into the woods, but being very careful to avoid being seen, Oscar discovered that three others were hiding there waiting for him.

In an hour the lad had taken the news to Sheriff James Glispin at Madelia, and within fifteen minutes the sheriff had organized a posse and was riding hard toward the place where the four men had been reported.

Minnesota is a land of beautiful woods and lakes, but it must have looked anything but charming to the starved, ragged, and wounded outlaws when they found themselves hemmed in at last in a small patch of timber only about five miles in extent and surrounded on all sides by open ground. About this a cordon of one hundred and fifty men placed themselves, and began shooting into the trees with rifles and shotguns. They could not see the bandits, but they hoped to hit them by accident. The fugitives, however, lay low, and the fusillades failed to flush them out.

Somebody had to "draw the badger." Sheriff Glispin called for volunteers to "go in and stir them up." Though the danger was well understood, he got them: Captain W. W. Murphy, G. A. Bradford, Ben M. Rice, Colonel T. L. Vought, C. A. Pomeroy, and S. L. Severson. All of these, or nearly all, were war veterans, lean, grim fighters every one. With the sheriff they made a party of seven. Colonel Vought, Sheriff Glispin, Rice, and Severson carried rifles. Bradford and Pomeroy were armed with double-barreled

[5] No mention of this is contained in the accounts of their capture. Perhaps one of them had a wounded foot and eased it by removing his boots at their camps.

shotguns loaded with buckshot. Captain Murphy had a Colt revolver.

Forming a skirmish line, each man a few yards from the next, they began a cautious advance through the brush, every nerve taut, every one of them knowing he might be killed at any instant.

Luck was with them. Nights of exposure in the cold Minnesota fall weather, with little food and the exhaustion of the long retreat and their wounds, had so weakened the outlaws that they were far from the dangerous fighters they once had been.

About fifty yards into the woods, Sheriff Glispin saw the first of the hunted men. He was Charlie Pitts. Almost simultaneously the officer and the bandit fired, but the sheriff's rifle was surer than the bandit's revolver. Pitts "ran a couple of yards in a cornering direction and fell dead."

Right after, the three Youngers were discovered, crouched in the bush. A furious little battle began, the seven possemen firing as rapidly as they could work their guns at the three outlaws, whom they could see but dimly, if at all. The brothers fought back. A bullet smashed a pipe in Captain Murphy's pocket, but the ball was deflected, so that his wound was slight. Another posseman had his watch shattered.

Meantime the three outlaws slowly retreated, shooting and keeping under cover as much as possible, until they found themselves exposed to fire from the men who were stationed on the north side of the thicket. A volley from these drove the Youngers back until they were within twenty yards of the men who stalked them.

In the blast of fire and lead that followed, Cole and Jim fell, helpless with wounds. Only Bob, with his broken right arm dangling painfully at his side, continued to stand and blaze away with the revolver in his left hand, "aiming first at one end of the line, and then at the other, then at the center, but apparently trying rather to scare the men off than hit them," as one account says.

It is more probable that Bob was doing his best to hit one of his enemies but was too unpracticed with his left hand to do much execution. Of the shots fired at him only one hit him, slightly wounding him in the side.

At last he called out, "Let up! The boys are all shot to pieces!"

"Throw down your gun," said Sheriff Glispin.

Bob obeyed. The weapon was empty. A moment later all three Youngers were prisoners.

The wounded men and the dead Charlie Pitts were taken to Madelia, where two surgeons, Dr. Overholt and Dr. Cooley, attended to the living. Bob had not exaggerated when he said "the boys are all shot to pieces." Cole Younger carried eleven wounds in his body, the most serious of which were a rifle ball under the right eye which paralyzed the optic nerve, a revolver bullet in his body, and a shot through the thigh. Jim had eight buckshots and a rifle slug in his body, an ugly wound in the shoulder received at Northfield, and his upper jaw smashed on the right side by a bullet in the same street fight. Bob was the only one able to stand at the surrender. His shattered right arm hung helpless. He had other wounds. Jim was at first thought a hopeless case, but his strong vitality carried him through.

None of the captured men would tell who were their two companions who escaped. They seemed resigned. Bob's comment was: "I tried a desperate game and lost. My brothers and I are rough boys and used to rough work and therefore must abide by the consequences."

All three brothers were sentenced to the Minnesota penitentiary at Stillwater. Bob died in prison, September 16, 1889, from tuberculosis. Cole and Jim lived out their twenty-five-year sentences and eventually were freed. Shortly after he was released from prison, Jim committed suicide by shooting himself in a hotel room at St. Paul. He was despondent over a hopeless infatuation with a young woman who would have none of him, and over his inability to get a good job. Cole survived the others. In his later years he became quite religious and would sometimes preach sermons, using "his own misspent life as a text." He died at Lee's Summit, Missouri, March 21, 1916.

Jesse and Frank James were still at large. After their escape from Minnesota they are believed to have gone all the way down into Mexico for a time. Then they made their way to Nashville, Tennessee, where Frank called himself B. J. Woodson and Jesse lived under the name J. B. Howard—the first recorded use of the famous name of the ballad. Two of the old gang, who had not been at Northfield, joined them: Bill Ryan, who used the alias Tom Hill, and Dick Liddil who went as Charles Underwood.

On the night of October 7, 1879, a Chicago & Alton train was robbed at Glendale, Missouri, twenty-two miles from Kansas City. A familiar pattern was present: a gang of seven bandits rode into the small town, put the entire little population into the station, compelled the station agent to signal a stop, and expeditiously removed $35,000 in money and valuables from the safe after beating the messenger, a man named Grimes.

There was no question of it: Jesse James was back!

But he was back with a far less efficient gang than he formerly commanded. Two of them were rank recruits, Tucker Basham, a reckless but none too bright young farmer, and Ed Miller, a younger brother of Clell Miller, who was killed at Northfield.

Basham was arrested. Then, one night early in 1881, Ryan got drunk in a village north of Nashville and was also arrested. As it turned out, these two arrests were the first of the downward steps that eventually ended the gang.

Back in Missouri, William H. Wallace, now a lawyer, had been elected prosecuting attorney of Jackson County. He and Whig Keshlaer, deputy marshal, read the description of the man taken in Tennessee and believed it was Ryan. Keshlaer went to Nashville, identified the prisoner, and brought him back to Missouri, where he lodged him in jail in Independence.

These arrests caused no great concern on the part of Jesse James. No member of his gang had ever been convicted in Jackson County, and he did not know that Basham had made a full confession of the Glendale robbery. He was sure Ryan would not say anything, and he still had his brother Frank, Wood and Clarence Hite, Ed Miller, and Dick Liddil.

But here, again, was a weak point. Liddil, of a good Jackson County family, was a dashing, handsome fellow with a well-groomed mustache and imperial, dreamy blue eyes, a high forehead, and a way with women. He had a mistress in Kansas City, one Mattie Collins, who had "lived as his wife" for some time. This did not, however, prevent him from exerting his undoubted attractions in other quarters.

Living on a farm called the Harbison place, near Richmond, in

Ray County, Missouri, was a young and quite comely widow, Martha Bolton, who kept house for her two brothers, Bob and Charley Ford. Liddil visited there, and caught Mrs. Bolton's fancy to the point that she was "madly in love with him"—to quote no less an authority than Judge Wallace.

Partly because of this alliance, the Harbison place became one of the new gang's hideouts. The Ford brothers were weak-faced, shifty, not courageous enough to be full-fledged bandits, but glad to be hangers-on, and they were to play a sensational role later. Their charming sister who succumbed to Liddil's blandishments also played her part in subsequent events.

Now robberies began to occur again. But this significant fact is to be noted: never, after Northfield, did Jesse James attempt to "hurrah" a town in robbing a bank. He had learned a lesson. Pushed too far, outraged citizens will rise and fight with deadly fury.

Ryan was indicted for participation in the Glendale robbery, and Wallace, in spite of threats and warnings, began to gather evidence, even in the home territory of the outlaws themselves.

On July 15, 1881, the bandits struck, bloodily.

That evening a Rock Island train left Kansas City for Davenport, Iowa. At Cameron, north of Kansas City, three bearded men boarded it. A woman who noticed them said later that their beards were so heavy that they looked "as though they wore false whiskers." This is hardly fair. The beards were genuine enough. One of the men was Jesse James. He was wearing that beard at his death a few months later.

When the train halted at Gallatin, sixty miles farther on, four men ran out of the shadows and leaped on it. Two of them climbed on the end of the baggage car right behind the locomotive tender. As soon as the train began to move again, they crawled over the tender and covered the engineer and fireman with revolvers. While they passed through Winston, they ordered the engineer to slow down and stop.

Back in the smoker, as the train began to slow down, William Westfall, the conductor, was taking tickets.

Suddenly the three bearded men leaped up, drawing revolvers, with a shout, "All aboard!"—evidently a signal. Westfall halted, paling.

One of the bearded men thrust his face forward and stared at him. Then he growled something, which one of the passengers later said sounded like "You're the man I want."

With that he fired. The bullet struck Westfall in the arm. Turning, the conductor stumbled down the aisle, grasping for the door at the rear of the car. Two more shots were fired at him, neither striking him.

Then the bandit behind the one who was shooting, "as if exasperated at this poor shooting," fired—once. The lead slug tore through the conductor's skull. With a dying effort, Westfall succeeded in getting the door open, and fell on the platform, rolling down the steps of the still moving train into the blackness of the night-shrouded ditch beside the rails.

In the smoking car the panic-stricken passengers leaped to their feet and tried to crowd into the aisles.

"Down, down!" yelled the bandits. Frank McMillan, a stonemason, trying to escape, was brought down by a shot, stone dead. The other passengers cowered in their seats.

By this time the train had stopped, about a mile beyond Winston.

The weather was oppressively hot, and in both the baggage car and express car the doors had been left open for ventilation. Taking advantage of this, the bandits ran forward. As they reached the express car, Charles Murray, the express messenger, was trying to close the door. It worked hard, and before he could get it shut, they were upon him. One fired a shot that splintered wood over his head. Another squeezed through the door and struck him a terrible blow on the skull with his revolver barrel.

Murray, half stunned, could not resist as they took his keys and rifled the safe. What they got is a matter of question. Buel, who as a reporter then working from St. Louis investigated the case immediately afterward, said between $8000 and $10,000. Horan, who had access to the Pinkerton records, says about $600.

It does not really matter. Wallace said that "it looked as though the bandits were defying the law as never before, because the law was daring to imprison one of their number [Ryan]."

But there may have been a deeper reason in the feud-steeped minds of Jesse and Frank James. It will be remembered that when the "secret" train carried the Pinkerton operatives into Clay County, to toss the explosive into the Samuel home which tore off the arm of Zerelda Samuel, killed Archie Samuel, and wounded others, the conductor was William Westfall—this same man.

Through their highly efficient intelligence system the James brothers would know that Westfall was in charge of the "secret" train, and they could easily learn that Westfall was on the later train. It would be a matter of blood vengeance to shoot down the man who took the Pinkertons in for their attack on the Samuel place.

It was Frank who first wounded Westfall, but it was Jesse who killed him. It was Frank who later faced a jury for killing McMillan, but there is still question who pulled the fatal trigger in that instance.

Whatever the motive, the Winston murders sealed Jesse James' fate. Missouri was outraged and furious. At Jefferson City the new governor, Thomas T. Crittenden, after consulting with railroad and bank officials, issued a proclamation offering rewards of $5000 for the bandits involved, and $10,000 apiece for Frank and Jesse James, *by name.*

Ten thousand dollars! That was a tidy sum for Missouri, or indeed anywhere in the nation, in that year of 1881.

But even yet the bandits were not unduly alarmed. It was well known that no jury had ever convicted a member of their band in any court in Missouri.

They did not reckon on Wallace, the prosecutor, an unterrified and remorseless fighter. Doggedly he sought information to convict Ryan. He tried to get officials of the railroad to identify the indicted man. Later he wrote:

> To my astonishment, the managers of the railroad refused. They said it was no use; that no man could convict one of the James Boys in Missouri, and if they tried to help me it would simply make the outlaws mad, and they would rob their trains more than ever, and probably shoot down their conductors and engineers.

Wallace's friends begged him to dismiss the case. They said it was worth his life to conduct the prosecution and it would only result in acquittal in any case. But the prosecutor did not waver. Ryan was brought to trial in Independence.

After fifteen years of unchecked robbery and bloodshed, here was a test case between the law and the bandit. It was one of the most thrilling trials in Missouri history.

The defendant was supplied with plenty of money, through various channels, and employed the best possible counsel. Throughout the trial the courtroom was crowded with friends of the James gang, "ready for an outbreak." Jesse James and his men were close by. At night skyrockets soared up from the woods near Independence, to signal to Ryan that his friends were near. Dick Liddil later said that a rescue of the prisoner was seriously planned, but was given up when the outlaws learned the names of the men who were guarding Ryan and the court.

Wallace had gathered about him as hard-bitten a group of fighting men as the country ever saw. Every man of them was an ex-Confederate, every man cool and game, every man deadly if it came to that, and every man determined to clear away the slur that the Southerners sympathized with the outlaws.

In that group were: Captain M. M. Langhorne, one of the hardest-fighting officers in General Jo Shelby's famed cavalry brigade; H. H. Craig, a Kentuckian; Cornelius Murphy, a Virginian; Colonel J. E. Payne, a Confederate regimental commander; Whig Keshlaer, whose brother was killed fighting in the Confederate Army; James Goodwin, once an officer on the staff of General Fitzhugh Lee; Captain James R. Timberlake, sheriff of Clay County; Major E. A. Hickman, who lost an arm (but not his shooting arm) in the Confederate Army; Colonel Upton Hays and his brother Amazon Hays, both of Shelby's Horse. These men could shoot as hard and straight as the bandits, and for once the bandits backed off.

More threats and warnings came to Wallace. Tucker Basham, who turned state's evidence, learned that his house was burned down and his family forced to flee to Independence for safety. But the trial went on. Wrote Wallace in his memoirs:

> I put my whole soul into an effort in the closing argument to inspire the jury with courage to convict, for I was afraid that some of them, knowing the danger of a vote to convict, might falter. I beg pardon for being specific, but I have always regarded this as the supreme hour in my practice as a lawyer.

The jury was stanch. It convicted Ryan, and he was sent to the Missouri penitentiary for twenty-five years.

It was a stunning blow to the outlaws. A member of the James band, convicted in open court, right in their own country? Nobody supposed a Missouri jury would ever dare bring in such a verdict. That single episode, more than any other one thing, broke the back of the gang.

No longer were they immune. Courage sprang into hundreds of hearts. Headed by leaders like Langhorne, Keshlaer, Payne, Hays, and Timberlake, squads of men began to comb the outlaw country.

Wallace was asked to furnish a list of those who had "harbored the James Boys." He refused. Later he learned that an armed invasion of the outlaw territory had been planned. A train of boxcars was to take a small army of men, guns, and horses from St. Louis to Jackson County, unload them, and let them ride out in squads to put to death every man on Wallace's list.

Under this new pressure the evil loyalties of the gang began to crumble. Jesse James grew suspicious of his own followers. Believing that Ed Miller was turning against him, he murdered him and left him by the roadside. Wood Hite was killed at the Harbison place by Dick Liddil. Liddil said it was because Hite accused him of "stealing" a hundred dollars from the loot of a robbery "before the divide." More likely the shooting was over a woman—Martha Bolton.

Hite, though unprepossessing in appearance, having bad teeth, was quite free with his attentions toward any woman for whom he took a fancy. The Ford brothers evidently preferred Liddil to Hite as their sister's lover, for Bob Ford was present at the shooting in which Liddil killed Hite—even claimed to have fired a shot himself—and helped bury the dead man afterward, wrapped in a dirty old horse blanket.

After the killing of Hite, Liddil began to fear for his own life. He had violated the code of the blood feud, since Hite was a first cousin of Jesse James.

It was at this psychological time that Sheriff Timberlake conceived the plan of using Liddil's two lady friends to pry an opening into the bandit ring. In some manner he induced Mattie Collins, the Kansas City woman, to visit Martha Bolton, her rival for Liddil's affections. Evidently the two were not jealous of each other, for shortly after Mattie's visit, Martha Bolton went to see the governor, with some queries about what would happen to outlaws who surrendered.

Crittenden promised that any of the gang, outside of the James brothers themselves, would be "amply rewarded"—in other words, given clemency—if they surrendered and gave information.

When his girl friend told him that, Liddil did not hesitate. He gave himself up and made a lengthy confession to Wallace, in which he gave dates, names, and facts. Many robberies over the country had been attributed to the James gang which in fact were not perpetrated by them. On one occasion, for example, two robberies on the same day but four hundred miles apart; both were charged to Jesse and his crew. Liddil pinned the list down to the following:

Liberty, Mo., bank robbery, Feb. 14, 1866, George Wymore killed.

Lexington, Mo., bank robbery, Oct. 30, 1866.

Savannah, Mo., bank robbery attempt, March 2, 1867, Judge McLain, cashier, wounded.

Richmond, Mo., bank robbery, May 23, 1867, Mayor Shaw, Jailer B. G. Griffin, and his fifteen-year-old son killed.

Russellville, Ky., bank robbery, May 20, 1868, Nimrod Long, cashier, and a man named Owens wounded.

Gallatin, Mo., bank robbery, Dec. 7, 1869, Capt. John W. Sheets, cashier, killed.

Corydon, Ia., bank robbery, June 3, 1871.

Columbia, Ky., bank robbery, April 29, 1872, R. A. C. Martin, cashier, killed.

Kansas City Fair robbery, Sept. 26, 1872.

Ste. Genevieve, Mo., bank robbery, May 23, 1873.

Adair, Ia., Rock Island train robbery, July 21, 1873, train derailed, John Rafferty, engineer, scalded to death; his fireman badly burned, and several passengers injured.

Malvern, Ark., stagecoach robbery, Jan. 15, 1874.

Gads Hill, Mo., Iron Mountain train robbery, Jan. 31, 1874.

Muncie, Kas., Kansas Pacific train robbery, Dec. 13, 1875.

Huntington, W. Va., bank robbery, Sept. 1, 1875.

Otterville, Mo., Missouri Pacific train robbery, July 7, 1876.

Northfield, Minn., bank robbery, Sept. 7, 1876, J. L. Heywood, cashier, and Nicholas Gustavson killed; A. E. Bunker, teller, wounded.

Glendale, Mo., Chicago & Alton train robbery, Oct. 7, 1879.

Winston, Mo., Rock Island train robbery, July 15, 1881, William Westfall, conductor, and Frank McMillan killed; Charles Murray, express messenger, brutally beaten.

Blue Cut, Mo., Chicago & Alton train robbery, Sept. 7, 1881.

Muscle Shoals, Ala., stage holdup, March 1881.

Riverton, Ia., bank robbery, July 10, 1881.

Liddil did not mention the San Antonio, Texas, or Mammoth Cave, Kentucky, stage robberies, both of which have been fairly well pinned on the James gang. For his testimony in later cases, he was given a conditional pardon by Governor Crittenden, after being held for some weeks.

The gang was going to pieces fast. Through Liddil's help, Clarence Hite was captured. He went to the penitentiary for participation in the Winston train robbery, but contracted tuberculosis and was released to die at home, which he did within a few weeks.

Meantime that offer of $10,000 apiece for the Jameses was gnawing at the Ford brothers, Charley and Bob. Bob Ford paid a secret visit to Governor Crittenden to make sure that the reward would be paid for the outlaw brothers *whether dead or alive*. The governor assured him that he would be as well satisfied with dead outlaws as living ones—maybe more so.

On the morning of April 3, 1882, the report of a single pistol shot was heard in a small house in a good neighborhood in St. Joseph, Missouri. It was followed by the screams and sobs of a grief-stricken woman.

Neighbors rushed in, followed by officers of the law. On the floor of a bedroom lay a man with a crisp brown beard and a great hole blown in his head. It was Jesse James.

Robert Ford was his killer. His own sworn account, given at a coroner's inquest, tells the story simply enough:

My name is Robert Ford and I am twenty-one years of age. My residence for the past three or four years has been in Ray County, Mo., near the town of Richmond. In January last I had a conversation with Governor Crittenden, the result of which I became a detective to hunt the James outlaws. My first meeting with Jesse James occurred about three years ago, when in company with Ed Miller he stopped at my house overnight and discussed the robbing of a railroad train. The members of his gang at that time were Dick Liddil, Wood Hite, Ed Miller, Clarence Hite, and Jim Cummins. I never met any of these except Dick Liddil, Jim Cummins, and Wood Hite.

Governor Crittenden asked me if I thought I could catch Jesse James, and I answered yes, and at this same interview I besought the governor to pardon Dick Liddil, and agreed to undertake the arrest of Jesse. The governor therefore agreed to pay $10,000 apiece for the production of Jesse and Frank James, whether dead or alive. This interview occurred in the St. James Hotel in Kansas City.

I have been with Jesse constantly since last Sunday night, but Charley [Bob's brother] has been watching for an opportunity to capture him since last November. I was with Jesse about ten days ago, when at his request I accompanied him to his mother's home and slept with him in the barn. We remained there for two days, then started on horseback for St. Joseph, stopping overnight in a church, and before reaching the town we hid in a patch of timber until night, so as to make our entrance unobserved. That was a week ago last night. I rode a horse that had been stolen from a man named Robinson, of Clay County.

Jesse and I had a talk yesterday about robbing the bank

at Platte City [Mo.], and which Charley and I both agreed to assist. Between eight and nine o'clock this morning while the three of us were in a room in Jesse's house, Jesse pulled off his coat and also his pistols, two of which he constantly wore, and then got up onto a chair for the purpose of brushing dust off a picture.

While Jesse was thus engaged, Charley winked at me, so I knew he meant for me to shoot. So, as quickly as possible, I drew my pistol and aiming at Jesse's head, which was not more than four feet from the muzzle of my weapon, I fired, and Jesse tumbled headlong from the chair on which he was standing and fell on his face.

. . . After the shooting I told Mrs. James it was accidental, but she would not believe me. I went directly from Jesse's house to the telegraph station and sent a dispatch to Governor Crittenden, informing him of what I had done. Jesse, at the time of his death, owned one .45 caliber Colt, one .45 caliber Smith & Wesson, one .44 caliber Derringer pistol, one Winchester rifle, and one double-barreled shotgun. I have heard him frequently declare he would never be captured alive.

Jesse James had just returned from the Indian Territory, where he spent some weeks hiding out, some of it at the home of Belle Starr, Cole Younger's former sweetheart. Unquestionably he was planning another major crime when he was killed.

The manner of his death, and the cowardly treachery of it, completed the Jesse James legend and gave him an imperishable place in American folklore.

News of the killing of the arch-bandit rocked the nation. One newspaper, the St. Joseph *Gazette*, carried this gem of a banner headline:

JESSE, BY JEHOVAH!

William Wallace, the tireless and fearless foe of the James brothers and all they stood for, said, "It was one of the most cowardly and diabolical deeds in history. Jesse James was a wonderfully lawless, bloodthirsty man, but that gave the Ford boys no right to assassinate him."

In the Kansas City *Journal*, Major John Edwards wrote that wonderful rodomontade which ends:

> Tear the two bears from the flag of Missouri. Put thereon, in place of them, as more appropriate, a thief blowing out the brains of an unarmed victim, and a brazen harlot, naked to the waist and splashed to the brows in blood!

So great was the public's emotional reaction to the treacherous nature of the act of men who wormed themselves into another's friendship to kill him from behind, that the brothers Ford had little enjoyment of their reward money.

Almost spontaneously sprang up the ballad with the refrain:

The dirty little coward,
Who shot Mr. Howard,
Has laid poor Jesse in his grave.

Four years after the murder of Jesse James, Charlie Ford, borne down by disease and remorse, was found dead, a suicide by shooting himself, in a weed patch near his home at Richmond, Missouri.

Robert Ford, the actual slayer, was forced by public opinion to leave Missouri. Here and there he wandered, eventually opening a tent saloon in the mining town of Creede, Colorado. There he was killed by an ex-police officer gone bad, Ed O'Kelley, in July 1892. The quarrel was said to be over a woman, no unusual cause of homicide. O'Kelley himself was killed at Oklahoma City, Oklahoma, while resisting arrest, June 4, 1904.

Jesse James was buried in the yard of the Samuel place. On the stone which marked the grave was this inscription:

> Jesse W. James
> Died April 3, 1882
> Aged 34 years, 6 months, 28 days.
> Murdered by a traitor and a coward whose
> name is not worthy to appear here.

Into the office of Prosecutor Wallace one day came two women. He later described them: "One of them was a large old lady with an empty sleeve. I had never seen her before. The face of the other lady was hidden by a thick veil."

The women asked for an interview in his private office. When the door was closed, the one with the veil removed it.

"Do you know me?" she asked.

Wallace nodded his head. "It's been a good many years since I saw you, but I certainly do. You are Annie Ralston, who I now understand is Frank James' wife."

"You are correct," said Mrs. James.

The one-armed woman was Zerelda Samuel, mother of the outlaw who was still at large, with a $10,000 reward hanging over his head.

They had come to make Wallace a proposal: that Frank James should surrender personally to him. If someone else took him, they said, they were "very much afraid he would be killed for the reward while in the act of giving himself up." They were sure Wallace had nothing to do with the assassination of Jesse James, and they believed he would protect Frank if he received the outlaw's surrender.

"Mrs. James," said Wallace earnestly, "if your husband surrenders to me, if he is harmed it will be over my dead body."

"Frank is living in perfect torment," she said. "He can't even cut a stick of wood without looking around to see whether or not someone is slipping up behind to kill him."

The prosecutor would not agree that her husband should go absolutely free, but he made the offer, "if he will give himself up and end the whole matter, the State will be satisfied with a short term in the penitentiary."

Those terms were not acceptable, and in a short time Wallace received a telegram from Governor Crittenden that the outlaw had surrendered to him, personally, and that he was sending James under guard to Independence to Wallace's custody.

The surrender of the last of the famous bandits created a national sensation. Frank James had chosen exactly the right time, when public feeling was still intense. Important men went to Wallace and besought him to release the prisoner on bond. But there was an indictment—written by Wallace's predecessor in office—charging James with murder, which under the Missouri law was not bailable. Wallace refused to permit his release on any kind of bond.

Now a new storm commenced. Was Wallace actually going to prosecute?

The answer was an unequivocal affirmative, and this in the face of the fact that the prosecutor was facing a new election with an apparently unpopular issue. It did not prove too unpopular. Wallace was re-elected by a convincing majority.

Now he prepared for the prosecution. The murder of Whicher, the Pinkerton agent, was first considered, but it was thought a better case could be made of the murder of Frank McMillan, during the train robbery at Winston, Missouri, when Jesse killed Conductor Westfall.

The scene of the trial was moved to Gallatin, county seat of Daviess County, in which the murder occurred, and the nominal chief prosecutor was a young man named William D. Hamilton, who held the office in that county. But from first to last it was Wallace's fight. As special prosecutor, he had all the evidence at his finger tips, and he had the courage to carry on the trial in the face of some very ugly threats and demonstrations.

The first clash was over the selection of a jury. Wallace was sure it was packed, and threatened to leave the case. He was persuaded to remain, which he did—with the statement, "We will simply try Frank James before the world. The verdict of the jury that is being selected is already written."

"There probably never was a trial where there was so much talk about 'honor,' 'duels,' and 'shooting on sight,' as this one," Wallace later recalled, "and I seemed to be the hapless victim of all the intended vengeance, although I had never done anything except to look up the law and the evidence, and push the prosecution."

Two different men wrote out challenges to duels, but Wallace said if they were delivered he would have the challengers arrested under the statute, and they never were presented.

The trial went on. Wallace hammered away, and later said,

"The State, in my judgment, had an overwhelming case—more than twice as strong as the case against Bill Ryan."

But he was fighting against something more baffling than any amount of evidence—emotion.

Into the witness chair one day climbed a witness for the defense, a bearded man with a lion look in his face. He was General Joseph O. Shelby, one of Missouri's heroes of the Confederate side in the Civil War, the man who took the last one thousand "no surrender" Confederates down into Mexico, whose name was associated with countless daring actions, one of the cavalry leaders dubbed "Wizards of the Saddle."

General Shelby, unfortunately, had fortified himself perhaps too well from the bottle, and as Wallace put it, "I will be charitable enough to say that General Shelby was not fully himself."

Nevertheless, the old general, asked if he knew Frank James, loudly answered that he did, with an addendum: "Where is my old friend and comrade in arms? Ah, there I see him! Allow me, I wish to shake hands with my fellow soldier who fought by my side for Southern rights!"

He was restrained from doing so, and there followed a bristling exchange of invective between him and Wallace, Jo Shelby storming furiously.

Nevertheless, from the moment the old general appeared on the stand, the case assumed a new dimension. It was not Frank James who was on trial so much as the Bonny Blue Flag, the Lost Cause, and a lot of other emotional matters that stirred people's hearts rather than their minds.

After Shelby was excused from the stand he left the courtroom. When the hearing closed that afternoon, a Dr. Black, of Gallatin, stopped Wallace and told him he had heard that Shelby threatened to shoot the prosecutor "on sight."

From most people, that threat might have been shrugged off. But fiery Jo Shelby was a man who could be expected to do exactly as he said he would.

Wallace, his arms full of lawbooks, left the courthouse for his room at the hotel. It had rained, and the streets were muddy. As was the custom of the times, a wide plank had been laid across the street to enable pedestrians to cross without stepping in the mire.

Just as Wallace came to one end of the plank, he saw General Shelby reach the other. It was a moment fraught with consequence, a spine-tingling instant when the prosecutor must have thought that fortune had played him the sorriest of tricks.

And then Shelby, instead of drawing a pistol, swept off his hat, and with a courtly gesture said, "Cross first, if you please, Mr. Wallace."

Shelby had never made the threat to shoot him, as the prosecutor instantly knew. He crossed over with his armload of books, received a pleasant greeting, and went on.

It was only one of numerous episodes that might have shaken the nerve of a lesser man than Wallace.[6] He was not shaken. At the end of the trial he made a brilliant oratorical summary of the case, but his opponent, Colonel John F. Philips (oddly enough, a Union officer, while Wallace was a Southern man), cleverly played on the emotional side of the case. As the prosecutor predicted, Frank James was acquitted.

Except for the few weeks he spent in custody awaiting his trial he did not serve a single day in prison for his many crimes. No other charges were made against him, and he died peacefully in 1915, when he was seventy-two years old. Of all the gang he alone escaped punishment.

John Younger, Clell Miller, Bill Chadwell, Charlie Pitts, Bud McDaniels, Payne Jones, and Tom McDaniels were killed by officers of the law or by citizens in arms; Andy McGuire, Arch Clements, and Dick Burns were lynched; Jesse James, Wood Hite,

[6] A pleasant little aftermath of the Shelby episode was when the general later hunted Wallace up and said to him, "What apology do you want from me?" He was referring to his behavior in court. Wallace smiled and said he did not know that any apology was necessary.

"Well," spoke Shelby, "the only apology I desire to make is that every man reserves the right to make a damn fool of himself now and then."

He then asked to present "a Wallace man." It turned out to be his wife. "Mrs. Shelby was a Wallace man all through the trial," said the general, "and she was right and her husband wrong."

Wallace and Shelby were devoted friends thereafter.

and Ed Miller were killed by members of their own gang; Jim Younger and Charley Ford committed suicide; Robert Ford was driven out of the state and shot down in a quarrel; Cole Younger, Bob Younger, George Shepherd, Bill Ryan, Tucker Basham, Dick Liddil, Clarence Hite, Hobbs Kerry, and Jack Kean served in prison for greater or lesser terms. Bob Younger dying in the penitentiary, and Clarence Hite being released to go home and die. Jim Cummins was a fugitive for a long time, not from the law, but from Frank James. They eventually dropped their feud and Jim Cummins died in the Missouri Confederate home.

One mystery has never been explained. Where did all the loot taken in the bank, stage, and train robberies go?

Exactly how much it amounted to will never be known accurately. Emerson Hough, in his study of the career of the band, estimated the total as not less than $275,000 and perhaps as high as $500,000.

It has been suggested that Jesse James was shot down from behind instead of being taken by a cordon of officers, who might have surrounded his house, "in order to keep him from talking." It also was hinted that the Ford brothers were killed—by this version Charley Ford's death was murder not suicide—for the same reason. In other words, there was a payoff somewhere that had to be hushed up.

But this does not hold water. Frank James knew as much as Jesse about the crimes committed, and he lived to a ripe old age. So did Cole Younger. Robert Ford was not killed for ten years after he murdered Jesse James, and it was officially established that Charley Ford did commit suicide.

Where, then, did all the money go? Perhaps the bandits spent freely, but in those simple times squandering that much money, it would seem, would attract too much attention to escape some comment.

There are persons today who believe that some of the loot is still hidden, perhaps in one or more of the limestone caves of Missouri which were gang hideouts, perhaps buried under floors of old Missouri houses, or in orchards or fields.

Buried treasure? It is the one thing that was needed to keep the legend of Jesse James forever new.

5. *A Brushwood Courtesan*

She was a wild young thing, black-eyed and dark-haired, rebellious at her mother's efforts to restrict her and "bring her up like a lady," and out of that rebellion going to the very opposite extreme—Myra Belle Shirley, who was to come down in history as Belle Starr.

Already, when she was eighteen, she had stepped over the bounds and suffered for it in a woman's way. It was she whom Cole Younger, at the very start of his bandit career, seduced while he visited at the home of her father, John Shirley, near Sycene, Texas. The seduction perhaps was not very difficult, for Cole was good to look upon, and throughout her life Belle seemed less than averse to attempts upon her so-called virtue.

The result might have been foreseen, for the lovers were young and lusty. After Cole Younger rode on, for his long career of outlawry, the girl remained behind, growing big with child, and when she had passed her nineteenth birthday gave birth to a girl baby, with her mother, rigid with disapproval and a sense of disgrace, as her midwife.

But Belle had an elastic nature. She abode the disgrace, if such she considered it, and also the desertion of her lover. She did not even seem to feel resentment toward the man who had fathered a child in her and then left her, as some girls would have done, for she named the little girl Pearl Younger, and later called her wild home in the Cherokee country "Younger's Bend." She even made vague pretense at times of being married to Cole, although this assuredly she never was. He was her first man, and she always cherished the memory of him in a secret little corner of her heart.

By far the best study of Belle Starr's career is Burton Rascoe's highly entertaining book, *Belle Starr, "The Bandit Queen."* In it Rascoe demolishes the dime-novel extravagances concerning her, and his findings are most valuable. Even when he falls back on conjecture he makes a good case for his theories. And yet, after she is stripped of her false legends—in which she was credited by lurid writers with numerous slayings (she never killed anyone) and hairsbreadth adventures that never took place—she emerges in Rascoe's book as a remarkable and somehow compelling woman, well fitted to perpetuate and disperse the infection of outlawry, of which she seemed to be a "carrier," like Typhoid Mary.

Facing the world with a fatherless child, Belle was in no wise discouraged. She was not pretty, in the classical sense, but she had the measureless vitality and attraction of youth, a body to make men fall to dreaming, and the instincts to use it for the purposes for which nature intended it. Reckless and promiscuous, she busied herself throughout her life providing, sexually, links and still further links with the Quantrill and James-Younger chain of crime—although she was not conscious she was doing it, being too much a creature of her impulses ever to arrive at a conclusion so abstract.

After Cole Younger—and the resulting accouchement—her parents tried to bring their daughter back to acceptance of the conventions and kept a rigid watch over her. But she was never one born for rules; only to follow the impulses of her inward flame, her woman's basic need for men.

The first, after Cole, was Jim Reed, a young bandit who took part in three of Jesse James robberies and engineered some of his own. Reed was a Missourian, brought up at Rich Hill, not far from

Carthage, where the girl grew up. He knew Belle when they were children.

From the first Belle warmed to him, probably in part because he relieved the boredom of her closely supervised home existence. But John Shirley, her father, still chagrined over having his daughter confer grandfatherhood on him with an illegitimate child, intervened. He ordered Reed off the place and shut the girl up in the second floor of his house. Not, however, before she had reached some kind of an understanding with her admirer.

Jim Reed, of middle height, with "sandy hair and a prominent nose," was a superb horseman. He also was ardent. One night, with twenty reckless young men to help him, he staged a "rescue," and released his inamorata from the parental custody. From that day on, Belle was her own mistress, as well as becoming the mistress of many men. But this is to be remembered of her: never was she a prostitute as her own daughter became. Throughout her life she chose her own lovers, and so strong was her nature that usually after she had given them her body, she dominated them for as long as she kept them.

In later years Belle claimed she was married to Reed, as she had claimed she was married to Cole Younger. But the wedding, if any, was strictly a piece of hippodrome. What seems to have occurred was this: When Reed and Belle, and the twenty "rescuers," were safely beyond the range of John Shirley's paternal shotgun, they decided to have a "ceremony." The "bride" and the "groom" both were mounted, and so was the "officiating" party, a horse thief and outlaw named John Fischer, who had no more authority or license to perform the rite than had the (probably stolen) animal he bestrode. Fischer pronounced them "man and wife," and the "witnesses" took a drink all around, and made some gross witticisms, and saw the couple off to their "nuptial" bed.

Nevertheless, whether she was *legally* married or not, Belle was Reed's consort long enough so that she could claim wifehood under the common law—which was about all that many other women had to go on in the outskirts of civilization in that day. And here arises a fascinating conjecture, first suggested by Rascoe.

There exists an autobiography of Frank James, *The Only True History of Frank James, Written by Himself.* Examining this, Rascoe at first discarded it as spurious. But later study of internal evidence convinced him that the "piece of shoddy," as he calls it, "maudlin, illiterate, vague, confused, pathetic," was probably genuine and actually written by the ex-bandit in his last days. It contains this about Belle Starr:

> When the civil war was over Bell [*sic*] married Jim Reed, a noted highwaymen [*sic*], who had served under Quantral [*sic*]. Jim Reed and my father were brothers. I was a base begotten child. It was never known to the world. My parents came from Tennessee[1] to Missouri. I was born only a short time after they arrived in Clay County, Missouri, and the people never knew or thought anything about the child that was called Frank James. My mother promised to be married secretly to a man named Edd Reed. He was killed before I was born, and to save the disgrace my mother married Robert James and then moved to Missouri. So the people of this old world did not know that Frank and Jesse James were only half brothers.

Looking back, it somehow rings true. It would account for many things: the sudden arrival of Robert James and his wife in western Missouri from their home in Kentucky, interrupting his theological studies; the birth of the first son to Zerelda shortly after; the utter difference in appearance, personality, disposition, even thinking of Frank and Jesse. And it is to be noted that Frank James had a "large nose and sandy hair," evidently Reed characteristics. It could very well be just as stated.

If it is true, Belle thus became Frank James' aunt by common-law marriage, although she was five years his junior. If so, also, her consort must have been a very much younger brother of the bandit's natural father. But this is easily possible. Families were large in those days and often as much as twenty or thirty years might separate the first and last of a given brood.[2]

In due time Belle gave birth to a second child, this time a boy,

[1] Actually, from Kentucky.

[2] As an instance, Benjamin Franklin was the seventeenth child in his family. Men and women in those days seemed to live primarily to procreate.

sired by Jim Reed. She named the baby Ed, perhaps after the "Edd" whom Frank said was his real father, or perhaps after her brother Ed, known as Bud, killed during the Civil War. Thus, through her offspring, she would be related by consanguinity, as well as by illicit connections, with the Youngers and the Jameses. And with those outlaws she maintained a constant contact in the years that followed.

The institution of "feuding" in the Hatfield-McCoy manner, which was characteristic of the Southern mountain white families, was inherited by the Jameses, the Youngers, and others, including the Reeds. But whereas before the Civil War it was confined to narrow areas, such as single mountain valleys, the dislocations of that conflict, with the spread of travel by railroad, stage, and horse, and the scattering of populations, introduced feuds and feuding to thousands of miles of the West.

Not long after taking Belle to his amorous but illicit bosom, Jim Reed felt called upon to exact some blood vengeance. The outlaw, John Fischer, who "married" him to Belle, had incurred the hatred of three brothers named Shannon (first names unknown). They arranged an ambush for him "at a point in the Indian Territory only a few miles from Fort Smith, Ark."

Another man, Scott Reed—fortunately for Fischer, but unfortunately for himself—chanced to ride by the ambush first. Mistaking him for their quarry, the Shannons shot and killed him.

Scott Reed happened to be an elder brother of Jim Reed, and the latter, on learning what happened, took Belle to Rich Hill, Missouri, left her there with relatives, and returned to the Indian Territory, where he joined the Fischers in their feud, bushwhacking and "participating in the killing of two of the Shannons in retaliation."

In this vendetta Reed became acquainted with a notable, even notorious, clan of Cherokee Indians, the Starr family and kin. The patriarch of the clan was a giant of a man, Tom Starr. He stood six feet five inches tall in his huge moccasins, had black hair and gray eyes "generally with the lashes plucked," great physical strength, and murderous hatred of a rival Cherokee clan headed by the sons of John Ross, chief of the Cherokee Nation. There had been killings on both sides since the 1830s, and during the Civil War these increased. Eventually Tom Starr gained an unusual distinction. A peace treaty was made between the Cherokee Nation and him, *as an individual*—one of the few in all history of this nature.

During the war some of Quantrill's guerrillas, including Jesse James and Cole Younger, operated for a time in the Indian Territory, and allied themselves with the Starr clan, at that time outlawed by the rest of the Cherokees. In this campaign Jesse James fought, and was wounded, in one of his hardest battles, against a body of Pin Indians.[3] The guerrillas defeated the Indians.

It was during this period also that Jesse became acquainted with some of the natural hideouts which later formed part of his string of refuges, spreading from Missouri into Arkansas and Tennessee, down into Texas, and through the Indian Territory. In particular the Indian Territory, now Oklahoma, was rich in caves that made ideal hiding places for outlaws.

After his "feuding" Reed returned to Rich Hill and took Belle to California, where their son Ed was born, in Los Angeles. When they returned to Texas, Jim learned that he was wanted by the law for, among other things, stage robbery. He therefore found it convenient, even urgent, to spend most of his time elsewhere—in the Indian Territory, living with the Starrs. Frequently Belle left her two children at Sycene with her mother—who seems to have become reconciled to her daughter's capricious conduct—and made visits to her consort in the wild country to the north.

It was through Jim Reed that she became acquainted with a member of the Starr clan: Sam Starr, described as "six feet tall, weighing two hundred pounds, a thorough Indian." There is some evidence that in this period she and Sam Starr became interested in each other—perhaps more than interested. The Indian was four years younger than she, a big man, and rather good-looking in his

[3] Anti-slavery Cherokees, favoring the Union. They were called Pin Indians because they wore pins, crossed, on their shirts to let others of their following know what side they favored.

way. She liked big men—throughout her life they seemed to appeal to something in her nature. And throughout her life she progressively became sexually interested in younger and still younger men.

In his book *Hell on the Border,* S. W. Harman, chronicler of the Fort Smith, Arkansas, federal court, reported as follows:

> During Belle's visits to Jim [Reed] they [Jim, Belle, and Sam Starr] often attended dances together, often riding twenty or thirty miles for the purpose, and it was not unusual that Sam Starr rode behind, *on Belle's horse,* the three attending the homely fetes together.

The great advantage to a man, in riding double behind an attractive woman, always has been that it was necessary to put his arms about her "to hold on"—at least that was the excuse. Belle at this time was in her early twenties, one would judge a ripe and luscious armful for any man.

On one of her visits, the night of November 19, 1873, Watt Grayson, an old Creek chief, was robbed of about $30,000 in gold coin and bills. Three men, Jim Reed, Dan Evans, and W. D. Wilder, broke into Grayson's cabin and tortured him and his wife by placing a rope about their necks, in turn, and "elevating" them until they were all but strangled to death. After Grayson suffered this seven times and his old wife three times, the stoicism of the Creeks broke down. The money, they disclosed, was under the cabin floor, through a trap door. One has less sympathy with the chief when the old rascal's method of getting it is known. It was an accumulation "which the Indian had secured by a system of official thievery from the tribal funds."

Years later descendants of Grayson brought suit against the government seeking to recover the money under provisions of a treaty whereby the government promised to make good any damages to Indians caused by white men. At that time Belle Starr testified in their behalf, said she was present at the robbery, and told how disappointed the robbers were to find that $12,000 of their loot was in Confederate currency, completely worthless. Disposition of this case is not known, but Belle's claim that she was present is probably true.

Wilder was afterward captured and sent to the penitentiary for twenty-five years for his part in the robbery. Evans was one of six men hanged at once on the Fort Smith gallows by the sinister George Maledon, official executioner for Judge Isaac C. Parker. He was executed for the murder of a boy named Seabolt, but during his trial confessed to his part in the Grayson robbery and the torture of the old Indians, adding an ugly detail: the inhuman robbers also burned the feet of their victims with pine torches to elicit the information as to the hiding place of the treasure. If Belle Starr was present and watched that unmoved, she was by that time hardened to crime in its extremest form.

It is time to take notice of Judge Isaac Charles Parker, and his hangman, George Maledon, for they played a chilling role in the history of the Indian Territory, from the year 1875, when Judge Parker took the federal bench at Fort Smith, Arkansas, to 1896, when his court was abolished and he died.[4]

This extraordinary judge was born in Ohio, in 1838, but was a Missourian by adoption, practicing law in St. Joseph, then holding several political appointments, besides occupying the bench in Missouri before being named judge of the newly created "Western District of Arkansas," by President U. S. Grant in 1875. The Western District of Arkansas in reality meant the Indian Territory, which until that time had no courts, except Indian tribal courts.

Judge Parker's appearance little prepared a stranger, seeing him for the first time, to realize that here was the man known over a vast area as "the Hanging Judge." He was plump, even rotund, and in his later years his snow-white hair and white beard, with his bulbous nose and pink round cheeks, gave him more the look of a jovial Santa Claus than one of the most fearsome judges since the notorious Justice George Jeffreys, of the "Bloody Assizes" in England in 1685.

[4] The great source not only on Judge Parker and his court but on much criminal history of the Indian Territory is a bloodthirstily interesting book, *Hell on the Border*, by S. W. Harman, a newspaper editor who was for many years a close observer of the court and knew the judge and many of its chief figures well.

The court of which he took charge in Fort Smith stood on the very border of the Indian Territory, which swarmed with ruffians—white, Indian, and Negro—who created a sort of criminal anarchy before the government placed it under the jurisdiction of the judge who ascended to the Fort Smith bench. To meet a condition like that, a man of unusual qualities was needed, and Ike Parker had them. He was singularly resolute and fearless, and he had none of the modern penologist's theories of "mercy" and "rehabilitation" toward criminals brought before him. Though he is reported to have shed tears on the occasion of first pronouncing a death sentence, he warmed to his work in the following years in a manner suspiciously suggesting zest.

In one respect Judge Parker's court was unique. The first fourteen years of the twenty-one during which he presided over it were free of interference by other courts, even the Supreme Court of the United States. His judgments were irrevocable. There was no appeal.

Power of life and death like that must have been a heady tonic. But it was a power needed to deal with the wild and lawless territory over which Ike Parker administered justice. To show what a problem was presented, it is only necessary to point out that in Judge Parker's twenty-one years on the Fort Smith bench, sixty-five law-enforcement officers were killed in his district. In that same period he presided over trials which resulted in one hundred and seventy-two convictions for capital offenses—murder or rape. Of the one hundred and seventy-two, eighty-eight suffered death on the gallows. Of the others, three died in jail before execution, one was killed trying to escape, two received presidential pardons, six were reversed by higher courts (in the later years) and on obtaining new trials were acquitted, two were adjudged insane and sent to asylums, eighteen forfeited bonds (but of these, two later were proved to be dead), and the rest had their death sentences commuted to prison sentences of various degrees of severity.

Judge Parker was a tireless worker. His court sessions lasted from eight o'clock in the morning to dark, "and when others grew weary he was still fresh and strong." As time passed he became more and more ferocious in the sentences which he pronounced on what he called "criminal intruders" in his domain. Excerpts from the exordium he delivered in sentencing the degenerate criminal Cherokee Bill to death for the second time, give a little of the flavor:

"The crime you have committed is but another evidence, if any were needed, of your wicked, lawless, bloody and murderous disposition. It is another evidence of your total disregard of human life; another evidence that you revel in the destruction of human life. The many murders you have committed, and their reckless and wanton character, show you to be a *human monster*, from whom innocent people can expect no safety!

"You have had a fair trial, notwithstanding the howls and shrieks to the contrary. There is no doubt of your guilt of a most wicked, foul and unprovoked murder, shocking to every good man and woman in the land. Your case is one where justice should not walk with leaden feet! It should be swift! It should be certain! As far as this court is concerned, it shall be, for public justice demands it!"

These are only parts of two paragraphs from the entire speech to the man who stood before the bench. After a burst of invective like that the prisoner must have felt that the gallows was not such a bad place after all.

The other half of the Fort Smith team was George Maledon, the lean-jawed, sinister hangman. He was small, five feet five inches tall, and spare, with a straggling beard that grew progressively whiter, and a gloomy, yet expressionless stare in his large dark eyes. Diminutive as he was, one is inclined to wonder if it did not give him a sensation of power to send to their deaths great strapping men who could handle him with one hand.

Maledon took a profound pride in his work of carrying out the death sentences pronounced by Ike Parker. He frequently explained to any who cared to listen his method of quickly and neatly putting his victims to death. The heavy hangman's knot, with its traditional thirteen wrappings of the rope to form the noose, was adjusted scientifically at the left side of the neck in the hollow just behind the ear. This, Maledon explained, was so that when the trap fell and the body went down with a jerk, the neck was broken, giving the condemned man a quick and easy death.

Altogether he personally performed the uncanny task of launching into eternity sixty criminals, besides shooting two others to death while they were attempting to escape from the jail, "gaining the unenviable reputation of having executed several times as many men as any officer in America, more than any known legal executioner of modern times, with the exception of the famous Deibler of Paris [during the French Reign of Terror] who is reported to have decapitated 437 persons."[5]

Maledon oversaw the building of the famous scaffold at Fort Smith. It had a platform thirty inches wide and twenty feet long, giving room for twelve men to stand upon it side by side. The master hangman, however, never was able to plunge that many to their death at once. On two occasions he did execute six men with one springing of his trap, three times five men, three times four men, and triple and double executions became too numerous to excite comment.

The first "six-man hanging" was, to him, his masterpiece. The victims were Evans (the associate of Jim Reed and Belle Starr), for the murder of young Seabolt; John Whittington, for the murder of John J. Turner; Edmund Campbell, Negro, for the murder of Lawson Ross and a young Negress; James Moore, for the murder of William Spivey; Smoker Man-killer, Cherokee Indian, for the murder of William Short; and Samuel Fooey, Cherokee Indian, for the murder of J. E. Neff, a schoolteacher.

Hangings at that time were public, and for an entire week before the execution people came to Fort Smith from other places, drawn by the unusual attraction as if it were some sort of an excursion. Some five thousand gathered to see the celebrated gibbet tested to "half its capacity." Hangman Maledon was equal to the occasion, performing his duty with skill and dispatch. "The entire lot of six convicted felons were lined up with their feet squarely across the line where met the two planks forming the death trap, and after prayer and the singing of gospel hymns, the last farewells were spoken, the black caps were drawn and at the word all were

[5] Harman, in *Hell on the Border*.

shuffled off together; their necks were broken and all died without a struggle." Eastern newspapers covered the event, and the reports in the press shocked many people over the nation. The episode did much to give Judge Parker a reputation for heartlessness.

Maledon, a Bavarian by birth, was convinced that all the men he executed deserved their fate. On one occasion he said, without any thought of the macabre humor of the statement, that "he has hanged few truthful men, for nearly all he has ever hanged persisted in declarations of innocence, even with their last breath." To an old lady who once asked him if he had any qualms of conscience or feared the spirits of the departed, he replied quite gravely: "No; I've never hanged a man who came back to have the job done over. The ghosts of men hanged at Fort Smith never hang around the old gibbet."

In spite of his grim efficiency in his official duty, he had little control in his own family. His daughter, Annie Maledon, described as "beautiful of face and figure, possessed of a wealth of long, heavy black hair, and soft, dark brown eyes," became at eighteen a much sought-after "unchaste woman." Frank Carver, a Muskogee gambler, found her in Fort Smith and took her back to Muskogee as his own personal *fille de joie*, lodging her within a few blocks of his home, where he lived with his wife and family. But Annie was of too ardent a nature to limit herself to just one man. She began secretly receiving another lover, Frank Walker. Learning of her relations with this rival, Carver got drunk on Jamaica ginger—his favorite tipple—and shot her to death.

George Maledon, the father, looked forward to the pleasure of personally hanging Carver, who was convicted of first-degree murder and sentenced to die by Judge Ike Parker. Unfortunately, however, the man was represented by excellent counsel, appealed the case, and it was commuted to life imprisonment.

Strangely, or perhaps not so strangely, Maledon had a sentimental affection for his hanging machine. When the court was abolished just before Judge Parker's death in 1896, he attempted to get possession of the scaffold, and failing that, at least the old trap doors, the last things on earth on which eighty-eight men had stood before they died. The city council of Fort Smith, however, ordered the ghastly structure burned.

Maledon managed to salvage a piece of the main beam of the gallows, together with the rope used in his first execution, one used in hanging ten different men, one used to hang nine men, one used to hang two men, one used to hang twenty-one men, and one used to hang Cherokee Bill. All six of these particular ropes figured in his first "sextette." It will be noted that Hangman Maledon was careful and economical. The ropes and beams, with some of the hardware of the mechanism used in his "drops," he displayed for some time as a traveling exhibit after his official duties came to an end.

These two men, Hanging Judge Isaac C. Parker and Hangman George Maledon, became names of terror in the Indian Territory. Harman tells of a sign at a crossing of the north fork of the Canadian River which read:

FORT SMITH
FIVE HUNDRED MILES

Beneath this some outlaw carved with his bowie knife:

TO HELL

To return to Belle and her affairs: Jim Reed, with a price on his head, was hunted for three months by John T. Morris, of McKinney, Texas, who was a somewhat shady character himself, but was specially deputized to bring the outlaw in. Morris used methods similar to those employed by the Ford brothers in killing Jesse James. He gained Reed's confidence by telling him that he also was running from the law, and traveled with him, waiting to "get the drop."

On the evening of August 6, 1874, the two stopped at a farmhouse fifteen miles from Paris, Texas, for supper. Morris suggested they leave their guns on their saddles, to avoid arousing suspicion. To this Reed agreed, but Morris made an excuse, went outside to obtain his Winchester, and returned, calling on the wanted man to surrender.

Wrote Harman:

> Reed sat at the opposite side of the table facing the open door, and as his betrayer stepped into sight, he, scenting the danger, cried "Traitor!" and reaching out with both hands grabbed the far

edges of the table and raised it between himself and the assassin, while dishes and contents went to the floor in a smash, echoing three shots which rang out in rapid succession, piercing the table top and releasing Reed's life blood.

Morris received the reward money of $1500. Though Belle besought Solly Reed, Jim's younger brother, to avenge the slaying, Morris seemed too formidable for the younger member of the family.

Belle was now a "widow," if living with Reed, under common law, could make her a "wife." But she appeared not to be entirely inconsolable. Returning to Dallas, for a time she cut quite a figure, keeping a stable of fine horses, and riding out in a black velvet habit with a plumed hat, always in the sidesaddle, for she considered it unladylike to ride astride.

It was during this period that Cole Younger and his brothers Jim and Bob made their residence for a time in Dallas, following the Muncie train robbery. Did Cole and Belle see each other clandestinely? Although there can be found no record of it, from what is known of both of them I think it more than likely that there may have been a brief interlude of warmed-over love between them. If it took place, however, it was brief, for the Youngers rode north again, to join Jesse James in the Otterville, Missouri, robbery, and from there go to the fiery ordeal of the Northfield disaster.

Perhaps out of frustration, Belle, with another woman named Emma Jones, deliberately set fire to a small store in a village near Dallas. Her companion lost her nerve and told of the arson, and Belle bitterly commented, when she was arrested, that "after that I never again placed confidence in a woman."

When she was being tried for this piece of malicious mischief, a Texas cattleman named Patterson, who had just shipped some cattle north, saw her in the courtroom and became infatuated with her. He not only secured her release but gave her a sum of money, said to be $2500.

What she gave him in return can only be surmised. One account describes the cattleman as "uncomely and notoriously amorous."[6] At any rate, when friends later urged him to sue her for

[6] Duncan Aikman, *Calamity Jane and the Lady Wildcats.*

fraud, he was quoted as saying, "Hell, let her keep it. I reckon after what she's had to put up with from me, she's earned it."

Meantime, Belle was looking around for what was to her a prime necessity of life—a permanent male consort. Her choice fell on Sam Starr, the burly Indian who used to ride double with her when she went to dances in the Indian Territory. The supposition is strong that he may have been her lover before she became a widow.

Belle was particular about her men. For one thing, they had to be sexually durable. One story about her is that when she was arrested on suspicion of horse theft, she prevailed on the jailer to release her on a promise that she would elope with him. A few days later he returned—alone. To his intense mortification a note was found, sewn in his side pocket without his knowledge: *Returned because found unsatisfactory.*

Sam Starr was of a different breed. He proved to be eminently satisfactory to Belle's ardent nature. He also proved to be jealous to a murderous degree.

In 1880 she "married" Starr—by the sketchy Cherokee custom, which meant simply moving in and living with him. At the time she was thirty-two and he twenty-eight. She thus became a member of the Cherokee Nation, and took an oath of allegiance to it.[7]

Word had come to her, of course, that Cole Younger and his brothers were in the Minnesota penitentiary after the Northfield fight and the long hunt following. One of the proofs that she carried a torch for her first lover, and an indication that the fire may have been rekindled on his most recent visit to Dallas, was that when she, with Sam Starr, took up land on the Canadian River, not far from Eufaula, she named her new home "Younger's Bend." There is no question that she also tried in many ways to secure a pardon for him and perhaps even helped finance his defense in his

[7] Interestingly, according to Burton Rascoe, the head of the Starr clan, the grim old giant Tom Starr, who was Sam Starr's father, was warned by an old Indian that he should kill the white woman who had come into the family "as he would a snake," because she would bring ruin on all who came into contact with her. Tom Starr talked to her. She must have impressed him, for he allowed her to remain.

trial. Until the day of her death she never forgot Cole Younger.

The new Cherokee alliance had a number of effects. It was at this time she adopted the name Belle Starr, and kept it for the rest of her life, no matter who happened to be her lover at the time. More important, she married into the clan feud. Only a short distance from Younger's Bend were the holdings of the West family, who belonged to the Ross clan.

In 1880 the Starr-Ross feud was still smoldering. Most members of the Starr family were upright citizens, some becoming tribal judges. But some also became outlaws, and all the males, even the youngest, learned the use of weapons. One of these novitiates into the skills of firearms was a boy who was the son of Hop Starr, Sam's brother. He would later become rather celebrated as Henry Starr, the bandit, and in that role provide a further link in the crime chain.

As Harman wrote:

> Gradually Belle gathered about her a set of male admirers as reckless as herself, to each of whom she was at one time or another especially gracious and who was for the time counted as her lover.

All of them, but one, were Indians, and all were progressively younger as time went on. From the first the imperious Belle assumed leadership over these illiterate outlaws. But she had higher ambitions than that.

On her place at Younger's Bend, she built not one but two "guest houses" for the shelter of more eminent criminals than the mixed breed Cherokees. One of her guests was none other than Jesse James, who spent some weeks with her after the Blue Cut train robbery of 1881. Sam Starr did not know the true identity of this honored guest, because Belle introduced him as "Mr. Williams," from Texas. Nor did Jesse share her bed, for he was faithful to his wife. It was from Belle's hospitality that Jesse James rode north to his rendezvous with the Ford brothers, and assassination in St. Joseph.

By no means should it be thought that she was a hostess, merely. During this period she directed a flourishing horse- and cattle-rustling business, besides purveying moonshine whisky on the side. At times she paid visits to Fort Smith, some sixty miles east, where she liked to sit in on gambling games and play with the best of the male gamblers for stakes as high as they desired. Unlike that other female gambler, Poker Alice Tubbs, of Deadwood, South Dakota, she did not smoke cigars. Belle did not consider cigars feminine, and she liked to keep her sex appeal.

Sometimes, too, she had business of another sort in Fort Smith—at the insistence of the law. But though she was charged several times with offenses ranging from horse theft to bootlegging, only once was she convicted. On that occasion she and Sam Starr had stolen a horse belonging to a neighboring rancher, Andrew Crane. John West, a member of the Cherokee tribal police force, and also of the Ross clan, was the chief witness against them, and this did not make for friendlier relations with the Wests. Convicted, they were sentenced, July 19, 1883, by Judge Parker, to serve a year apiece in a house of correction at Detroit, Michigan. There, for nine months, Belle wove cane bottoms for chairs and Sam performed uncongenial toil on the prison rock pile, after which they were released for good behavior.

When, following this interval of confinement, they returned to Younger's Bend, Belle's wayward whims again began to assert themselves, and trouble followed.

Very soon after they were freed, Sam Starr was implicated in the robbery of the Creek tribal treasury, and found it highly convenient to absent himself from his usual haunts. Time passed. Sam, enthusiastically sought by the authorities, rarely came home. And Belle? She grew increasingly discontented, until at last she began to appease her discontent by taking into her bed whatever handy outlaw most appealed to her.

John Middleton, a cousin of Jim Reed and nine years her junior, finally ousted all the others. For six months he was the favorite of the "bandit queen," who seemed to have an appetite for new bedmates exceeded only by that other celebrated "royal" nymphomaniac, Catherine the Great of Russia.

Middleton was from Arkansas, where he did some petty thievery and helped burn down the Scott County courthouse. In order to escape going to prison for arson, he skipped to Paris, Texas, stealing a horse or two on the way, and promptly wound up in jail. But the bastille at Paris was not strong enough to hold him. He escaped, returned later (on another stolen horse), called on Sheriff J. H. Black, and when that official came to the door, shot him down.

When first he appeared in Belle's ken he was described as a "young man, of heavy build [Belle's well-known predilection for big men!] with a heavy mustache." Furthermore, he had made himself a genuine outlaw, with a price on his head. To such a surplusage of charms Belle readily succumbed. Her six months idyl with him, however, was not without its concerns. For one thing, Sam Starr came home once in a while—usually embarrassingly unannounced. He professed friendship for Middleton, but she never could be quite sure that he did not know what was going on. And he was, remember, of a jealous nature.

Furthermore, the law was sniffing around for Middleton, too close for comfort. Two deputies, Jack Duncan and J. H. Millsaps, of Paris, Texas, had traced him to the Cherokee country. There they enlisted the aid of John West, the Indian policeman who helped send Belle to prison. It was only a matter of time until they found and probably killed the man who murdered Sheriff Black, and to Middleton it obviously was time to "shove."

But Belle, enamored to an unusual degree, for her, proposed to go along. She said she would go to Arkansas, leave her daughter, Pearl, now in her middle teens and "quite pretty and charming," with relatives, and then vacation at the springs near Chickalah with Middleton until the annoying Texas lawmen wearied of a fruitless search in the Cherokee country and went home.

To this end she rented her farm, loaded whatever she thought necessary in clothing and other articles into a covered wagon, and hired a boy named George Cook to drive.

And then—just before the start—Sam Starr suddenly appeared and said he also was going along. He was hardly a welcome addition to the company, but neither Belle nor Middleton could well refuse. They set forth.

One can imagine that the woman, riding in the wagon with her daughter and the hired driver, was much more concerned about those two rivals for her favors than she was about the road ahead. She could hear them on their horses behind the wagon; even catch glimpses of them, as they paced side by side with a smooth assumption of friendship.

But how long would it last? She knew Sam Starr's jealousy, and every unusual sound, any lifting of voices, would be enough to startle her. When would the dreaded outbreak come between the two men to whom she had rendered her joys and who therefore must be inwardly smoldering toward each other? And what could she do? Nothing, except try to seem innocent of any suspicion of the state of affairs and hope that if and when violence occurred it would not involve herself or her daughter.

The journey began May 3, 1885. As they neared Fort Smith, May 4, Middleton suggested that he had better take a roundabout way and meet the party on the other side of the city, since he might be recognized in that stronghold of the fearsome Judge Parker. The wagon, with Belle, Pearl, and the Cook boy, proceeded by the direct route, while Middleton, riding a horse later proved to be stolen and with a saddle borrowed from Belle's stable, turned off.

Now a sinister thing occurred. Sam Starr insisted on turning off with Middleton, still protesting friendship, and asserting, rather logically, that he also had to avoid possible recognition in Fort Smith.

On May 7, three days after the two men rode away from the wagon, a horse, saddled and bridled, was found on the banks of the Poteau River, twenty-five miles north of Fort Smith. A search was made for its rider, and presently a body, badly decomposed, was found washed up on the bank and partly covered with mud, about two hundred yards downstream. The face had been almost eaten off by buzzards, but the corpse was identified as that of John Middleton. He had been murdered.

The murderer? Sam Starr, without much question, although he never was charged with the crime.

Belle later was accused of stealing the horse, whose owner proved his brand, because a saddle and pistols belonging to her were found on it, but of this she was acquitted.

Short one lover, Belle returned at once to Younger's Bend with Pearl. She found Sam Starr already there, with not a line in his expressionless Indian face to indicate that he knew anything of Middleton's death.

Nor did she accuse him. Perhaps she was a little afraid of him.

Very soon she was taken to Fort Smith to face the horse-theft charge, and was freed, largely through the testimony of Fayette Barnett, who took oath that, whoever stole the horse, it had been paid for by the deceased Middleton to the tune of fifty dollars in gold coin. The animal was the property of A. G. McCarty, a rancher, who recovered it. Barnett himself may have been the thief.

To celebrate her acquittal, Belle took part, with considerable fanfare, in a Wild West show at the fairgrounds near Fort Smith. Wrote Harman:

> Judge Parker, always a public spirited man, requested her to arrange and take the leading part in a mock stage robbery; he offered himself as one of the passengers to be robbed. Belle consented and the affair was carried on to the satisfaction of the large crowd who came to the fair, in response to the widely advertised "stage robbery," and whose coming added to the profits of the association.[8]

Belle returned once more to Younger's Bend—and to increasing trouble. A new lover had fascinated her, a white man known only by his fantastic alias, Blue Duck.

Blue Duck was of a pattern with Belle's other lovers—burly and powerful. He was slightly popeyed and wore a small mustache, and he had qualified for Belle's favors by a career including horse thievery, some highway robberies, and a murder.

The murder was what interested her. Blue Duck was convicted of killing a youth named Wyrick on June 23, 1884, during a drunken spree in which he also took pot shots at an Indian named

[8] Rascoe is inclined to doubt that Belle was the lady holdup artist in this case, at least that Judge Parker, who previously sent her to prison, "requested her" to make the arrangements. I respect Rascoe, but on the other hand, Harman, who worshiped the judge, is authority for it. I am inclined to think it may be true.

Hawky Wolf and his little son named Willie Wolf, missing because he was too inebriated to shoot straight. He was sentenced to die, but Belle employed counsel for Blue Duck, his sentence was commuted to life imprisonment, and in some manner the remarkable woman obtained for him a pardon after a year, to return to her arms.

The new romance, however, flowered only briefly. Blue Duck had scarcely rejoined his paramour when he was killed in July 1886, "by an unknown party." That party, in all probability, was the jealous and murderous Sam Starr, who hunted Blue Duck down and shot him because of his relations with Belle. The poor woman was always losing lovers by violent ends, and having to find new ones, which must have been annoying, not to say unsettling.

There is a photograph in existence showing Blue Duck and Belle Starr, probably taken after their reunion. She looks far from beautiful. A straight, thin-lipped mouth, somewhat hollow eyes, and an expression of rather fierce determination make her appear a much stronger personality than the man, in spite of her print dress, lace jabot, knitted jacket, flowered hat and earrings. One wonders why a man, even in a country where white women were relatively scarce, would go to the risk and trouble of shooting another man over her. But then, she did not have the services of cosmeticians, hair dressers, and couturières, who seem to achieve miracles in enhancing the appearances of her sisterhood of today. Nor did other women of her time. Perhaps she was handsomer when compared to her contemporaries than she appears to a modern eye, accustomed as it is to enameled countenances, plucked eyebrows, lipstick, eyeshadow, permanents, hair shaping and shading, girdles, and other appurtenances of current femininity.

Within five months of Blue Duck's murder Sam Starr himself was dead, killed in a duel with Frank West, brother of John West who had dogged his steps so long. The battle was an outgrowth of the tribal feud, and occurred after Starr was arraigned for robbing a post office. He was on bond (probably arranged by Belle) and attending a dance at Whitefield, Indian Territory, December 18, 1886, when a violent quarrel broke out between him and West. The men were both drunk and Starr accused West of killing Belle's horse, Venus, some time previously. In the gun battle that followed they succeeded in mortally wounding each other, thus ridding the Territory of two quarrelsome and dangerous men, but further complicating Belle's emotional life.

Just at this time she faced another problem. Pearl Younger, her daughter, now seventeen, was attractive and of warm temperament. She wanted to marry a youth of the neighborhood, but Belle forbade it. The daughter had her mother's inward flame. In July 1886 she somehow managed to slip away with the young man and get herself pregnant.

At first the girl tried to hide the unfortunate circumstance. But by February 1887 this became no longer possible.

Belle should hardly have been surprised, considering her own career, but the discovery of her daughter's condition seemed to outrage her very latent sense of the conventions. There was, of course, a scene—the angry mother, and the weeping daughter.

Next Belle attempted a shotgun wedding—with the substitution of her menacing six-shooter for the shotgun—in which the intended groom was a terrified elderly man named Kraft. Pearl frustrated this effort to restore the conventions by flatly declaring that Mr. Kraft was not the father of her unborn child. Kraft scuttled away to safety, and in the stormy interview that followed, the girl absolutely refused to name the man.

Presently Belle quieted down and thought things over. Her next proposal was an abortion, and she even suggested as a candidate to perform the illegal operation—without as yet consulting him—a prominent physician in Fort Smith.

But Pearl, by this time about seven months along in her pregnancy, was afraid of the dangers involved and refused to undergo the operation.

At that Belle, losing all patience, ordered her daughter to leave home. This the girl did at once, having some of her mother's spirit, and promised Belle that she would never see her again.

The baby, a little girl, was born in Siloam Springs, Arkansas, the following April and was named Flossie. Though Pearl later relented and returned to her mother's home, Belle Starr never set eyes on her grandchild.

To a degree Pearl's absence was made up for by the appearance at Younger's Bend of Belle's son, Ed Reed. The boy, who had been farmed out to relatives in Missouri, ran away, became a bootlegger at fourteen, and a horse thief soon after.

Before long Pearl abandoned her child to an aunt at Wichita, Kansas, who allowed it to be legally adopted there, and returned to her mother, so for a time Belle Starr was united with both her children.

For the next couple of years after her quarrel with Pearl, Belle relieved her unhappiness with a succession of lovers. All were Indians, and all came to bloody ends, although all outlived her.

The first was Jack Spaniard, a strapping Choctaw, who murdered a man named William M. Irwin. He was rounded up by the deputies, tried and convicted at Fort Smith, and sentenced to die. His execution was not until August 30, 1889, but his incarceration in the celebrated jail removed him as a mate for Belle.

Next came Jim French, a young Creek Indian with almost feminine grace and eyes as large and brilliant as any girl's, but an outlaw and killer to the last. French had a flair for pretty colored scarfs, which he knotted in becoming fashion about his neck. Apparently Belle dallied with him as a lover for a short time only. He was later killed while robbing a store in 1895.

Jim July, a powerfully built Cherokee, more in keeping with Belle's taste in paramours, succeeded French in her affections—and her bed. He was killed resisting arrest in 1890.

But Belle preceded all of these to the grave.

On February 3, 1889, her riderless horse came trotting into the yard of her home at Younger's Bend. Pearl was there at the time, and at once became fearful that something had happened to her mother.

She was right. A neighbor, Milo Hoyt, found Belle lying in the mud beside the road, terribly wounded but still alive. She had been shot from behind, in her back.

The slayer evidently used a double-barreled shotgun, one barrel loaded with buckshot, the other with heavy turkey shot. The buckshot charge knocked her from her horse, four of the large pellets taking effect. Thereupon the murderer walked up to her and blasted the charge of turkey shot into her as she lay on the ground. It ripped into her face, neck, and one arm.

When Hoyt found her, Belle gasped out a word or two, but she did not name her assailant. A moment later she was dead.

Who killed her? Suspicion pointed at Edgar Watson, a neighbor with whom she had quarreled over some land and who was afraid she might inform against him for a murder he committed in Florida. Her lover, Jim July, a fine-looking Indian, was in Fort Smith facing arraignment on a charge of horse stealing. At news of her death he secured a continuation of his case and hurried to Younger's Bend.

Belle Starr was buried with Cherokee Indian rites, her jewelry in the casket, her hand grasping a fine revolver said to have been given her by her first lover, Cole Younger.

As soon as the body was lowered into the grave, July pointed his Winchester at Watson and arrested him for the murder. The prisoner was taken to Fort Smith, but not even in Judge Parker's court could enough evidence be produced to convict him, and he was released.

Watson later was convicted of horse stealing at Van Buren, Arkansas, and sentenced to fifteen years in prison. He escaped and was killed while resisting arrest.

Jim July, incidentally, failed to return to Fort Smith to answer the charges against him. He was trailed by Deputy Marshal Heck Thomas, and elected to fight it out with that hard-shooting officer. It was an error of judgment. July received mortal wounds from which he died, January 6, 1890, four days after Thomas landed his bullet-punctured frame in jail.

But Watson was not the only one suspected of murdering Belle Starr. It was whispered that she was killed by her own son, Ed Reed. He was at the time about eighteen, and Belle tyrannized over him, dominating him completely, even whipping him on occasion with her riding quirt.

Burton Rascoe, who interviewed many of the old settlers in the vicinity, among them R. P. Vann, a former member of the Indian police, had this to say in his book *Belle Starr:*

> Among the people in the Belle Starr country it is commonly accepted belief that there were incestuous relations between Belle

and her son and that she complicated this with extreme sadism . . . They say also, with perceptible lowering of their voices, that Ed hated his mother's domination and yet was jealous of Jim July.

Rascoe is too careful and thorough an investigator not to be taken seriously in such a statement, unpleasant as it is. And there is to be considered Harman's description of the terrain where Belle was shot:

> [After leaving Watson's] Belle continued her journey, riding along a road leading around Watson's field to a point where it intersected an old road that had been fenced off, near a corner of another field, 150 yards from Watson's house. Inside the fence, at the corner of this field, stood the assassin whose bullets took the life of Belle Starr. As there was no brush or other means of hiding she must have seen him as she passed and a moment later she was shot in the back.

Was that killer, standing in full view in the corner of the field, Watson? Is it likely that Belle Starr, accustomed as she was to the lawless ways of the frontier, would calmly have ridden on past a man armed with a gun, whom she considered an enemy? But what if the man were her own son, Ed? She might perhaps have spoken to him and gone on, not suspecting a murderous design until the blast of the shotgun struck her.

There is another circumstance of interest: Belle spoke one or two words after she was found, *but she did not name her assailant.* Would she have protected Watson, if he had shot her? But what if the murderer were her own son?

Of course, this is all surmise. Nobody ever was convicted of the slaying.

Belle Starr was no "bandit queen," as romantic writers of the times entitled her, except insofar as she harbored bandits, and furnished them with ideas, and acted as an intermediary and often as a bedfellow for them.

But she left some unholy legacies.

Her daughter, Pearl Younger, abandoned her child Flossie to an aunt, and Flossie dropped out of sight. For a time after her mother's death Pearl lived respectably, having married a man named Will Harrison. But respectability was dull. She had no scruples about cuckolding her husband, whenever the opportunity and whim suited her, and they were soon separated.

At the time she was twenty-two years old, a young woman with manifold charms. Those charms were so much sought after that presently she discovered a calling whereby she could dispense them for profit: she became one of the girls in a brothel at Fort Smith. So popular did she make herself with the clients of that establishment that in a few months she was able to lease a building in the "Bad Lands"—as the city's red-light district was called—and run a place of her own for seven years. When finally she grew tired of being a madam, she married again, and according to Harman, lived quietly and ostensibly conventionally thereafter. She was only twenty-nine when she married for the second time and had not lost her looks.

Ed Reed, whose name was whispered so darkly in connection with his mother's death, suffered a fate more violent. He was caught purloining a horse which did not belong to him, and Judge Parker sentenced him to an Ohio penitentiary for seven years.

Pearl gave as her "reason" for taking up prostitution that she wanted to make money to hire lawyers for her brother. Evidently she did pay some legal fees, and Ed eventually received a pardon.

When he returned to Fort Smith he obtained an appointment as a deputy marshal. During the three years he served in that capacity he killed two drunken part-Indian brothers, Dick and Zeke Crittenden, who were trying to "paint up" the town of Wagoner, Indian Territory. They were both former deputy marshals.

After a time he married a pretty half-Cherokee schoolteacher, Jennie Cochrane. But Ed Reed could not stay out of trouble. One November day in 1896, he quarreled with two owners of a saloon in Wagoner and tried to throw them out of their own place. They very properly shot him and the community gave them a vote of thanks.

It is interesting to note that almost everyone who had any sort of close relationship with Belle Starr, sexually or through blood relationship, suffered a melancholy fate. Here is the record of her lovers:

Cole Younger (Jesse James gangster), crippled by bullets at Northfield, Minn., and served twenty-five years in prison.

Jim Reed (Jesse James gangster), killed by Deputy Sheriff John T. Morris, Aug. 6, 1874. It was after this that she went to the Indian Territory and "married" Sam Starr under Cherokee "sharing the blanket" custom.

Sam Starr (Belle's Indian husband), killed by Frank West, whom he also killed, Dec. 18, 1886.

John Middleton (cousin of Jim Reed, and Belle's lover), murdered about May 5, 1885, probably by Sam Starr out of jealousy.

Blue Duck (horse thief, murderer, and Belle's lover), murdered July 1886, "by unknown party," possibly Sam Starr, for same reason as above.

Jack Spaniard (Choctaw Indian, and Belle's lover), hanged for the murder of William M. Irwin, Aug. 30, 1889.

Jim French (Creek Indian, and Belle's lover), killed while robbing a store, Feb. 7, 1895.

Jim July (Cherokee Indian, and Belle's last lover), killed by Deputy Marshal Heck Thomas while resisting arrest, Jan. 6, 1890.

Others closely connected with Belle Starr ended up in the following manner:

Pearl Younger (Belle's daughter by Cole Younger), became mother of an illegitimate child, then a prostitute, and later madam of a bawdy house in Fort Smith.

Ed Reed (Belle's son by Jim Reed), after serving a prison sentence, killed in a saloon fight at Wagoner, 1896.

Flossie (Belle's granddaughter, Pearl Younger's illegitimate child), never seen by Belle after her birth. Final fate of Flossie unknown.

Ed (Bud) Shirley (Belle's brother, a Quantrill guerrilla), killed by Federal irregulars near Sarcoxie, Mo., 1863.

Preston Shirley (Belle's other brother), killed in a gun fight with Joe Lynn, at Spring Creek, Tex., 1867.

It is fairly evident that, to anyone having much to do with Belle Starr, she was about as healthy as a cobra's bite.

One of her lovers, Jim French, became a member of the Cook gang, which was organized after Belle was dead, and was its last unimprisoned survivor. A nephew of Belle's, Henry Starr, son of Hop Starr, who was Sam Starr's brother, was a clean-cut, very gentlemanly young man, but he had enough of the traditions and teachings of Belle and her lawless retinue so that he, too, became a member of the Cook gang and had a career of alternate prison and outlawry which lasted for twenty-five years.

Meantime, very soon after Belle Starr's death, a new and furious outbreak of outlawry occurred which was connected directly with the James-Younger bandits and the curse of Quantrill.

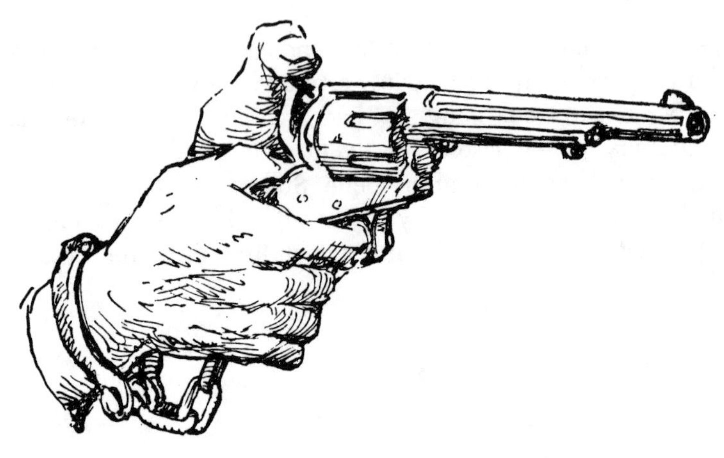

6. *"To Beat Jesse James"*

Not the least of the evils which Jesse James and his Missouri bandits bequeathed to their generation and the generation immediately following it, was the example they set, with all its fanfare, which tempted wild, and usually ignorant, young men to go into outlawry at one place or another. The spectacular career of the Jameses and the Youngers kept the nation in an uproar for fifteen years and was celebrated in countless newspaper articles and many books which frequently were more interested in sensationalism than in the strict truth.

It is not surprising that such literature and the constant talk about the famed brigands caught the imagination of restless and reckless youths. A few of those who achieved notoriety in other parts of the nation but hailed originally from the James-Younger stamping grounds were:

> Harvey, Lonny, and Johnny Logan, members of Butch Cassidy's celebrated Hole-in-the-Wall gang, all of whom were killed. All were from Missouri.

> Bill, Tom, and George McCarty, Western outlaws and train robbers. Bill, the eldest, got his first experience in holding up a train while riding with Jesse James. They gave Butch Cassidy his apprenticeship in banditry. All from Missouri.
>
> Tom Horn, adventurer, sometimes scout against the Apache Indians, sometimes hired killer in the cattle wars, hanged at last for murder in Wyoming. A Missourian.
>
> Nick Ray, killed with Nate Champion, who was called "King of the Cattle Rustlers," in the K. C. Ranch fight in Wyoming. A Missourian like the others.

The list can be lengthened, and each name would lead to an outlaw trail of its own, running from Canada clear down into South America, and spanning the continent east to west. But we are following only one line, and that one stemming from Quantrill through the Midwest and West.

Living in Jackson County, Missouri, at the beginning of the border troubles, was Louis Dalton, a farmer who was a veteran of the Mexican War. In 1851 he married a Cass County girl, and at about the start of the Civil War he took her and their growing family to Kansas, settling finally near Coffeyville, just north of the border of the Indian Territory, a wild and lawless frontier town. The girl he married was Adeline Younger, a sister (or half sister) of Colonel Henry Washington Younger, father of the outlaw Youngers; who therefore was an aunt of the Younger brothers and a blood relative of the James brothers.

Thirteen children were born to this couple, nine sons and four daughters. Of these, eight sons and three daughters reached adulthood. Concerning the father, Louis Dalton, Harman wrote:

> His one passion was for fast horses, and it may be that their imitating their father in becoming expert horsemen was the means by which the sons cultivated the company which resulted in their becoming criminals.

More likely it was because they grew up on tales of the exploits, romantic in their youthful eyes, of their outlaw kinfolks. Clannishness was inherent in the family, and they naturally sided with their outlaw relatives, exulted in their deeds, perhaps boasted of their relationship, and regretted their deaths and imprisonments.

In their veins ran the same wild blood that spurred their cousins to reckless and murderous acts, and four of them felt the urge of it with strength sufficient to pattern their lives after their notorious kin. Their familiarity with the James-Younger saga is unquestioned, for it was a desire, expressed to his companions by Bob Dalton, to "beat anything Jesse James ever did," that led to their final and bloody downfall. So, with the call of blood, and the example of the Missouri bandits, began the weaving of another thread in the pattern of outlaw descent.

When the new Oklahoma Territory was created in 1889,[1] the family joined the land rush, and the father and older sons obtained claims near the town of Kingfisher. But times were hard, and Louis Dalton returned to Coffeyville, working at various jobs to support his wife and younger children while his claim was being proved up. He died in 1890 and was buried in Coffeyville.

Mrs. Dalton and the family continued to live near Kingfisher, where she and three of her sons, Charles, Henry, and Littleton, each obtained title to claims, and lived quiet, hard-working lives. With the other five sons it was a different story.

Every one of the Dalton boys had plenty of nerve, and four of them served as deputy marshals, at one time or another, while the fifth went to the Montana gold fields and became a member of

[1] To define the various territorial limits in the present state of Oklahoma, at the time the Oklahoma Territory was created in 1889, is a complicated task. The Oklahoma Territory itself occupied only a relatively small area in the center of the present state. East and south of this were the lands of the Cherokees, Creeks, Choctaws, and Chickasaws—each larger than the area known as the Oklahoma Territory—together with eighteen smaller Indian reservations. West lay the reservations of the Cheyennes, Arapahoes, Wichitas, Kiowas, Comanches, and Apaches. A wide strip of territory known as the Cherokee Outlet or Strip ran across the northern part of the present state, cutting the Oklahoma Territory off from Kansas. In addition to these there were the Public Land Strip, comprising the present Oklahoma Panhandle, and generally called No Man's Land; and in the extreme southwest corner, between the forks of the Red River, an area known as Greer County, claimed both by Texas and the United States government, which the government later obtained title to by a court decision. All of these disparate sections were incorporated into Oklahoma when it became a state in 1907. To avoid endless confusion, the single term "the Territory" will in general be taken in this book to mean all that country which later became Oklahoma, regardless of its varied designations at that period.

the state assembly (legislature) in California before turning outlaw.

Frank, one of the elder brothers, was killed in 1884 while serving as a deputy in a fight with Indian horse thieves. Grattan, usually called Grat, received a wound in 1888 while acting in a similar capacity. Both Bob and Emmett, the two youngest brothers, did brief service for the law. Bill, older than Bob and Emmett, but younger than Grat, made a venturesome journey west, spent some time trying to make a fortune in the gold mines around Helena, Montana, and finally went to California, where he settled in Tulare, married, became interested in politics, and was elected to the state assembly.

From the very beginning Bob Dalton was the reckless leading spirit among the brothers. He killed his first man, Charles Montgomery, when he was not yet twenty. His story was that he caught the man in the act of stealing horses. But there was a whisper that Bob had been in love with Minnie Johnson, a sprightly cousin of his; and Montgomery "cut him out" with the girl; and that was the real reason why Montgomery was shot. Since Bob was a deputy marshal at the time, his version was accepted, especially in view of the fact that Montgomery had a bad record, having served jail sentences at Fort Smith for thefts and selling liquor to the Indians.

By 1890, the year of his father's death, Bob Dalton, although only twenty, was secretly organizing a gang of thieves. Horses always were a temptation, being easy to transport and readily salable, and at first horse rustling appears to have been Bob's aim. There may be some slight reason for this in the miserably low remuneration the government paid its deputy marshals. To quote from *The Dalton Brothers,* by "Eye Witness":[2]

> For arresting a suspected or guilty party the U. S. Deputy Marshal receives the munificent sum of *two dollars!* And remember that, out there, he faces death with every arrest, and remains, besides, the marked victim of the arrested outlaw's friends.

[2] "Eye Witness," the anonymous author of *The Dalton Brothers,* is believed by Burton Rascoe to have been a reporter on the Coffeyville newspaper, and may have known the Daltons personally and been present at their last fight.

> The Deputy Marshal is allowed *six cents per mile* when on the trail after a criminal, all expenses of transportation, board, etc., to be paid by him out of these six cents.
>
> When he returns with his two-dollar prisoner in charge, he is allowed *ten cents,* and has to feed and transport himself, the assistants he may require, and the prisoner himself, all at his [the Deputy Marshal's] own expense.
>
> Now listen; this is not all. When the accounts are rendered, the Marshal deducts thirty-five per cent of the gross amount as his fee. Then the bill is sent to Washington—and sometimes allowed!
>
> In the meantime, the Deputy Marshal has had to advance all the money spent, borrowing it from friends—or usurers; very happy he is indeed if he finally gets in hard cash *just one half* of what is legitimately due him. And, mind, the man receives *no salary!*

It is a grim picture, surely, yet perhaps it was not quite so bad as that, for scores of deputy marshals served for years at great risk and made few complaints. And, of course, Bob Dalton could have gone to work on a legitimate job, but this seems not to have occurred to him. A job lacked excitement and glamour, and besides it was hard work, something that failed to appeal to his nature.

Presently some excellent horses which had disappeared from the Territory turned up later in Kansas, where they had been sold. Suspicion pointed at the Daltons. When Grat Dalton was found "prowling about the range" of Charles McLelland, he was promptly arrested and taken to Fort Smith. "Prowling," however, was no crime, no matter how strongly the officers felt that it was a prelude to rustling. Grat was regretfully released.

When he returned to his brothers, they felt that things had grown too warm for comfort. Suspicion continued to focus on them, and in that day horse theft was a lynching offense, if the thief was caught with the goods. Grat and Emmett, and perhaps Bob, decided to take a "vacation" in California—to preserve their health and their necks—and pay a visit to their brother Bill.

The "vacation" proved a turning point in their careers. On the night of February 6, 1891, a Southern Pacific passenger train running from San Francisco to Los Angeles was stopped by a waving red lantern at the small station of Alila (now Earlimart), south of Tulare.

Shots fired in the air and wild yells convinced the passengers in the sleepers that they had better remain where they were. Several masked men surrounded the train, held the conductor and engineer under guard, and marched the fireman, George Radliff, back to the express car with his coal pick. This circumstance made some people later believe that Bob Dalton was in the holdup, since it was a device he seems to have thought up.

With a gun at his head, Radliff broke open the door of the express car with his pick. Then he ducked, as if to escape. Two shots killed him.

The express messenger had time to escape from the opposite side of the car, diving into the bush and hiding, with the combination of the safe and the keys. As a result the bandits got very little, and they rode away disappointed in their hope for loot, leaving George Radliff dead by the side of the train.

It was the first of the Dalton train robberies—and it occurred in California, whereas all the rest were in what is now Oklahoma or in states or territories immediately surrounding it.

Detectives trailed Grat Dalton, whose horse fell in the getaway, severely bruising him, to the home of "a California gentleman of political prominence in these parts"—Assemblyman William Dalton. Both of the brothers were arrested. Bill proved an alibi, and used his political influence to help Grat. But in spite of this, Grat was identified as one of those in the Alila holdup. He could not be convicted of murdering Radliff, but he was found guilty of armed robbery and sentenced to twenty years in Folsom Penitentiary.

It was hard, however, to hold a Dalton, and very soon a spectacular escape took place, which set everyone in California to talking. When Grat was placed on a train at Fresno, to be taken to the prison, he was guarded by two deputies. To one of these he was manacled, while the other sat in another seat conversing with a passenger.

The day was oppressively hot, and the windows of the car were open as the train roared northward at full speed. Somewhere between Fresno and Berenda, the prisoner's seat companion, to whom he was manacled, nodded and took a nap. Suddenly Grat Dalton was seen to rise to his feet. A second later, while all the startled passengers looked on, and before either of the guards could raise a weapon, he plunged *headfirst* through the window of the speeding train.

His timing was perfect. Had he struck the ground he would have been killed, but the train at the moment was crossing a bridge over a river, probably the San Joaquin (not drained of water for irrigation as it is most of the time in these days). Headlong, the outlaw plunged into the water, disappearing under the surface. The swirling current bore him rapidly downstream as his head reappeared.

The train was halted as soon as possible, but Grat Dalton was gone. It was an almost incredible feat, and only a superb athlete with tremendous nerve and cunning could have accomplished it.[3]

With his brother Emmett, who was known to have helped in the holdup of the train at Alila, he fled back to the Oklahoma Territory.

Now Grat and Emmett were full-fledged outlaws, and their careers were immediately enriched by a reward of $6000 for each of them, dead or alive, offered by the Southern Pacific.

Whether or not he accompanied them to California, Bob forgathered promptly with them in the Territory, perhaps a little jealous of their notoriety, and the real story of the Daltons began.

The gang was ready and organized, but its scope and objectives were changed. Instead of a mere group of furtive horse thieves, it was henceforth to operate on a much loftier criminal level, as bank and train bandits, modeled on the James-Younger plan.

Bob had recruited some "long riders" who could be depended on to run any risk with him and his brothers. Not far from Guthrie,

[3] There is still mystery as to how Grat Dalton freed himself from the guard to whom he was handcuffed. The most likely theory is that somehow he quietly took the key to his manacles from the pocket of the sleeping guard, unlocked himself, and waited his chance to leap from the car window when the river would receive his body and both break his fall and carry him out of sight.

the Territorial capital, lying along the Cimarron River, was one of the great cattle spreads of the area, the HX Bar Ranch, owned by Oscar Halsell. It possessed a rather remarkable group of cowboys, from a standpoint of recklessness and lawlessness, even in an era when reckless and lawless men were numerous in the West. At least seven HX Bar cowboys are known to have gone into outlawry, and there probably were more.

Bob, always the leader, although he was nine years younger than Grat, knew the HX Bar outfit, and from it drew three men. Most important of these, from a historic standpoint, was Bill Doolin, who in spite of an almost complete lack of education had a magnetic personality, was popular with his fellows, and later became noted as a bandit leader in his own right.

A second was Dick Broadwell, just a happy-go-lucky young cowpuncher, who did anything Bob Dalton told him to do, holding the outlaw leader in almost childish admiration. The third HX Bar hand was Bill Powers, of a stamp very different from Broadwell. He was a "cold proposition" in the language of the West, not ruled by friendship or loyalty, but a man who turned to crime with his eyes wide open, for what there was in it for him.

A fourth recruit, Blackface Charley Bryant—so called from a powder burn on one cheek received somehow in a shooting scrape—came into the gang by ways less direct. He worked on a ranch near Hennessey, about twenty-five miles north of Kingfisher, where the Dalton clan dwelt. Bryant had a sister, a divorcee, in whom Bob Dalton had a more than sentimental interest. It is probable that Bryant and Dalton joined forces through acquaintance formed through the girl.

It did not take the gang long to get into operation. Grat and Emmett could hardly have been home more than a few days when, May 9, 1891, a Santa Fe train was held up at Wharton (now Perry, Oklahoma) and the express car robbed. Once again the fireman was forced to tear open the door of the car with his pick. The loot was small—about $1500—but it was a sort of "shakedown run" for the band, and Bob Dalton could take satisfaction in the way his gang worked, smoothly as well-oiled machinery.

As they retreated from this exploit, the gang passed through the country near Orlando, on Beaver Creek, and spotted eight or ten fine horses grazing. It was a deep temptation, and for the last time the bandits became rustlers and took the animals along.

But horse larceny, in the mind of the West, was slightly worse than murder and a good deal worse than train robbery. An indignant posse pursued, equipped with convenient lengths of rope for hanging purposes, and caught up with the outlaws near Twin Mounds.

They quickly found, however, that they were not dealing with ordinary horse thieves. Bob Dalton and his brigands were waiting for them, lying in a heavy growth of woods along a creek bank, protected by a sort of breastwork of dead timber.

As the posse moved forward through the trees, there was a sudden spatter of rifle shots, and the men hit the ground. A flurry of firing followed in which it became very apparent to the posse that they were faced by men who shot quick and close and were very willing to kill. One member of the posse, indeed, did not come out of the woods with the others when they retreated. He was W. T. Starmer, and Bill Thompson, who was with him when the bandits opened fire, said he had been hit and probably was dead.

While the posse hesitated about going back in after those murderous men, the bandits neatly slipped away with their stolen horses. After they were gone, Starmer was found. He was dead, struck by three bullets, all so well aimed that any one of them would have been fatal.

Not until June 1, 1892, did the Daltons appear again, this time to waylay another Santa Fe train at the little station of Red Rock. The technique perfected by Jesse James was employed by Bob Dalton with almost clockwork efficiency. When the train halted at the station, Blackface Charley Bryant and Dick Broadwell clambered into the locomotive cab and held the engineer and fireman under their guns.

While Bob and Emmett Dalton and Bill Powers went through the passenger coaches, relieving the passengers of their valuables, Bill Doolin and Grat Dalton entered the express car, the door of which stood open, and found the express messenger and his guard playing checkers.

Across the floor spilled the red and black disks as the two men rose trembling, hands in the air, when they saw the bandits' menacing guns. The outlaws tumbled the safe, a small one, to the ground outside the car, to open it there.

As they did so, Blackface Charley saw through the window of the station the telegraph operator, hardly more than a boy, frantically rattling his key, calling for help. The bandit lifted his gun. At the shot there was a shivering of glass, and the bullet, shattering the pane, killed the young man.

Then, the safe opened and looted, the bandits rode whooping away. They had gained only a few hundred dollars and some watches and jewelry from the passengers, but two murders, one at Twin Mounds and the second at Red Rock, set the law more grimly on their trail.

Down at Hennessey was stationed Deputy Marshal Ed Short. He had been a "gun" in the Stevens County War in Kansas, where several persons were killed while the towns of Hugoton and Woodsdale fought to see which would be the county seat. It was said that Short went to the Oklahoma Territory from Kansas, looking for some of the men who committed murders there. Failing to find them, he took a deputy marshal's commission.

When the Dalton gang scattered after the Red Rock robbery, Blackface Charley Bryant went to the ranch not far from Hennessey where he had worked off and on—between robberies—to "hole up." Evan G. Barnard, who knew Bryant, wrote of him in *A Rider of the Cherokee Strip:*

> Very frequently he [Bryant] shot at a mark and practiced pulling his six-shooter to see how quick he was on the draw. Many of the men in camp thought he was just a slow, easy-going fellow, and just had that habit. Now and then he left camp and was gone for a month. Then he turned up again and said very little to anyone. The last trip he made was when the Santa Fe train was held up at Red Rock. At this time none of the boys thought of him in connection with this holdup.

But Ed Short, the deputy marshal, did. Both the fireman and engineer of the train had seen the shooting of the telegraph operator at Red Rock, and the powder burn that gave Bryant his nickname was too evident to be missed. Short received a description of the murderer, including the telltale powder mark, and also notification that the Santa Fe offered $1000 for the wanted man, dead or alive. At once he was sure that "the man with the powder burn" was Blackface Charley.

He also knew of the close connection between Bryant and Dalton. Daisy Bryant, Charley's sister, an expert horsewoman who knew how to handle a gun, was the bandit leader's mistress. Dalton had bought her a place near Hennessey, where he frequently visited her, although at other times she joined him elsewhere. She was described as "a full-blown beauty," and she was much enamored of the reckless, good-looking bandit chief. Putting these details together, Short decided to arrest Blackface Charley.

The exact details of Bryant's capture are a matter of dispute. One version has it that Short took him at his sister's place. A better and more circumstantial story is that he was ill and went to Hennessey, for treatment, taking a room in the Rhodes Hotel, which was managed by an old cowman, Ben Thorne. Jean Thorne, the manager's pretty sister, acted as a nurse and brought Bryant's meals to him in his room.

Short went to the hotel and asked Jean Thorne to let him take a tray into Bryant's room. She refused. Did she know her "patient" was wanted by the law, and was there some kind of an attachment between her and Bryant? Short did not ask, but he was equal to the occasion.

Waiting until she went back to the kitchen to get the tray, he removed his boots and stole up the stairs and down the hall in his socks. There he hid around a corner until Jean Thorne came up with the dinner.

Her knock and her voice were all the assurance the outlaw needed. As she entered the room Short noiselessly stepped in just behind her.

Bryant was sitting on the bed. On one side of him lay a revolver, on the other a Winchester. Had Short attempted to enter alone he would certainly have been shot down.

"Hands up!" ordered the deputy, his six-shooter ready.

Stunned amazement, then fury, showed in the powder-burned

face. But it was too late for Bryant to make a movement for either of his guns, and besides, Short was standing behind the girl and thus was protected.

After a heart-stopping moment of hesitation the bandit slowly raised his hands and felt the handcuffs clamped on his wrists.

The marshal now had a slight transportation problem. Overland, Hennessey was not far from Guthrie. But if he conveyed his prisoner there by rail, he must go a roundabout way, north to Enid, and then double back to the Territorial capital. Short elected, instead, to take Bryant to Wichita, Kansas, where there was a federal jail, and to which the Rock Island railroad ran directly from Hennessey.

Perhaps Blackface Charley's easy surrender made his captor overconfident. He was concerned about a possible rescue attempt, and when the train stopped at Waukomis, he decided to go out and look around. He did not take the precaution of fastening the prisoner to one of the iron rods at the side of the car. After all, Bryant looked dejected and harmless, sitting slouched in a chair in the baggage car, his wrists fastened together by their manacles. So the officer handed his six-shooter to the baggageman, said "Keep an eye on him," and carrying only his Winchester, stepped out on the station platform.

Inside the car the baggageman was busy with his work. He glanced at Bryant, who appeared cowed and harmless and half asleep. After a few moments the baggageman placed the revolver Short had given him in a pigeonhole in his desk and became occupied with his job.

But both he and the deputy had misjudged Blackface Charley. He seemed to be drowsy and cowed, but he was intensely alert, his body tensed for action. Hardly had the baggageman laid aside the gun and turned his back when the outlaw made a leap for the weapon. His hands were handcuffed together, but he seized the revolver in both hands, and in an instant made his quondam guard climb out of the car on the side opposite from the station platform.

Then Bryant hurried to the end of the car and stepped out, standing at the top of the steps which led down from its platform.

Ed Short stood in front of the station, and at first he did not see the desperate man with the gun.

Lifting the six-shooter with both shackled hands, Bryant fired it as rapidly as he could cock it and pull the trigger. Of the three or four shots, one struck the deputy marshal in the body.

A grimace of pain went across Short's face. Nevertheless, stricken and staggering as he was, he whirled and fired twice. Down, bumping and rolling on the car steps to the ground, toppled Blackface Charley Bryant. As he did so, Ed Short, already collapsing, made a dive for him, caught him by a leg, and held him.

He need not have made the effort. The powder-marked outlaw, with two bullets in him, was already dead when he was stretched out.

"Jim, he got me, but I got him, too," Short gasped to Conductor James Collins as he was eased down upon his back.

He was shot through the chest, the bullet tearing through his lungs, and in a few minutes he, too, was dead from internal hemorrhage.

The Dalton gang had taken another life, but this time it had lost one of its own in exchange.

Blackface Charley Bryant's sister had been arrested and held as a material witness, but when he was killed she was released. Leaving the vicinity of Hennessey, she is supposed to have joined Bob Dalton in Greer County, almost down into Texas. After its custom, the gang had scattered and disappeared. But in the latter part of July, that same year, they gathered again, for one of the strangest of train robberies, at Adair, not far from the Arkansas line.

What made it exceptional was the cool daring of the robbery. The train, a Missouri, Kansas & Texas (or "Katy") express, carried that night about $17,000 in cash in the express car, and an armed guard of several Indian police and special detectives rode in it for the reason that the Daltons had been reported as camping near the line.

At about nine o'clock on the evening of July 14, 1892, the gang, heavily armed, rode into the small village of Adair. Eight men later were reported in it by frightened witnesses of what followed. It is certain that the three Dalton brothers, Doolin, Powers, and Broadwell were there. But who were the other two? They never were named. Excited imaginations sometimes exaggerate numbers. I am inclined to think the robbers were the six named, no more.

They proceeded with the utmost confidence. People in Adair were still up, sitting in their homes, talking or joking. Paying no attention to these few houses, the outlaws went direct to the station.

Winchesters menaced him, and the station agent made no resistance. The bandits tied him up securely, gagged him, and made him sit in a corner. Then they carefully and systematically looted the place, taking everything of any value they could find, from the agent himself and from the packages and parcels in the express and baggage room.

They were in no hurry. The train from the south, which they had come to rob, was not due until 9:45 P.M. Having finished the preliminary filching, which seemed to be done more to occupy the time than for any real value in the shape of swag they expected to get, they went out on the platform, and calmly sat down, Winchesters across their knees, talking in low voices and smoking cigarettes, while they waited for the train to arrive.

It was on time. As it drew up to the platform, two men swung on the steps of the engine and climbed up to the cab. A moment later Glen Ewing, the engineer, and his fireman were prisoners. The conductor, George Scales, and a porter came down the platform, perhaps to get orders from the telegrapher. They, too, were taken captive.

Meantime others of the gang were at the door of the express car, demanding that it be opened. George Williams, the express messenger, at first refused, but he was informed that the car would be blasted into flinders with dynamite if he did not obey. At that he opened the door, and the bandits leaped in.

For some reason never explained, the armed guard, consisting of eleven men, was riding *in one of the passenger cars some distance to the rear of the express car.*

One of the guardsmen, La Flore, a half-blood Cherokee, seeing men running about with lanterns, thrust his head out of the car window. Instantly he jerked it back, for it drew a salvo from two or three bandit Winchesters.

Captain J. J. Kinney, commanding the guard, did not lead his men out of the car, but directed them to fire at the freebooters from where they were. The result was a curious battle, the officers and Indian police shooting out of the car windows at the flitting forms of the bandits, and the outlaws blazing back at them.

Toward the end of the blistering little fight, in which some two hundred shots were fired, a few of the guards dismounted on the side of the train *opposite* from the bandits, and tried to shoot between or under the cars, with absolutely no effect.

So far as is known, not one of the robbers was hit. But others were.

Dr. W. L. Goff, a local physician, who was in a drugstore near the station with another of his profession, Dr. Youngblood, was struck by a stray bullet and fatally wounded, the bullet severing an artery in one of his thighs. Dr. Youngblood also was hit by a flying bullet, and for a time it was thought he also would die, but he eventually recovered.

Of the guard, Captain Kinney and two of his men, La Flore and Ward, were wounded, none seriously.

Throughout the affair the bandits appeared to be supremely contemptuous of their opponents, in effect holding off the guard with one hand while they robbed the train with the other. With complete effrontery they backed a spring wagon up to the express car and in an almost leisurely manner loaded the loot into it. They made no effort to rob the passengers, but when the spring wagon was loaded they fired a few more shots, gave some derisive whoops, and disappeared into the darkness, one man driving the team, the others careering along as escorts.

Once again bandit terror gripped the West. The Daltons had added another killing to their list, and the boldness of the Adair robbery caused people to couple their name with those of James and Younger, to whom they were successors by blood and tradition.

For months thereafter every train which crossed the Territory carried heavily armed guards.

And the robbers? They simply dropped out of sight. It was as if they were swallowed up by the earth—which is exactly what happened. Along the extensive breaks of the Cimarron River were a number of caves, all known to the bandits. Into these they disappeared to divide the loot and rest between robberies.

One such cave, near Mannford, Oklahoma, is still pointed out as the "Dalton Cave." The local story is that a half-breed Creek Indian named Tom Bartee would bring food to the Dalton crew hiding there, while U.S. deputy marshals fruitlessly combed the country for them. It is also locally believed that considerable sums of money are still buried somewhere in the vicinity of this cave, and not a few treasure hunters have tried to locate the "cash cache," but without success so far as anyone knows.[4]

With such retreats the band might have continued its career indefinitely had it not been for a piece of sheer vainglory on the part of Bob Dalton. Twenty-two years old at this time, he was a wonderful rider and marksman, was never known to step back from danger, and his personality gave him a special mastery over his men.

But he had some weaknesses. He was a little too interested at times in women to suit some of his followers, who believed feminine connections spelled danger. And he thirsted for publicity like some of his predecessors; was even beginning to have delusions of grandeur. At length his mania for notoriety caused him to plan an exploit designed, more than any other one thing, to fix his name imperishably in men's minds.

As he himself expressed it, he was going to "beat anything Jesse James ever did—rob two banks at once, in broad daylight."

Emmett Dalton phrased it somewhat differently in his statement made after he was wounded and captured: "Bob said he could discount the James boys' work and rob both banks at Coffeyville in one day."

There it was—the family pride in the exploits of those of the

[4] It seems unreasonable to think that any large sums were concealed for any length of time at this place. For one thing, in spite of their notoriety, the Dalton bandits never made many extremely big hauls. For another, if any cache was made, Bill Doolin undoubtedly would have appropriated it after Coffeyville eliminated his companions.

blood who had gone before, coupled with the instinct to rival or excel them, and thus win fame.

Bill Doolin and Emmett Dalton were a little dubious about it at first but soon fell in with the plan, which the others accepted with enthusiasm. For his proposed "double holdup" Bob selected Coffeyville, Kansas. His reasoning was logical. Coffeyville had two banks, quite close to each other, which would simplify a simultaneous robbery. Coffeyville, also, was a town in which he and his brothers were brought up. They knew its streets, alleys, and principal edifices. Bob, in fact, sometimes visited in Coffeyville on the quiet, even after he had a price on his head.

The boss bandit believed the two banks could be rifled quickly and with a minimum of trouble, and he knew that each carried so much cash that a successful robbery would provide his gang with a "stake" that would permit them to hide out for a long time, or even leave the country, if they desired, and live in what to them would be luxury.

The strange thing about the Coffeyville affair was that the town had received a warning from law officers in the Territory that the town might be raided by the Daltons. The warning was not believed, or people forgot about it, for the community was totally unprepared when the blow fell.

It was October, and the nights were frosty, when the band set forth from "a rendezvous near Tulsa," the location of which Emmett, the only survivor of the bloody fight, refused to reveal. It might easily be guessed. The "Dalton Cave" was only about twenty miles west of Tulsa. Emmett would naturally not tell its location because others of the gang might still be using it.

There were six riders in the party, and they made their first camp on the night of October 2, 1892, about twenty miles north of Tulsa. Next morning they saddled up and made another easy twenty-mile ride toward Coffeyville, camping in the timbered hills at the head of Hickory Creek, about twelve miles south of their destination. That night (October 4) they moved on up to the Onion Creek bottoms, within two or three miles of the town.

The men were beautifully equipped. Their horses were thoroughbreds, racing stock. Their saddles were new and expensively hand-tooled, with bearskin-covered saddlebags. Behind each cantle was a bedroll, and all the men wore black wide-brimmed cowboy hats and long coats, buttoned closely, not only because of the nip in the air but to conceal their deadly six-shooters. Each man also carried a Winchester rifle in a scabbard under his left leg. In appearance and accouterments they seemed almost to be in a sort of uniform—recalling the James-Younger gang in the fateful ride to Northfield, just a little more than sixteen years before.

They were all lean, tough, and deadly. Bob Dalton, his face hard in spite of his youth, was smooth-shaved. Grat Dalton, bat-eared and grim-mouthed, wore a dark mustache. Emmett Dalton, youngest of the brothers, just twenty years old and not a bad-looking youngster, but as reckless as any man in the crowd, also had a mustache—a little fuzzy adolescent decoration which he was proudly cultivating. Bill Powers' mouth was almost hidden by his heavy mustache, but Dick Broadwell's careless, easy-smiling face was clean-shaved. Bill Doolin's appearance on this date is not known, but he was always careful in his grooming until the latter part of his career.

That night of October 4 was cold in the woods of the creek bottom, and Emmett later told of how he could not sleep, partly because of his thoughts concerning the morrow, and how at last he rose and walked about uneasily while the others slept. Presently his brother Bob, who was his closest pal in the family, awoke and told him he had better get some rest.

Morning, October 5, 1892. In their camp the outlaws were astir early, making coffee and frying bacon and potatoes. After they ate, *each man carefully shaved himself*. Why this care in appearance? Was it that the Coffeyville raid was to be a dress affair in keeping with its expected historic importance? No one ever knew, but the outlaws, without exception, were clean and neatly shaved when they were laid out after the fatal battle that was fought later that day.

All six saddled up and mounted as the sun rose in the sky. They were seen—six limber, keen-eyed men—riding in a little clump, by a man and his wife, and a few moments later by two men, all of whom were driving along the road about half a mile west of the outskirts of Coffeyville. These witnesses agreed later that there were *six* men. Yet persons who saw the squad ride into town half a mile or so farther on agreed just as positively that there were only *five* men.

What happened? Bill Doolin discovered that his horse had somehow gone lame as they approached the town. A horse that could run was an imperative in this sort of adventure, so he pulled over to the side of the road and told his companions that he was going to stop and try to steal another horse. He had seen, in a pasture just a little way back, a sorrel gelding that "looked as if it could step." As soon as he had it, he promised to follow, probably only a few minutes behind.

Bob Dalton saw sense in this, and agreed. He knew Doolin would keep his promise and follow—as, in fact, Doolin did.

Just after nine o'clock on that morning the five men trotted their horses down Coffeyville's Eighth Street, turned to their right on Maple Street, just a block from the Plaza, where stood the two banks, and then down an alley, where they dismounted and tied their mounts at a fence which, it later turned out, was at the rear of the residence of Police Judge Munn.

Now came a delay, odd in its way. The Daltons, who were known in Coffeyville, made an effort to disguise themselves. Grat and Emmett donned false beards, dead-black in hue. Bob put on a stage mustache and goatee. They waited, mind, until they were in the heart of the town to don this mummery. Broadwell and Powers, being strangers in town, needed no disguise. As soon as the Daltons had completed their arrangements, the five walked boldly east along the alley, the three brothers in front, Broadwell and Powers side by side, just behind them.

Those false whiskers! They must have been decidedly amateurish in appearance, for they were the very cause of the downfall of the gang, which they were supposed to prevent.

A laborer, who fell in behind them, seemed to think nothing of five men, all carrying Winchester rifles, walking along the alley, for he turned north at the end of the block, to go unconcernedly on to his job. There was considerable hunting, especially in the wild country south of the state line, and the laborer perhaps thought this was a group of peaceful hunters going for supplies or ammunition.

Not so Alex McKenna, lounging in front of his dry-goods and grocery store on the street at the alley's mouth. He noticed the five men come into the street, gave a second look, and then a start as they passed him. Some of those men very obviously wore false whiskers!

Why should grown-up men fix themselves up that way?

McKenna smelled mischief, especially when the five all at once broke into a trot, holding their rifles ready for action. He watched, and saw three of them (Grat Dalton, Powers, and Broadwell) enter the large C. M. Condon Bank, which stood just south of the small "Opera House." The others (Bob and Emmett Dalton) passed on, through a vacant lot, around the Condon Bank, headed for the First National Bank, which stood just across the street east of the Condon institution.

Cautiously McKenna followed and peered through the plate-glass window of the Condon Bank. What he saw confirmed every suspicion he had felt. One of the men inside was pointing a Winchester at the cashier!

So great was the reputation of the Dalton gang that the name leaped involuntarily to McKenna's lips. Up the street he ran, yelling, *"The Daltons are robbing the bank!"*

One of the astonishing phenomena of the frontier was the celerity with which a community could arm itself and go into battle. Men, almost universally, were accustomed to weapons and many were expert in their use. It was natural to keep a rifle or revolver handy in the business place or home, if only to pick it up now and then, run a greasy rag through the barrel, and feel the pleasing weight of it in the hands. When something electric occurred the first move was toward that gun, and the second toward the scene of action, wherever it was.

Now history, already written at Northfield, repeated itself. At McKenna's cry of alarm the citizens of Coffeyville came boiling out of their places of business like hornets from a newly prodded nest, and they came shooting.

As soon as they entered the Condon Bank, Grat Dalton, Broadwell, and Powers went about their work briskly. It was Grat whose Winchester McKenna saw covering the cashier, C. M. Ball.

With Ball in the bank were T. C. Babb, a bookkeeper, and C. T. Carpenter, one of the owners. These men, their hands held high, were backed toward the rear while Grat entered behind the counters. Broadwell stood guard at one door, and Powers at the other.

"Put all the cash in that," Grat said. He produced a grain sack—the old, standard container made classic by the James gang—and the banker placed in it about $1000 in currency and $3000 in silver, which was in sight. But the bandits were not satisfied.

"Open the inner safe," Grat ordered.

The cashier was thinking fast. "I can't open it," he said. "It's set on a time lock and won't open before nine forty-five."

Actually it had been open since eight o'clock, as Grat could have easily discovered simply by trying the door. But the bandits accepted Ball's word for it.

"That's only three minutes," said Grat, looking at the clock on the wall. "We can wait."

Had he known it he could *not* wait. He could not afford those three minutes. They were all the difference between life and death to him and the men with him.

Nevertheless, cool as ice, he prepared to sit out those three minutes with disaster threatening every second, in the very center of a busy town. One after another, two customers entered, J. D. Levan and a clerk named James. They were lined up with the bank officials.

Slowly the three minutes ticked past in dead and breathless silence. Suddenly there was a nerve-tingling crash as one of the bank windows was shattered. A bullet had splintered the glass, fired probably by P. L. Williams, the first citizen to get into action.

A moment later other men were firing—Cyrus Lee, an iceman; J. H. Wilcox, a cattle dealer; and Hank Miller, a harness maker. Their rifles smashed more glass in the bank windows, and one slug slightly wounded Broadwell's arm.

"I'm hit," he said, hardly flinching. And then, looking sardonically at the frightened men held prisoner in the bank, "You'd better get under the counter, or you might get killed by some of those people."

By now the three minutes had passed and the vault was opened.

Grat, with a new idea, ordered Carpenter to pour out all the silver in the grain sack, saying it was too heavy, and replace it with currency, which was lighter. More and more bullets came searching in through the broken windows, and the bankers and their customers flung themselves on the floor.

Grat had completed the looting of the vault. Now he calmly tied up the mouth of the bag and prepared to lead the dash to escape.

Across the street, in the First National Bank, matters at first moved more smoothly for Bob and Emmett Dalton. They covered Thomas G. Ayers, the cashier, W. H. Shepherd, the teller, and a customer, J. H. Brewster. Bob knew the cashier and addressed him familiarly by name.

"Tom," he said, "get into that safe damn fast and get out all the paper money—and the gold, too."

His brother Emmett held his rifle on the others, and routed out of a small office at the rear, the cashier's son, Bert S. Ayers, and made him join the prisoners.

By now the racket of gunfire was heavy, as Coffeyville directed its fusillade against the Condon Bank. Ayers tried to delay as long as possible, but Bob impatiently followed him into the vault, seized two packages each containing $5000 in currency, and about $1000 in gold, all of which he dumped into his grain sack.

By this time men were rallying from every direction to repel the raiders, borrowing rifles and shotguns from hardware and general stores if their own weapons did not happen to be handy. The roar of guns rose to a pitch that sounded like a full-scale battle. Gray smoke wreathed store fronts and hung from second-story windows. Flying lead splintered wood and sent glass crashing into slivers.

Not all the citizens, however, were brave and determined. "When the firing broke out, rheumatic old men who had hobbled with difficulty a moment before dived into convenient barrels with acrobatic agility. Pedestrians crawled headfirst under culverts and remained there trembling, unmindful of protruding hindquarters. Men of wide girth squeezed behind thin hitching posts or scrambled under porches. Scarcely a box, fence, or doorway in the Plaza was unoccupied."

In both banks the robbers knew it was time to go. Grat Dalton in Condon's asked Ball if there was a back door, and the cashier, now more than anxious to get the bandits out of his place, where the lead sang so thickly, showed him an exit at the rear.

Out burst the bandits and found themselves in the midst of as deadly a street fight as outlaws ever encountered. There was nothing to do, however, but brave the withering cross fire. Carrying their sack of money, they ran across Walnut Street, to the mouth of the alley in which their horses had been left.

At about the same time Bob and Emmett, with their sack of loot, attempted to leave by the front of the First National, driving before them some of their prisoners as a screen. As they appeared, however, George Cubine, a shoemaker, and C. S. Cox fired at them. The bullets missed, but the brother desperadoes dodged back into the bank.

"Let us out the back way!" yelled Bob, flourishing his Winchester.

The door to the alley behind was opened for him by Shepherd, and the two dashed out, meeting, as did Grat and his two companions, instant fire from men who had been posted to cut off just such a retreat by Charles T. Connelly, the city marshal.

One of these was Lucius Baldwin, a youth who clerked in Isham's hardware store right next to the bank. Seizing a revolver from the store's stock, and loading it, he dashed out of the rear entrance in time to see the two bandits running north down the alley. Tremendously excited, he pursued, trying to head them off, running toward the two Daltons, firing wildly.

"Stop!" yelled Bob Dalton at him.

Baldwin plunged on.

"I'll have to kill you!" said Dalton.

He pulled his trigger and the Winchester bullet tore through the youth's chest, bringing him to the ground. Three hours later Baldwin died.

When they made their exit through the back door of the First National, Bob and Emmett were placed at an additional disadvantage. They were now on the opposite side of a block of buildings from the Plaza, which meant that they had to run a gantlet of two blocks to reach the place where the horses were tethered. And from every direction, it seemed, men were shooting at them.

They bolted north, leaving Baldwin sprawled behind, and turned west on Eighth Street, past Mahan & Custer's grocery. Looking south at that point, they could see men still shooting wildly at the Condon Bank. It gave them hope that they might run down the street unnoticed, and turn south through an alley to reach the horses, their sole means of escape.

But as they reached the open street they were spotted by George Cubine, revolver in hand, who stood with Charles Brown, an elderly man, who also was a shoemaker but was unarmed. Cubine fired at them and missed. Both Bob and Emmett returned his fire and Cubine pitched forward, dead.

Brown, although gray-haired and retiring in disposition, was on this day as full of fight as any of the younger men. When Cubine fell, he stooped and picked up the revolver. But before he could get into action he crumpled up, dying, near Cubine's body, another victim of Bob Dalton's deadly rifle.

The exchange of shots, brief as it was, had attracted to Bob and Emmett the attention of citizens who had been concentrating on the Condon Bank and the three outlaws in it. Ayers, cashier of the First National, with his son and Shepherd, ran into Isham's store next door and seized weapons.

Ayers looked down the street and saw Bob and Emmett. He knelt and steadied his rifle against the door jamb, his body concealed by a variety of articles, including harness, displayed for sale. But though he was already aiming, Bob Dalton saw his head, and the outlaw's snap shot was quicker. Ayers, wounded severely in the head, fell sidewise, his blood spurting over the sidewalk. Strangely, he did not die but eventually recovered from this apparently mortal wound.

Bob and Emmett Dalton ran on.

From the front door of Isham's, just south of the bank, jumped Mat Reynolds, a clerk. He had seen Ayers fall, but did not know the direction from which the bullet came. Looking toward the south, he failed to see Bob and Emmett north of him as they sprinted across to the lee of the "Opera House."

Instead, Reynolds' eyes were fixed on the three men running from the Condon Bank. He raised his rifle and fired, hitting Bill Powers, a center shot. The outlaw was mortally wounded, but he turned, black-browed and fierce, and shot, his bullet smashing Reynolds' foot.[5] Then he reeled on toward his goal—the horses.

The course taken by Grat Dalton, Broadwell, and Powers led them directly down the alley from which they first had issued into the street to enter the Condon Bank. This alley was lined in part by stables, including the livery stable belonging to John J. Kloehr, and in part by a board fence. About midway down the alley stood the small city jail, and just beyond that a lumber yard, and beyond that the fence to which the bandits' horses were fastened. Kloehr, a picturesquely mustached individual, wearing that day a battered derby hat, had seized a rifle and run west toward the horses, or he might have killed some of the outlaws when they passed his place. When he stationed himself, he was within fifty feet of where the outlaws met a little later.

Isham's hardware store faced west, looking directly down the alley. Partly for this reason, and partly because guns were available in the store, quite a little squad of men had gathered on the porch of the place, firing very rapidly, their bullets sweeping down the narrow alley, tearing bits of wood out of the fences and kicking up jets of dust from the ground about the fleeing bandits.

Powers already had a death wound, though he kept going, and Joe Uncapper sent a slug into Broadwell's back, crippling him badly. The outlaw tumbled into hiding in the lumber yard on the alley, and crawled forward among the stacks of boards toward the horses.

Charley Gump, a laborer, raised his pistol, but Powers, still on his feet, lifted his Winchester and fired. The bullet crippled Gump's wrist and disabled the weapon he held.

Up to this time the shooting of the civilians had been poor,

[5] It is to be remarked here that all of the bandit shooting was with rifles. They all carried revolvers, but evidently considered them too uncertain at any distance, and relied on their Winchesters. Not one of the gang used a six-shooter during the entire battle.

considering the number who were doing it, while that of the bandits had been deadly. But about this time John Kloehr, the best shot in town, took a hand, and the execution measurably improved.

Bob and Emmett Dalton, running south from Eighth Street along a small alley, met Grat Dalton and the staggering Powers coming west, at the intersection of the two alleys, just in front of the small jail. There, for the first time, a bullet struck Grat, inflicting a deadly wound. He dodged into a shed stable off the alley, where he kept his feet and turned at bay with his Winchester, hoping to cover the retreat of the others, who were running toward the horses.

Connelly, the marshal, was watching the horses, his rifle ready. Not knowing Grat was in the shed, he ran across the alley to it. The outlaw's wound was such that he could not lift his rifle to his shoulder. Shooting from his hip, he fired, and Connelly dropped, dying.

By this time Kloehr, behind the board fence where he could look out into the alley, was joined by Carey Seaman, a barber, who had a shotgun loaded with buckshot.

A team of horses drawing an oil tank had halted in the alley, the driver evidently diving into hiding somewhere. Frightened, the horses plunged and reared. They obscured Kloehr's view of the bandits' animals, and he coolly shot them down. He did this just in time, for the outlaws were about to reach their mounts and escape.

Left behind, Grat Dalton knew he was dying, but he had the dying creature's instinct to get away. He staggered out of the shed, past the body of Marshal Connelly, and still firing from his hip, shot at Kloehr and Seaman. Weakness made his aim unsteady and he missed. An instant later Kloehr's rifle sent a slug through his throat, and the bandit dropped right beside the marshal's body, in a dying condition.

Though mortally wounded, Powers tried to get into a door on the alley, found it locked, then ran stumbling on. He was the first to reach the horses. Feebly he tried to mount, and actually got into the saddle, but a volley of bullets sang down the alley and he was struck again. For a moment the bandit clung to the saddle horn, then he pitched off into the dust of the alley, dead.

Now suddenly Dick Broadwell, who had crept through the

lumber yard, appeared. Agonizingly he crawled through the fence and climbed on his horse.

Both Kloehr and Seaman fired. The outlaw reeled in his saddle, but he managed to stay in it, and his horse, frantic with fear, galloped out of town, carrying him. Later he was found dead, about a mile from the city, his horse standing beside him. Both Kloehr's rifle and Seaman's shotgun had inflicted such dreadful wounds that only Broadwell's wonderful vitality kept him in his saddle that far, before death blacked out everything for him.

Bob and Emmett Dalton were hurrying along some little distance behind Powers when the latter was killed. Emmett carried the sack of loot and Bob was guarding him with his Winchester. Neither of them had thus far been wounded.

From an upstairs window F. D. Benson shot at them, and missed. So quick was Bob's return bullet that it almost got Benson, and he ducked down out of sight.

But the bandit chief had run out his string of luck. From his position behind the alley fence Kloehr aimed at him just as he was ejecting the shell with which he had fired at Benson. Bob saw the livery-stable man, and worked his lever so fast that when Kloehr's bullet struck him, he discharged his own rifle, though the shot was wild.

The outlaw, shot through the bowels, was seen to lurch. Then he walked, very slowly, across the alley. All at once, seized with wound vertigo, he sat down on a pile of stones. Yet he did not drop his gun.

When the first paroxysm of sickness had passed, he rose again, staggered a few paces, and leaned for support against the corner of the shed where Grattan and Connelly had been killed.

Half standing thus, he tried to fight his thronging foes, and got off two shots. But darkness was closing about him, and neither took effect. Again Kloehr fired, the bullet ripping through his chest and bringing him to the ground near his dead brother and the marshal.

Last of the bandits on his feet, young Emmett Dalton had run on and mounted his horse, apparently not realizing that Bob was down. He tied the sack of money to the saddle horn before him while a perfect volley of shots direct at him killed the horses belonging to both Bob Dalton and Bill Powers, on either side of him.

Then a bullet went through Emmett's arm, another through his hips. Hard hit, he spurred his animal to escape. It was at this time that he seemed to realize that Bob was not with him. His brother and closest friend was back in the alley, lying by the barn, dying.

In the midst of the murderous fire, Emmett made a brave effort to save him. Turning his horse, he rode to where Bob lay, and reached down a hand, hoping to pull his brother up behind him. But Bob was too far gone to respond. As Emmett leaned over, his hand extended, Seaman blasted both barrels of his shotgun into his back.

Down to the ground slid the youthful outlaw, beside Bob. His effort to save his brother would have been futile in any case, for Bob died immediately from his hemorrhaging wounds.[6]

Twelve crowded minutes of shooting—and the Dalton gang was no more! The Coffeyville battle was fiercer, bloodier, and more disastrous to the outlaws than was the Northfield fight to the James-Younger gang. Four bandits were dead: Bob and Grat Dalton, Dick Broadwell, and Bill Powers. Emmett Dalton, the fifth, with a bullet through one arm, another through his hips, and at least a dozen buckshots in his back, was so fearfully wounded that physicians said he certainly would die. It was this medical verdict that probably prevented him from being lynched by the furious citizens that night.

Emmett, however, managed to survive. He was sentenced to life imprisonment, was pardoned after fourteen and a half years in the penitentiary, and later wrote a book, *When the Daltons Rode,* which received a wide sale and was made into a motion picture. He died when he was sixty-five years old, July 13, 1937, in Los Angeles, California.

Of Coffeyville's fighting citizens, four were dead or dying: Marshal Charles T. Connelly, Lucius M. Baldwin, George Cubine,

[6] Rascoe denies that this rescue attempt was made by Emmett Dalton. Nevertheless, I interviewed surviving persons who were in the fight, some years back, and I am convinced it took place. Almost every account of the battle mentions it. I went over the entire ground and took notes in the early 1920s, when details were still vivid in the recollection of the participants.

and Charles Brown. Three others were wounded: Thomas G. Ayers, Charles T. Gump, and Mat Reynolds.

Of the money taken by the bandits—$11,000 from the First National Bank and $20,000 from the Condon Bank—every cent was recovered except for one twenty-dollar bill which never was found.

But saving the money was insignificant compared to the real achievement of the battling citizens who wiped out a lawless and ruthless gang of criminals which was daily becoming a greater and still greater threat to the peace and security of the country.

Within minutes after the end of the bloody street battle excited riders galloped out along every road leading from Coffeyville, carrying news of the great fight with the bandits.

One of them met a lone horseman, cantering along on a sorrel gelding toward the town from the west.

"Fight! Big gun fight in Coffeyville!" yelled the citizen, almost incoherent with excitement. "The Dalton gang's wiped out! Four dead, and one's going to die, sure!"

The silent rider from the west turned his horse, put spurs into it, and rode back to the Territory in a cloud of dust. He was Bill Doolin.

He had managed to steal the fine thoroughbred he had seen back on the road, changed to it the saddle and accouterments from his own lamed horse, and was coming to join his companions as he promised. But so rapidly had events moved in Coffeyville that he had no time to reach the others before he thus accidentally learned their fate.[7]

[7] There is considerable conjecture as to just where Doolin halted on the way to Coffeyville. E. D. Nix said Doolin's horse wrenched its foot "during the night" and he stayed behind to get another mount when the band left the Onion Creek camp. Mrs. Tilghman has it that the halt was made the day before and Doolin was to join the others at the rendezvous, but they left before he came, so he followed. But four persons, Mr. and Mrs. R. H. Hollingsworth and J. M. and J. L. Seldomridge, in two vehicles, met *six* riders half a mile out of town, while those who saw them enter the outskirts of the city later agreed there were only *five* horsemen. The conclusion is unavoidable that Doolin, who was the sixth man, turned back within half a mile of Coffeyville to get the "sorrel gelding," although he may have ridden back a mile or even more before he reached the pasture where he had seen it, hence his delay.

Doolin rode hard for safety. The stolen sorrel was good and game. Until he crossed the border he kept his mount at a gallop. Then, according to his story later told to Bill Tilghman, the great marshal, and preserved by Zoe A. Tilghman, the marshal's wife, in her writings, he kept on at an easier pace, stopping now and then to breathe his horse, "crossing the Territory like a flying wraith."

At last he reached a haven.

What might have happened had Bill Doolin gone into Coffeyville with the others? Would he have died with them, ending the outlaw succession?

As in the nursery rhyme of the lost horseshoe nail, a limping mount that October day in 1892 changed criminal history. With him, as he fled into the fastnesses of the Territory, fierce Bill Doolin carried the seed of a still greater wave of outlawry that was to follow.

7. *The Oklahoma "Long Riders" Take Over*

It should be stated that the outlaws of the West, after the first post-Civil War period, were almost without exception cowboys. And it should be further explained that this was in no wise due to any inherent criminal streak in cowboys as a class.

Rather it was a result of the lives they led, and the resentments they held, chief of which was the way in which barbed wire and settlements were constantly restricting their ranges to smaller and smaller dimensions, thus depriving them of their livelihood, and more importantly, their way of life.

There was, in point of fact, a condition in the Oklahoma and Indian Territories in the 1890s that was strikingly similar to that existing in Missouri which led to the outbreak of outlawry immediately following the Civil War. Here again was a population ready-made for lawlessness. To be a good cow hand, a man had to develop a certain hardihood, even to the point of a reckless willingness to risk both life and limb. The cowboys in the Territory in the 1890s could ride as well as any men who ever lived, were accustomed to every kind of hardship, had almost limitless endurance, and were skilled with weapons, in some cases to the point of virtuosity.

They hated the "sodbusters" who were plowing up their grazing lands, and they hated the little towns that were springing up everywhere. Furthermore, they had the example of other hard-riding, hard-shooting men, who as outlaws had defied society and *almost* got away with it.

By 1890 Jesse James was a full-scale legend of the roundup camps—an attractive legend to the lean riders, with overtones already gathering about it in which the old Robin Hood characteristics were attributed to the Missouri brigand and his men. With such a tradition and such a background, the cow country was a ready-made recruiting ground for a man like Bill Doolin in forming an outlaw band of his own.

Oscar Halsell, owner of the great HX Bar Ranch, which lay for miles along the Cimarron River, was an eminently respectable and law-abiding man—a business partner, in fact, of E. D. Nix, who became United States marshal in the Oklahoma Territory. Yet for some reason his ranges furnished more outlaws than any other single cattle outfit in history.

It was to the Halsell range, after the Coffeyville disaster, that Doolin, himself a former HX Bar cowboy, rode to hide. He had friends there and for some time he lived in various outlying line camps of the Halsell outfit, where he knew a few of the riders, and where almost nobody came, and where those who did come asked no questions.

But there was an even safer place for him. East of the Halsell ranch, near the Cimarron River, was a large cave, which had been one of the fastnesses of the Daltons during their career. It was situated in a fantastic tangle of heavily wooded, rugged hillocks, deep gullies, and creek bottoms, and was so isolated that almost nobody knew of it.

The nearest community to it was a little joy spot known as Ingalls, which consisted chiefly of a couple of saloon-gambling places, two small stores, a blacksmith shop, a livery stable, and a "hotel" (for other purposes than sleep). From Ingalls the outlaws needed to have no apprehensions, since it subsisted almost entirely on their spending, and hence was highly friendly to them.

In that cave on the Cimarron, Doolin presently went to live—with an occasional visit for relaxation amid the joys furnished by Ingalls—and there he brooded and planned his next move. There, after a time, he was joined by another member of the Dalton clan—Bill Dalton, from California.

After Coffeyville the notoriety of the family name became such that Bill gave up politics and the California state assembly, disposed of whatever property he had in that state, and returned to the Oklahoma Territory. He was married, and for a time he lived quietly near Kingfisher, where his mother and other members of the family resided. But presently he searched out Doolin, informed of the outlaw's whereabouts by the curious "underground wireless" that spreads news among criminals. To a casual observer Bill Dalton would hardly have looked like a bandit, potential or otherwise. He was "a respectable-appearing man," with short chin whiskers, chunky in build and sober in dress, who might have been taken anywhere for a merchant or a land dealer, both of which he had been. But he had the Dalton eyes, restless and piercing, and also the Dalton instinct for lawless action, which was released in him by the bloody fate that overtook his brothers.

Black-browed Bill Doolin, whom he found in the cave, was by all accounts a fine-looking man, and a top hand when he was working cattle. The only photograph of him was taken after he was killed, when he had allowed his beard to grow as a disguise, and it is hard to judge exactly how he appeared in life. But this much is certain: he was a born leader, who combined great daring with a killing instinct; and after his peculiar code, with a certain sense of honor.

His father, Mack Doolin, was an Arkansas farmer, who never made any money, and brought up his family in a primitive environment, with almost no education. Bill could hardly read or write, but illiterate as he was, he possessed a personality so engaging that it won him close friends. Oscar Halsell was very fond of the young man and profoundly regretted it when he learned that his former cowboy had gone into outlawry.

Bill Doolin and Bill Dalton . . . names very similar and easily confused, though the men who bore them were vastly different.

At first Doolin was suspicious of Dalton. He had succumbed to the insidious lure of the doubtful "glory" and the lurid publicity that went with outlawry. He wanted to be the boss bandit, and he wanted his gang to be called the Doolin gang. As Gordon Hines commented in his book *Oklahombres:*

> Some peculiar quirk in the minds of these outlaw leaders caused them to visualize themselves as romantic heroes. They were extremely jealous of the peculiar prestige that belongs to such predatory characters.

But very soon Doolin found that Dalton had no ambitions to be the leader. By tacit agreement the newcomer took a subordinate place. They trusted each other fully after that. As Doolin went about the choosing of the other men he wanted they each learned at once that he was chief. There was no question about its being the Doolin gang. Some of his choices were interesting.

The first man approached was George Newcomb, a handsome, devil-may-care cowboy with an eye for a pretty girl. He was a son of a respected family which lived near Fort Scott, Kansas, but he had not been home for a long, long time. In his younger days he worked for C. C. Slaughter, a noted cattleman, and was called the Slaughter Kid. Later, however, he was far better known as Bitter Creek Newcomb.

With him came a strange anomaly in the range country—a college man from Pennsylvania, of a fine family, who contracted tuberculosis, went West and regained his health in the fine dry atmosphere of the plains, fell in love with cowboy life, became a close friend of Bitter Creek's, and for sheer adventure followed him into outlawry. His name was Bill Raidler, alias Little Bill, to distinguish him from the two bigger Bills, Doolin and Dalton. Sometimes, when the mood was on him, Raidler would dreamily quote Wordsworth, or Keats, or Shakespeare, and often at nights around the cow-camp fires, he kept the hands listening open-mouthed to his strange tales of persons about whom they had never heard, such as Marco Polo, and Hernando Cortés, and Genghis Khan. Raidler was small, rat-faced and unprepossessing, a contrast to the great, handsome Newcomb; and it is likely that Bitter Creek was drawn to him because of his culture and education, which the big cowboy, denied them in his own life, admired.

Others from the HX Bar Ranch were Roy Daugherty, alias Arkansaw Tom, a youngster with a boyish idolatry for the magnetic Doolin; and Richard West, alias Little Dick, undersized and deadly, with a peculiar prejudice against sleeping under a roof, who was said to be the fastest gun in the Territory.

Also recruited by Doolin were George Waightman, alias Red Buck, a man with a streak of homicidal deviltry in him; Dan Clifton alias Dynamite Dick because he was said to use dynamite cartridges; Oliver Yountis, alias Crescent Sam; John Blake, alias Tulsa Jack; and Charlie Pierce, who, strangely, had no alias at all. All were cowboys, and it is possible that some of these last five may have worked with the Halsell outfit at one time or another.

But Doolin was impatient. He did not wait to gather all his new gang together before he embarked on his first raid, a daring foray up into Kansas in November 1892, only a month or so after the Coffeyville affair. Thereafter his hard-riding and dangerous bandit crew blazed a gaudy trail of crimes through Kansas, Oklahoma Territory, Arkansas, and Texas.

The first bank robbed was at Spearville, Kansas, a small town on the Santa Fe Railroad between Dodge City and Kinsley. Only four bandits rode on that raid, "since some of the members were still busy arranging their affairs to join the outfit permanently." The four were Doolin, Dalton, Newcomb, and Yountis.

The robbery was a success and $18,000 was taken, which the robbers divided equally among them as they headed south. To confuse pursuit, Dalton rode for his mother's home near Kingfisher; Doolin and Bitter Creek fled to the gang's cave in the Creek Nation; and Crescent Sam Yountis made a beeline for the home of his sister, near Orlando, twenty miles north of Guthrie.

The first three made clean getaways, but Crescent Sam was not so lucky. His horse was poor and slow. Behind him, pawing up the dust in furious pursuit, was Sheriff Chalk Beeson, of Dodge City, a very colorful and somewhat impatient officer, who believed in "due process of law" but was not so fanatical about it that he might not be willing to forgo "due process" in favor of a rope and a convenient cottonwood tree if he caught the outlaw.

Frantic with fear, Yountis rode his horse too hard, flogging the animal along until it utterly failed. His situation now was very serious. Leading his broken mount, Crescent Sam began to stumble along in his high-heeled cowboy boots. The cowboy boot is not designed for walking, at least for any distance, and the weather was raw and unpleasant. Not only did Yountis presently acquire blisters on his feet but he became more desperate and angry as time went on.

He was still fifteen miles from his sister's home, and tired and footsore, when a stranger rode up on a good horse and asked if he could be of some help. For answer Crescent Sam savagely drew a six-shooter and demanded that the friendly stranger trade horses with him. When the other demurred, in surprise, Yountis shot him dead, left his body on the prairie, and rode hard on the new horse for his sister's place, where he intended to hide until the uproar of the Spearville robbery died down.

Sheriff Beeson, however, was not easily shaken off once he took a criminal's trail. A "convention" of buzzards brought the pursuit to the dead man. Near the body was a ruined horse which Beeson, because of a peculiarity in its hoof marks, identified as the animal he had been trailing. To the sheriff the story was plain: the fugitive had ridden this horse into the ground and murdered the owner of a fresh horse to make his escape. Beeson noted the direction of the trail of the new horse, and since he had no authority to make an arrest in the Territory, rode directly to Guthrie for help.

Help was prompt and efficient. Chris Madsen, deputy marshal, already had a federal warrant for Yountis, for some previous offense. They seemed to agree that Crescent Sam was the man they wanted, for Madsen took two more good men, Heck Thomas and Tom Houston, and rode directly for Orlando. Leaving Guthrie in the evening, they made the twenty miles or so without stopping, and reached the ranch house they were seeking just before daybreak.

Silently, in the pre-dawn gloom, the officers took positions which commanded every exit. Thomas posted himself behind a stone wall not far from the barn, Madsen behind the corner of the barn itself.

As the first glimmer of the rising sun cut the horizon, a man came out of the house and started for the barn with a feed bag in his hands. It was Crescent Sam.

"Throw up your hands! You're under arrest!" called Thomas.

Yountis reached into the feed bag, drew from it a revolver, and a long spurt of flame leaped from the barrel. Behind the stone fence ducked Thomas, while bullets chipped pieces from it.

At this moment Madsen stepped from behind the corner of the barn and fired. The bullet from his revolver drilled through Yountis' heavy coat pocket and the thick roll of bills he was carrying in a pocketbook, and into his body. It did not kill him, but it spun him around, and a moment later Thomas and Houston, using Winchesters, brought him to the ground.

Out ran Crescent Sam's sister, hysterically crying, "Don't kill him! Don't kill him!" and threw herself on his body. But he was done for. He died hard, grimly cursing the officers as he lay helpless and wounded to death. He was taken to Orlando for medical treatment but he died that night.

On his person was found $4500 in cash, his share of the Spearville loot, which had broken the force of Madsen's first bullet.[1] The money was identified by officials of the bank and returned to them.

Just at this time occurred a spectacular event which had an important bearing on the activities of the outlaws, and at first seemed to give them a temporary advantage.

Across northern Oklahoma stretches what once was known as the Cherokee Strip. It was guaranteed to the Cherokee Indians when they were removed into the Indian Territory in 1828, as a "perpetual outlet, west," to enable them to travel to the buffalo-hunting country. But times changed. After the Civil War, in 1866, the Cherokees were compelled to sell the eastern part of their Strip—the government, of course, paying the bill—to various

[1] In a letter written October 8, 1942, shortly before his death, to Lon Ford, another old-time peace officer, at Ashland, Kansas, Madsen said he still had a photograph of one of the bills with the bullet hole through it, but the bill itself with the others went back to the bank. He made it clear that his bullet did not kill Yountis.

tribes, the Osage, Kaw, Ponca, Tonkawa, and Pawnee, for reservations.

Cut off from their hunting grounds and with the buffalo killed off anyway, the Cherokees in 1883 leased their wild and beautiful domain for $100,000 a year to a group of big ranchers, who formed the Cherokee Strip Livestock Association, and it became a vast cattle empire.

Pressure by land-hungry settlers caused the government to negotiate a sale whereby the Cherokees disposed of what remained of their Strip. Originally it had comprised about 12,000 square miles, or 7,680,000 acres, but by 1891 it had shrunk to 5,698,140 acres, for which the government paid $8,595,736.12. Part of the money was placed in the Cherokee tribal treasury and the rest was distributed on a per capita basis among members of the tribe.

It was announced that this area of fine arable land would be opened for settlement on September 16, 1893, on a basis of first-comers receiving the claims they staked out.

On that day a dense, black fringe of people, horses, and vehicles stretched mile on mile all around the Strip. Hysterical excitement was in the air, for this was to be a race, maybe the biggest race in all history, and for prizes of free land. Men—and many women and children—poised in every kind of rig, or on horseback, for the starting signal.

At noon a soldier fired a carbine to release the surging crowds. With a roar that could be heard for miles, a sudden, terrific avalanche of wagons, buggies, carriages, riders on horseback, and even a few men on foot leaped forward. Whips rose and fell as the vast company rolled into the Strip. There were, inevitably, accidents—wagons tangled wheels, horses fell and their riders were flattened under the rush of vehicles and hoofs coming up behind. Numbers of persons were injured and lives were lost.

But by nightfall the Cherokee Strip was occupied, its entire territory staked with claims. Though there would be innumerable disputes over priority rights, court actions, fist fights, and some shootings, the Strip had ceased to exist as open public domain.

Before the "Run" a new U.S. marshal's district was created with headquarters at Guthrie. E. D. Nix, who was appointed marshal by President Grover Cleveland, was not a gun fighter. He was the reverse, a sober, hard-working businessman, running a wholesale grocery business in Guthrie, in partnership with Oscar Halsell, owner of the HX Bar Ranch.

The Halsell outfit, it will be remembered, furnished some of the outlaws for the Dalton gang, and most of those for the Doolin gang, a circumstance which in no way reflects on the high character of the owner. It was Halsell, in fact, who persuaded Nix to take the office of U.S. marshal and helped him get the endorsements which he presented to President Cleveland.

But though he was not a gun fighter, Nix was an administrator. Realizing his great responsibilities in that wild country, he combed the West for the best men he could find, and succeeded in getting together a group of officers who were to be famous for their courage and skill, and also for their integrity, in enforcing the laws against great dangers and difficulties.

The names of some of these are household words in the West today: Bill Tilghman, Chris Madsen, Heck Thomas, Bud Ledbetter, Frank Canton, and John Hixon. The first three, in particular, became celebrated as the "Three Guardsmen." Their deeds are part of the folklore of the country.

Bill Tilghman was a clean muscular six feet in height, as handsome as he was fearless, had blue eyes, wore a crisp mustache, and was as fast and accurate with either rifle or six-shooter as any man in the West. He was born at Fort Dodge, Iowa, in 1854; had been a buffalo hunter when it was worth a man's scalp to go out in the wild Indian country; was an army scout fighting hostile Cheyennes, Arapahoes, and Comanches; city marshal of Dodge City for three of its bloodiest years, and undersheriff of wild and woolly Ford County, Kansas. Tilghman was universally respected, for his incorruptibility, his cold courage, and his fairness—even by the criminals he hunted down—and to this he one day was to owe his life.

The second of the Guardsmen, Chris Madsen, was a real soldier of fortune. He was born in Denmark, fought in the Danish Army against the Prussians in the Schleswig-Holstein War of 1864, and later enlisted in the French Foreign Legion. About 1870 he came to the United States, enlisted in the United States Army, and by ability rose to be chief of scouts against the Apaches in Arizona,

Sioux and Cheyennes in Wyoming and Montana, and Nez Percés in Idaho and Montana. He had gray eyes, a face which appeared rather heavy and stolid—giving a false impression, since he was lightning-quick in action—and was as lethal as he was brave.

Third of the trio was Heck Thomas. Born in Georgia, as a youth he served as a soldier in General Stonewall Jackson's immortal Confederate brigades. After Appomattox he went to Texas, became a Texas Ranger, made an impressive record for daring and efficiency, and later was a top deputy in the district over which Judge Parker presided, being the man who shot it out with, and killed, Jim July, Belle Starr's last Indian lover.

There were many others in the deputy force of the same stamp. It was a force designed to quell outlawry in the Territory; but before it came to grips with that problem, it first had another task to do. It policed and handled the tremendous crowds that gathered on the borders of the Cherokee Strip to make the sensational "Run," and later saw to it that the claims were legally taken, prevented "claim jumping," and kept order in the new tent settlements that sprang up. The task kept the entire force, plus hundreds of special deputies, busy for months.

That was just what Bill Doolin and his crowd were looking forward to.

The killing of Ol Yountis did not daunt the outlaws. Their headquarters cave in the breaks of the Cimarron River, not far from the present Cushing, Oklahoma, was large, safe, and secret—big enough to shelter the whole gang and a *remuda* of twenty-five horses, remote and inaccessible, warm in winter and cool in summer, with a good supply of pure water. It was, in fact, a natural fortress which could be defended, if necessary, against a small army.

After Doolin gathered all his men there—including those who had to make "last arrangements"—he led his second raid, again into Kansas, in the belief that the marshals would be too busy to bother with him. This time the gang held up a Santa Fe train at Cimarron, Kansas, May 28, 1893, taking about $13,000 in cash, with which they rode south.

They counted wrongly, however, on the supposition that the marshals would ignore them. When a telegram reached Chris Madsen at Guthrie, telling of the robbery, he thought back on his old scouting experiences with the Army to figure the route they probably would take down into the Territory, and then, having no time to raise a posse, wired the commanding officer at Fort Supply (now Supply, Oklahoma) to send some Indian scouts and some cavalry to meet him at a point where the trail made a bend near where Buffalo, Oklahoma, now stands.

He had guessed the outlaw route exactly, but unfortunately he and the military arrived just minutes too late to cut them off. The Indian scouts first saw the bandits, but they were four hundred yards away. A running fight took place, in which Doolin got a bullet in one foot from Madsen's gun,[2] but the superior horses of the outlaws rapidly drew away, leaving their pursuers, bitter with disappointment, in the dust far behind.

Doolin stopped at a ranch owned by a man named Jim Riley, in the Strip, where the bullet was removed. The others rode on to the bandit cave, but young Arkansaw Tom remained with his chief and took care of him, until Doolin could ride again, when they both rejoined the gang.

Save for the bullet that punctured Doolin's foot, the brigands had escaped scotfree, and the $13,000 they divided was a juicy plum to them. For a time they lay low, but presently they began to ache for amusement and took to making occasional visits to their old playground, Ingalls.

At this time Orrington (Red) Lucas, who held a deputy marshal's commission, had gone "into the brush" to try to find where the outlaws were hiding. He learned of their visits to Ingalls, and posing as a harmless and none too bright fisherman, selling yellow channel catfish for a living, put up an old tent in the town itself. There he became acquainted with the outlaws, sometimes played

[2] Years later, after he was captured by Tilghman, Doolin made Madsen a present of the bullet he got in the fight. It was easily identified as from Madsen's gun, because the marshal was using steel-jacketed bullets while the soldiers and Indians were using army carbines with black powder and lead bullets.

poker with them, sold them fish, and meanwhile checked them as to weight, height, scars, and other identification.

"They won the goodwill of the people around Ingalls," Lucas later said, "bought food and provisions for the needy, and set themselves up as 'Robin Hoods,' taking from those who had plenty and giving to those who had nothing. That's why peace officers received no cooperation in their attacks on this gang."

Ingalls was twelve miles east of Stillwater, and the road from that town ran through it, on the way to Tulsa. It wasn't much of a road, just a wagon track across the country, but it served as one of Ingalls' two streets, running east and west. The north-and-south "street" was even less of a road, being no more than a wide space between two very short and scattered rows of jerry-built buildings.[3]

On the main road stood a livery stable, where the outlaws kept their horses. Across the street to the south was the Pierce Hotel, conducted by Mary Pierce, which appears to have had as its chief tenants a few prostitutes and the outlaws who came to frolic with those sirens, although Mrs. Pierce also had three young children in the place. Next to the "hotel" was the Trilby Saloon, where swashbuckling desperadoes "bellied up" to the bar, or gambled their money at poker, seven-up, and faro. It was owned by a portly, jovial man named Murray, but, as Lucas said, "it virtually belonged to the Doolin gang."

There was another saloon, two small stores, a blacksmith shop, and a few shacks. In the middle of the street was a curb well—the town pump—with a horse trough.

It was Red Lucas, in his daring role as a scout masquerading as a simple-minded fisherman, who got word to Guthrie that the outlaws might be expected in Ingalls at almost any time. At once Nix called some of his officers away from other duties and organized a posse to investigate.

Bill Tilghman was to have headed the force, but he broke one of his legs in a runaway accident and was confined to his home. Chris

[3] I visited Ingalls years ago, before World War II, and at the time it was a ghost town, the buildings all falling into ruins. The Trilby Saloon was still standing then, and the bullet scars could be seen in its walls. The small town of Signet stands near the old site of Ingalls.

Madsen, Heck Thomas, and Bud Ledbetter were busy elsewhere, but John Hixon was available and was given the command. He was a fighting man when fighting needed to be done, and he had some good men with him, including Lafe Shadley, Tom Houston, who had been with the party that killed Yountis, Jim Masterson, brother of the famous Bat Masterson, Dick Speed, and others specially deputized.

The posse traveled in two covered wagons, the men remaining concealed under the canvas except for the drivers, so as not to attract attention in the towns. They gave out word that they were a party of hunters. It was some forty miles from Guthrie to the outlaw hangout, over rough, almost roadless country, but the men took their time, and they had supplies to last for weeks. At one place they halted, and hunted two or three days, awaiting word from their scout.

Lucas rode into camp September 1, saying that the outlaw gang had landed in Ingalls and was engaged in a big jollification that looked as if it would last for some time. At once the wagons were hitched up, the hunters of game, now become hunters of the most dangerous game of all—armed men—concealed themselves under the canvas tilts, and the party was quietly on its way.

The approach to Ingalls was made from the Cimarron River, to the south, up a small creek which allowed the wagons to come near to the town without being seen. At last a halt was made in a concealing draw. The tense moment of action had arrived. Out crawled the deputies, each carrying two six-shooters and a Winchester, with two belts of cartridges.

From the town the howl of a drunken desperado told them that the outlaws they sought were still there. Hixon began directing his men in a low voice, sending them to the best possible vantage points.

The Trilby Saloon had been indicated by Lucas as the chief gathering place for the gang, but it was necessary also to watch other buildings—the "hotel," the livery stable, the stores, wherever one of the bandits might be idling his time at the moment.

In different directions the deputies snaked their way, seeking places where they could command the saloon's exits or get a good shot down the "street." As it turned out, the Doolin gang was scattered over the town at this hour. Some were in the Trilby Saloon, at least one was in the "hotel," and two or three were purchasing supplies or ammunition at one or the other of the little stores.

Accounts differ as to how the fight started. According to one story, the first shot was fired from the saloon by an outlaw who saw a suspicious movement as a deputy crawled forward. Another says that a messenger was sent to tell Bill Doolin that he was surrounded and must surrender, and that he answered, "Go to hell!" This sounds incredible, primarily because the outlaws were not surrounded at all, as events proved, and also because it would have been pretty hard to find anyone on the law's side with any desire to commit suicide by carrying such a message to Doolin.

Lucas said a boy from a neighboring place had warned the outlaws that the deputies were about, and the outlaws were trying to get to their horses and escape when the shooting began.

However it started, the officers were not yet ready, because they had not all reached their assigned positions, but now it was too late for much maneuvering. The battle, one of the most interesting affairs of its kind in the outlaw West, was on.

The squalid little huddle of shacks seemed almost deserted under the pale bright autumn sky, and there was a crispness in the air. The Trilby Saloon and Pierce Hotel were like blank faces, except now and then for puffs of smoke accompanied by the crack of Winchesters.

Lead sang through the air, causing the deputies to lie very close. They were at a disadvantage, since they were seeking cover in the open while their enemies were for the most part concealed. As often as possible, however, the officers got in return shots, and their bullets went through the thin plank walls of the buildings as if they were cardboard, making the interiors perilous.

Here and there, dodging across open spaces and working from house to house, some of the outlaws tried to reach the livery stable. Each time a figure was seen darting past one of those vacant spaces half a dozen rifles cracked, but the appearances were so brief, and so impossible to predict, that the brief volleys inflicted no damage.

Both sides knew this fight was deadly serious. The outlaws could look for little mercy if they were captured; the officers must take those men at the risk of their own lives.

At first there were no casualties. Speed, Houston, and Shadley concentrated on trying to drive the outlaws out of the saloon. Though they were shooting blind, their bullets kept puncturing the wooden walls, smashing glasses and bottles on the bar—behind which, flat on his face and trying to make himself as small as possible, lay trembling the fat saloonkeeper, Murray.

Presently the saloon became too warm to stay in. Bitter Creek Newcomb was the first to make a dash for the livery stable. As he did so there was a small fusillade. Just as he reached the town pump the outlaw fell, with a bullet through his leg from the rifle of Tom Houston. He fired back, and his shot took Houston's hat off, without inflicting a wound.

As Bitter Creek fell, Bill Doolin, broad-shouldered and game, jumping, zigzagging, one after another, Bill Dalton, Red Buck companion and drag him over to the livery stable. He had lifted Newcomb, and partly carried him to that haven, when he was seen to wince as a bullet found him, and then sag down beside Newcomb. For a moment the officers whooped, thinking they had got both men. But amazingly, Newcomb and Doolin scrambled to their hands and knees and thus reached concealment in the stable without being further wounded.

The deputies, indeed, hardly had been able to shoot at them, because a very hot covering fire was poured upon them by the other outlaws to save the two by the pump. Jim Masterson, behind a tree, heard lead strike again and again in the trunk or rip up the sod around his feet. Hixon, in a shallow ditch, hugged the ground as the bullets combed the grass just above him.

At this time the officers began to notice that someone was shooting from Mary Pierce's place. Hixon and Masterson turned their guns toward that building, smashing windows and riddling doors with Winchester slugs.

Now a sudden eruption came from the saloon. Dodging, buckjumped out from the saloon, and ran across the road to pick up his

Waightman, Dynamite Dick Clifton, and Charlie Pierce made the dash across the street, past the horse trough and pump, to the livery stable. Every one of those men reached the stable safely. Little Dick West and Bill Raidler had crossed, probably from one of the stores, and were there with Doolin and Newcomb.

The sudden shift in position gave the outlaws an advantage. From the livery stable their bullets could reach positions where officers lay which had been protected from direct fire from the saloon. And a single rifle from Mary Pierce's place continued to make any movement deadly dangerous for the deputies.

In the "hotel" was young Arkansaw Tom Daugherty. One story is that he was sick at the time. More likely he was dallying with one of Mary Pierce's girls when the shooting began.

Mrs. Pierce and the girls, with her children, took refuge on the second floor, at the rear of the building, where they cowered, although the bullets of the deputies apparently did not actually penetrate that far through the intervening walls.

Meantime the young bandit in the front of the building had barricaded himself behind a bureau and washstand, from which he could shoot out from his window. Bullets smashed the water pitcher and bowl, and water splashed over him. The mirror was shattered and glass slivers spattered him. But Arkansaw Tom kept shooting back until the firing from without grew so heavy he had to change his position.

Carrying his Winchester, he crawled up a ladder which led through an opening in the ceiling to the attic. There he punched a hole with his rifle muzzle through the shingle roof.

It was just at this time that Deputy Tom Houston found his position too hot, as the bullets searched the area about him from the new direction of outlaw fire from the stable. He tried to dodge over behind a tree for better protection.

As he did so he suddenly crumpled up, shot through the stomach. As he fell he said, "I'd like to see the man who shot me."

A strange wish that was, expressed by a man who must have known he had received his death wound, and it was said without any apparent malice, but only with an odd, withdrawn curiosity.

The other officers said later that the shot came from Mary

Pierce's establishment. If so, it was Arkansaw Tom who fired it, for by this time all the other outlaws were in the livery stable.

Hardly had Houston fallen when Lafe Shadley made a gallant effort to reach a place from which he could get a better shot. Stooping low, he dashed forward and threw himself behind the carcass of a horse which had been killed early in the fight. But there he found himself so pinned down by the fire from the livery stable that he hardly dared raise his head and was for the time being ineffective.

Now occurred a dramatic episode, concerning which there has been much romantic writing. Bitter Creek Newcomb, the finest-looking man in the Doolin gang, had, as has been noted, an eye for a pretty face and a way with women. One of Mary Pierce's feminine "tenants" was a very pretty girl, who was known as the Rose of the Cimarron. She was at this time about eighteen years old, and the especial sweetheart of Bitter Creek, who probably was among the customers who regularly patronized Mary Pierce's place.

Rose had seen her lover fall, then scramble to the livery stable. She knew that his Winchester and cartridge belt were in his room on the second floor of the hotel, at the rear of which she and the other women were huddled. Braving a possible probing bullet, she ran to the room and brought back the rifle and ammunition. The only possible regular exit from the second floor was exposed to the marshals' fire, so with Mary Pierce's help she tied the gun and belt in a corner of a sheet and lowered them to the ground from a window on the sheltered side of the building. Then, tying two more sheets together, slid down herself.

Quickly she picked up the Winchester and cartridge belt. A moment's hesitation, and pretty Rose darted from her shelter, and ran across the lead-swept open area toward the livery stable as fast as her fluttering skirts would permit.

Those fluttering skirts, while they may have impeded her speed, saved her life. The astonished deputies saw a woman crossing over to where the outlaws lay, and though they could also see that she was carrying a rifle and extra ammunition to their foes, not one of them pulled a trigger on her. She reached the livery stable in safety, bringing much needed cartridges to the beleaguered bad men, and the story of her race to save her lover is still one of the legends of the West.[4]

At about this time Deputy Dick Speed attempted to cross the street to take shelter behind the dead horse where Lafe Shadley already lay. Doolin had been seriously wounded when he helped Newcomb to safety. A bullet had torn through his neck, lodging at the base of his skull but not severing any arteries. Nevertheless, the pain of it half dazed him.

He was still, however, the leader. Looking around a corner of the stable, he saw Speed make his dash. He fired at the officer and missed. Then, gathering all his will power to steady himself, he knelt and leaned against the side of the building, taking careful aim. This time when he pressed the trigger his bullet sang true. Speed, hit squarely between the eyes, pitched forward, dead without a cry.

Doolin and Dalton, behind the livery stable, saw where Arkansaw Tom had barricaded himself, in the attic of the hotel, and knew he could not hope to join them. There was only one thing to do—escape with those who could.

Bitter Creek, weak from loss of blood, was helped on a horse,

[4] There has been a lot of mystery about this girl. Long after, when he was captured, Bill Doolin said of her, "She was a sweet little girl who was unfortunate enough to fall in love with an outlaw. She would have laid down her life for Bitter Creek Newcomb, and he worshipped her. She was as good a girl as ever lived, and the whole gang worshipped her." The last, about her being "as good a girl as ever lived," is a little hard to believe, considering the character of Mrs. Pierce's establishment and the type of men she associated with. But the West was always a little top-heavy with gallantry where women were concerned, and Doolin can be forgiven if he perhaps stretched the facts a little in pretty Rose's favor. As to the assertion that she would have laid down her life for Bitter Creek, she proved it that day.

There was a lot of mumbo jumbo about how none of the men who knew her true identity would ever reveal it because she later married and became a good wife. But old Chris Madsen was more realistic. Her real name, he said, was Rose Dunn, and she came originally from Texas. That she was amazingly brave and loyal is beyond question. But good? Madsen says, "She was said to have been the sweetheart of Doolin but only for a short time and then became the mistress of Bitter Creek." After her bandit lover was killed and she served a term in prison, she married a man named Noble, moved out of Oklahoma, and lived a completely upright and normal life as a wife and mother.

and Rose mounted one also. Together they rode for cover, trying to keep the buildings between them and the law.

But Bitter Creek could not stay in his saddle. After a few minutes he lost his seat and tumbled to the ground. Rose did not even think of deserting him. She caught his horse and rode back to him, to try to revive him and get him mounted again.

Doolin and Dalton told the remaining outlaws at the stable to get away while they covered the retreat. When the others had mounted and gone, the two took horses and followed. Dalton was unhurt, but Doolin's neck wound was very painful. About a quarter of a mile from the town they caught up with Red Buck and Dynamite Dick.

"Where's Bitter Creek?" demanded Doolin.

"Hell!" snarled Red Buck. "We ain't got time to fool with him and that girl! They're back there——"

He started to ride on when Doolin's revolver flashed out and a bullet sent the hat sailing from Red Buck's head.

"Come back here, you yellow dog!" shouted Doolin. "We're not leaving Bitter Creek and that girl behind!"

The four outlaws turned and rode back toward the town looking for their missing mate.

Meantime Deputy Shadley had seen Bitter Creek's fall from the saddle and the return of the girl to help him. Leaping from behind the dead horse which had sheltered him, he ran forward, Winchester ready, to kill or capture the wounded outlaw.

As he did so, Bill Dalton, on his horse, came careering at full speed over a short rise, his Winchester in one hand, looking for Bitter Creek.

Both he and Shadley must have fired almost at once. But though Shadley, on foot, had the better shooting stance, he missed. The report of Dalton's rifle sounded almost at the same instant as that from Shadley's gun, but the outlaw's bullet struck its mark, and the deputy dropped to the ground, dead.

Almost at the same moment Doolin, Dynamite Dick, and the cursing Red Buck arrived from a slightly different direction. They helped Bitter Creek on his horse, and with Doolin and Dalton riding on each side to support him in his saddle, they galloped away, followed by Red Buck, Dynamite Dick, and the Rose of the Cimarron.

Shadley lay alone, where death had found him.

The deputies were not mounted and could not pursue the outlaws. But they could turn their attention to the "hotel," where Arkansaw Tom still lay in the attic. He had not fired recently, and they did not know whether he was wounded or dead. As a matter of fact he had run completely out of ammunition.

For a time the officers kept up a barrage of bullets, but the youth lay low and none of the slugs hit him. At length Jim Masterson proposed that they dynamite the building, or set it on fire.

When she saw the men gathering kindling and wood, Mary Pierce went out with her three children and pleaded with them not to destroy the place. "It's got everything I own in it," she said.

"How many are up there?" asked Hixon.

"Just one—Arkansaw Tom."

"Well," said Hixon, "it's up to you. Bring him down with his hands up, or we'll blow the building, and him in it, into the sweet bye and bye."

She entered the building and talked to the boy. His cartridges were all shot away and it did not take much persuasion to get him to surrender. After a few minutes he came down the ladder, stepped into the open, and was at once shackled.

They took the long, gangling youth over to where the dying Tom Houston lay. "This is the man who shot you," they said.

Houston looked at him, but did not speak. The young outlaw put a white handkerchief to his face.

"I have often noticed outlaws doing this," said Lucas later, "but do not know the significance of the sign."

Perhaps it was merely to wipe the cold perspiration from the fear-stricken youth's face.

Hixon and another deputy climbed the ladder to the attic to make sure nobody else was there. When they returned, carrying the outlaw's empty rifle and revolvers, they said that the place "literally was shot to pieces. It was a miracle that any man could have come out of it alive."

Arkansaw Tom, not yet twenty years old, was the sole bag of the posse in the bitter Ingalls battle, in which they lost three deputies, Tom Houston, Dick Speed, and Lafe Shadley, killed by outlaw bullets.[5] He was born Roy Daugherty in Arkansas (whence his alias) and, strangely, in a very religious family. Two of his brothers became ministers of the gospel. His mother died when he was quite young, and after his father remarried, his stepmother made life so miserable for him that he ran away from home when he was fourteen. He worked on various ranches until he became a fair cowhand, and he admired Bill Doolin above all other men. He had begged to join his idol's outlaw band, and at last was accepted. The lone stand he made in the attic of the Pierce "Hotel," covering the retreat of his friends, was his payment for the privilege of associating with Doolin and his gang.

Because of the killing of Tom Houston, he was tried on a murder charge. It was not conclusively proved that he fired the fatal shot, but the presumption was so strong that he was found guilty. He was sentenced to serve fifty years in the federal penitentiary at Leavenworth, Kansas.

Of this, Arkansaw Tom actually served fourteen years, after which he was pardoned through the efforts of one of his ministerial brothers. He went straight for several years, but then was involved in a bank robbery at Neosho, Missouri, and went to prison again. When he got out he held up a bank at Asbury, Missouri, and was killed by Joplin officers while resisting arrest, August 16, 1924. By that time the Doolin gang had long ceased to exist. He was the last member of it to die.

[5] Red Lucas said that a "thirteen year old boy" (name not given) also was killed in the Ingalls battle, but I can find no record of this in any of the other accounts. Tom Houston died shortly after the battle.

8. *To the Bloody End*

The Ingalls battle was the first round, and in its way it was a victory for Doolin and his men. They had killed three officers and escaped with a loss of only one of their own gang, captured.

Other rounds, however, were to follow. The Ingalls fight was only the beginning of a long, grim hunt which never ceased until the outlaw gang was destroyed. It is hard for the modern mind to conceive of the bandit country as it was then, and the conditions existing that made outlawry possible but which have now disappeared. Roads were few; most of them mere meandering wheel tracks, where they existed at all. The small settlements were widely scattered, many of them no more than Indian villages. Habitations in the open country were far apart, largely of the dugout variety,[1] and the people were either unfriendly to the law

[1] The dugout was the most primitive of dwellings. It was made by digging a hole in the side of a hill or embankment, squaring the walls as much as possible, and roofing it over with logs slabbed with sod. The front was of logs, usually standing upright, and contained the only opening, a door,

or afraid of the outlaws, so that it was almost impossible to get information from them.

The fastest travel was by horseback only—the automobile, the plane, and the paved road were for future generations. A horse could leave the trail in any direction, and a cunning rider could lose himself with ease in the wild and broken, almost deserted country. While the telephone had been invented, there were no telephones except in the very largest towns, and certainly no two-way radios or any of the other means of communication which aid modern law-enforcement agencies.

At times in the years that followed the Ingalls battle the prospect must have seemed very discouraging to the courageous officers, doggedly following the mocking trail left by the bandits, a trail studded with robberies and murders. But their deadly determination never faltered and they did not quit until they had hunted the last of the outlaws down to the bloody end.

After the Ingalls fight the wounded Doolin and Newcomb rode some miles to a small Indian town, where they had their wounds dressed. Bitter Creek was so weak that he could not ride farther, and that night a rancher named Will Dunn, a suspected cattle rustler, came with a buckboard and hauled him to his dugout, within a few miles of Pawnee. The outlaws rode into that town, kidnaped a doctor, blindfolded him, took him out to the Dunn ranch, and had him treat Newcomb, stopping the bleeding; and then took him back, releasing him minus the blindfold near his house.

Newcomb recovered fully, but the ball at the base of Doolin's skull remained there for the rest of his life. At times it gave him pain and severe headaches, and even occasionally caused seizures, similar to short epileptic fits, due probably to the pressure on some important nerve. Yet, so far as his adversaries were able to tell, it

---

usually open for light, and closed with a curtain consisting of no more than a steer hide or piece of canvas. This formed a cavelike room usually about 10 × 12 feet, with a dirt floor, bunks or animal skins to sleep on at either side, and a fireplace always at the end opposite the door. It shed dirt from the roof continually in dry weather, and often dripped mud in wet weather. Yet it was fairly warm in winter and many families knew no better.

never cowed him or broke his spirit, and the most complete tributes to his gameness were those given by the officers who hunted him.

Having efficiently mixed up their trail, the outlaws holed up at the ranch of Bee Dunn, brother of Will, who had a slightly better house than the dugout of the latter, and there they were able to rest.

Fortunately for the Doolins, another gang, the Cook gang, to which attention will be given later, was at this time having its brief but spectacular career of crime in the eastern part of the Territory, and the activities of law-enforcement agencies were divided, so that for a period the outlaws could recuperate. During this "recess" Bill Doolin and his men had the services of two of the most unusual "scouts," to bring them warnings and information, in the history of Western crime.

One day, when a posse was working near the gang's hiding place it encountered a girl on the trail. She was quite pretty and mounted on a good horse, but the fact that she carried a Winchester rifle caused the officers to stop her and question her. She seemed sullen and uncommunicative. They let her go, but from her attitude and evident hostility, they had reason to believe that she went straight to the outlaw hideout they were then seeking, and warned the gang of the posse's movements.

At once, after this encounter with the girl, Doolin and his men disappeared entirely from the Territory. Later it was learned that they went to Arkansas. Doolin and Bitter Creek, still bothered by their wounds, visited the curative baths at Hot Springs, and they for a time debated robbing a bank there, but gave it up because the institution was too centrally located in the city.

The fact of the sudden departure of the outlaws, of which the officers soon learned, caused inquiries to be made about the girl who was seen on the trail. Now it appeared that instead of one, there were two girls. The one the posse had met, about seventeen years old, was known as Cattle Annie. She had a friend, a couple of years younger, who always wore men's pants and was called Little Breeches. Both went about heavily armed, and it was reported that they had sold liquor to the Osage Indians. More important, it was quite evident that they were in close touch with the outlaws, acting as spies and lookouts for them.

There was enough evidence to warrant their arrest, and two deputies, Bill Tilghman and Steve Burke, were sent into Indian country to bring them out.

The two little wildcats gave the officers more trouble than they expected. Inquiry led the officers to a ranch near Pawnee, where the girls were said to be living. But when the deputies rode up to the place they saw the younger one, Little Breeches, run suddenly out of the house and mount her horse.

Tilghman left Burke to find the other girl, and rode after the fleeing Little Breeches. He was a great horseman, and specialized in fine riding stock, and his mount was much faster than the girl's.

Rapidly he began to overtake her. As he came up, however, she drew a revolver and fired back at him. Again and again she shot, and though the bullets went wide, there was always the uncomfortable possibility that one of them might strike its target.

Tilghman was in an embarrassing and exasperating situation. He felt that he could not shoot a woman—it was one of the things that you just did not do in the frontier West. But the girl seemed to have no such scruples about shooting him. And small as she was, her six-shooter was as dangerous as if she were six feet tall, and at any instant one of her shots might kill him. Meantime, he was riding behind, helpless to reply.

Eventually he saw he must act. Drawing his Winchester, he shot and killed her horse. The animal in falling pinned one of the girl's legs under it, and the shock of the fall shook loose her hold on the pistol, which flew just out of reach. Raging, she clawed the grass frantically in an effort to reach it.

Tilghman dismounted, picked up the revolver, and took out the shells, then lifted the horse enough to free the girl's leg. Up she came, a spitfire to the last, scratching and clawing, and threw a handful of dirt into his eyes, almost blinding him temporarily. But he managed to seize her arms and subdue her, though her eyes still seemed to spark fire. She was not seriously hurt by her fall, and after giving her a lecture, Tilghman put her on his horse, mounted behind her, and returned to the ranch house.

Burke, meantime, had an almost equally brisk experience with the other girl. He dismounted when Tilghman rode after Little Breeches, and walked along close beside the house, when he saw Cattle Annie, with a Winchester, put her head out of a window, looking after Tilghman and the other girl. Fortunately her gaze was in the direction opposite from where Burke was crouching.

Before she could use her rifle, he leaped forward, seized her about the shoulders, and pulled her out through the window. In the struggle she dropped the Winchester, but tried to get at a six-shooter she was carrying. When Burke took that away, she resorted in her fury to very feminine scratching and kicking before she was subdued.

Burke came out of the melee with a long scratch across his cheek, and Tilghman was still wiping dirt out of his eyes when they started to Perry with the girls. Once they saw they were helpless, the two young prisoners gave no further trouble, although they became somewhat tearful. Cattle Annie gave her real name as Annie McDougal, and Little Breeches said she was Jennie Metcalf. They were daughters of poor, but respectable enough, white families living in the Osage country. The father of one of them told the officers that the girls met their outlaw friends at country dances, and became attached to them to the point that they acted as "scouts" for them and sometimes smuggled food and liquor to them.

Both girls were sentenced to a female reformatory at Framingham, Massachusetts. It is pleasant to record that, far from being depressed, the two little "criminalettes" thoroughly enjoyed the train journey East, being continuously excited and interested as they crossed the continent, and exclaiming delightedly over the sights. Neither of them had ever been far from home, and the outside world was a revelation to their starved little minds.

At Framingham they were model prisoners. After she served out her term Annie McDougal returned to the West, married, and settled down as if she had never lived anything but a normal and decorous existence. Jennie Metcalf went into religious work in the slums of New York. While engaged in it she contracted an illness from which she died, about a year and a half after her release from the reformatory.

The Doolin gang was not inactive during this time. After they visited Arkansas, they robbed a bank at Southwest City, Missouri, almost on the Territorial line in the extreme southwest corner of Missouri's "Boot Heel." There was some shooting, and Doolin received a slight wound. But the bandits escaped, with $15,000.

J. C. Seaborn, former state auditor of Missouri, and his brother, hearing the guns, ran out on the street in time to see the brigands riding by. One of them fired at the two Seaborns. The bullet passed through the body of the former state auditor's brother, without inflicting a fatal wound, and then bored into J. C. Seaborn, killing him.[2]

Crossing the Indian Nations, the outlaws paused in Pawnee and relieved a bank there of $10,000. Soon they were back in their old haunts.

Winter came on, cold and blizzardy. Then, in January 1895, the hideout at the Will Dunn ranch was discovered—quite by accident—and in finding it Bill Tilghman gave one of the greatest exhibitions of chilled-steel nerve in the annals of the frontier.

It was during an extremely frigid spell, with snow deep on the ground, but Tilghman with Neal Brown, also a deputy marshal, and an Indian driver named Charlie Bearclaw headed in a covered wagon for a ranch southeast of Pawnee, where it was reported some cattle rustlers were hanging out. At this time the Doolin gang had not been heard from for months and the deputies expected to deal with nothing more vicious than some sneak stock thieves.

As they neared the Cimarron River, Tilghman noticed smoke

[2] One version says Little Bill (Raidler) fired this shot, but I think it was Little Dick (West), because Raidler was never charged with the murder. The names are easily confused, and they were of a similar size.

Raidler's college education came in handy on one occasion, when the outlaws took what looked like a windfall—$50,000 in bank notes in one of their robberies. As they gloated over it, Bill Raidler glanced at the notes and gave a bitter laugh. They were no good, he told his stunned companions, because they had not been signed by the bank officials. It was a close thing, for if one of the ignorant bandits had tried to pass one of those notes he would immediately have drawn the law upon him. Newcomb and Doolin both highly admired Raidler's "eddication," and considered it an asset to the gang.

apparently coming out of a snowdrift a short distance from the trail. It was, of course, a dugout covered with snow from which the smoke came, and the officers and their Indian friend were cold.

"Stop here," said Tilghman to Bearclaw. "I'll go in and see those folks."

He probably intended to ask if he and his companions could get warm and perhaps stay the night, since evening was coming on.

As he approached the dugout there was no sound or sign of anyone. He pushed open the door. The interior was dark, except for flickering flames from a few blackjack logs in the open fireplace opposite the door. One man sat near the fire, a rifle across his knees.

"Howdy," said Tilghman. He got a grunt in reply.

The deputy walked the length of the room to the fire. As his eyes adjusted themselves to the darkness he saw that both sides of the rather long dugout room were lined with bunks, curtained with burlap. It was a typical cow camp with accommodations for fifteen or twenty cowboys.

Then, as he stood before the fireplace, holding his hands out to the warmth, Tilghman saw, from the corner of his eye, something else.

From behind the burlap curtains of several of the bunks, rifle or revolver barrels peeped out, *all aimed at him.*

In that moment he knew that he had walked, with no warning, right into the outlaw hideout. What happened in those next few minutes proved the caliber of a man Bill Tilghman was. A fool, or a man with less than perfect control of himself, might have leaped for the door, or tried to draw his guns. In either case he would have been blasted to death, for he was covered by half a dozen weapons, in the hands of murderous men.

But not a muscle of Tilghman's face, or a flicker of his eyes, showed that he had any inkling of the situation.

He spoke, and his voice was that of a man with an infinitude of time, and no pressing concerns of any kind.

"How far is it to Bee Dunn's ranch?" he asked the man by the fire.

"Find out for yourself," growled the man.

Tilghman rubbed his cold hands together and stamped his feet. He had forgotten all about asking shelter for himself and his friends. Only to get out of this place alive!

Yet he showed not a trace of haste, nor did he make one false motion. As if he had all the time that was to come, he continued to stand there, warming his hands, knowing that bandit fingers were crooked on triggers, itching to press them and send a death volley into his back.

His very calm seemed to hold them. For a few minutes there was a complete silence, broken only by the crackle of the blazing logs and the howl of the wind in the fireplace chimney. And every second of that time seemed an eternity to Bill Tilghman.

"Well, I reckon I'd better be getting along," he said presently.

His mind was asking: Why don't they shoot, and be done with it?

"I reckon you'd better," said the man by the fire, in the same surly tones.

Very politely, Bill Tilghman thanked him. Then, turning, he walked toward the door.

Without question it was the longest walk he ever took. At every step he expected the fatal blast, the volley of bullets that would tear him to pieces, and fling him, a bleeding corpse, on the dirt floor of the dugout.

But he was an old poker player, schooled in keeping any trace of emotion out of his face. Without a sign of hurry he paced toward that far door. In some of the bunks, as he passed, he could even hear the low breathing of the inmates. Not once did he look back.

When would they pull those fatal triggers? Were they cruelly allowing him to get as far as the door, only to kill him at the last instant?

He reached the door. Slowly, very slowly, as if reluctant to leave the warmth of the interior, he opened it. As deliberately he stepped outside, and closed it carefully behind him.

Not a shot had been fired!

Now, Tilghman acted. No sooner was the door closed than he

sprang back and whipped out both revolvers. There was no rush from inside to open that door.

Keeping his six-shooters ready and his eyes on the door, he began to back away as rapidly as he could through the snow, toward the waiting wagon.

"Get out of here fast!" he said to his companions as he vaulted in. "That dugout's swarming with outlaws!"

Bearclaw, the Indian driver, needed no other prompting. His whip cracked, and the horses surged forward. Rapidly the wagon rolled away from that place of deathly peril.

Bill Tilghman's superb courage and self-possession had saved him when nothing else in God's earth could have done so.

Once clear of the ranch and its venomous crew, Tilghman directed Bearclaw to drive directly for Pawnee instead of heading for the Bee Dunn place. There he found another deputy, John Hale, and together they formed a posse. But already it was night, and bitter cold. They could not move until daylight the following morning.

As Tilghman, Hale, and their men rode up to the dugout ranch house, next day, they saw the man with whom the deputy marshal held his bloodcurdling colloquy while the guns were pointed at his back. The man came toward them, and told them that he was Will Dunn, owner of the ranch, and added that the outlaws had left his place the previous night, very soon after Tilghman's visit.

There were eight of the outlaws, he said. They included Doolin, Dalton, Red Buck Waightman, Bitter Creek Newcomb, Bill Raidler, and three others—probably Little Dick West, Tulsa Jack Blake, and Charlie Pierce. When the wagon drove up, he said, the outlaws, not knowing who was in it, went into the bunks and let the curtains down. Tilghman, of course, was recognized by them as soon as he entered.

Dunn told Tilghman, and Tilghman believed him, that he had purposely shown the surly lack of hospitality and good manners because he was praying that the officer would leave at once, before he was murdered.

But there was more: As soon as Tilghman was out of the dugout, Red Buck, the man who liked to kill for the sake of killing, leaped out of his bunk, swearing that he was going to "kill that damn lousy marshal."

Doolin and Bitter Creek seized him and restrained him.

He cursed them for cowards.

Dunn said to him, "If you shoot Tilghman there'll be a hundred men on your trail inside of twenty-four hours."

And Doolin added something that showed the odd streak of something far better than mere criminality that was in him: "Bill Tilghman's too good a man to be shot in the back."

Tilghman heard that, and remembered it.

But the outlaws knew they had to move on, for a posse would infallibly return, looking for them. They left the Dunn place, with Red Buck still wildly cursing.

It was the second time he and Bill Doolin had clashed. The first time was when he wanted to ride off and leave Bitter Creek to his fate after the Ingalls fight, when the boss bandit shot off his hat and compelled him to return with the others to rescue their wounded mate.

Doolin by this time had come to despise Red Buck, but for the present he did nothing about it.

Winter passed and spring came. On May 4, 1895, Bill Doolin and his gang signalized the arrival of the vernal season by holding up a Rock Island train near the little town of Dover, a few miles north of Kingfisher. They robbed the express car and the passengers, getting several thousand dollars.

But this time the law was amazingly quick and efficient. At El Reno was stationed Chris Madsen, and as the wires hummed with news of the robbery, he acted like a born general. Commandeering an engine and a boxcar, he had the track all the way to Dover cleared by telegraphic order, loaded on the car himself, Deputies Prather and Banks, two Indian scouts, and three other men who could shoot and were game, together with their horses and weapons; and within minutes the one-car "special" was puffing northward as fast as the engineer could speed his engine.

They arrived at Dover only a few hours after the crime was committed. Evidently the bandits did not dream that anyone could trail them so quickly. They had camped not far from the scene of the holdup, in a glen below a low hill, to divide up the loot.

Just before sundown, to their utter astonishment and consternation, Madsen and his posse came riding over the hill.

There was a sharp, irregular rat-tat-tat of gunshots as the outlaws sprang to their horses, trying to reply to the first fusillade from the men who were riding down upon them. Two of the bandits' horses crumpled down, killed by the pursuers.

One was Tulsa Jack Blake's mount. The other was Red Buck Waightman's.

Both men ran for life, heading for a timber. Before Tulsa Jack could reach it, he was hit and fell, dying shortly after.

Red Buck was luckier. As he reached the edge of the woods Bitter Creek Newcomb—the very man he would have deserted at the Ingalls fight—wheeled his horse beside him and took him up behind. A moment later the bandits had disappeared in the gathering dusk, scattering in the thick timber.

Waightman was the coarsest, lowest-minded member of the gang. He was a horse thief before he joined Doolin, and admitted he had been a hired killer, saying he would "kill any man for five hundred dollars." On one occasion he was offered two hundred dollars for a murder. Turning away from the man who made the offer, he shrugged scornfully. "Kill him yourself" was all he said.

He was foul-mouthed and bad-humored, and more than once Doolin had thought of getting rid of him. The occasion came soon after the Dover robbery.

Mounted behind Bitter Creek, Red Buck as usual was making himself unpleasant with his constant cursing and complaining of other members of the gang. The next day they passed the cabin of an old backwoods preacher, and Waightman saw a horse that was to his liking.

Jumping off Bitter Creek's animal, he went to the corral, took a saddle and lariat from the pole-and-mud barn, and roped the horse.

As he did so the preacher came out of the cabin, and began to protest that the horse and saddle belonged to his son. Red Buck drew his six-shooter and with cold heartlessness that shocked even his companions, shot the old man to death. The name of the inoffensive old minister who was thus murdered does not even come down in history.

With his victim sprawled on the ground before him, Waightman threw the saddle on the stolen horse, bridled him, mounted him, and rode away.

A short distance on, Doolin stopped the gang and told them to dismount. Squatting on their heels in the cowboy manner, they carefully divided the loot, and Doolin meticulously counted out to each man, including Red Buck, his share and gave it to him.

Then he stood up and said to Waightman, "Now you get out! You're too damn low to associate with a high-class gang of train robbers!"[3]

Red Buck rose and glared. But few men could look Bill Doolin between the eyes and defy him, man to man. And here were four other men backing their leader's judgment, all fast with a gun. Sullenly Red Buck walked away, mounted his stolen horse, and rode off, ousted by his own fellows.

The Doolin gang had lost four members. Tulsa Jack and Oliver Yountis were dead, Arkansaw Tom in prison, and Red Buck ostracized. But those who were left still had plenty of gusto. Not long after Red Buck was driven out, three of them, Bitter Creek, Bill Raidler, and Charlie Pierce, committed a clever robbery at Woodward. Learning that a shipment of money had come in, they lay outside the town, rode in at night, kidnaped the express agent from his home, forced him to go to his office and unlock the safe, and took from it $6500. All this was done so quietly that

[3] More than one officer had a kind of admiration for Doolin as a worthy opponent. When he was ninety years old, two years before his death in 1944, Chris Madsen wrote a friend, Sheriff Lon Ford, of Ashland, Kansas: "I was told that after I and my posse had killed Tulsa Jack, some of the others [of the gang] were talking about killing me, but was told by Doolin that if they did he would kill the man that done so. That I had only done my duty as an officer, and he would not have a murderer in the outfit. If they got into a fight with the officers they might kill to get away, but they must not kill an innocent person. And he showed that he meant it." That was a tribute of one fighting man to another whom he respected though he was outside the law.

nobody in Woodward knew anything untoward was happening. Leaving the agent bound and gagged in his office, they rode slowly out of town, and then galloped gleefully back to the gang to tell their friends, and justly divide the loot with them. After that the gang disappeared once more.

That French crime expert who coined the phrase *Cherchez la femme* had nothing on the marshals of the Territory, and it was women who eventually brought an end to the Doolin reign of terror.

The outlaws presently began to find that one by one their various hideouts were being discovered and it was harder and harder for them to lose themselves.

The first break from the distaff side came when Mary Pierce, who ran the "hotel" at Ingalls, agreed to help the officers in return for not being arrested and tried on a charge of harboring the bandits. She it was who told them the exact location of the secret cave which long had been the Doolin headquarters. That favorite place thereupon ceased to be a haven.

Bill Doolin's wound from the Ingalls fight continued to bother him. He had married, in 1894, a girl named Edith Ellsworth, daughter of a minister at Lawton.[4] They had a baby, and during his Ingalls days, his wife had visited him there, so Mary Pierce knew her. But though Mrs. Pierce gave the officers all the information she had, they were at first unable to locate either the outlaw or his wife and child.

Following the Woodward robbery Doolin told his followers that they should disband for a while until the "heat" cooled down. The result was a general scattering, with an understanding that

[4] Zoe A. Tilghman wrote of this affair: "Doolin courted her as ardently as any girl was ever courted, and finally won her. While their love affair was progressing, Doolin ran more risks of death or capture when he went to visit her than he did in all his subsequent bandit career. Swimming his horse, he crossed swollen streams many times to see his sweetheart, and often rode silently through the night, avoiding the marshals only by the fraction of a minute, to visit the girl he loved." Mrs. Tilghman was not sure Edith Ellsworth knew at first that her suitor was an outlaw, "but even after it became known to her he was the leader of a bandit gang she held to him all the more."

the gang should meet at an agreed time at the ranch of Bee Dunn, a suspected cattle thief, who was a brother of Will Dunn and lived a few miles from him. What the bandits did not know was that Will Dunn, the rancher who sheltered them the night Tilghman walked into their power and out again, had agreed to help the law against them. They could not have chosen a more dangerous place for a rendezvous than his brother's place.

On the day scheduled, Bitter Creek Newcomb, Bill Raidler, Dynamite Dick Clifton, and Charlie Pierce met at the Bee Dunn ranch as agreed. But Doolin, their leader, did not appear. They scattered again.

Will Dunn, who now had been commissioned a special deputy, learned from his brother that they would return in a few days. He conveyed the information to Tilghman. The result was a trap, set for the outlaws.

With Tilghman and Thomas, and three possemen, Will Dunn went to his brother's place and the officers showed the rancher a warrant charging him with cattle theft and the harboring of outlaws. At the same time Will Dunn revealed that he was an officer and advised his brother to co-operate, to save himself. Bee Dunn thought it over, and agreed.

His house was somewhat more pretentious than his brother's dugout, being a two-story frame building, with two rooms on the ground floor, and a single room on the second floor, lined with bunks. A severe hailstorm had recently broken the glass of the windows on the east side, and they were boarded up temporarily.

Within the house, by the windows on the west side, Tilghman, Will Dunn, and two of the possemen hid themselves to watch. Since the east side was blind, being boarded up, a rifle pit was dug outside the house there, and in this Thomas, Bee Dunn, and the third posseman lay.

It was a long and weary wait. Two days and nights passed, with no results. The men began to wonder if the outlaws would turn up after all.

Then, on the third night, they heard the sound of horses' hoofbeats approaching in the darkness. There was no way to know how many bandits were coming. As it turned out, only Bitter Creek and Charlie Pierce were riding up, but it might have been the whole band and the waiting officers were tense.

Now the horsemen were quite near the house. They halted and dismounted. Suddenly Heck Thomas called out:

"Surrender! You're surrounded!"

The outlaws did not even think of trying to mount again and flee. Instead, drawing their guns, they turned to fight.

From the rifle pit a Winchester flashed. Instantly the outlaws, game as men ever were, not knowing what odds were against them but wishing only to close with their enemies, charged toward where they had seen the orange streak of fire, shooting as they charged.

Heck Thomas and the others in the rifle pit were shooting, too.

Bitter Creek fell first.

Then Charlie Pierce sprawled forward, his head within a foot of the rim of the pit.

Both were quite dead. They had shown nerve to the last, preferring death to being taken.

In some manner Dynamite Dick and Bill Raidler received a warning of the trap in which their comrades were killed. They were to have joined the others at the Bee Dunn place, but instead they separated, each trying to find a hiding place.

It was Dynamite Dick's great ill fortune to blunder right into three deputy marshals, Steve Burke, W. M. Nix, and W. O. Jones, at a country store between Pawnee and Perry, where they had stopped for lunch.

Burke recognized the outlaw when he rode up to where the deputies' horses were tied. At the same moment the bandit knew he had made a terrible mistake.

Guns were out and shooting, but the deputies had the advantage of being first to draw. Dynamite Dick fell with three bullets in him, one in his gun arm, one in his hip, and the third in his lungs. He was taken to Perry and then to Guthrie, where he died in jail from pneumonia caused by the lung wound.

Very shortly after this a friendly Indian brought word that Bill Raidler was hiding out near the Sam Moore ranch, just below the

Kansas line and twenty-five miles northeast of Pawhuska in the Osage reservation. Tilghman and Thomas went to get him.[5]

The Indian had reported that Raidler hid out in the hills during the day, but in the evening went to the small log house of the Moores, to eat. On September 7, the two marshals arrived at the ranch, talked to the rancher and his wife, and prepared to take the outlaw who was a college graduate, a quoter of poetry, the devoted friend of the dead Bitter Creek Newcomb.

They were told by Moore that Raidler habitually put his horse in the corral before coming in for supper. The officers posted themselves, therefore, in the corral.

Evening came, and the waiting deputies heard a horse coming. A little later Raidler appeared, put his horse in the corral, and started toward the house. Tilghman, standing by one of the corral posts, ordered him to throw up his hands. Later, Tilghman was quoted as saying:

"Did you ever see a dog creep stealthily up on a cat in the sun, and suddenly bark, and that cat would spring up in the air, with its back arched and spitting fire? That's the way Little Bill [Raidler] acted. When I shouted he went up into the air as if he'd been thrown from a springboard, and as he went he pulled a six-shooter in each hand, and he shot at me before he hit the ground. I never saw a man draw and shoot so quickly before."

But Tilghman was the better shot. His Winchester spoke twice, and Thomas also fired. Tilghman received a shoulder wound, but Raidler fell, shot through the body.

He was taken to Elgin, Kansas, just a short distance north, for medical treatment, and then to Guthrie, where the bullet was

[5] Bill Tilghman and Heck Thomas were boon campanions, worked on many cases together, and loved to "rib" each other. Chris Madsen told of one time when Thomas got the joke on Tilghman. There had been a brush with some Mexican outlaws, in which Tilghman received a slight wound in one leg. Said Madsen, "Heck Thomas told Bill [Tilghman] he did not get the wound fighting but when he was running away. Bill showed that he had been shot from in front. Then Heck told him that he was running so fast getting away that he ran into the bullet after it had passed him." It brought a roar of laughter in which Tilghman, who was never known to step back from any danger, laughed as heartily as anyone. "They were both good men," said Madsen. "They never came any better than those two."

removed from his body. It had grazed one of his lungs, and his wound was believed by the physicians to be fatal. But the educated bandit was a tough little pine knot of a man. He, who once had been expected to die of tuberculosis, won this second battle with his lungs, and lived to serve a term in the penitentiary at Columbus, Ohio. He was sentenced to twenty-one years—no mention being made of the Seaborn murder at Southwest City, Missouri—but he was pardoned after a few years, through the influence of Bill Tilghman. Later he married and lived for ten years after his release from prison.

In the penitentiary Raidler met another inmate, William Sydney Porter, later to become famous as one of the world's greatest short story writers under the pen name O. Henry. They were joined in prison presently by another bandit, who turned writer, Al Jennings, and the three became friends. O. Henry began his real writing career in prison and some of his best stories came from the reminiscences and characters of these two men.

The country was becoming more settled, and the marshals were gaining in numbers and acuteness. With the outlaws it was like the childhood rhyme of the "Ten Little Indians"—one after another they were being picked off.

There now remained four of the original Doolin gang: Bill Doolin, Bill Dalton, Little Dick West, and Red Buck Waightman. Red Buck, of course, had been thrown out of the outfit, but he still had to pay for his crimes.

First of this quartet to go was Bill Dalton, and a woman was the direct cause of his fall. He had married a girl in California, and they had a child. In vain the officers had tried to trace this woman, believing she would lead them to her husband. But Dalton had taken a deserted ranch house about thirty-five miles west of Ardmore, where he remained with his family so secretly that for a long time the deputies were completely baffled.

Then, one day in September, Mrs. Dalton and another woman from a neighboring ranch drove in a buggy to Ardmore for groceries and supplies. The "supplies" included a case of liquor which Dalton had ordered, and which came by express. It was illegal to bring alcoholic beverages into the Territory, and officers had received word of this shipment, although they did not know for whom it was intended.

They were watching when the two women came to the express office and asked for the consignment, and arrested them. Even then Mrs. Dalton was not known by her true name, nor was her connection with the much wanted outlaw suspected. But when she was brought into court to be arraigned for having the liquor in her possession, someone in the courtroom recognized her as Bill Dalton's wife.

At this the other woman was questioned closely. She broke down and told where the outlaw was hiding. Mrs. Dalton mercifully was spared the experience of seeing her husband killed.

Saddling up, a posse led by Deputy Loss Hart rode out to the ranch. They reached it September 25. Dalton did not have the flair of his brothers, and his death was almost an anticlimax. When he saw the officers ride up, he jumped from a window in an effort to escape. Hart's Winchester came to his shoulder and the rifle spoke—once. The last of the outlaw Daltons plunged forward to the ground, killed by that single shot.

His body was hauled to Ardmore in a wagon and delivered to his wife, who was released from custody. She and her baby soon left for California, from which she originally came, to live with relatives and try to forget.

Three of the outlaw band were still at large. Bill Doolin had not been located, and Little Dick West, the deadly little man who refused to sleep under a roof, likewise had disappeared.

Red Buck Waightman, the third of the trio, and the most inhuman member of the gang, had been up to his old tricks, and the Territorial marshals ran into a piece of luck with him. Chris Madsen, in the southern part of the Territory, received in September a communication asking for a conference. It was signed by a Texas Ranger.

Madsen at once met the man and found that he was one of a party of that force, which had traced two outlaws from Texas, where they had killed and robbed a man on the road, north into the Territory. One of the men they were after they knew—his name was Beckham and he once had been a member of a sheriff's force in Texas, but went bad. The other they did not know, but from the description they gave, Madsen at once concluded he was Red Buck Waightman.

The Rangers were in a position of some little embarrassment. "We really have no business here," said their leader in a polite drawl. "Y'all know, and so do we, that us Rangers have no authority in the Territory."

Madsen thought for a minute. "I can fix that," he said. "I'll just deputize the whole bunch of you as my posse. That will give you any kind of authority you need."

The Texans considered this a highly excellent solution, and with Madsen they resumed the trail they had been following. In Comanche County, in the southwest part of the Territory, they "jumped" the two men they were after. Texas shooting proved as proficient as advertised. Beckham, the former undersheriff from the Lone Star State, was killed in the running fight, and Red Buck was believed to be wounded.

"We got our man," said the Rangers to Madsen. "We'll receipt for Beckham and take him back with us. The other fellow belongs to you."

Madsen nodded. Red Buck *did* belong to the Territorial marshals, and this form of interservice courtesy he could appreciate as much as the next man. The Rangers departed, amid mutual expressions of good will all around.

But meantime Red Buck once more had disappeared.

Madsen, with a new posse, took up the pursuit. The deputies wanted the killer very badly, because they knew his murderous tendencies and that he had to be stopped before others were slaughtered by him. The trail led north toward Arapaho, in the Cheyenne country. There, on October 2, 1895, they located through an Indian scout the dugout in which Red Buck was hiding.

Carefully the dugout was surrounded, the officers with their guns ready. After a time Red Buck came out, to get a bucket of water.

One look of surprised recognition, the bucket was dropped, and out came the man's deadly revolvers.

But Madsen and his deputies were taking no chances. Knowing

that he was perhaps the most desperate member of the entire gang, they fired before he could pull a trigger.

Red Buck went down, shot through by several bullets. He was dead when he hit the ground.

But where was the boss bandit, Bill Doolin?

He seemed to have vanished, nor could the authorities locate his wife and baby, of whom he certainly was very fond.

Again women were the key to the solution of a perplexing mystery. It was through Mary Pierce, turned informer, that the first line on him came. And that line was through his wife.

Mrs. Pierce had received a letter from Mrs. Doolin, asking her to mail a certain ring she had left at the hotel in Ingalls, with instructions to address it to "Mrs. Will Barry, Burden, Kansas." This the Pierce woman did—and immediately reported it to the officers.

It appears that Doolin was trying to reform and cut loose from his past. Since he left them he had not communicated with any of his band. Instead he went up into Kansas, bought a farm near Burden under the assumed name Will Barry, and to it took his wife and two-year-old baby son.

Unfortunately for his good resolutions, a criminal past cannot be so easily shed. Society demands payment for crimes committed, however sincere the repentance of the criminal.

And now began a strange personal story.

Both Bill Tilghman and his arch-quarry, Bill Doolin, were, without question, remarkable men. Between them, in spite of their life-and-death duel of hunter and hunted, there was a sincere streak of mutual admiration.

Doolin it was who saved Tilghman from being shot by Red Buck in the Dunn dugout that wintry day the previous January, with the remark "Bill Tilghman's too good a man to be shot in the back."

This Tilghman knew—it was related to him the following day by Will Dunn. And he also knew that his adversary was one of the most dangerous men in the world, who would shoot it out if given the slightest chance rather than surrender.

In spite of this, he announced that he was going to bring the outlaw in singlehanded. Other officers protested, saying it was death for one man to go alone after Doolin. But Tilghman, remembering the episode in the dugout, was determined.

"If a posse goes, there will be shooting and Doolin will be killed," he said. "He saved my life once. He's got to be brought in, but I want to take him alone—and alive."

Nothing could dissuade him, so at length Marshal Nix rather unwillingly let him go, giving him a federal warrant for Doolin which could be served anywhere in the United States.

For this expedition Tilghman attired his tall frame in a very different style of apparel from what he customarily wore. He donned a long-skirted Prince Albert coat, and a derby hat, and assumed the character of a traveling preacher. Under the Prince Albert, of course, were his six-shooters in their holsters, and he carried credentials that would gain for him co-operation from postmasters and other federal officials.

At Burden the "minister" at first was unable to locate the "Barrys." But after a little inquiry, he learned that a certain Mrs. Barry was getting her mail at Winfield, a town not far away. He therefore traveled to Winfield and there enlisted the help of the postmaster.

Through this official he learned that Mrs. Barry was regularly receiving letters from Eureka Springs, a small spa in the extreme northwestern part of Arkansas. The letters bore the return address of Will Barry.

Bill Doolin still suffered periodically from the leaden ball at the base of his skull, which sometimes brought on seizures, and also produced a condition akin to rheumatism. He had gone to Eureka Springs for the baths, hoping to derive some help from them.

At once Tilghman took a train for Eureka Springs, arriving there the morning of December 5, 1895. After registering at a hotel, he went to one of the bathhouses, to enjoy a bath and relax before he began a serious hunt for his man.

To his astonishment, as he walked into the place, he recognized Bill Doolin.

Tragedy could have occurred at that stark moment. But Bill Doolin was reading a newspaper, and besides he had never seen

Tilghman in anything but a plainsman's hat and garb, so the derby hat and Prince Albert coat, if he casually noticed them, did not register with him.

At once Tilghman averted his face so that a second look would not reveal his identity, and stepped quickly into the bath booth assigned to him. There he took out a six-shooter, examined it, and walked out of the booth directly toward the outlaw.

Doolin was sitting on a couch, with his newspaper. His first warning that his greatest adversary stood before him was when he heard the marshal's voice.

"Bill, you're under arrest," said Tilghman.

In amazement the outlaw glanced up from his paper. "What do you mean?" he asked.

Then he recognized the man who was speaking to him.

With a bound he was on his feet, reaching for a revolver that he carried in a holster under his left armpit. Tilghman grasped his gun arm by the sleeve of the coat, and thrust his own pistol muzzle against the other's side.

Calmly, without excitement, though he was straining to hold his man, he said, "I remember what you did for me in the Dunn ranch dugout, Bill. Don't make me kill you."

They were both powerful men and for a few moments Doolin continued to try to reach the revolver, his gun arm held by Tilghman's grip on his sleeve. Then the sleeve began to rip.

"Good-by, Bill," the officer gasped.

Doolin, looking him in the eye, saw it was death if he resisted for another instant.

"You win," he said.

Tilghman disarmed him and took him to the hotel to pack up his things. Among the articles there was a small cup, of a child's size.

"Yours?" he asked.

"Yes," said Doolin. "I bought it for my baby."

It made a deep impression on Tilghman, who was fond of children. He felt that a man who had such affection for his child could not be all bad.

"I'll see that the baby gets it," he said. And then he added, "I believe you'll keep a promise, Bill. If you give me your word that you won't try to escape, I'll take you back to Guthrie without humiliating you by putting the handcuffs on you."

Doolin gave him a look of gratitude. "I wouldn't go back on a trade like that," he said. "I promise."

So Doolin, the boss bandit, rode back to Guthrie sitting by his captor, chatting in a friendly manner. Few on the train dreamed the famous outlaw and equally famous gun-fighting lawman were there side by side, talking like two old friends. They exchanged experiences, and Doolin told much of the history of his band, now all but wiped out.

"You almost got us that time," he would say, and describe an occasion when the deputy posse narrowly missed him and his men. Or, "We were watching you from the woods on the hill," as he related another episode. "We really had you fooled, didn't we?" He could even laugh, and so could Tilghman, over these reminiscences.

But if the passengers on the train did not know the eminence of the personages with whom they were riding, word had gone on ahead that Doolin was captured, and five thousand people were at the station at Guthrie to see him. Police and deputy marshals had to clear a path for the outlaw and his escort.

One woman exclaimed, "Why, Mr. Doolin, you don't look so terrible. I believe I could have captured you myself."

Doolin smiled. "I'm sure, lady, that I believe you could," he said with a twinkle.

In the Guthrie jail the outlaw talked freely of his past career, giving little side lights on his men, almost all of them now dead. He had, at one time, planned to rob the bank at Guthrie, he said, but did not do so when he found "my old friend Halsell kept his account there." He was speaking of Oscar Halsell, owner of the HX Bar Ranch, for whom he once worked and with whom in his pre-bandit days he had been a favorite.

At another time he told the story of the Red Buck episode in killing the old preacher, and how he threw him out of the gang. "That dog wasn't fit to black the boots of a respectable train robber," he said.

Asked why he prevented the killing of Tilghman at the Dunn ranch, the prisoner said, "It just wasn't my idea of how an officer should be killed—not that I love you fellows any too well." And he grinned.

He was in prison, facing robbery and probable murder charges, but Bill Doolin seemed perfectly serene. And with good reason. He did not intend to stay long in jail.

Highly gifted as a talker, he fascinated all about him. He made a special friend of the jailer, a rather simple-minded fellow, even drawing a map for him, showing where he had buried some treasure near the town of Mulhall—but omitting to put in the final key to locate it.

After a time he began to complain of being ill, and the sympathetic jailer, knowing the history of his head wound and its effects, did what he could for him. On a cold night early in January 1896, Doolin called the jailer to his cell. He was clinging to the bars, as if very weak, and talked in a voice so low and husky that the turnkey leaned close to make out what he was saying.

Like a flash Bill Doolin's hand went through the bars and snatched the jailer's pistol from its holster. A few minutes later the foolish turnkey found himself locked in Doolin's own cell, while the outlaw, with the keys, liberated all the prisoners in the jail.

Most of those who thus escaped were quickly recaptured. But Doolin, in the outskirts of the town, stopped a buggy in which rode a young couple "out sparking," made them get out, unhitched their horse, and rode away bareback. It was many long weeks before the officers heard of Doolin again.

One aftermath of this daring escape was the arrest of Rose Dunn, alias the Rose of the Cimarron. Since Bitter Creek's death she had nothing to do with the outlaws, but it was feared she might in some way communicate with the leader of the band. To Bill Tilghman fell the distasteful task of arresting her at the home of her parents, who had located on a claim not far from the Halsell ranch in Payne County. It was not a job of which the brave marshal was proud, but he followed orders and did it.

Rose was very young—hardly twenty at this time. But she had been, without any question, a consort of outlaws, and she pleaded guilty to a charge of being an accessory to crime.

"That girl has no business being in any jail," Tilghman had snorted. The court gave her a light sentence in the institution at Framingham, Massachusetts, where Cattle Annie and Little Breeches had preceded her. In a few months she was released and returned to the West. Because of her charm and good conduct the officers admired her and were glad when she married and had a home and children.[6]

But "Seek the woman" was still the motto of the marshals on the trail of Bill Doolin. Since the outlaw had escaped prison once, it was recognized that he would never surrender again, unless he was helpless, and the men who went after him would do so at extreme risk of their lives.

Mrs. Doolin had left the Burden, Kansas, farm with her child and returned to the Territory, where it was learned she had gone to live with her father, the Reverend Ellsworth, near Lawton. There, if anywhere, Doolin might be expected to appear.

A round-the-clock watch was set on the place, with Indian scouts assigned to the task. Late in June came the first word. Bill Doolin, drawn by the irresistible magnet of his love for his wife and baby, had appeared at his father-in-law's home.

Heck Thomas, with a small posse, was assigned to take the outlaw. On August 25, 1896, they closed in on the house where the Doolin family was reported to be staying. Some discreet inquiry in the neighborhood had disclosed to the marshal that their outlaw quarry was planning to take his wife and child and get out of the country for good, perhaps to Canada or Mexico. Clearly it was now or never if they were to capture their man.

As they neared the house the officers found a wagon, already loaded and outfitted for a long trip, with a team hitched to it, and

[6] In his later years Chris Madsen kept in touch with her. In a letter he wrote October 8, 1942, he spoke of an effort to get her to Hollywood to play a role in an outlaw film. She refused, for which he applauded her. "Rose was considered to be about the finest looking girl in Oklahoma in her days but she was wild and romantic," he concluded his letter.

a riding horse, saddled and tethered to a front wheel. They were not a minute too soon.

It was night, but the moon was shining brightly. The men took stations where they could command with their guns both the house and the wagon.

Almost as soon as they reached their various positions the door opened, and Doolin appeared. He had allowed his beard to grow, to disguise himself, but Thomas immediately recognized him. Behind the outlaw came his wife with the sleeping baby in her arms.

By so small a margin did Bill Doolin fail to make his getaway.

He carried a Winchester in the crook of his arm, and he kissed his wife and baby, then helped them into the vehicle. Next he turned to get the saddle horse and mount it.

At that moment Heck Thomas stepped into view from the shadows of some trees and bushes where he had been standing.

"Drop your gun and hold up your hands!" he shouted.

For answer the outlaw swung his rifle around and fired—missing.

But Thomas was ready. The heavy roar of the shotgun echoed once, twice, as the officer emptied both barrels.

Down, death-stricken at last, Bill Doolin measured his length on the ground, his body riddled by twenty-one buckshots.

With a heartbroken wail his poor wife jumped from the wagon and threw her arms about his neck.

But he was already dead.

The officers were sympathetic. They took the body to Guthrie, and thousands viewed the remains of the great outlaw in the morgue. Hundreds more, including most of the deputy marshals who had so long hunted him, attended the funeral.[7]

[7] As to the fate of Mrs. Doolin, a fine woman who was loyal to her husband and deserved better things, Madsen had this to say: "[After Doolin's death] Bill Tilghman and I passed through Stillwater and talked to Doolin's wife. She then had a baby with her. That same boy, now nearly fifty years old, a great big fellow looking just like his father, called on me about a year ago [1941] to learn something about his father whom he did not remember ever having seen. After Doolin's death in 1896 his widow married a preacher and the boy was adopted by him under the name of John Doolin Meeks, the last name that of his stepfather. The second time he called on me he had his family with him. He is now himself a preacher at Ponca City and a good citizen."

It was the end of the Doolin gang, and with it people believed the reign of outlaw terror was ended. But they were wrong. One member still remained to carry on the infection of crime—Little Dick West, who had disappeared like a wraith and would not reappear until he thought the time was proper.

9. The Hanging Judge Does His Duty

Throughout all this time the celebrated gallows at Fort Smith had been kept busy, the melancholy clatter of its fatal trap—dubbed "the Gates of Hell"—dropping men to their deaths at the end of a rope with sinister periodical frequency.

George Maledon, the undersized little hangman with the gloomy, blank stare, never had the opportunity to test his gibbet to its full capacity of twelve victims simultaneously. But he did well enough. Twice—September 3, 1875, and January 16, 1890—he plunged six men into eternity at one pull of his lever that released the fatal trap.[1] Three times he performed his distinctive services for five men at once, thrice he assisted four into the hereafter, and on four occasions three men simultaneously experienced Maledon's efficient, though fatal, ministrations.

[1] It has been claimed that Maledon's two six-man hangings were a record for the United States. But on December 28, 1862, at the conclusion of the Sioux outbreak in Minnesota, thirty-nine unfortunate Indians, for proved cruelties and murders, were executed *at once* on a specially built gallows at Mankato, Minnesota.

Between these major, or "wholesale," hangings, the diminutive hangman was by no means idle. Two executions at one time constituted no job at all for him, and single hangings were too numerous for comment. When he retired, in 1894, he had presided over the uncanny task of watching sixty condemned criminals march up his scaffold stairs, after which he caused them to descend again suddenly through the trap to their deaths.

There was good reason for this carnival of hangings. At first Judge Ike Parker's court had jurisdiction over the entire Indian Territory, which was filled with lawless men. Even when, after the opening of the Oklahoma Territory in the central part of the state, the Fort Smith tribunal handled only cases from the eastern part, known still as the Indian Territory (or Indian Nations), it was dealing with the worst of the population.

One example of the conditions and crimes, some of them of the most degenerate variety, with which the officers of the eastern district had to cope gives an idea of the type of criminals in that area, and because of its singularly flesh-crawling sequel, is worth briefly reciting.[2]

On April 20, 1882, two Negroes, named Henry Loftus and Martin (Bully) Joseph, made arrangements with a white man, Bud Stephens, a fugitive horse thief from Texas, to go with them to steal some horses in the Chickasaw Nation.

Stephens, in escaping from Texas, brought with him a sixteen-year-old white girl, quite pretty, twenty years younger than he, who had run away from home with him over the protests of her parents. They lived together in a cabin in the Arbuckle Mountains and set themselves forth as married, although no marriage between them had occurred.

The Texas horse thief took his youthful mistress along when they went on the horse-stealing expedition. She carried a basket of food, for a lunch, and the three men left her beside a brook in a pleasant spot, while they went down into a ravine to round up the animals they had seen. They were some distance away from the girl, and engaged in running the horses into a rope corral, when Loftus shot the white man in the back, killing him.

[2] For this story I am indebted to S. W. Harman's *Hell on the Border.*

Loftus and Joseph next rode back to the girl and told her that her husband had fallen from his horse and was seriously injured. He wanted her to come to him, they added.

She did so. They took her to a sequestered place and there, pulling her from her horse, both of them violated her.

Now they were in a dangerous situation, for if the girl testified against them, both might be hanged, rape being an offense with a death penalty attached. The inhuman beasts therefore shot the poor weeping creature, and when they made sure she was dead they carried her into a narrow cavern in the rocks, at the far end of which was a deep pit or "well." Into the pit they dropped her body, and after it threw her saddlebags filled with clothes, a bed-quilt, and other identifying articles, and departed in haste.

Henry Loftus not long after, while drunk, told of the triple crime of a rape and two murders, to his brother, William Loftus, who was as law-abiding and hard-working as he was not. When Bully Joseph learned of this, he killed Loftus and left the country.

William Loftus notified officers, and the bones of Stephens were found where he was killed. Meantime Joseph was arrested and placed in the Fort Smith jail.

But according to the story of the surviving Loftus, and Bully Joseph's account also, Stephens had been murdered by Henry Loftus, now dead.

To prosecute the prisoner it was necessary to obtain evidence of his crimes against the girl. Deputy J. H. Mershon was assigned to this task. With a few men he accompanied William Loftus to the cavern, which led downward at a slanting angle, until at the end the rays of a lantern showed the "well" down into the bowels of the earth, some sixty feet deep.

As he peered down, Mershon jumped back.

"Great God!" he exclaimed. "That well is full of rattlesnakes!"

The rattlesnake has the curious habit of living in large colonies in "dens," for protection from both extreme cold and extreme heat. Down in that hole Mershon could see the curling forms of deadly reptiles, on ledges in the rocks.

But what was left of the murdered girl was in the bottom of the well. Who would go down after it?

One man, John Spencer, was brave enough to make the attempt.

A strong rope was tied about his body, under the arms, and the others in the posse "slowly lowered him into the dismal and foul-smelling sepulcher."

Down he went. Then suddenly they heard him cry out in horror: "Lift me out, for God's sake!"

They obeyed. In a few minutes he stood on the floor of the cave, pale-faced and shaken. He had seen along the walls the twisting bodies of huge serpents, swaying their heads back and forth or darting them in and out, and even the glitter of their eyes from the dim light above.

But Spencer was unhurt. A man of extraordinary nerve, he waited for a few minutes to regain his composure, and then said, between his clamped teeth, "Give me that lantern!"

Again he descended, lowered by the rope into the noisome depths. But this time he carried a lantern, and his six-shooter in his hands.

Once more the rattlesnakes, some of enormous size, darted their heads out, and angrily buzzed their warnings of death.

Spencer held the lantern out toward the head of the biggest, and taking advantage of the temporary blinding of the reptile by the light, thrust the muzzle of his revolver at its eye and fired.

The result was indescribably hair-raising. At the explosion of the gun, the lantern went out. In the same moment the snake which had been decapitated by the bullet flung its writhing body out and coiled itself about one of his arms.

In the darkness, with the serpent twisting and wrapping about his arm, Spencer could imagine loathsome creatures by the scores crawling, hissing, preparing to strike and send the deadly poison from their dripping fangs into him. Yet with incredible determination he lighted the lantern again, and told the men above to lower him onto the bottom.

His bravery was rewarded. The blast of the revolver shot, in the narrow space of the "well," so frightened the rattlesnakes along its walls that they drew back into the interstices and crevices between the rocks as far as they could get. Holding a grain sack, Spencer rapidly gathered up all the grisly remains that had once been a lovely young girl—her delicate bones, her clothes, the saddlebags, and other articles thrown by her murderers down into the pit. Then, tying the body of the still writhing rattler he had killed by a string to his wrist, he signaled to be brought up.

"When he appeared above the mouth of the well with one end of the great rattler attached to his wrist and the other wrapped about his neck, he presented an appearance that nearly caused a stampede among the posse."

But the corpus delicti had been secured. Bully Joseph was convicted. Before he was hanged, June 29, 1883, by the ever efficient Maledon, he made a full confession of his crime.

The case just cited was only one of many scores in that lawless area. Judge Isaac Parker, who sentenced the men whom George Maledon hanged, took note of the many and terrible crimes committed in his jurisdiction, the Indian Territory, and summarized the causes of this condition in his famous charge to the grand jury which indicted the outlaw Cherokee Bill, in the following words:

> The reason for it in our jurisdiction is, because we have had to contend with almost the whole earth—the criminals, at least, of all the country. It has been the custom for all these years that when a man committed a crime in an older state, or in any state, and he could get away from the officers, he would run to the Indian country. He became a refugee criminal. And while there are many good men . . . there are hundreds and thousands of others who are stained with crime, whose tendencies are corrupted by the crimes they have committed elsewhere, and it is with this corrupt element assembled from all the states of this Union that this court, and the juries of this court, have had to contend with. That is why the volume has been so great. That is why it has been said: "You convict so many men there; you must be cruel, you must be harsh, you must be tyrannical."

Later on, in that same charge, he enunciated his own personal theory and philosophy in dealing with crime:

> *It is not the severity of punishment but the certainty of it that checks crime nowadays.* The criminal always figures on the chance of escape, and if you take that away entirely he stops being a criminal. The old adage of the law, "Certainty of punishment brings security," is as true today as it ever was.

Out of an area like that, the eastern part of what is now the state of Oklahoma, at about the same time as the Doolin gang began its operations in the western part, another outlaw crew sprang up, for a time flashed across the scene in the Southwest, and came to its end with Judge Parker as a final arbiter in most of its cases.

It was called the Cook gang, from its leader, a mild-appearing ex-cowboy, Bill Cook. Of him, Harman wrote:

> Personally, he [Bill Cook] was not an aggressive appearing man, having rather the mien of a very ordinary cowboy, and the close observer of him would wonder that the government was ever compelled to use such extreme measures to bring him to a state of docility; yet he accomplished what the Fort Smith Chamber of Commerce could not—forced the railroad company operating between Fort Smith and Coffeyville, Kas., to run a day train between those two cities, as it became unsafe for valuable express matter, or even passengers, to travel over that route at night.

Cook's father, James Cook, was a Southern man who fought in the Union Army during the Civil War. After the war he went West and settled near Fort Gibson, where he married a quarter-blood Cherokee woman. She bore him two sons, William Tuttle (Bill) Cook, on December 19, 1873, and Jim, about four years later.

Both father and mother died while the boys were young, and they were brought up in an orphanage. When he was fourteen, Bill ran away, worked a couple of years on farms, then drifted to a cattle ranch, where he became a top hand. But he took to drinking, and from that to selling liquor to the Indians, which landed him in jail.

After serving a forty-day sentence for bootlegging, he tried to reform, even doing posse duty for law-enforcement officers. But presently his younger brother Jim got into trouble in the Cherokee Nation and fled to the Creek Nation to escape tribal justice. Bill Cook, not yet twenty-one, joined him and they became outlaws.

In a way it seems odd that Bill Cook should be the leader of the somewhat desperate men who gathered about him, some of whom were far more murderously inclined than he was. The one photograph of him that exists shows a face that appears sleepy rather than alert. He was five feet nine inches tall, with a light complexion and hair, light-blue eyes, and a mild manner. Yet he was the moving spirit and director of the gang. There is this footnote to his character, by Harman:

> He was not an inveterate horse thief . . . for, as he valued his life too highly to become a murderer and thus place his neck in a halter, so, too, he took little chances of inviting pursuers to his own lynching by violating the unwritten law of the plains, except . . . when immediate personal safety demanded.

And here arises once more an intricacy in the threads weaving the pattern of outlawry. Two who had felt the influence of Belle Starr helped, almost as if by an inevitability, in the organization and growth of Cook's band. They were Henry Starr, Belle's nephew by her marriage with her Indian husband, Sam Starr; and Jim French, next to the last of Belle's lovers, who at times called himself Jim Starr at her behest, and was ousted from her affections (and her bed) by the superior attractions of Jim July, her current consort when she was killed.

Others in the gang included Henry Munson, Lon Gordon, Curtis Dayson, Elmer Lucas, alias Chicken Lucas, Sam McWilliams, alias the Verdigris Kid, and Thurman Baldwin, alias Skeeter. Baldwin, who was very tall and almost ludicrously lean and skinny, got his odd name one day when he rode a horse in a match race such as were common in the cow country. His opponent in the race, looking over his cadaverous form, said scornfully that "he had not undertaken to ride against a muskeeter," and the name stuck.

All of these, including Bill Cook, were cowboys. But there was one who was never a cowboy, but who became the worst and most bloody-minded of the lot. His name was Crawford Goldsby, alias Cherokee Bill, and he murdered several persons, including his own brother-in-law, was twice sentenced to death by Hanging Judge Ike Parker, and at last died on the famous Fort Smith gallows—although in his case George Maledon did not officiate.

Interestingly, there existed a sort of interlocking relationship between the Cook gang and the even more notorious Doolin gang. Bill Cook knew the Daltons, and also Bill Doolin, and it was their example he followed in his banditry. Another link was a no-good named Ben Howell, who was kicked out of the Doolin gang early, "because he lacked sand." After that he went over to Cook, who tolerated him as a hanger-on. Howell was to play a baleful part in the final series of events that led up to Cherokee Bill's last murder, and finally put an end to that felon's career.

At first the Cooks began in a modest manner, robbing stores and express stations. But from this they graduated to train and bank robberies, and rose to their greatest height in 1894. A brief record of some of their crimes in that year gives an idea of their activity:

July 14, held up and robbed the Muskogee–Fort Gibson stage; July 16, robbed a Frisco train at Red Fork; July 31, robbed the Lincoln County bank at Chandler, killing J. M. Mitchell, a barber who sounded the alarm; September 21, raided the Parkinson store at Okmulgee; October 5 and 6, two holdups near Fort Gibson; October 10, held up and robbed a Missouri Pacific train at Claremore, and later the same day held up the agent of the Katy Railroad at Choteau, twenty miles away, and looted his safe; October 20, wrecked and robbed a Missouri Pacific train at Coretta, five miles south of Wagoner, wounding two passengers in a volley fired after the robbery was completed and they were riding off; October 25, held up and robbed three travelers between Vinita and Fort Gibson; November 9, help up the Schufelt store and post office at Lenapah, and killed Ernest Melton, a painter.

It is small wonder that the Cook crowd so impressed the people that at times the Doolin gang, a far better run and more sinister outfit, was almost obscured in the public mind.

Crawford Goldsby, better known as Cherokee Bill, by far the most vicious of the Cook gang, was, I believe, a psychopathic killer, who murdered at times in a sheer insane lust for blood.

His father, George Goldsby, was a trooper in the Tenth Cavalry, a Negro regiment, although Goldsby seems not to have been a Negro, being of mixed Mexican, white, and Sioux Indian descent. He married Ellen Beck, half Negro, a fourth Cherokee, and a fourth white, and their son Crawford was born at Fort Concho, Texas, February 8, 1876. A second son, Clarence, was born about two years later.

The eldest boy received some schooling, attending for a time the Catholic Indian school at Carlisle, Pennsylvania. But he did not take to study, soon returned to the Territory, and as rapidly got into trouble. His father was by this time dead, and he lived with his mother at Fort Gibson. There he had a quarrel with a Negro youth, Jake Lewis, shot him twice, left him for dead, and took to the Cookson Hills in the Creek Nation, to escape arrest. Lewis eventually recovered, but by that time Crawford Goldsby had met the Cook brothers, joined their gang, and become known for all time as Cherokee Bill.

In the early summer of 1894 a memorable event took place in the Cherokee country. After long negotiations, the government had purchased from the Cherokees their rights to the Cherokee Strip, which was opened to settlement September 16, 1893, with the great Cherokee Strip Run and its dramatic scenes.

Certain portions of the payment were reserved for the Cherokee tribal treasury, but a total of $6,640,000, known as "Strip Money," remained to be paid out in shares to all who could make legitimate claims to having the required one-eighth Cherokee blood to qualify. Individual payments amounted to $265.70.

The distributions were made amid scenes bizarre and lawless. With all that money being given out, sharpers, gamblers, bootleggers, highwaymen, even murderers, gathered from every quarter to defraud the Indians of their money. Weeks before the distribution, slick-talking salesmen passed through the country, with goods "ranging from thread and calico to household utensils, furniture and agricultural implements," urging the Indians to buy on credit —or "on the strip," as it was termed—payment to be made when they received their shares of the distribution. Prices asked often were ruinous, sometimes with high interest rates added, and "many homely habitations were graced with high grade musical instruments, sewing machines, and so on," which the Indians really did not need. Horses, cattle, and all kinds of personal property were sold on a similar basis. When the Cherokee treasurer arrived at each of the several points in turn where the distributions were made, the collectors were there with their stacks of bills, to take the top off the moneys the Cherokees received.

At every distribution point a circus atmosphere prevailed, with merry-go-rounds, dance halls, "cat wagons," and all the usual carnival devices to take money from the unsophisticated Indians. Through the crowds slipped pickpockets and many a Cherokee never knew where his funds disappeared. Liquor sellers, in spite of the laws, did a huge business. Gamblers labored night and day to "peel" the Indians at crooked poker, chuck-a-luck, loaded dice, and other skin games. There were many holdups, and even murders. One of those killed in a holdup was Mrs. Nancy Duncan, an aunt of Henry Starr, the bandit, and sister of Watt Starr, a much respected Cherokee tribal judge.

The first payment was made at Tahlequah, where more than $1,000,000 was distributed, beginning June 4, 1894. Since Cherokee Bill and both Cook brothers had enough Cherokee blood to qualify, they naturally wanted their $265.70 apiece. But the difficulty was that all three of them were wanted by the law. If they went in person to Tahlequah they might receive their payments, but they also might find themselves immediately thereafter occupying cells in the jail. None of them wanted to face fearsome Judge Parker in the Fort Smith court; and none of them wanted to be tried and punished by a tribal court, the alternative.[3]

Some fourteen miles from Tahlequah, near the former home of the Cooks, was an eating house and primitive hotel called the Halfway House. It was operated by Effie Crittenden, the estranged wife of Dick Crittenden, part Cherokee, who with his brother Zeke held deputy marshal's commissions. Working for Mrs. Crittenden as a cook was Bob Hardin, whose wife, Lou, was a half sister of the Cook brothers. Because of this connection

[3] There were frequent jurisdictional disputes between the white men's courts and the Indian courts. On more than one occasion Judge Parker himself yielded jurisdiction in purely tribal matters. Indian punishments were severe. Indian policemen were called Light Horse, and Indian courts whipped horse thieves—so many lashes for first offense—more for the second—death for the third. W. F. Jones, a deputy marshal, described the punishment: "The victim's hands were tied to a small tree, feet tied together, a fence rail placed between—long way. Indian fastened to rail—then a Light Horseman with a well seasoned hickory gave 25 lashes, then another gave the next 25, and so on, 150 lashes being the limit." Executions were by shooting. The condemned man stood by the tree, a white card marking his heart. Five Indian marksmen fired at an order. The card and the heart were riddled by the bullets.

Cherokee Bill and the Cooks stopped at the Halfway House rather than go on in to Tahlequah.

They debated the best way to get their allotments, and finally appealed to Effie Crittenden, asking her if she would go to the town and collect their shares. She agreed, having other business to do in Tahlequah, and after taking written orders from the three outlaws, departed on her errand.

When Mrs. Crittenden appeared before the tribal treasurer and presented the three orders, even though the men did not come in person, Ellis Rattling Gourd, the Cherokee sheriff, got the information he was looking for—that the outlaws were in the vicinity. Two days after Mrs. Crittenden returned to her home, he called together a posse of seven men, consisting of Dick and Zeke Crittenden, Bill Nickel, Isaac Greece, Sequoyah Houston, and two others, named Hicks and Brackett. With these he rode to the Halfway House.

Cherokee Bill and the Cook brothers were still there. They had received the money, and supposed its collection had passed unnoticed. The appearance of the posse, therefore, was a nasty surprise. But they did not intend to be taken. Leaping for their Winchesters, they opened fire from around the corners of the house, which was returned by the posse, and a brisk little battle took place in the late afternoon sunlight.

At the very first volley Jim Cook was severely wounded, his rifle being dashed out of his hands by a bullet from Dick Crittenden's gun, while other slugs struck his body, as he tried to shoot from around a corner.

But a moment later Sequoyah Houston, of the posse, was killed by Cherokee Bill.

With Houston's fall, Sheriff Rattling Gourd and four of the posse retreated, leaving the two Crittendens to fight it out with Bill Cook and Cherokee Bill. Darkness was falling, and as soon as they could escape, the Crittendens[4] did so, leaving the outlaws in possession of the field.

Bill Cook insisted on taking his wounded brother to Fort Gibson

[4] These were the same Crittendens who later were killed, October 24, 1895, by Ed Reed, Belle Starr's son, at Wagoner, Indian Territory. At that time they no longer held deputy marshal's commissions.

for medical treatment. With the help of Cherokee Bill, Jim Cook was conveyed to that town, and left in care of a physician, while the other two rode away to escape capture.[5] It was after this that the gang was mustered and began its career of crime briefly listed above; and after this also that Cherokee Bill turned morose killer.

During a gang holdup of a train at Nowata, he shot to death the station agent, a man named Richards. On another occasion, he murdered his own brother-in-law, George Brown, "for no other cause than that Brown's father, the owner of a hog ranch, had given Brown's wife, Bill's sister, a few more hogs than he had given him."

In killing Brown, Cherokee Bill exploded in a very frenzy of passion, pumping his body full of bullet holes after it was apparent that there was no life left in him.

The killing of Mitchell at Chandler also was generally ascribed to him, although he was never tried for it.

It was November 9 when Cherokee Bill and one or two others of the gang robbed the general store of Schufelt & Son, at Lenapah. The store was chosen for robbery because a post office was run in conjunction with it, and there was always money in the safe.

Boldly, in broad daylight, the bandits rode up to Lenapah from the south. They entered the store, and John Schufelt, the junior member of the firm, under the compulsion of a Winchester, opened the safe, which yielded several hundred dollars. But Cherokee Bill had a fancy for some new clothes. He compelled the store owner to go to the rear of the store, where garments were displayed and where also was a rack of guns with ammunition, giving him a chance to lay in a supply of cartridges.

[5] Jim Cook recovered and was tried in the Cherokee tribal courts for the killing of Sequoyah Houston. He was found guilty of manslaughter and sentenced to eight years in the Cherokee prison, escaped once, but was recaptured and served out his term. The odd thing about this is that Jim Cook did not kill Houston. At the time the deputy was shot dead Jim was lying helpless, his gun smashed and several bullet holes in his body. Since Bill Cook, according to Harman, never committed a murder, it could only have been Cherokee Bill who slew Houston. Jim Cook probably was tried under a tribal law that considered a man who was a party to a murder guilty, to a degree, of that murder. After his sentence was served no more was heard of Jim Cook.

Next door to the store, with a vacant lot between, was a restaurant which was in the process of being painted and wallpapered. While he fingered the goods, Cherokee Bill glanced out of a window and saw one of the painters, Ernest Melton, staring across at him from a glass door in the other building.

As if in sheer pique that he should be stared at in this manner, Cherokee Bill threw his rifle to his shoulder, fired, and Melton dropped dead. There was no logical reason for killing the painter, unless the outlaw also killed everyone else who saw him, because others besides Melton could identify him, nor did he seem particularly to care about that. The murder was a senseless exhibition of inhuman ferocity.

With a few shots fired as warning, the bandits rode away in the direction from which they came.

Cherokee Bill, of course, was positively known to be the murderer of Melton, and additional rewards were offered for him, until he was worth $1300 to anyone who took him, dead or alive. By this time, although he was not yet nineteen, the outlaw had grown into a bull-shouldered powerful man, six feet tall and weighing perhaps 190 pounds. His face showed both his Indian and Negro blood, being very dark, with wide cheekbones and jaw, thick lips, a low forehead, kinky hair, and eyes with a peculiar wild-beast glare in them at times, although on most occasions he seemed perfectly impassive.

Most men who were fast with a gun have been of the slender type, or at least rawboned in their muscularity. But Cherokee Bill, for all his bulk, was known to be so quick with his weapons and so ready to kill that he was the most feared desperado in the Indian Territory.

Nevertheless, the marshals were after him, and two deputies, W. C. Smith and George Lawson, searching through the rough country of the eastern part of the Territory, induced a man named Charles Patton, who personally knew the fugitive, to try to learn if Cherokee Bill was in those hills. Patton agreed to inform the deputies at Sapulpa, where they would wait for him, if he obtained any information.

He was one of the natives of the country, knew everyone, and could therefore move freely without exciting suspicion. Nevertheless, his errand, as he set out on horseback, was a perilous one.

Within a day or two, he actually stumbled on Cherokee Bill himself, together with Sam McWilliams, alias the Verdigris Kid. They were camping in a ravine in the remote wooded hills, deadly and watchful. They did not dream Patton was a spy. He dismounted, had supper with them, and remained with them until about nine o'clock that night, when he said he must "shove off," and they allowed him to ride away.

Had they known his errand they would have slaughtered him without compunction. But instead they became so friendly with him that before the evening was over Cherokee Bill confided to him that he had "got about $164[6] in a little holdup at Lenapah and had to shoot a fellow," and later gave Patton a locket he took from John Schufelt, whom he robbed the day of the murder, with an injunction "to be careful or it might get him in trouble."

Patton went directly to Sapulpa, met the deputies, told them where Cherokee Bill and the Verdigris Kid were hiding, and turned over the locket and information. This was important evidence in connection with the murder, and the law was more anxious than ever to close with the murderer.

A posse led by Deputy John McGill rode to the place Patton had described. Sure enough, Cherokee Bill was there, although now alone. There was some shooting, and the outlaw's horse was killed, but he scrambled into the brush, leaving his hat as a trophy. The posse did not follow him into the tangle in which he had disappeared—for reasons of discretion.

Months passed. At last Deputy Smith learned something that might be the desperado's weak point. Five miles east of Nowata lived Ike Rogers, a mixture of Cherokee, Negro, and white blood, who once was a deputy marshal but was considered a friend, even an intimate, by Cherokee Bill. One reason for this friendship was a girl named Maggie Glass, half Cherokee and half Negro, who was frolicsome and alluring, and had captured the outlaw's affections. The desperado, even when he was being hunted, was unable to prevent himself from taking the risk of frequent meetings with the girl, usually at Rogers' place.

[6] His share of the loot.

But Rogers was a man who would do anything for money, and Deputy Smith knew him. He encountered him at Nowata, and made a compact, on a promise to divide the reward, whereby Cherokee Bill was to be trapped. The girl, Maggie Glass, was the bait. Rogers was to invite her to his house, then send for Cherokee Bill. While the outlaw was there, completely off his guard, enamored by his feminine idol, Rogers and another man, Clint Scales, who also was in the plot, were to capture him.

Rogers carried out the plan, getting the couple together at his house January 29, 1895. It turned out to be a hair-raising experience.

In the first place, Maggie Glass was suspicious of Rogers, and though she came to spend the evening with Cherokee Bill, she warned her lover to be on the lookout for his host. The outlaw laughed at the warning, telling the girl that "if Rogers made a break he would shoot him in his tracks."

Scales arrived at the cabin, and Rogers, knowing the desperate character of his outlaw guest, played the generous host while he waited for a chance to catch Cherokee Bill off guard.

Once he suggested that the outlaw lay down his Winchester.

"That's something I *never* do," replied the desperado.

Next Rogers offered him some whisky doctored with morphine, which he had obtained from Smith, but Cherokee Bill refused to drink.

At supper the bandit took his place at the table, his back to the wall, his Winchester across his knees.

Later, while Maggie helped with the dishes, he played cassino with Rogers and Scales. The game must have had overtones of tension far greater than most sessions with cards, but it continued far into the night.

Maggie grew weary of waiting for her lover and went to bed with Mrs. Rogers, her aunt. The men played on, Cherokee Bill with his Winchester across his knees, Rogers and Scales with their weapons concealed.

At four o'clock in the morning they at last retired, and the outlaw shared a bed with his treacherous host. Even there he took his gun, lying with it beside him. Most of that night Rogers lay awake, hoping to catch Cherokee Bill asleep. But every time he stirred, the renegade would "instantly rise in bed, ready to use his Winchester."

The long night ended in a stalemate. By breakfast time it began to appear that Cherokee Bill would certainly escape, because neither of the other two men dared make the first move. Breakfast over, they sat for a time before a fire in the open fireplace, for the January weather was cold. To get rid of Maggie, Rogers sent her on an errand, to buy some chickens at a neighbor's.

After a time Cherokee Bill remarked that he would have to go. It was a tantalizingly desperate moment. Rogers suggested that he wait for Maggie to return, so he could say good-by.

At that the outlaw rolled himself a cigarette. He had no match, so he stooped over to get a light from the fireplace, turning his head away just an instant. That was the first and only mistake he made.

In that mere breath of time, Rogers seized a stick of firewood and struck him a terrible blow across the back of his head.

"I must have hit him hard enough to kill an ordinary man," he later said, "but it only knocked him down. Scales and I jumped on him but he let out a yell and got on his feet."

There followed a terrific struggle in the cabin. Rogers' wife seized the outlaw's gun, but Cherokee Bill, with his bull's strength, almost overcame both men who were wrestling with him. He was half stunned by the blow on his head or they might never have held him. At last, however, they managed to get handcuffs on him and he quit struggling and begged them to kill him or release him.

He was not yet through fighting. On the way to Nowata, Scales drove the wagon in which the prisoner rode, while Rogers followed on a horse, carrying a double-barreled shotgun loaded with buckshot. All at once Cherokee Bill, in some manner, broke his handcuffs apart and with a leap reached for Scales' gun.

"Scales had to fall out of the wagon to keep from losing his Winchester," Rogers related, "while I kept Cherokee covered with my shotgun."

After that, though he was now unshackled, the outlaw rode quietly the rest of the way to Nowata. Wrote Harman, in explanation of this:

Down in the Indian Territory men only draw their guns when they intend to shoot, and a citizen of that country, when a gun is drawn upon him, realizes on the instant that the weapon is in dangerous hands and though he might be heavily armed himself, he knows better than to make a movement after a weapon so long as his opponent has him covered. This fully accounts for the fact that Cherokee Bill remained riveted to his seat; he knew that his every act was being closely watched by Ike Rogers who rode silently behind him, with a loaded, double barrel shotgun.

The prisoner was delivered to Deputies Smith and Lawson at Nowata. Rogers and Scales received their share of the reward, while Cherokee Bill was taken to Fort Smith to stand trial for the murder of Ernest Melton.

As a digression, let us take a look at the ultimate fate of Rogers. His capture of Cherokee Bill was valuable, but the treachery he employed in achieving it turned the people of the country against him.

Rogers, according to a contemporary account, "was not a munificent provider, and had it not been for the supplies often brought to them by the reckless Cherokee Bill, when returning from his raids, they [the family] would often have suffered for the bare necessities. More than that, it is claimed, Rogers looked for opportunities and planned burglaries . . . and after divulging his plans to Bill, sat down to await his return, well laden with the fruits of his crime." Under the circumstances, public feeling can be understood.

Cherokee Bill's younger brother, Clarence Goldsby, was expected to avenge his brother, but at first the youth made no move. Rogers, a bullying sort of man, lived under an oppressive fear, which he wished to bring to an end. He attempted to pick a quarrel with Clarence, in order to have an excuse to shoot him. But the boy was taken away by friends and sent elsewhere.

Early in August 1898, Clarence Goldsby was serving as a guard for a goverment paymaster at Fort Gibson when Rogers sent him a notice that he was coming to kill him. The youth calmly waited on the station platform for the train in which Rogers was to arrive, and when the man stepped from the car—in which he had been riding and somewhat drunkenly boasting of what he intended to do—Clarence fired a single shot with his revolver, breaking the betrayer's neck and killing him.

Young Goldsby then dove under the train, and as several shots were fired at him, ran for the heavily wooded hills. Several men followed him, shooting, but he was so far ahead that none of the bullets brought him down.

The only one of the pursuers who was mounted was Deputy Smith. He was far ahead of the others, but when he came to a fence he dismounted and ran across a field to cut the fugitive off. But Clarence, "with exceptionally keen cunning, discovered the situation and ran back, mounting the officer's horse and rode away, much to the officer's discomfiture and chagrin."

The killer of Ike Rogers disappeared from the country, and no real effort was made to discover where he had gone and arrest him. In fact public sentiment was so strongly in his favor that it was freely stated that "as soon as quiet was restored and cool judgment prevailed, he could openly have returned, with perfect impunity."

Before Cherokee Bill arrived in the Fort Smith prison, Henry Starr had preceded him there. Starr, born December 2, 1873, at Fort Gibson, was a son of Hop Starr, half-blood Cherokee. His mother was only a quarter-blood, which made Henry more white than Indian.

Like all the young Indians in the feudist Starr clan, which was led by that fierce old patriarch Tom Starr, Henry Starr early learned to be an expert with weapons. He did not use liquor, tobacco, tea, or coffee, and he had an Indian's agility and endurance, and also an Indian's ability to find his way through a wilderness, live on roots, berries, nuts, and what game he could trap, and sleep wherever night overtook him, so that he could become independent of ordinary food sources, and correspondingly hard to locate.

In him was an innate streak of lawlessness. As early as June 1891 he was fined for "introducing liquor into the Indian Territory," and the following year, in February 1892, he was arrested on a charge of horse stealing, but released.

Starr was described as "five feet nine and one-half inches in height, had straight black hair and black eyes and a good-looking beardless face." Throughout his life he displayed a remarkable quality of making friends and keeping their friendship. He was courteous, acquired before his end an education which gave him an almost cultured conversational grace, liked to read good literature, and was a pleasant companion. Yet he was destined to span two generations of outlawry and die in the end, shot while holding up a bank.

One of the first men to come under Henry Starr's peculiar charm was Albert Dodge, a rancher living near Nowata, who gave him a job as a cowboy. Starr was a good enough cow hand, until in August 1892 he was again arrested for horse theft. This time he was released on bond, furnished by his cousin Kale Starr and J. C. Harris, the tribal chief of the Cherokees.

When he failed to appear for trial, the bond was forfeited, and his bondsmen offered a reward for his capture. "On the scout" now, for certain, and an outlaw even among his own people, Starr wandered about in the Verdigris Valley country. It was at this time that he first fell in with some of the men who later formed the Cook gang, notably Cherokee Bill and the Verdigris Kid; perhaps also Jim French.

It was at this time also that he committed his first and, so far as can be discovered, only homicide. A store at Lenapah and an express office at Nowata had been robbed, and because of his previous record Starr was suspected of the crimes. Since he was known to have worked for Dodge, two officers, Floyd Wilson, a deputy marshal, and an express-company detective, H. E. Dickey, rode to Dodge's ranch.

When they arrived, Starr was not there. In fact the rancher did not expect to see the young Indian, and it was a coincidence that Starr rode up while the officers were inside talking to Dodge. Suspicious that detectives were at the house, Starr rode past the windows, peering in to see who were there.

As he did so Dodge caught a glimpse of him. In spite of his friendship for Starr, he was a law-abiding man.

"There's the fellow you're looking for," he said.

Wilson ran out of the house as Starr rode away. He jumped on a horse, already saddled and bridled belonging to Dodge, and pursued.

To his surprise Starr suddenly halted and dismounted. Wilson did likewise. The two men faced each other not thirty yards apart, and in full view of the house.

There are two versions of what followed. Starr said that he offered Wilson the first shot, saying, "If you miss and I kill you it will be in self-defense." Wilson fired and missed, and Starr killed him.

To those watching from the house, however, the two men appeared to be parleying for some minutes. Finally the officer fired a shot, apparently over Starr's head to frighten him. At that Starr began shooting with intent to kill. Wilson's first shot was from a Winchester, but the shell became clogged in it, so he threw it down and drew his revolver. Two of Starr's bullets hit him, the second knocking him down. Then the outlaw walked over to him and shot him in the breast, killing him, the muzzle of his gun so close that the clothing of the prostrate man was burned by the powder.

Meantime Dickey, trying to follow, found that the horse he saddled and mounted did not want to go. The animal began to buck, and by the time he had it under control, Starr had remounted and gone. Wilson was dead when Dickey reached him.

Slaying an officer was a crime so serious that Starr knew if he were captured he might suffer capital punishment. He aided the Cook gang, then in formation, in one or two robberies, and then, on June 5, 1893, embarked on a bank robbery of his own, with his own gang.

With six men, Frank Cheney, Bud Tyler, Hank Watt, Link Cumplin, Kid Wilson, and a man known only as Happy Jack—all cowboys—he entered Bentonville, Arkansas, to hold up the People's Bank. In this raid Starr and Cheney drove in a buggy, in which were concealed the rifles of the group, with two riding horses led behind. All the others were on horseback, but strung out on the road to avoid attracting attention.

Starr chose 2:30 P.M. as the hour for his robbery, reasoning that a good deal of money would be in sight at that time, and also that it would be only six hours until dark, which would give his men a better chance for a getaway. Meeting behind the bank, the outlaws scattered to stations assigned them by Starr.

Tyler and Watt were posted between the bank doors and the horses. Happy Jack held the seven mounts. Cumplin stood watch at the front door, and Starr, Kid Wilson, and Cheney made the actual entry.

Cheney and Wilson leaped over the counter, while Starr held up six men who were in the bank and ranged them in a row against the wall. He intended to use them as a screen when he and his companions marched out of the bank.

But the town roused quickly, and citizens were armed and shooting by the time Cheney and Wilson, each carrying a sack of money, climbed back over the counter and indicated they were ready to go. Cumplin was wounded in the eye and body but still was shooting back at the citizens as Starr and the others came out.

One of the sacks, containing $11,000 in gold and paper money, was carried by Wilson. The other sack, though it contained only $900 in silver, was the heavier of the two, and the bandits compelled the assistant cashier to carry it as they backed toward their horses, shooting.

As the assistant cashier, with his load, walked toward the rear of the bank, he passed a door which opened into the office of the Bentonville *Sun*. Miss Maggie Wood, business manager of the paper and a lady of considerable determination, was standing just inside the open door as the banker passed. Reaching out, she seized him by the shoulders, and with the strength of an Amazon pulled him and the sack of money inside, then slammed and bolted the door before the outlaws could interfere or do much of anything except stare at this astonishing feminine intervention.

The bandits reached their horses and escaped, although a posse followed them for miles, until dark. Except for Cumplin, none of them was hit. Three or four citizens were wounded in the street fight, but none seriously.

The raid netted the robbers less than $1500 apiece, "trifling pay for such a desperate venture," as Starr said. Nevertheless, he married a girl named Mary Jones on his share of the proceeds, and took his bride to Colorado Springs, being accompanied there by Kid Wilson, another Indian, about his own age, and his closest pal.

Less than a month after the robbery, July 3, 1893, William Feuerstine, who lived at Fort Smith but was in Colorado Springs on business, saw the bandit on the streets and recognized him. Police, notified, discovered that Starr, his wife, and Wilson were registered at the Spaulding House as Frank and Mary Jackson and John Wilson, all giving their home address as Joplin, Missouri.

That evening Starr and his wife were arrested in the dining room of the hotel.

"Who do you think you've got?" the outlaw calmly asked the officers as he submitted to arrest without resistance.

"Henry Starr," one of the police replied. He then admitted his identity.

Kid Wilson did not go to the hotel. He was traced to a bawdy house, where he was captured without difficulty in one of the rooms with a girl.

A search of Starr's room disclosed a sack containing $1460 in paper money and $500 in gold coin, hidden under the pillow on which Mrs. Starr slept. The girl, only eighteen years old, was not held, but the two men were taken to Fort Smith to stand trial. Fourteen separate indictments, including one for the murder of Floyd Wilson, were lodged against Starr. He was convicted of that murder and Judge Parker sentenced him to hang by the neck until dead. But Starr did not hang. The date set for his execution, February 20, 1895, passed, and many other years came and went with devious happenings, before his time arrived at last.[7]

After Starr was in prison, sentenced to die, the Cook gang rapidly went to pieces. During the shooting which followed the robbery of the Chandler bank Chicken Lucas was wounded in the hip and captured.

The Creek Light Horse took the trail of the bandits, and caught

[7] The ultimate fates of the six men who helped Starr rob the Bentonville bank were as follows: Wilson was convicted of several robberies, went to prison, was paroled, and was killed when he went back into banditry. Link Cumplin joined the gold rush to Alaska, tried to hold up an express messenger, and was likewise killed. Happy Jack was shot to death by officers only a few months after the Bentonville robbery. Frank Cheney was killed by marshals a year after the robbery. Hank Watt also died with his boots on. Only Bud Tyler died, of natural causes, in bed.

up with three of them at the house of Bill Province, west of Sapulpa. In the battle that followed, the quite efficient tribal cavalry killed Lon Gordon and Henry Munson, and captured Curtis Dayson. Dayson and Lucas were tried before Judge Parker, the former being sentenced to ten years and the latter to fifteen, both in the prison at Detroit, Michigan.

Heavy rewards were offered for the gang members still at large, several persons including Province had been arrested for harboring them, and the country was growing too hot to be healthy. It seemed wise to depart for less fervid climes.

At this point Bill Cook made a bad mistake—about as bad a mistake as an outlaw leader could make. He took his men down into Texas, where they promptly ran afoul of the Texas Rangers, led by fierce-eyed, fierce-fighting Captain Bill McDonald.

On the way down into Texas the gang held up a German family named Beckley on the road to Tecumseh, robbed them, and, according to one charge, assaulted the eldest daughter, holding the father at bay with six-shooters while the act was committed. It gave the Territorial marshals a clue to their direction, and a wire was sent to the Texas Rangers to be on the lookout for them.

The Rangers obliged. Near Wichita Falls, Texas, there was a shooting flurry, and Jess Snyder and Will Farris were captured. Returned to Fort Smith, both of them were convicted of robberies and sentenced by Judge Parker to long prison terms.

Bill Cook and Skeeter Baldwin escaped from the Rangers that time, but they were really being hunted now. They separated, and Cook headed over into New Mexico, while Skeeter elected to try his luck in the arid mountain country of western Texas.

Hot on Cook's trail was Sheriff T. D. Love, of Burden County, Texas. He did not stop at the New Mexico state line, but crossed over and enlisted the help of Sheriff C. C. Perry, of Chaves County, New Mexico, with a posse. Clear across New Mexico they trailed Cook, by a broken place in the hoof of his horse which left a distinctive mark.

Cook thought he had shaken the officers off his track, and took a job as a cow hand on the Yates ranch, not far from old Fort Sumner, where lay buried Billy the Kid and two of his pals, Tom O'Folliard and Charlie Bowdre.

Early on the morning of January 11, 1895, Cook rose to feed the horses. As he came to the barn the officers stepped out and confronted him. He made no attempt to resist. Returned to Fort Smith, he was tried on twelve counts of robbery, convicted, and sentenced by Judge Parker to forty-five years in the federal penitentiary at Albany, New York.

Meantime, Skeeter Baldwin was still on the loose. His cadaverous figure finally was located in Clay County, Texas, south of the Red River, evidently heading back for the Indian Territory. Three Texas Rangers jumped him. They were Bob McClure, W. J. L. Sullivan, and W. J. McCauley, and one look at them was enough for Skeeter, although he was heavily armed. He surrendered and pleaded guilty to robbery before Judge Parker, who promptly sentenced him to thirty years in prison. When he heard that sentence, Skeeter made a heartfelt remark:

"Well, this is a hell of a court to plead guilty in."

Only three members of the Cook gang remained at large: Sam McWilliams, called the Verdigris Kid, George Sanders, and Jim French—who also had the distinction of being the last surviving lover of Belle Starr, except of course for Cole Younger, then still in the Minnesota penitentiary.

French did not go to Texas with Cook. Instead he hid out near Tulsa, which then was little more than a Creek Indian village, this being prior to the discovery of oil in its environs. Around that town were a number of hideouts formerly used by bandits, including the Daltons and Doolins, in which French could secrete himself. A lone wolf now, he had to plan his own forays on a less ambitious scale than when he had been a member of the Cook crowd.

Of the tough towns of the Territory, one of the toughest was Catoosa, which for a time was the railhead of the Frisco line. The arrival there of Colonel Thomas M. Reynolds, a Missourian who was brave enough to face the desperadoes and willing to shoot it out with them if it came to conclusions, somewhat changed the complexion of the place. Reynolds became mayor and chief law officer of the beautifully situated little hamlet, looking down upon the wooded bottoms of the Spunky River, and boasting, as an early account says, that "in the vicinity live some of the prettiest Indian girls ever seen."

But even Colonel Reynolds could not entirely tame the town. A typical episode of wild and woolly Catoosa was recounted by Charles Myers, conductor of a Frisco train which ran through the place, to S. W. Harman. One evening while his train was halted at the station, some drunken desperadoes began whooping and riding back and forth, "corn shelling," which meant shooting at the bunches of corn ears hung in front of the stores where feed was sold, until nothing remained of the corn except the husks which had been drawn back, the kernels being scattered far and wide for vagrant hogs or chickens to find the next day. About this time a solitary man rode in from the Spunky bottoms. To quote Myers on the ensuing events:

> With a yell, one of the revellers started for the new arrival, who had pulled up in front of the post office and dismounted. Immediately the "corn sheller" began shooting at the man, who was wrapping his lariat around the horizontal hitching post. The party attacked pulled his gun, and soon unhorsed the bad man and his load of whiskey with a well-aimed shot. No sooner had the man struck the ground than he bounded to his feet, and began pumping lead at the intended victim. One of his shots cut a deep furrow across the scalp, another passed through his right shoulder. The victim of the assault staggered forward and grappled with his assailant, his gun having fallen from his hand when the bullet entered his shoulder; he was practically helpless in the hands of the ruffian burning with alcohol. The "corn sheller" grasped his victim by the hair, pushed his head back over the hitch-rail, drew his murderous looking knife, *and deliberately cut the poor devil's head off,* and stuck it on a post. The murderer then picked up his own and his victim's gun, and started yelling down the street, shooting as he went; but before he reached the Lone Star Hotel John [*sic*] Reynolds' gun cracked and the side partner of the Verdigris Kid fell forward with a curse. He was not more than forty feet from the headless trunk of his victim.

Just what occasioned the seemingly causeless attack, Myers did not discover, nor did he learn the name of the murderer who was felled by Reynolds' shot. His train was pulling out and what probably was the culmination of a blood feud such as was prevalent in the country was never explained to him.

The episode illustrates the brisk and eventful lives that the citizens of Catoosa lived. In the spring of 1895 Jim French, needing money, decided to rob the store there of W. C. Patton and Company, since it was the largest emporium in the town.

With an Indian stripling, Jess Cochran, French, on the night of February 7, 1895, slipped into Catoosa, held up two citizens, and forced them to break open a window in the Patton store. Still holding their two prisoners, cowed into silence, and forcing them to go before, French and the Indian boy entered through the broken window.

The office was in a small room at the back, separate from the store, but connected to it by a short passageway. Seeing a light in this room, French went to a side window while his partner stood at the door which opened into the store. Through the window French saw Colonel Sam Irwin, the manager, sitting at a desk, working on his accounts, his back toward the door.

French raised his Winchester, but at that moment he caught sight of the muzzle of a double-barreled shotgun. It was in the hands of a night watchman, named Wilkins, who was sitting in a rocking chair facing the door.

At this moment, for some reason, the Indian youth outside the closed door fired, his bullet crashing through the thin panels and just missing the night watchman. Instantly Irwin sprang to his feet, and flung the door open. At almost the same instant the night watchman's shotgun bellowed, and the young Indian bandit fell forward on the sill "with the roof of his head blown off."

With the explosion of the shot, there was a crash at the window as Jim French shattered the pane with his Winchester butt. The night watchman whirled and fired his second barrel, but the charge went too low, shattering the window frame but failing to wound French.

At the report from the outlaw's Winchester a slug tore through Irwin's lower abdomen, inflicting a fatal wound. As the manager sank to the floor with a groan, French bounded into the room, while the night watchman, his gun now empty, dodged behind a dresser.

"Come out of there!" ordered French. "You've killed my partner. Help me put Irwin on the bed; I don't want to hurt him any more."

Wilkins obeyed and helped carry the dying Irwin to a cot near the wall.

"Now help me bring in my partner, and then I'll take care of you," snarled French, cursing the trembling watchman.

The young Indian's body was brought into the office and laid on the floor, his face literally shot away, so that later there was difficulty in identifying him.

In spite of the ghastly sight, French was cool and deadly.

"Now, you coyote," he said grimly, "I'm going to kill you."

The watchman began to beg for his life, protesting that he had no weapon to defend himself. French paid no attention. Holding his Winchester at his side, he drew a revolver and deliberately aimed at the helpless, pleading man.

Before he could pull the trigger, however, Colonel Irwin, who was bleeding to death on the cot, made a final effort, drew a revolver that was concealed under the pillow, and fired twice.

Both bullets tore through French's neck, just below the ears. Dropping his two guns, he staggered about for a moment, and then, with the blood spouting from his wounds, ran out of the door toward the Spunky River.

After him came pursuers, led by the vengeful watchman.

Just outside of town, the bandit fell and crawled into an Indian hut. There they found him. He was dying, but Wilkins, who had reloaded his shotgun, blasted both barrels of buckshot into his body and finished him.

Jim French was a son of a well-regarded Creek Indian, Tom French, who was "recognized as a good friend but a dangerous enemy." The father died about 1890.

The outlaw seemed to regret shooting Irwin after the deed was done; and it was evident that he knew him, for he called him by name.

Before his end, French must have realized the terrible position in which he had placed himself by defying society, for on the back of a letter found in his pocket after his death, he had written two sentences:

It is hard to live in hell and then go to hell, but it looks like such a fate is in store for me.

A fool never knows nothing until it is too late; so, boys, beware, and look before you leap. J. K. FRENCH.

A month and a half later, on March 28, the Verdigris Kid, Sam McWilliams, was killed in a store robbery at Braggs, near Fort Gibson. With him died George Sanders. A nondescript youth named Sam Butler, who was with them, shot to death Joe Morris, a clerk, and escaped.

He was not a regular member of the gang, but he wore the brand of outlaw now. On August 1, John Davis, a deputy marshal, found Butler, lying under an apple tree at his mother's home near the Verdigris River. Butler leaped to his feet and his shot knocked Davis from his horse, penetrating his right side.

Though mortally wounded, the brave deputy staggered to his feet and fired at the outlaw youth, his bullet going through Butler's heart and killing him instantly. Davis died about an hour later.

The Cook gang was wiped out. Six of its members, Jim French, Henry Munson, Lon Gordon, Verdigris Kid McWilliams, George Sanders, and the last recruit, Sam Butler, were dead. Chicken Lucas, Curtis Dayson, Jess Snyder, Will Farris, Skeeter Baldwin, and Bill Cook himself, all had been "put away" for most of their natural lives in various prisons. Cherokee Bill and Henry Starr were under death sentences in the Fort Smith jail.

With the death of Jim French the strange and crime-streaked entourage of Belle Starr came to an end, save for young Henry Starr, who, though condemned to hang, was destined to escape the gallows and still be heard from for more than a quarter of a century in the world of outlawry.

Meantime, Cherokee Bill was further engraving his name on the annals of the Fort Smith court. From the moment he landed in the jail there seemed to be a personal feud between him and the Hanging Judge. From the first Judge Parker appeared to feel (with somewhat less, I fear, than the ideal judicial impartiality) that the big, scowling prisoner was guilty of the crimes alleged, and should be disposed of for the good of humanity in general. For his part, Cherokee Bill hated the judge with everything in his dark nature. The result was a sort of conflict of personalities between the two rarely seen in a court of justice.

During his trial for the Melton murder, Cherokee Bill's witnesses were "restricted by Judge Parker," according to the record. He also rigorously limited the attorneys—on both sides—in the length of their final arguments, and delivered a thirteen-minute charge to the jury of such a bristling nature that it took only a few minutes for that body to arrive at a verdict of guilty.

When he heard the verdict, Cherokee Bill smiled ironically. His mother, however, wept.

"What's the matter with you?" he said to her. "I'm not a dead man yet by a long ways."

There was some reason for his confidence. Because of Judge Parker's highhanded rulings in the case, his attorney, J. Warren Reed, appealed to a higher court—this being after the dread power of irrevocable judgments had been taken from the Fort Smith tribunal.

It was while this appeal was pending that Ben Howell, the hang-dog ex-Doolin man who had joined the Cook gang, played his maleficent part.

Howell, who stole some groceries from a store in the little town of Ingalls—the Doolins' hangout—was captured and sent to prison for ninety days. Since he was cowardly and believed to be harmless, he was made a trusty with "outside privileges." Early in June 1895 he simply "walked away."

Some time later, on July 10, a startling discovery was made. There was a loaded revolver in Cherokee Bill's cell!

How did such a weapon get into the cell of a known killer like Cherokee Bill? Later, before his execution, the murderer stated that Howell smuggled in to him two six-shooters, by means of a pole, putting them through the cell window, together with some extra ammunition, which the prisoner received and hid.[8] One of

[8] Howell, recaptured soon after, denied smuggling the pistols, but he received a heavy sentence for breaking his parole as a trusty, which evidently was in part a punishment for the plot to get the guns to Cherokee Bill, which they must have hatched together.

the weapons, Cherokee Bill hid in a bucket—where it was found, as he planned. The other he secreted in the wall of his cell, in a hole made by removing a brick, placing the gun and extra ammunition within, then replacing the brick. As he had cunningly reasoned, this weapon was not discovered, nor was its presence suspected, because the first revolver had been found and nobody dreamed of a second.

The day of July 26, 1895, was sultry hot, and in sheer mercy the prisoners in the Fort Smith jail were allowed to come out in the corridors, where it was cooler than in their stifling cells. They had to return to their cells, however, at seven o'clock in the evening, to be locked up for the night. The hour of locking up, when there was a certain amount of confusion in the prison, was chosen by Cherokee Bill for his desperate attempt, probably long planned, to make his escape.

Two men always passed down the corridors together, side by side, to attend to the locking of each cell. The corridor known as "murderer's row," in which Cherokee Bill's cell was situated, was attended to by Turnkey Campbell Eoff (pronounced Ofe) and Lawrence Keating, a guard. Keating was armed with a revolver, but Eoff left his weapons outside the corridor cage.

When they reached Cherokee Bill's cell, the prisoner, who had taken his pistol from the hole in the wall, suddenly aimed it at them through the bars and demanded Keating's gun. If the guard had surrendered it, the murderer could have held both men as hostages.

Instead of obeying, Keating, with a great deal of courage, reached for his own revolver. Instantly Cherokee Bill's weapon crashed out its report, and Keating staggered back, fatally wounded.

Eoff, who was unarmed, turned when the shot was fired and ran up the corridor, while Cherokee Bill stepped out of his cell and fired at him twice, but missed both times.

With the shooting, perfect bedlam broke out in the prison. Convicts howled and threw their weight against their bars. From some of the cells still unlocked, men issued, at least one of them armed with a club made from the leg of his table, ready for a full-scale prison riot. Above the frenzied yelling of the prisoners, and the shouts of officers ordering them back into their cells, rang out again and again the reports of firearms, as Cherokee Bill tried to drive the guards from the gate, and they replied to him.

Smoke so filled the corridor that it was almost impossible to see, which was the reason why more persons were not killed or wounded.

Out of this smoke suddenly appeared a dreadful figure, Lawrence Keating, still carrying his revolver, the blood cascading from his body, his face drawn and pale, like the ghost of a man already dead.

Dead he really was, except for the effort of will that kept him staggering on, carrying the weapon which the murderer behind might have used, until he collapsed by the gate, gasped "I'm killed," and died.

Now Heck Bruner, a deputy marshal, came up with a shotgun and blasted with it down the corridor. The "scatter gun" would have done some execution, if it could have been brought into play sooner. But when Bruner fired, Cherokee Bill and all the other prisoners had already retreated into their cells, so the buckshot whined and rattled down the passageway without finding a living target.

Yelling, hooting, and howling still continued from the prisoners, and the scene was one of wildest excitement. Cherokee Bill had barricaded himself in his cell, and in the now darkened corridor he fired at any sound of a step. With each shot he "gobbled like a turkey."

The "gobble" was pure Indian, described by Harman as "a curious mixture of sounds, unearthly to the hearer, and is much like a combination of the howl of a coyote and the gobble of a turkey-gobbler. Coming from the lips of a full-grown Indian it can be heard at a long distance and it signifies *Death.*"

Still shots echoed, mingled with Cherokee Bill's weird outcries, the yells of the convicts, and the shouts of guards who called to each other as they tried to reach a position where they could get at the barricaded desperado.

It was at this moment that Henry Starr stepped unforgettably into the picture.

He had been sentenced to hang for the murder of Floyd Wilson, but his lawyer had appealed the case, and he was awaiting a decision on the appeal in his cell in the Fort Smith jail. Now, he managed to get the attention of one of the guards, and made this proposal:

"If you'll keep the men who are watching the corridor from shooting at me, I'll go into Cherokee Bill's cell and get his gun for you."

He knew the desperado from their association in the Cook gang, and after a consultation was held, the guards agreed not to fire. Released from his cell, young Starr walked steadily down the corridor to the cell occupied by the cornered murderer. He entered it, and for a few minutes there was some sort of a colloquy within. When Starr reappeared, he carried the outlaw's revolver, which he turned over to the officers. What he said to Cherokee Bill thus to tame him will never be known.

For his courage the death penalty against him was lifted, and he was permitted to plead guilty to a charge of manslaughter, for which he was sentenced to fifteen years in prison, being pardoned by the President after five years.

At the time of Keating's murder, Judge Parker was in St. Louis. The old man was in failing health, partly, I am sure, because he knew that very soon his beloved court, in which he had ruled virtually as a personification of Fate for so many years, would soon be abolished.

But the news was like a strong stimulant to him. Now at last he had an iron-clad case against Cherokee Bill, and he aroused himself to a final burst of the old energy that had characterized him.

He paused only long enough for a press conference, during which he gave a snorting excoriation of the Supreme Court, which had reversed many of his decisions and sentences:

"These reversals have contributed to the number of murders in the Indian Territory. First of all, the convicted murderer has a long breathing spell, before his case comes before the Supreme Court; then when it does come before that body, the conviction may be quashed, and whenever it is quashed it is always upon the flimsiest technicalities. The Supreme Court never touches the merits of the case. As far as I can see, the court must be opposed to capital punishment, and therefore tries to reason the effect of it away. That is the sum total of it."

History does not record what the Supreme Court of the United States did or said when this scorching denunciation reached the ears of that august body. Meantime Judge Parker had taken a train back to Fort Smith.

He was his old implacable self as he presided over the trial of Cherokee Bill that followed. The case was called at once, and any symptom of pettifogging tactics on the part of the defense counsel was sternly stopped. Judge Parker permitted the very minimum of legal juggling, called down lawyers if they tried to speak longer than the time allotted to them, turned down with high indignation a demurrer which, he felt, implied that a "fair and impartial trial could not be given in his court," and insisted that the usual delays be cut short.

When the testimony was in and the pleas of the attorneys for both sides heard, he gave the jury a brief, grim charge, and sent them to their deliberations. They required only thirteen minutes[9] to arrive at a verdict of guilty, and Judge Parker complimented them on their speedy decision.

"Give these men a good dinner," he told the bailiff. "They deserve it."

Cherokee Bill listened while Judge Parker, with an almost

[9] S. W. Harman, was foreman of this jury. He wrote, somewhat whimsically: "There is much comfort here for those who believe that the number 13 is an unlucky one, for the number occurs many times in connection with Cherokee Bill and his conviction and sentence. First, Cherokee was believed by some to have killed thirteen persons during his career; the offer of $1,300 reward affected his capture for killing Ernest Melton; his first sentence to die was pronounced on April 13; he killed Keating on the 26th day of July, or twice thirteen; Bill was said to have fired thirteen shots during his fight with the guards; Judge Parker occupied thirteen minutes in charging the jury in the Keating case; the foreman of the jury, myself, boarded at a house numbered 313; the actual hours occupied in the trial numbered thirteen; the jury were thirteen minutes in arriving at a verdict; the jurymen and deputy who ate and slept together during the trial made a company of thirteen; there were thirteen witnesses for the prosecution."

furious review of his crimes, pronounced the sentence of death, ending: "May God, whose laws you have broken and before whose tribunal you must then appear, have mercy on your soul!"

Reading the conclusion to the pronouncement of that sentence today, one is inclined to the belief that Judge Parker had little expectation of any mercy for Cherokee Bill, even from the heavenly judgment seat—and would have dissented from it as strongly as he dissented from the Supreme Court's rulings, if it was extended.

As it happened, Cherokee Bill was not hanged for the murder of Lawrence Keating after all. His lawyer had appealed from the second conviction, but before the appeal could be heard a decision came down from the Supreme Court rejecting the previous appeal that had been made from the conviction in the case of Ernest Melton. So the desperado died for the Melton murder after all.

The hangings at Fort Smith, which at first had been public, were by this time restricted to the prison yard and only about one hundred persons, who received official passes, were admitted to it. But thousands packed themselves about the jail, and many climbed to the tops of walls to see the execution of the notorious criminal when Cherokee Bill was led out to the gallows on the afternoon of March 17, 1896. The roofs of the nearest buildings were covered with morbid watchers, and one shed collapsed under the weight it carried, several neck-craners being injured.

Upon the scaffold, Cherokee Bill's burly figure took its place. On this occasion there were no others to stand upon the fatal trap. The limelight was reserved exclusively for him.

Some who watched might have missed the diminutive form of Hangman George Maledon fussing around. The executioner had resigned more than a year before.

Several persons took part in this, the most celebrated of the Fort Smith hangings. The ropes, binding his arms and legs, were adjusted by Deputies George and Will Lawson. A Catholic priest, Father Pius, was present to give the last prayers. Turnkey Eoff, whom the condemned man had tried to kill in the prison riot, was assigned the duty of springing the trap.

Cherokee Bill turned his broad, impassive face, with its gleaming eyes, about and said, "Hell, look at the people; something must be going to happen."

Before the hood was placed over his head he was asked if he had any final word to say.

"No," he replied gruffly. "I came here to die, not to make a speech."

A final prayer was said, the hangman's noose was adjusted, the black cap pulled over his face.

"Move over a little, Bill," said Eoff, his hand on the lever.

Cherokee Bill obediently moved his huge feet until he stood directly over the center of the trap.

The lever was pulled, his figure shot down through the opening, dropped ten feet, and that was the end. His neck was broken and he died without a struggle.

Exactly eight months later, November 17, 1896, Judge Isaac C. Parker died. What he considered his mission in life was ended. On September 1, prior to his death, the jurisdiction of his court ceased by congressional enactment. He had no wish to continue his existence after that, and his own and his court's expirations very closely accompanied each other.

10. *Amateur Outlaws— and the Death of a Marshal*

Criminal succession somewhat resembles certain noxious plants that leave their indurated seed in the ground to lie latent, perhaps for a lengthy period, then spring up anew after the parent stock has been destroyed.

In the final roundup of the Doolin gang, only one outlaw escaped. He was Little Dick West, an undersized weasel of a man, dark of face and hair, ignorant, none too neat or clean, and tough. He also had a reputation for being murderous. To use an old expression, "You could smell 'bad' off of him like smoke in a house."

Yet I wonder if this deadliness, perhaps, was not more a matter of reputation than the cold truth. Men who should know said that he was close to being a genius in his lightning speed with his six-shooters; and he probably was. But in spite of this I have never found any clear-cut evidence that he killed anyone—unless it was J. C. Seaborn, at Southwest City, Missouri, during a bank holdup there, and that slaying was credited in at least one account to Bill Raidler. He was, to be sure, in holdups and fights where men were killed, and he may have provided some of the corpses on those occasions; but that it was Little Dick's bullet which took such and such a life, and not the bullet of someone else in the gang, cannot be absolutely demonstrated.

Of his bravery, also, there has been some question. As an old-timer put it, "Little Dick had courage, but it was more like fear-bit ferocity than sand." In other words, when cornered he was desperate; but he had to be in a corner before he would fight. Nevertheless, it was generally believed that he was the fastest gun in the Territory; and furthermore, he was known to be ambidextrous with his six-shooters, a rarity then and always in the history of the West.

Originally, Little Dick came from Texas. As a scrubby homeless waif, he got a few scraps of food and a place to sleep by washing dishes in frontier "beaneries," or by chopping wood and doing other menial odd jobs. Perhaps he did not always have a place to sleep, for somehow he picked up a dislike for sleeping indoors. In later years it grew into what amounted to an obsession, as if he felt that being in a house was in some manner a trap. Even in severe weather he usually spread his blankets and slept under the open sky. When he used a roof at all, it was always a shed or barn, not the roof of a house.

Oscar Halsell gave him his first chance. He found him, a wizened little runt sixteen years old, working as a roustabout on the Three Circle Ranch in Texas, just south of the Red River, and felt sorry for him; so much so that he offered him a job as a horse wrangler, to go with a herd of cattle he was trailing up into the Territory for his HX Bar Ranch on the Cimarron River. The boy took the job. He could handle horses, and he cared for them and treated them well. It was perhaps Little Dick's most redeeming feature—a man who was good to horses in the horse-riding West, which was sometimes cruel with spur, and quirt, and bit, could not be entirely bad. But it also was the immediate cause of his downfall at last, this friendship toward a horse.

When the herd reached the HX Bar, Dick West stayed on as a permanent hand, and came to know Bill Doolin, Bitter Creek Newcomb, Bill Raidler, and other riders of the outfit who later took to the outlaw trail. They at first tolerated him, then accepted him; and perhaps in sheer gratitude he followed them when they went into banditry.

Always he was like a little lone wolf, without any real friends, staying much to himself. Inarticulate and incommunicative, he had no loyalties, except perhaps toward Bill Doolin. And when the boss bandit was killed, he was completely on his own.

The marshals wanted him, and they beat the country for him. But with all his handicaps of appearance, character, and lack of education, Little Dick excelled in one thing—he could "lose" a pursuing marshal, or a posse, better than any other outlaw in the whole Territory. His penchant for sleeping outdoors and away from others sometimes stood him in good stead. Nobody knows how many times officers "jumped" the Doolin gang or some of its members and did not even know Little Dick was near. He was off somewhere alone, and slipped quietly away.

Yet though the fighting marshals, who successfully ferreted out every other member of the gang, were so baffled by him that they for a time gave up the hunt, in his limited mind there remained always the memory of what he considered the great days of his life; the days when he "amounted to something," when he was not merely Dick West, an undersized nonentity, but Little Dick West the Bandit, whose name people spoke with a touch of fear and even awe. And though he might have lost himself so completely that he could have lived out his life to the end, his discontent ate into him like a canker, until at last it had its way with him.

The manner of Little Dick's return to banditry was roundabout, and began in a courtroom—a place he sedulously avoided as long as he lived.

One of the most picturesque figures in the Territory at that time—or, indeed, any other time—was Temple Houston, a lawyer. He was the youngest son of the great General Sam Houston of Texas and his wife, Margaret Lea Houston, whom the general married when he was forty-seven and she but twenty.[1] Temple,

[1] One of the strange errors in Burton Rascoe's *Belle Starr* is this extraordinary statement concerning Temple Houston: "Houston was a handsome, brilliant but eccentric grandson of General Sam ('Old Fuss and Feathers') Houston,

the last of their several children, was born at Austin, Texas, in 1862, when his mighty father was sixty-nine years old and had just been impeached as governor of Texas for his tremendous, almost singlehanded battle to try to keep the state from seceding from the Union at the start of the Civil War.

Temple Houston graduated from Baylor University, took up law, and was for a time district attorney of the "Jumbo District," made up of several of the sprawling counties in the Texas Panhandle. After a term in the Texas state senate, he moved to Woodward, Oklahoma Territory, where he specialized in criminal practice.

The youngest of the Houston clan inherited his famous sire's fighting qualities, eloquence, and flair for theatrical appearance. A built-in scowl only enhanced his handsome face, and he sometimes (although not always) wore his hair long, so that it fell about his shoulders. Often he indulged in sartorial eccentricities, such as buckskin coats, beaded vests, rattlesnake cravats, and similar originalities in costume. Six feet three inches tall, with a resonant voice and a penetrating eye, he seemed to dominate any courtroom in which he appeared. He was fearless, quick and accurate with a gun, and an orator without peer in the Territory.

One of his forensic feats, which was levied upon by Edna Ferber in her *Cimarron,* occurred as follows: A woman, charged with prostitution, was brought into court one day while Houston was present on other business. She had no counsel, no money, apparently no friends, and the judge asked him to represent her. Until that time Houston had hardly paid any attention to the case; but when he was appointed to defend the poor lonely feminine prisoner at the bar, he delivered on the spur of the moment, and entirely extemporaneously, a speech so masterfully

---

father of the Texas Republic. Temple's mother and grandmother were full-blooded Cherokee Indians."

Aside from the important facts that Temple was Sam Houston's *son,* not grandson, and that he did not have one drop of Cherokee or any other Indian blood in him, there is a trivial but amusing mistake in that Sam Houston never in history was referred to as "Old Fuss and Feathers." It was a nickname of General Winfield Scott of Mexican War fame.

eloquent that it not only gained her acquittal but became a classic of the times. After the trial the court stenographer was besieged for copies of the speech, and it was printed and widely circulated. Yet for this brilliant service in behalf of his client, Houston neither received, nor expected, any fee.

In trying a case, Houston was inclined to be overbearing, tough on witnesses, and frequently he cut up his legal adversaries with biting sarcasm that led to bitter clashes. Yet he was as clever as he was domineering.

As an instance of this combination of qualities, on one occasion, while defending a man charged with murdering a well-known gun fighter, in the midst of his speech Houston demonstrated the speed with which six-shooters could be brought into action by a lightning use of his own weapons. Whipping them from their holsters, he fired one set of six shots point-blank at the jury, and the other set at the judge.

Out of their seats fell the terrified jurymen, and wildly walked upon each other in their haste to get away, scattering in every direction and fleeing from the courtroom. With equal celerity—and panic—the honorable judge dove under his desk and took refuge there.

When order was restored, Houston explained with a smile that he had used blank cartridges and only wanted to illustrate the point that if his client had not fired when he did, the gun fighter could have drawn his revolvers and killed him almost in an instant. Both judge and jury, quite naturally, were furious at him for thus ruffling their dignity. They convicted his client without further ado.

But here was where the Houston cunning came into play. Blandly, he moved for a new trial, on the ground that "the jury had been allowed to separate and leave the courtroom during the hearing of the case." This was manifestly true—they fell over each other as they bolted for the doors and out. The judge did not like it, but the law was on Houston's side and the new trial was granted. When it was held, Houston, with a new jury and without any pistol pyrotechnics, got his client acquitted on a plea of self-defense.

More than once in his legal practice he met as opposing counsel members of a family named Jennings. The father, J. F. D. Jennings, was a judge at Woodward for a time, and later a judge at Tecumseh. There were four sons, Ed, John, Al, and Frank, the first three being lawyers. Ed and John had law offices together in Woodward, Al was briefly county attorney at El Reno, and Frank was a deputy court clerk at Denver, Colorado.

Al Jennings, next to the youngest of the brothers, born in Virginia, November 25, 1863, was a curious combination of conflicting traits. He was more of a gambler and a drinker than a lawyer, a great talker, histrionic, and eager for publicity and attention. He should have been an actor—which he eventually was for a short time—because throughout his life Al Jennings played a role, envisaging himself as bold and dashingly romantic, whereas he was a lean, wispy little man who was only trying to make up for his lack of inches by vainglorious boastings. Eventually he published a couple of books, full of assertions that he was deadly as lightning with a gun, and telling of how he faced down this or that notable killer. But there is no corroboration for any of this; in fact quite the contrary. In the last act of his outlaw career, he, with two other armed men to back him, surrendered as meekly as a lamb to one businesslike officer, standing in the road with a gun. Al Jennings the desperado was only a creation of the imagination of Al Jennings the frustrated little man.

Apparently at the very time he was county attorney at El Reno, he drifted into the acquaintance of another little man—unlettered, unclean, very quiet, with ferocious mustaches, and with no more home than a lost dog. He was Little Dick West. Why or how Little Dick, cautious as he was, divulged the information remains a mystery, but he set Al's eyes to bulging when he told him that he had been a member of the Doolin gang.

Al Jennings was an officer of the court, sworn to uphold the law. Did he inform the marshals of the whereabouts of the most wanted outlaw in the Territory? He did not. He only swelled with pride, secretly, at being a personal friend of a real, sure-enough, rootin'-tootin' bandit!

Just at this time, like a *deus ex machina,* Temple Houston stepped into the scene.

Jack Love, an opportunist of the era and sheriff at Woodward, had been appointed corporation commissioner through the influence of Houston, which made enemies of the Jennings clan, who wanted the job for one of their own members. When Love sued a certain Frank Garst for $3000 back rental on pasturage, he asked Houston to represent him, and Garst retained Ed Jennings as his attorney.

Both lawyers were of a belligerent nature, and repeatedly they clashed over legal technicalities. At last, in a heated argument over a question Houston asked of a witness, he rose, slammed his fist on the table, and shouted, "Your Honor, the gentleman is grossly ignorant of the law!"

From somewhere in the courtroom came an exclamation, "That's a lie!"

Al Jennings later, in one of his books, claimed that he was assisting his brother in the case, and it was he who gave the lie to Houston, adding, "His hand was on his forty-five and mine was leveled at him."

Actually, it appears that Ed uttered the words, and though he and Houston came near to blows, they were separated (without any drawing of forty-fives by anyone), received a reprimand from the judge, and made due apologies to the Court.

Whoever passed the lie, it was a fighting word to Houston, and nobody thought the matter would rest there. Best evidence that Ed uttered the word was the fact that the feud became a personal one between him and Houston.

That very evening Ed Jennings and his brother John were playing poker in a saloon when Houston entered. Immediately Ed jumped up and reached for his gun. It was a mistake. Houston was much quicker. At his instantaneous shot, Ed Jennings pitched to the floor, dying almost at once. John Jennings also tried to draw, but another shot from Houston's revolver smashed his left shoulder, disabling him. He later recovered from his wound.

Houston surrendered, asked for a trial, acted as his own attorney, and was acquitted by a jury on the grounds of self-defense when all the witnesses testified that Ed Jennings was the first to draw.

Al Jennings attended Houston's trial, and left the courtroom bitter over the acquittal. Having taken a few drinks, he uttered some threats in public; and then, appearing to realize that Houston might resent his animadversions in a manner most unpleasant, left hurriedly for Tecumseh, where his brother Frank soon joined him, coming from Denver.

In his "memoirs" Al Jennings told how he "hunted" Houston to revenge his brother. But Houston, a highly conspicuous figure in the Territory, went where he pleased, made no attempt to conceal his presence or his destination, and never encountered Al. The "hunting" could not have been too zealous. In fact, after some sober consideration, Al decided that a feud with a man like Temple Houston, who was so notoriously deadly with his guns, was very unsafe, and he kept out of Houston's way.

But in so doing, his peculiar nature required some sort of self-justification. It was perhaps then that a safer and more lucrative form of enterprise suggested itself to him, an outgrowth of his acquaintance with Little Dick West. He and his brother Frank were broke—and Little Dick was an experienced bandit! With Little Dick to show them how, they could gain headlines and presumably wealth by the spectacular (a very important point to Al) robbing of banks and trains. Little Dick was willing. With the addition of two brothers, Pat and Morris O'Malley, and a shifty character named Sam Baker, the so-called Jennings gang was born.

From the first it was a feckless, fumbling, futile crew. And mark that it was not called the "West gang." Very early Little Dick became disgusted with his amateur followers, whose career was a comedy of bungled efforts.

Their first essay was a nighttime holdup of a Santa Fe train near Edmond. The "bandits" crawled into the cab of the engine while it was taking on water, forced the engineer to pull the train a mile out of town, and broke into the express car. To their intense disappointment they found only a few hundred dollars in the cashbox; and they were so unnerved by their own unwonted boldness that they forgot even to rob the passengers.

Two weeks later came an even greater fiasco. They piled a stack of ties on a railroad track to stop a Katy train south of Muskogee.

But the engineer saw the barricade, opened his throttle—and the train roared through, scattering ties in every direction. After this Baker deserted them, though he still kept in touch with them.

Next they planned to rob a train at Purcell. But while the five would-be bandits were hiding in the switchyards, they saw the approach of what they took to be a posse, and decamped. They were lucky, for there actually was a posse—*on the train.* Bill Tilghman lay hidden in the locomotive tender, and in the express car rode Heck Thomas and several special deputies. Had the gang boarded that train its career would have ended right there.

They did not know it, but there was a leak, and that leak was Sam Baker, who kept the officers informed of what the "bandits" intended to do. From the beginning Tilghman, who was used to dealing with professionals in brigandage, was contemptuous of this amateur aggregation, and so were Thomas, Ledbetter, and other officers.

Thus far the gang's effort at train robbery had only been humiliating, so they decided to try bank robbery, with a raid on Minco, a small town not far from El Reno. But before entering the village they cautiously halted outside and sent Pat O'Malley to ride in and reconnoiter. Pat saw some men, who seemed suspiciously alert and well armed, standing about in the streets—and rode straight on out without hesitating. A posse was guarding the bank, he told his companions, and he was right. Word of their project again had reached Bill Tilghman, and he placed about the bank a number of men who strongly disliked bank robbers and were ready to back up their distaste with hot lead.

Nothing but fiascos had occurred thus far, but the gang at last struck luck. They blasted open a Wells Fargo chest at Berwyn, south of Ardmore, and got a wad of money. Al Jennings said it was $35,000. Allowing for his inclination to exaggerate, it may have been $10,000. Still, it was a stake, and the gang decided to scatter for a time.

The brothers Jennings boarded a tramp freighter at Galveston, Texas, and landed in Honduras. There they met a plump, somewhat rumpled personage, who greeted them with drunken gravity and introduced himself as William Sydney Porter, self-exiled to beat a bank-embezzlement charge at Austin, Texas. With him they embarked on a lengthy spree which ended when, completely out of funds, Al Jennings proposed that they rob a bank.

Porter refused to have anything to do with the robbery, which did not take place. Instead, he went back to Austin to face prosecution on a charge that his biographers have since said was unjust—in which he was made to suffer for carelessness or peculations by higher officials of the bank in which he was working. He was sent to prison, where he began the writing which was to rocket him to world-wide fame under the pen name of O. Henry.

Al and Frank Jennings returned to the Territory in the fall of 1897, and the gang gathered again for one more effort to get rich quick. Since most of their night holdups had been conspicuous failures, they decided they must not have the secret to that form of enterprise. This time, therefore, they would try robbery by daylight.

So, shortly before noon, October 1, 1897, five masked men galloped down upon a section gang which was working on the Rock Island track near Pocasset, eleven miles from Chickasha. Flourishing six-shooters, they ordered the foreman to flag down a train, due to arrive soon, while they hid in the underbrush, ready to charge out.

With interest, but without any sense of personal responsibility in the matter, the section gang sat down to wait while the foreman did as ordered. The train appeared, came to a halt at the waving red flag, and the bandits held the conductor and engineer at their gun points while Al Jennings and Little Dick scrambled into the express car. Not one, but two safes were there, a small one standing on a larger one, but they were both locked and could not be opened.

With extraordinary foresight, however, the robbers had brought along four sticks of dynamite. They now prepared to blow the safes, and they proceeded with their usual inexpertness. One of the dynamite sticks was placed between the upper and lower safes, at a point they thought might be vital, the fuse was lighted, and the bandits leaped out of the car and ran to a safe distance.

What followed astounded them. It was a really noble explosion—far greater than anyone could have expected from a single stick of dynamite. The car was splintered to bits.

Either Al Jennings or Little Dick had forgotten the three extra sticks of dynamite, which had been laid on the floor beside the larger safe when the explosive was fixed. All four sticks blew up at the detonation.

Worse, neither of the safes had been opened by the blast. The would-be robbers were out of dynamite and nothing remained for them but to take a few watches and about $400 in cash from the passengers. A bunch of bananas and a gallon of whisky also were salvaged from the train, and with this they disconsolately rode away.

It was too frustrating—a bunch of bananas as loot for a train robbery! Little Dick West's pride was utterly scarified. One evening he mounted his horse and without a word of explanation rode off all by himself. They never saw him again.

The four tattered and chapfallen "bandits" he left behind drank their whisky and ate their bananas and wondered what they were going to do next. They speedily found out. They had to run for it—the marshals were on their trail.

Banditry ceased to be fun. Their horses gave out and they stole a farm wagon, in which, not only ragged but nearly starving, they rode behind a team of plodding nags. Where was the glamour now?

One night as they wandered from one hiding place to another, they passed through the little town (at that time) of Cushing. Here they completely lost caste, robbing a clothing store of some clothes to replace their tatters, and taking about fifty dollars from the till. From train and bank robbery to common store theft is a long way down for men who once claimed to be of the "elite" in brigandage.

The Cushing robbery gave officers a new clue, and Sam Baker soon told Bud Ledbetter where to find them—at the ranch of some people named Harkless. The place was surrounded, Mrs. Harkless and her hired girl were allowed to depart, and the outlaws were commanded to surrender before the officers opened fire.

After a few shots the fugitives escaped,[2] when one of the possemen got a shell stuck in his gun and was too busy trying to eject it to report their flight. Ledbetter and the other deputies poured bullets into the house for several minutes before they knew their quarry was gone.

Al Jennings received a slight wound in his knee, and Frank Jennings' clothes were punctured by buckshot although he was not injured. The fleeing outlaws sought refuge at the home of their false friend, Sam Baker, who went to Checotah, five miles away, and brought back a Dr. Parmenter to treat Al's wound.

It happened that on the same trip he also made arrangements for delivering his guests into Ledbetter's hands.

Three days later he put the Jenningses and Pat O'Malley into a covered wagon, and on horseback, with Morris O'Malley, also mounted, accompanied them to a place near the crossing of Carr Creek. There he told them they were "on the right road," and cantered back, Morris O'Malley accompanying him while the wagon went on.

In the wagon the three now thoroughly miserable fugitives started to cross the creek. A log had been placed across the trail, and on this the wagon stalled.

Out into the road stepped a single stark figure with a Winchester.

"Surrender!" came the voice of Bud Ledbetter.

Meekly the "bad men" scrambled out of the wagon, leaving their weapons inside, and without a shot or any semblance of a fight gave themselves up with every evidence of relief.

Ledbetter had made a bet with Tilghman that he could capture the whole gang singlehanded. But he had a posse on hand, in ambush, should the outlaws show more spunk than he expected.

[2] Later, in one of his books, Al Jennings made a great battle of this. The truth is that at the place where he stood before he fled, the officers found one empty shell and half a dozen loaded cartridges, all belonging to a .38-55-caliber Marlin—Al's rifle, since the others were armed with .40-72-caliber Winchesters. Evidently Al had been so excited that he stood there and pumped his gun nearly empty, while actually firing only one wild shot. Al later said, "Not only was the house shot full of holes, but even the shots went to playing *Home Sweet Home* on the piano." If so, he did not wait to see or hear either of these interesting developments.

He won his bet because until the posse came out of hiding the crestfallen fugitives had no knowledge that they were dealing with anyone besides that one deputy marshal in the road.

Morris O'Malley was captured soon after. All of them served five-year sentences in the penitentiary at Columbus, Ohio, although Al Jennings received a life term, from which he was pardoned at the end of the five years. In prison he was reunited with O. Henry, and also came to know Bill Raidler. The future great author confided that he was trying to write.

"I had started to write the memoirs of my bandit days," recalled Jennings later. "At the moment I felt myself far the greater writer of the two. I had not even known that Porter hoped to write. I felt really sorry for the man who was destined to write the finest stories America ever read."

The wry humor of that statement indicates a change which had taken place in Al Jennings. Prison gave him time to think things over and he achieved a sense of proportion that had been no part of him before he did enforce penance for his wrongdoings.

All four of the prisoners, after they were released, had learned their lessons well. There was no more outlaw trail for them—they remembered the vicissitudes which in no way were paid for by the small results they gained. Every one of them lived an honorable and industrious life and made a place in society.

Al, the true extrovert of the lot, remained the most publicized. He tried writing; went into evangelistic work, with his own sinful career as an example *not* to be followed; got his citizenship rights restored; and even ran for governor of Oklahoma (most unsuccessfully).

Eventually he drifted to California, where he attended all the Old Settler barbecues, appeared on the stage in vaudeville, played a bit part or two in Hollywood movies, and gave interviews to newspapers.

As this is written he is still living—at ninety-seven the last of the old-time outlaws, quite willing to give his version of every event in which he participated, with large numbers of friends, well liked and respected, though very superannuated. His home is in Tarzana, California, and it is filled with relics of his "wild days."

The treacherous Baker, I am glad to report, was killed not very long after he betrayed the Jennings crowd, by a man named Torrence, in a dispute over a wagon.

While the four unlucky tatterdemalions were being hunted, all trace of Little Dick West was lost. It is hard to find a man who dislikes sleeping in any house and is as much at home in a patch of woods or out on the prairie as anywhere else; and Little Dick was cunning as a coyote. He knew the law was after him; and he knew what probably would happen if the law ever caught up with him.

"I won't be took," he had told his companions.

In this period he must have regretted bitterly "throwing in" with those amateurs, for it started the hue and cry for him all over again. And yet perhaps some of the failures were his own fault. He had participated in numerous robberies, but never led one. The others depended on his "know-how," and he probably lacked the mentality to plan and lead a successful holdup.

For three months after the capture of the Jenningses and O'Malleys the marshals had not the slightest notion of where Little Dick might be. It was supposed that he had left the country, perhaps had gone down into Texas or even Mexico. Yet all the time he was prowling through the Territory, moving chiefly at night, getting his food nobody knows how.

He knew a few men, former associates of his pre-outlaw cowboy days. One of these was an old cowman named Fitzgerald. Another was Herman Arnett, also a rancher, whose place was about five miles from Guthrie and half a mile from Fitzgerald's. These two men Little Dick sometimes saw briefly, perhaps out of sheer desire for some human contact.

Since the days when Little Dick and he rode together on the old cattle range, however, Arnett had taken to himself a wife. And a wife makes a considerable change in a man's habits and ways of life.

Mrs. Arnett had a woman's somewhat typical suspicion of the wild days of her husband's younger manhood—before he met *her*, and became respectable. In particular she disapproved of his former companions, having a natural feminine fear that they might lead him to depart from the straight and narrow path upon which she had set his errant cowboy feet.

One of those previous associates, who appeared now and then, spent a few minutes with Arnett, and then disappeared, she especially disliked. He was dirty, and she was an admirer of cleanliness. He wore a shirt too big for him, and a mustache out of proportion to his small, rather round face. His eyes were set unusually wide, but they were small and to her they seemed to glitter. Above all, his ways were so furtive, and he spoke so seldom if at all in her hearing, and his comings and goings were so unpredictable, that she was sure he was up to some skulduggery.

All this she confided one day (in strictest confidence) to a neighbor woman, saying she was afraid the disreputable stranger might get Herman into trouble. The neighbor woman (also enjoining absolute secrecy) mentioned it to a friend of hers, Mrs. Hart, who lived in Guthrie. Mrs. Hart (as might be expected) told her husband. And Hart, who happened to be clerk of the district court at Guthrie, at once reported it to the U.S. marshal's office.

The description Mrs. Arnett had given—undersized, unclean, big mustache, small wide-set eyes—all fitted someone the officers were looking for. Could it be possible that Little Dick West was actually hiding within half an hour's ride of the U.S. marshal's office in Guthrie? It seemed improbable . . . and yet that description . . .

Bill Tilghman, Heck Thomas, Frank Rinehart, and a man named Fossett rode out to see.

Little Dick's love for a good horse had been mentioned. He took the very best care of any he happened to possess or be using, and that was one thing that brought him to Herman Arnett. Even though he himself slept out, he wanted his horse under shelter, and asked the rancher's permission to put his animal in a stable.

On the morning of April 7, 1898, he came to the barn, from wherever he was camped, led his horse out to the corral, and began lovingly to curry him. In one hand he held a currycomb, in the other a brush. These two simple implements of horse grooming were made each with a wide strap over the back, into which the user slipped his hands while he employed them.

Behind the Arnett barnyard was an orchard, and it was through this that the officers approached, dismounting and stealing up through the trees. Unaware of any danger, Little Dick plied his currycomb and brush.

All at once Tilghman and Thomas stepped into view, guns ready. They recognized the little outlaw, they knew of his statement "I won't be took," and they were aware of his reputed quickness on the draw. But they gave him his chance.

"Hands up!" called one of them.

At the words, Little Dick "shucked" the currycomb and brush from his hands, and pulled both six-shooters. But the straps on the backs handicapped him for just the fraction of a second that meant the difference between life and death.

Both Thomas and Tilghman were deadly shots. Together their guns rang out. Little Dick slumped to the ground, dying.

He would have killed, without any question, had not the bullets of the deputies brought him down, the swift-striking paralysis of death curbing the flexing fingers on his triggers.

"If he hadn't had to drop the currycomb and brush before he reached, one or both of us might have gone with him," said Heck Thomas, afterward, in sincere tribute to Little Dick's amazing speed with his guns.

It was the last check-off for the Doolin gang.

But there was new trouble.

Henry Starr was the last of the notable Territorial bandits, and he extended his activities for many years after Oklahoma attained statehood. Yet, because he began at the same time as Doolin and Cook, and even the Daltons, his subsequent career belongs here rather than with the newer generation of outlaws which followed.

The associate of Jim French, Bill Cook, and others of that ill-omened crew, and the man who went unarmed and singlehanded into the cell of kill-crazy Cherokee Bill and disarmed him, Starr was allowed to plead guilty to manslaughter and was sent for fifteen years to the penitentiary at Columbus, Ohio, where so many federal prisoners went. There, from the first, he put into play his gift for winning the regard of others. He was such a model prisoner, and his conduct was so dignified and courteous, that on the recommendation of the warden he was pardoned by President Theodore Roosevelt, about 1902.

Starr returned to the Territory, found his wife, and took her to Tulsa to live, going into the real estate business. After a time they had a baby son, whom he named Roosevelt, for the man who pardoned him.

Then, in 1907, Oklahoma achieved statehood, with Charles N. Haskell as its first governor. As soon as Oklahoma ceased being a territory, the neighboring state, Arkansas, applied to Governor Haskell for the extradition of Starr, over whom still hung an indictment for the Bentonville bank holdup. At the same time a rash of robberies of stores, small eating houses, and even banks broke out; and because of the publicity he received from the renewal of the Bentonville case, the newspapers began to suggest that Starr was guilty of the outbreak of crime.

"I had the name of robbing *banks*,"[3] he later said. "I thought I might as well have the game."

[3] Starr was making a distinction between bank robbing and lesser crimes. One of the curious characteristics of old-time bandits was their pride in their self-assumed role and their sense of injury whenever they were accused of a "minor" offense. The shame of the Youngers, in demeaning themselves by robbing a hen roost for food, has been mentioned. In the 1920s I had an experience with a bank robber named Ray Majors that illustrates the point. He had been released from prison and was known to be in Kansas; and the police of Wichita, Kansas, jittery over his presence, began to ascribe every petty store and hamburger-stand burglary to him. It nearly drove Ray Majors crazy. At last, simply because, as he said, "I couldn't stand having every candy-store robbery charged to me," he secured the services of a highly reputable lawyer, Hal Black, who was a personal friend of Henry J. Allen, former governor of Kansas and publisher of the Wichita *Beacon*. Through Black, Majors arranged a meeting with Allen at the latter's home one night, in which he dramatically handed over his pistol to the former governor and asked him to announce that "Ray Majors has gone straight and forsaken a life of crime." Allen, a good newspaperman, suggested that Majors' life career would be a good feature for the *Beacon*, and Majors, who, like most of his ilk, loved publicity, agreed. I was on the staff of the newspaper and was assigned to write the story. Ray Majors was very proud of my effort, which appeared on the front page, and ordered many extra copies. Unfortunately, however, the story led to the digging up of a forgotten charge—he had once robbed a bank at Rose Hill, Kansas. For that he was sent to the Lansing, Kansas, penitentiary, and it seemed to break his spirit. He wrote me several times, quite sadly. Later he was paroled, but presently was arrested again and convicted of robbing—of all things!—*a candy store*. It was as if the matter had preyed on his mind until he just had to do it. Majors died in the penitentiary while serving time on this last conviction.

Actually, Starr never was a highly successful bank robber. He was so articulate and personable that he impressed many persons and gained a far greater reputation than he actually earned.

Now, before he started anew on the outlaw trail, he went into hiding and sent a friend to see Governor Haskell at Guthrie (still the capital until 1910) and ask if, after Starr's record of five years' law-abiding existence, he was going to grant the extradition. The friend telephoned a message which Starr understood as "He [the governor] has granted it [the extradition]." At once Starr embarked on a new career of banditry.

What his friend really said was "He hasn't granted it." But when Starr learned of the mistake he had made in his understanding of the message, it was too late. He held up a bank at Webster Groves, Missouri, and then headed for California. On the way, he paused to rob a bank at Amity, Colorado, was caught, and sent to the Canon City, Colorado, penitentiary for twenty-five years. It was after he arrived at this prison that he learned the true tenor of his friend's report on the extradition proceedings in Oklahoma.

Once again Starr was the exemplary prisoner, likable, courteous, and co-operative. Within a year he was a trusty, in charge of a road-building camp with a hundred convicts in it; and so faithfully and well did he administer this task that after five years he was paroled on his promise not to leave Colorado.

He did not keep that promise. Instead, he returned to Tulsa, looking for his wife, only to find that she had divorced him. Already the newspapers were saying that Henry Starr, the parole violator, was at the bottom of every robbery in the state, and the Oklahoma legislature offered a reward for him. To use his own words, he "became desperate."

On March 27, 1915, with five other men, he attempted what the Dalton brothers had failed to do—the robbery of two banks at once—at Stroud, Oklahoma. It was done in broad daylight. As he later told Tilghman:

"When I came to Stroud to look it over, I saw it was just as easy to rob two banks as one, so I decided to kill two birds with one stone."

The chief defect in all of this was that while he was making his escape after the twin holdups, he was shot and captured.

Starr once said, "There's a sort of hypnotism about a man or a bunch of men who come coolly into a town in the middle of the day, walk up the main street, rob a bank, and walk out again, doing just enough shooting to show they can hit anything. The very daring of it puts a spell on people, paralyzes them with surprise and awe. Before they recover, the bandits are gone."

At Stroud that day, his formula seemed to be working. As the bandits walked toward their horses after the robbery, Starr in the rear holding the citizens at bay, nobody seemed disposed to lift a finger to stop them.

But there was one who was not "paralyzed with surprise and awe"—a sixteen-year-old boy named Paul Curry.

As the bandits were retreating up the street, the youngster stepped into a butcher shop, picked up a sawed-off rifle which was used for killing hogs, aimed at the menacing rearmost bandit, and fired.

The bandit collapsed in the dust of the street. He was Henry Starr, and Paul Curry's bullet had gone through both his hips, temporarily paralyzing him. The others got to their horses and fled, leaving their leader behind. Starr threw aside his gun and surrendered.

The five others of the gang made their escape for the time being. Later a posse directed by Bill Tilghman killed one, Lewis Estes, and captured two, Bud Maxfield and Claude Sawyer, who went to prison with Starr. The remaining two got away cleanly. One of them, from a statement made by another criminal, was a young man named Al Spencer, then about twenty years old, who had come under the influence of Starr and became a first-class desperado as a consequence.

Stroud was wildly excited after the robbery, and some of the men who had been very meek and inconspicuous until Starr was dropped by the courageous boy, now became suddenly brave—with the outlaw disarmed and in jail—and began an agitation to lynch him. But Bill Tilghman arrived in town, and before that impressive figure of the law lynch talk died quickly.

For safety Tilghman transferred Starr to the jail at Chandler, the county seat of Lincoln County, in which Stroud is located. There, while he was recovering from his wound and awaiting trial, the bandit was visited by E. D. Nix, the former U.S. marshal. Nix later told Gordon Hines, who recorded it in his *Oklahombres:*

> Starr had used his years in prison to complete the education that had begun in his childhood and I was surprised to hear him quoting great literary classics. He talked like an intellectual. I do not wonder that he was always able to interest influential people and number them among his host of friends.

After he was well enough to stand trial, Starr was convicted of bank robbery and once more sentenced to twenty-five years in prison. At the McAlester, Oklahoma, penitentiary, the prisoner began "interesting influential people" again, and about the end of 1920 he was out once more on parole.

By this time he was forty-seven years old and showing the effects of his hard life, alternately as an outlaw and a convict. He had spanned almost thirty years with his career, had been sentenced once to death and on three other occasions to a total of sixty-five years in prison, of which he served about fifteen years, being pardoned once and paroled twice. Of the fifteen years he was free, only five had been spent in lawful pursuits—the years he lived with his wife at Tulsa. All the rest of the time he was hiding from the law, or committing banditries.

It might be thought that he would be willing to give up the obviously futile business of defying society. But the old urge for crime had not left him. Once he had said:

"I don't know what's the reason that I do the things I do. You've known men who craved drugs or liquor or tobacco. I must have excitement. I crave it and it preys on me until I just step out and get into devilment of some kind."

Starr might have become a first-class hero if he had been a soldier, fighting in a war. But in peace his peculiar daring and desire for dangerous action only led him into trouble. He could not reform.

Hardly was he out of prison when, February 18, 1921, he made his last mistake.

Harrison, in northern Arkansas, is about one hundred miles east of Bentonville, where Starr held up his first bank. On that February day business was slow, and there were only two persons in the small bank, William J. Myers, cashier, and a bookkeeper.

They looked up as three men pushed the door open and entered. In a moment the situation was coldly clear. The three men had drawn guns and were menacing them—the bank was to be robbed.

"Get into the vault," said the leader, gesturing toward it with his six-shooter.

Helplessly the two bankers backed toward the open vault. Starr, who was conducting the holdup, intended to rob the vault, and then lock the men in it while he escaped.

But Myers, as he stepped backward, had a very different plan in mind. Bank robbery had been too common of late, and he had prepared for just such a contingency as he now faced. Inside the vault, leaning in a corner where it was concealed from the view of anyone outside, he kept a shotgun, well oiled and in good order, and loaded with buckshot.

Starr was following close upon the two bank men. One of them—the cashier—seemed to retreat rather quickly, as if he were thoroughly terrified. The bandit probably thought nothing of it, unless perhaps that such fearful obedience to his commands simplified the robbery.

Into the vault stepped Myers. An instant later, with his last fleeting vision in life, Starr looked into the black double muzzle of the shotgun.

The bandit had no chance to move. With the shocking bellow of the banker's shotgun, Henry Starr was blasted out of existence.[4]

His two accomplices fled without taking any money. They were too busy putting daylight between themselves and the angry banker with the shotgun to worry about loot.

[4] Starr died penniless, but he was not buried like a pauper. Years before, he had paid a Tulsa undertaker the money for a decent burial, saying, with foresight: "Some day you'll read in the paper that Henry Starr has been killed. When you do, give me a decent funeral." The undertaker carried out the compact and Henry Starr went to his last rest in a good coffin, with Christian rites.

Even before the death of Henry Starr the work of the great deputy marshals of the Territory was finished. It might, in fact, be called completed when Little Dick West went down with a six-shooter in each hand.

What of those marshals? "They who live by the sword shall die by the sword." Was it true in their case?

In most cases, no. Heck Thomas died peacefully at Lawton, Oklahoma, August 15, 1912, when he was sixty-two years old. He was the first of the "Three Guardsmen" to go.

Chris Madsen lived out his life at Guthrie, Oklahoma, near the scenes of some of his greatest adventures. I knew him in his old age, a blunt, realistic veteran, with still a very slight Danish accent, who answered truthfully, sometimes explosively, questions he considered worthy of an answer. He died at Guthrie, universally honored, at the serene old age of ninety-two, on January 9, 1944. He was the last survivor of the famous trio.

Of the "Three Guardsmen" only Bill Tilghman, perhaps the greatest of the fighting marshals of the Territory, died in harness. And he died a martyr to his own code: he never shot unless it was absolutely necessary, and he tried to give even criminals a fair break, which one of them did not give him.

After statehood in Oklahoma, Tilghman was for a time chief of police at Oklahoma City, by that time the capital. He wished to retire, his interests being in farming and horse breeding, but again and again he was called back to duty.

I met him in his later years, not long before his death. His hair and mustache were gray, but he still had the erect, spare figure of his active days, and the look from his eyes was direct and piercing. He possessed an old-fashioned graceful courtesy, but while he was glad to talk of current matters, whenever the subject was directed to his own deeds he would turn it aside with a dry witticism or simply by ignoring it. So quiet and unassuming was he that in his later years few of the new generation knew him as the grim and deadly nemesis of the outlaws. He would have been regarded as a splendid gentleman in any stratum of society.

Oil had become one of the spectacular features of Oklahoma. With each new wildcat gusher, there sprang up among the sprouting derricks little scrofulous shanty hamlets. And the residents of those towns were not oil workers. To the wild hysteria of oil excitement was added a new element—oil-field criminality. Like carrion crows there flocked to the new oil towns hordes of bootleggers, harlots, gamblers, highjackers, thieves, dope sellers, a shifty, sinister population.

One of the towns thus born was Cromwell, in Seminole County, where conditions grew so desperate that in 1924 a delegation of citizens implored Tilghman to restore order there. At the time the marshal was seventy years old, and friends advised him against accepting the post. But he took it, although I believe he had a premonition.

"If I don't get killed in a gun fight," he said, "I'll have to go to bed some day and die like a woman, and I don't want to do that."

To Cromwell he went, as a special representative of the governor, and once more Bill Tilghman was marshal of a wild and lawless town. But times had changed since he first put on a star. The whole sorry aspect of corruption due to the national mistake of the prohibition act, which gave to crime its widest and most profitable field of operations in the history of the world, had arisen. With it came a new generation of lawbreakers, underhanded, cowardly, the type that would shoot in the back, which Bill Doolin would not do. Tilghman's greatest problem was the underworld oligarchy of bootleggers and narcotics peddlers in Cromwell.

Four different officers were successively hired to help him, and one after another all four resigned. Still Tilghman remained on, and his presence in some measure quieted the town.

The bootleg-and-dope ring wanted him out of the way. It was the day of the prohibition agents, that curious breed, part fanatical, part venal, that sprang up in conjunction with prohibition and built their careers upon it. One of these, in Cromwell, was a man named Wylie Lynn, who drew a salary for "enforcing" the prohibitory laws, yet could not keep away from the bottle himself. He knew the bootleggers and the bootleggers knew him—and worked on him, playing upon his gullibility and jealousy until they built up a genuine hatred for Tilghman in his mind. Tilghman heard of this feeling on Lynn's part, but he went quietly about his duties.

On the night of November 1, 1924, he had dinner with a friend, W. E. Sirmans, president of the Cromwell Chamber of Commerce. Having finished their meal in a restaurant which stood next door to the Murphy Dance Hall, one of the more notorious establishments of the town, they stood outside on the board sidewalk talking.

Suddenly a car came roaring up. It contained Wylie Lynn, two women known as "notorious," and one of his bootlegger friends. They had been on a "party" and Lynn was crazy drunk and irresponsible, as they had planned to get him.

Out of the car jumped Lynn and started toward Tilghman, shooting into the ground and yelling.

Tilghman met him. To disarm the man was no problem for the marshal. Easily he wrested the weapon from the other's hand, and then, carrying Lynn's gun in one hand, began to conduct him to the police station, to sober him up, talking to him soothingly as he did so.

He knew Lynn was a prohibition agent and supposed he would come to his senses. It does not appear to have occurred to Tilghman that the other might have a second gun.

But Lynn did have one, in the side pocket of his coat. Putting his hand in this pocket, and without drawing his weapon, he turned the muzzle on Tilghman and fired—twice.

Sirmans caught the tall figure of the marshal as he staggered back, and eased him to the sidewalk. The long legs twisted once in agony. Then Bill Tilghman was dead, killed by a drunken fellow officer.

It was tragic that he should lose his life to a sneak when he had faced and shot it out with stand-up bad men so often. Bill Tilghman was a target for would-be killers scores of times, and carried at least four wounds on his body. Yet he continued the dangerous game of law enforcement until death took him.

Why did he keep at a task which had small rewards, great risks, and many discouragements?

I have in my possession a letter from John E. Rosser, an old-timer of Dallas, Texas, written January 8, 1941, to Guy J. Giffen, which makes a comment on this general question:

> I've known a flock of the trigger gents. I've known some Texas Rangers who simply don't know the emotion of fear. I don't know how the psychology boys would explain or rate this attribute. To me it often looks like amazing dumbness. I once asked Captain Cook, Texas Ranger, whether he had ever been hit rounding up the bad boys. He said simply, "Oh, yes, here and there." "Did it ever occur to you when, as you say, the boys slightly teched you up, to go into some less dangerous calling, like making dynamite caps or training tigers, for instance?" "No-o-o, I jest figgered each time that I had that one coming and I wouldn't get any more lead." . . . He said he got the [bad] boys, because that was his instructions.

That last sentence tells the story. There was no "dumbness" in Bill Tilghman. It was very much the reverse—he was a highly intelligent man, gifted with a magnificent sense of humor and a real enjoyment of life. He had one other thing: an extremely lofty sense of duty. He did the things he did "because that was his instructions."

For him was reserved an honor never before paid by Oklahoma to a private citizen. His body was taken to Oklahoma City, where for three days it lay in state in the capitol building, with a guard of honor.

During those three days thousands of citizens passed by for a last look at the peaceful, handsome face of the hero of a hundred adventures, the steady and fearless defender of the rights of his fellow citizens and the laws that protected them, the man who better than any other personified the taming of the old wild and lawless West.

11. *Automatics and Automobiles*

Al Spencer had several dubious distinctions. He might be called the last of the old-style Western bandits. He was a sort of a bridge between the "classic" era, when outlaws used horses, six-shooters, and Winchesters, and the new age, when they employed automobiles, automatic pistols, and submachine guns in their crimes. He was, moreover, a connection with the older brigands, notably Henry Starr, and therefore a link in the particular lengthy chain of crime going back to Quantrill and his desperadoes.

John Callahan—of whom more presently—said that Al Spencer was a member of Henry Starr's gang during the period ending in the Stroud bank robbery and Starr's capture in 1915. I think this statement was probably true, since it was made late in Callahan's life, after Spencer's death; and Callahan knew Spencer very well, having acted as a "fence" for him in disposing of hard-to-cash loot, and otherwise co-operating in his banditries.[1]

[1] Callahan, as a fence and trainer of crooks, knew more outlaws in his day than any other man in the West; and allowing for the fact that he could lie

But even if Callahan's statement about the Stroud affair is wrong, there can be no question of the Starr influence in Spencer's life. He was born in 1893, on a farm near Lenapah, Oklahoma. The town is in Nowata County, just south of Coffeyville, Kansas, where the Daltons met their doom. Through it, north to south, runs the Verdigris River. Always a turbulent area, this part of the old Territory was a ranging and recruiting ground for the Cook gang. Sam McWilliams was called the Verdigris Kid because he hailed from the Verdigris Valley. At Lenapah, Cherokee Bill murdered Ernest Melton, for which he later paid with his life on the Fort Smith gallows. At Lenapah, also, Henry Starr committed his first robbery, and it was near Nowata, a few miles south in the same county, that he killed Floyd Wilson, the deputy marshal, and then went abroad as a highwayman.

Later, in his periods of banditry, the rough country surrounding the Verdigris Valley was a favorite hiding place for Starr when the chase grew too warm. It was there he probably awaited the message about his extradition—the message he misunderstood—that sent him into outlawry after five law-abiding years at Tulsa. Starr had friends in Nowata County, and he was a hero to some of the young men who lived in the area.

Al Spencer grew up in this atmosphere, and he knew the outlaws who tarried in it or passed back and forth through it. For the bandits the Verdigris country was strategic. Southeast of it were the Cookson Hills, an outthrust of the Ozark Mountains, a region of deep, narrow valleys and numerous clear streams, today a favorite place for anglers. The deeply cut watercourses formed steep, picturesque bluffs, and the whole rugged country was heavily timbered with oak, ash, hickory, elm, walnut, sycamore, and other trees. It contained natural caves, and its scanty population was recessive and clannish, many of the families being Indian.

To the immediate west of the Verdigris lay the Osage Hills,

as fast and far as anyone I ever knew, there really was no reason for his lying in the case of Spencer and Starr. Throughout his career old John Callahan used falsehood as a valuable commodity, not to be frittered away on trivialities, but to be used when it could do him some good.

then as now cattle country, wild and remote. Ted Schumaker, a special agent of the American Railway Express Company, who later was one of the men who trailed Spencer, said of this area:

"There were places in that country where you could stand on a rocky mound, look for twenty miles in any direction, and see no trace of human habitation. Then, in a deep canyon three hundred yards away, you might stumble on a previously invisible ranch house."

The Osage Hills made an ideal retreat to which many an outlaw, among them Bill Raidler, fled when the law was hot on their trails. In Spencer's day the entire area surrounding Lenapah was as if it had been especially designed for a bandit's operational base. His favorite headquarters and the place where he met his death were both less than fifty miles due west of his birthplace in the Osage Hills.

Al Spencer was a hard-faced little man—five feet six inches tall, weighing 131 pounds, with gray eyes, chestnut hair, and irregular teeth. Like some undersized men, he appeared to feel, because of his slight stature, some sort of a compulsion to demonstrate to others that he was especially to be reckoned with.

From the very first he was restless and reckless. Through the Osage Hills ran the old "Thieves' Road," so called because of its use by horse thieves for decades in transporting stolen animals, and it was as a horse thief that Spencer began, when he was less than twenty years old. He found it not too difficult to take horses from the eastern part of the Territory, do a little skillful brand blotting on them, and dispose of them to cattlemen or Indians in the Osage Hills, or in Kansas as the Daltons had done.

From that he turned to store thefts. At the time of the Stroud bank robbery he was twenty-two years old, and already a veteran horse thief and store robber. It will be remembered that two of Starr's gang escaped and were not identified in the Stroud affair. I think it reasonable to believe Callahan's statement that Spencer was one of those men. He was not then well known and could easily shake off pursuit, as he later demonstrated beyond any argument. Perhaps the other man who thus escaped was Grover Durrell, his brother-in-law, who lived in the Osage Hills and was one of Spencer's followers later.

By 1917, Spencer was an outlaw, dodging officers, who wanted him for a number of robberies, and in 1920 he was captured and convicted of horse stealing. Sentenced March 8, 1920, to the Oklahoma state penitentiary at McAlester, he was able to renew his acquaintance with Henry Starr, who was serving time in the same prison.

At this period Starr, though maintaining an exemplary attitude toward the prison authorities and using every friend outside who could pull strings to get him released, was aging, bitter, and actually had no intention of trying to reform and rebuild his life, ever, as was proved when he was killed attempting to rob the bank at Harrison, Arkansas, within a few weeks after he was paroled from the penitentiary. From Starr, the inveterate bandit, Spencer gained some useful instruction in the techniques of robbery, and they may have made plans for a partnership when they both got out. As it happened, Starr's suave attitude toward the prison staff and outsiders obtained for him a parole late in 1920. He was killed in February 1921.

Shortly after Starr's death, occurred an incident of some mystery. The story of it is vague, but in substance it is as follows: Spencer became concerned over a "business matter." The nature of the matter is not of record, but he asked the warden to give him a leave of absence from the prison, promising to return. The warden, curiously, released him on this promise, for thirty days. Spencer left the penitentiary July 26, 1921, and even more curiously, he returned to the prison as he had promised, August 27, 1921, overstaying his leave by only one day.

Both Spencer and the warden are now dead, and the nature of the "business" transacted will never be disclosed. Could he have known of where some of Starr's loot was hidden, and "took the vacation" to locate it and put it in a safe place where nobody but himself could find it? We know that during the time he was out, he appeared in Nowata and talked to the chief of police, W. F. Davis. Davis suggested that when he served out his time he ought to settle down and go to work—Spencer had learned the electrician's trade.

The paroled bandit sneered. "Watch me when I get out" was all he said.

Having kept his promise to the warden, Spencer appeared to consider that he had discharged his obligations. On January 27, 1922, he "went over the wall," and escaped. From that day to his death he was one of the most active and daring bandits on the road.

In the McAlester penitentiary his closest associate was a tall, rather homely man, with a big nose and thinning hair, whose name was Frank Nash. Sometimes he was called Jelly Nash. He was a smooth-talking, polite man, at that time serving his second term in prison. The first was for killing an associate in a store robbery, Nollie Wortman, who "squealed." He was pardoned from his life sentence to enlist in the Army during World War I. The second sentence was for the robbery of a bank at Corn, Oklahoma.

Nash was well educated, and read widely—including the poets. Following Spencer's example, he applied for a leave of absence "for business reasons." Again the warden granted the odd request and released him in December 1922.

This time the "business" soon became evident. Nash simply joined Al Spencer and became his right-hand man. He was a thinking bandit, who became known as an expert in planning robberies, "casing" banks, and mapping "getaway charts."

Frank Nash had a special significance. On a bloody day in 1933, he was destined to be the central figure in a shocking episode of criminal violence that led to a new era in crime detection and punishment—the Kansas City Union Station Massacre.

The 1920s and early 1930s were the heyday of bank robbing. Small towns had little police protection, and the old days when citizens generally kept weapons handy were gone. Country banks were vulnerable with almost none of the modern protective devices. In a fast car bandits could roar in, hold up a bank, and roar out. Municipal authority ended at the town limits, sheriff's authority at county lines, and even state authority at the state boundaries. Wrote Don Whitehead in his book *The FBI Story:*

> Many of the gang operations were not in violation of federal statutes and there were some curious inconsistencies in the laws. For example, a bank official who embezzled $50 or $50,000 from a federal bank in 1933 (or before) had violated a federal law. But

> a gang of bandits might rob a federal bank of $100,000, machine-gun the bank officials and escape into another state without violating a single federal statute. And the bandits could be reasonably sure that pursuit would end at the state line.

It was not until 1934 that it became a federal crime to rob a federal bank, which made such a robbery the business of the dreaded "G men."[2] Yet, though the bandits paid small attention to it, the weapon already was being poised which would become their greatest check. The Department of Justice, in 1924, had reorganized its investigative force, placing at the head of the Federal Bureau of Investigation a young lawyer named J. Edgar Hoover. The new director proceeded at once to rebuild that organization, divorce it from politics, and create a personnel of highly trained agents, most of whom were educated in law or business. Not for ten years did it gain the wide authority and jurisdiction whereby it became such a terror to criminals, but in the very years when bank robbers seemed to have things much their own way, their nemesis was preparing one day to combat them on their own terms.

The day of the FBI, however, was still to come, and meantime Al Spencer, Frank Nash, and others, including Grover Durrell and Earl Thayer, boldly took advantage of the situation. In the year and eight months between Spencer's escape from McAlester and his death, he and his gang robbed twenty banks by actual knowledge, and he was accused of robbing twenty-two more, a total of forty-two—although Alva McDonald, the U.S. marshal who finally ran him down, was of the opinion that "Spencer was a good publicity man and only participated in a small portion of the crimes he was credited with."

Whatever the actual number of his robberies, his love for publicity is well established. He was an exhibitionist, and loved to make "wisecracks" which later would be quoted.

One of his famous remarks occurred during the robbery of a

[2] G men, the underworld nickname for Government men, was given to the FBI agents by Machine Gun Kelly, when he was captured after the Urschel kidnaping, September 26, 1933. Cringing, Kelly cried out, "Don't shoot, G men! Don't shoot, G men!" Newspapers, radios, movies, and magazines popularized the name, and the publicity proved helpful to the FBI, since it dramatized its efforts.

bank at Chickasha, Oklahoma. He and his gang entered the place and herded the bank employees into the directors' room, where they ordered them to lie face down on the floor while the looting took place.

A girl, one of the stenographers, lay down on her back, staring up at the robbers. Spencer pointed his six-shooter at her.

"I said for you to lay face down!" he yelled. "Where the hell do you think you are—in a directors' meeting?"

The story got into the newspapers and so did some of his other gibes. Sensational journals gave him great publicity, headlining him as the "Phantom Terror," "King of the Osage Bad Lands," "Wild Rider of Oklahoma," and so on. It was balm for his notoriety-seeking soul.

But it also intensified the search for him. Several times officers thought they had him cornered, but he always managed to slip away. On March 26, 1923, he was wounded in a fight with a posse after robbing a bank at Mannford, Oklahoma. In that same fight he shot and fatally wounded J. B. Ringer, a Mannford secondhand man. One of his gang, Bud Maxwell, was killed, but Spencer and others escaped through the blackjack undergrowth and wooded river bottoms. Once more the story ended with "escaped into the Osage Hills."

It was the bandit's vanity, and his inordinate love for publicity, that brought about his downfall. Oklahoma newspapers began to compare him with the old-time bandits, like the Doolin, Cook, and Dalton gangs. He was, they agreed, in the tradition of those notable predecessors.

All this was well and good enough. It pleased Spencer, who was an avid reader of accounts of his own doings.

But presently the newspapers began to temper their descriptions of him. He might be in the old tradition, they said, but he lacked the real daring of the others. His robberies were all of banks—easy game, the newspapers gibed, compared to robbing trains.

There was an excellent reason why Spencer and his gang had not done any train robberies. As holding up banks—in those years—seemed to become easier, train robbery had progressively grown more dangerous. Railroad companies had developed their own staffs of trained investigators, who were supplemented by equally trained agents of express companies. The government added its long arm, where mails or cars carrying mails were tampered with. County and state lines did not hamper these crime hunters. Furthermore, the railroads combined forces, offered rewards, and furnished every facility, including transportation and quick message service, to those who set out to capture train robbers. Spencer was wise to confine himself to banks.

Yet the editorial gibes stung him. As they continued he grew more and more restive.

"Sure Thing Bandit," "Petty Bank Robber," "Cash and Carry Outlaw"—epithets such as these ate into his soul. At length, goaded beyond endurance, he decided that he must rob a train—just one—to prove to the world (and those sneering newspaper writers) that he could perform such a feat if he wanted to do so.

In the Osage Hills hideout, there was a dramatic council. Frank Nash, the cunning and practical, protested against the idea. Why run unnecessary risks? He pointed out that they had been amazingly successful and could continue to be so almost indefinitely, barring some sort of accident. But train robbery—that was a different matter.

Spencer listened to him, then overruled him. He was the boss. The train robbery was to go through, and plans were carefully laid.[3]

On the night of August 20, 1923, two men boarded the Katy Limited at Bartlesville, Oklahoma, for Okesa, about fifteen miles west. One of the men was Charley Carson, a section foreman who lived near Okesa. The other man had bought a ticket at Bartlesville solely for the purpose of causing the train to stop at Okesa, which was a flag station only, where the Limited only paused to discharge passengers.

[3] It was so thoroughly planned, from a publicity angle, that Spencer invited some of his friends from the Osage Hills to watch it. Officers, investigating next day, found a place on a hill overlooking the scene, where the grass was trampled down and burned matches and cigarette stubs had been dropped, which marked the spot where the "audience" had stood and observed the proceedings below. Spencer took no chances that the train holdup should be credited to anyone else.

As the train halted at the station shortly after midnight, two other men came out of the shadows and boarded it. They did not have tickets, but the conductor who saw them board took his time about collecting their fares, for this kind of passenger traffic was not unusual.

The train resumed its way. About a mile from Okesa, Byron Tower, the fireman, going to the tender, found himself looking into the barrel of a pistol held by a man who was masked by pulling a portion of a woman's silk stocking over his head and face. At the same moment a second bandit, with a red bandanna handkerchief tied about his features just below his eyes, scrambled over the coal in the tender, and covered William Miller, the engineer. These were the two men who had boarded the train at Okesa, and they had made their way forward to the engine.

Tower's cry of protest was silenced by a blow from the stocking-faced bandit's pistol that dropped him to the floor, unconscious. The man who struck the blow was Al Spencer.

"Stop the train," crisply commanded the red-masked bandit. He was the taller of the two and throughout the robbery he commented on various topics, such as the then recent death of President Warren G. Harding, and appeared better educated than his shorter, blunter companion. This was Frank Nash.

The engineer could do nothing but comply with the order. By the time the train stopped, the fireman recovered consciousness.

"Get down and cut the train for us," he was told.

Other men ran out of the woods, where they had awaited the train. They fired a volley of shots down the sides of the passenger cars, to keep anyone from coming out.

Tower was forced to uncouple the front part of the train, including the engine, mail and baggage coaches, from the passenger coaches, and the engineer then was made to pull the forward section some distance ahead from the rest of the train.

Working with complete deliberation, the bandits entered the mail car and forced Warren Burke, the postal employee, to turn over the registered mail. The chief item they garnered was a package containing $20,000 in Liberty bonds, readily negotiable, which were consigned from a Muskogee bank to the state treasurer at Oklahoma City. Otherwise the loot was small.

The Pullman cars all had been locked before the robbers turned to them. One proposed that they blow the sleepers open.

"And kill women and kids, maybe?" said the leader. "We don't do that."

While they debated, the whistle of another train—a freight—approaching from the rear, was heard. At that the bandits climbed into automobiles, which were by prearrangement waiting at the place, and drove rapidly away.

A terrible disaster was averted when a train flagman ran back along the track and with a frantically waving red lantern managed to halt the oncoming freight train just in time to keep it from crashing into the rear of the standing Pullmans, filled with passengers.

Charley Carson, the section foreman, left the train at Okesa, and was walking toward his home, when he saw the train slowing down and stopping, and a little later heard the shots fired by the outlaws at the place it stopped a mile away. Knowing immediately what was happening, he ran to a telephone box beside the right of way, and sent a frantic message which apprised the railroad authorities of the Okesa robbery almost while it was being committed. But the bandits disappeared in the pitchy black night and for the time being all trace of them was lost.

All Oklahoma was in a high state of excitement next day. The train robbery was the first for some time, and Al Spencer at last gained the full recognition he craved—his name was bracketed with those of Doolin, Dalton, Cook, and Starr without reservations.

But he also got something far less desirable, which had been forecast by Frank Nash. The mails had been robbed, and United States marshal's forces, aided by postal inspectors, took his trail. Operatives of the express company and the railroad, together with local authorities, augmented the scope of the work. A concentrated man hunt began—with Spencer as the central quarry—far more intense and prolonged than any he had thus far experienced.

Alva McDonald, United States marshal, and his men, together with special investigators of the Katy Railroad and the American

Railway Express Company, with all available local officers, were at Okesa by dawn next day. At least one hundred and fifty men were out scouring the country, at first without much result.

Then came a break. Ike Ogg, a tenant farmer, living close to Okesa, under questioning admitted buying a ticket at Bartlesville for Okesa, though he denied any part in the robbery. Pressed still further, he finally confessed he bought the ticket for "the boys" and named five of them: Grover Durrell, Curtis Kelly, Earl Thayer, Frank Nash—and Al Spencer.

Posses, numbering twelve men each and all heavily armed, began to comb the Osage Hills. An astonishing bag of men with police records came from that apparently uninhabited country—of sixty-two who were questioned, only one was without some sort of criminal past. There were bootleggers, highwaymen, petty thieves, confidence men, crooks of all kinds, "combings of the underworld from Oklahoma City, Wichita, Kansas City and even St. Louis."

But no Al Spencer.

Someone remembered that at least one, perhaps others, of the bandits were masked with a woman's silk hose drawn over their faces. A search began for the "lady of the stockings," and she was found—at Ogg's home.

When officers entered the house she tried to get to a rifle that stood in a corner, and it required three men to hold her in her furious struggles until she was exhausted. Her name was Goldie Bates, she was part Indian, not unattractive, and Spencer's sweetheart. She had furnished the stockings, all right, but otherwise she gave her captors no information.

Earl Thayer was known to live in Oklahoma City, and two or three days after the robbery he was picked up there.

By that time rewards totaling $10,000 had been offered by Governor J. C. Walton of Oklahoma, the federal government, and the railroad. For years the Osage Hills people had been silent, but that $10,000 made things different. Where before there had been not one hint of Spencer's whereabouts, tips now began to come in to Alva McDonald, the U.S. marshal, and L. U. Gaston, chief of police at Bartlesville.

At last a woman, whose name was witheld by the authorities, told them that she knew where Spencer and his gang were hiding. So accurate was her description of the bandits that her story was believed, and she added this:

"Spencer doesn't take part in the little robberies. He leads the big ones."

To the amazement of McDonald and Gaston, the location she named was only a few miles—about ten—north and west of Bartlesville, in a broken area of the Osage reservation.

That was late in the day, September 15, 1923, and the Katy train robbery was less than a month old. Immediately a carload of men, consisting of McDonald, Gaston, M. L. Adamson, a postal inspector, and three others, started out in the gathering night, to investigate the place described by the woman.

The country road they had to take to reach it was rough and full of twists and turns. It had rained recently, so that in places the going was slippery and trapped with mudholes. To keep from being bogged down travel was slower than the man hunters would have liked and it was full night before they reached their destination.

As the car seesawed, snorting, around a corner, the headlights picked up a solitary figure, walking beside the road. The man was carrying a rifle.

His body tensed as the lights bore down upon him, and he began to run.

"Drop that gun!" someone shouted as the car came to a skidding stop.

For answer he turned and fired at them.

From the automobile burst a sudden crescendo of sound—six rifles blasting at once at the figure caught in the headlights.

They saw him take two or three wavering steps, then fall heavily in the mud at the side of the road.

It was Al Spencer. Three bullets had torn through his body and he was dead when they reached him.

He was wearing an old yellow shirt and overalls, and apparently had been out hunting when he was seen. In his clothing they found stuffed $10,000 worth of Liberty bonds which later were identified as part of the Okesa train robbery loot. His vanity, which lured him into the train holdup, had been his death.

Grover Durrell and Curtis Kelly were located by officers at

Durrell's ranch southwest of Pawhuska, and surrendered without a fight. Another member of the gang, Riley Dixon, described as a "small-time crook, out of his depth in the Oklahoma bad lands," surrendered soon after. Earl Thayer already was in custody. Frank Nash, who had protested against the train robbery, was captured months later by McDonald almost on the Mexican border, on the Texas side of the Rio Grande River. All of these men were sent to the federal penitentiary at Leavenworth, Kansas, for terms of twenty-five years each.

Of his entire gang only Al Spencer, when the showdown came, tried to fight it out and died. With him died the era of frontier outlaws.

One thing Al Spencer did was to have far-reaching effects. In his early, store-robbing days, perhaps in 1915 or before, he made a business contact with a gross, unsavory man named John Callahan, and thereby the weft of the crime fabric swung northward to Wichita, Kansas.

Close by the railroad tracks near the Union Station in Wichita was a junk yard, with an old, two-story frame house. In this place lived Callahan. I knew him tolerably well, for I was a police reporter in Wichita in the 1920s. He was a portly old Irishman, with close-cropped white hair, a smooth white face, a double chin, and a potbelly. Usually he was smoking a short black pipe, and he was a smooth talker with a slight hint of Irish brogue on his tongue. Partly, I suppose, because it is hard for most people to imagine a fat man as very sinister, for a long time few suspected that he was other than the honest Irish junk dealer he seemed to be.

Yet Callahan was a criminal, and a very cunning one. I do not believe his importance in the history of outlawry in the West has ever been fully appraised, because he was careful, wherever possible, never to figure as a headliner in any of the crimes in which he participated. He used the junk yard as a "front" for every kind of devious lawless enterprise.

There is no reason in this account to go at length into his record, for it contained few spectacular episodes, but it was a long one and a bad one. He began as a bank robber, served two or three prison sentences, graduated to become the "brains" of a gang of bandits and burglars, at one time was the largest wholesaler of illicit liquor in Kansas, developed an interstate trade in stolen goods, and wound up his career as an importer and seller of narcotics.

Callahan, a singular and unappetizing genius of the criminal world, was a man of many gifts. At his height, he was the best-known "fence" in the Midwest, which is why Spencer came to him. Callahan had mysterious connections, all over the country, through which he could dispose of almost any kind of stolen articles, ranging from postage stamps to automobiles. He was known as the man who could sell securities taken from banks—giving the robber twenty cents on the dollar, the rest going to the receiver of the stolen securities, with, of course, a comfortable "cut" for John Callahan's own capacious pocket.

In his unctuous, cunning way, he established working contacts with police officials, secondhand dealers, pawnbrokers, handlers of "hot" money, and store owners, even bankers, not only in Kansas but in other states.[4] Early in his career as a crime impresario he arranged a "treaty" with the Wichita police, whereby he undertook to keep banditry out of Wichita, if the constabulary, in return, refrained from bothering him and the "boys" who visited him. For a period, under this agreement, the city was singularly free from major crimes, but the crooks were free to use it as operating headquarters for crimes elsewhere, ranging as far as 400 miles away for bank robberies at times, but returning to Wichita as a haven of safety. Wichita thus became a part of what

[4] A weird case grew out of Callahan's "connections" in Wichita, including the city hall and a banker. In 1910, after his emissaries had robbed nineteen stores with post offices in conjunction, he found himself with stamps to the value of $6261 in his possession. He arranged with Frank Burt, then police chief, to take the postage stamps off his hands at a considerable discount. Burt sold them to a prominent Wichita banker for a slight profit, and the banker disposed of them to a patent-medicine manufacturer for his "cut." The banker was arrested, convicted of selling stolen postage stamps, and sentenced to a year in prison. Before he served time, however, his influential and moneyed friends persuaded President William Howard Taft to pardon him. He went back into the banking business and died many years later, successful and highly respected in the community. Callahan served a sentence for dealing in the stamps, but Burt, who turned state's evidence, was not prosecuted, although he "resigned" from the police force.

Maurice M. Milligan, U.S. district attorney in Missouri, called the "corridor of crime," including, among other cities, Kansas City, St. Paul, St. Louis, Chicago, and Detroit.

Nobody will ever know how many noted criminals Callahan sheltered or had dealings with, but in addition to Al Spencer, Frank Nash, Wilbur Underhill (who killed a policeman named Merle Colver in Wichita), Diamond Joe Sullivan, the Majors brothers, the two Poffenbergers, Eddie Adams, Frank Foster, and Pretty Boy Floyd, with whom his relationship is established, there were many others. It is more than a mere conjecture that among these were Al Karpis (a Kansas product and a "graduate" of the Hutchinson, Kansas, reformatory under his true name of Raymond Alvin Karpavicz), Jake Fleagle, Fred Barker, and others of that stamp who unquestionably operated at times in the Wichita area.

Two of his associates in the dope racket were Clyde and Nellie Miles, man and wife, both of whom were later convicted and sent to a federal prison for running narcotics up from Mexico. Nellie Miles kept a house in the southern part of Wichita, where criminals could hide from the law and at the same time be entertained.

Late in the 1920s John Callahan's sins caught up with him at last. He was arrested with a shipment of narcotics he was bringing up from Mexico, by Oklahoma officers, and sentenced to the penitentiary at McAlester for twenty-five years, which would have meant the rest of his natural life. After serving seven of those years, however, he was paroled because of old age and physical infirmity, to go home and die.

Old and broken, he returned to Wichita. It was in this period that Captain W. O. Lyle, of the Wichita police force, in an effort to put together some of the pieces of the criminal jigsaw puzzle, talked with him repeatedly. Curiously, Callahan was fairly willing to discuss his past with a police officer who, as he well knew, had brought about his arrest more than once. He had no such willingness to discuss such matters with newspapermen, which indicates that he was too canny to desire publicity as some other criminals have done.

He told Lyle, for example, of his association with Al Spencer and of Spencer's relationship with Henry Starr. He also discussed other outlaws, all of them at that time dead. But he revealed no secrets to Lyle or anyone else concerning any man who was living.

Callahan died alone in his house, June 8, 1936, when he was seventy years old. His body was not discovered for some time after his demise.

Perhaps John Callahan's most sinister importance was in his role as a sort of modern Fagin—a trainer and schooler of criminals. He silently observed the young men who hung about Wichita pool halls and dance halls, and who seemed to have no visible means of support. When one of them seemed to show promise along his peculiar lines, he would often draw him into his web like a fat, unhealthy spider, and by showing him how "easy money" was to be obtained, start him on a career of crime.

Bootlegging was the first step. Kansas had a state prohibition law since the early '80s, and had therefore, through all that time, been a happy hunting ground for bootleggers. None supported more heartily or contributed more heavily to the political fights against any symptom of repeal of the state prohibition law than those same gentlemen, who considered it their prime source of income, since they controlled the liquor supply and could ask what they wanted for it.

The prohibition laws never were unanimously approved or desired by the people. General public and private agreement is necessary for the strict enforcement of any law. Thus, all but a small criminal group are behind the laws against theft, murder, and fraud, which have the full support of public opinion. But the prohibition laws never were more than effort by a majority by a rather small margin, to enforce its will upon a minority, often a very large minority. The inevitable corruption and venality among law-enforcement officers that such a law produces existed for decades in Kansas. In Wichita, major bootleggers usually had informers in the city hall, even on the police force itself, so that when perfunctory raids were made, warnings went out in sufficient time so that the "evidence" could be removed to some other place, not mentioned in the search warrant.

After national prohibition went into effect in 1920, the situation which had existed in state-wide dimensions became nation-wide.

Almost immediately the federal government began to find difficulty in enforcing the Volstead Act (which had been passed over the veto of President Woodrow Wilson, who considered it unenforceable).

The result has been seen. A new criminal population appeared, as bootleggers and racketeers organized to supply illicit liquor by smuggling or manufacture, at the cost of crime, even murder. Wrote Herbert Asbury in *The Great Illusion:*

> The appalling moral collapse which followed in the wake of the Eighteenth Amendment and World War I caused the almost complete breakdown of law enforcement throughout the United States, and made it possible for the underworld to take over the importation, manufacture, distribution, and sale of illegal liquor . . . The criminal gangs required only a comparatively short time to perfect the setups of their new booze departments, to establish sources of supply, and to secure their operations against undue interference . . . In considerably less than two years the whole vast machinery of underworld domination was running smoothly and peacefully, and the money was pouring in at the rate of millions of dollars a month. The shooting began when greedy captains encroached on the territory of others.

Prohibition was the greatest money windfall crime ever received, in any country, in all history. Leo Katcher, in *The Big Bankroll,* describes the vast financing of the liquor syndicates; and relates how the underworld went into the corruption and control of governments of important cities and even states, and how the gangsters "policed" their own organizations through such professional killers as the deadly Murder, Inc.

More appalling, the criminal czars became so powerful and so rich that they continued to operate after prohibition ended. Lacking the enormous revenues of illicit liquor, they turned to other sources, including labor racketeering, "protection" extortions, various "numbers rackets," mulcting of the gullible public through gambling centers, controlled prostitution, operation of slot machines, preying on food, laundry, and other sources, and worst of all, the widespread, well-organized, intensely and malignantly evil traffic in narcotics.

Frederic Sondern, Jr., in his *Brotherhood of Evil: the Mafia,* has detailed the shocking extent of that traffic today, its international scope, and the vast network of enterprises—many of them apparently legitimate—which have been built up to conduct the dope racket.

John Callahan was one of the first to perceive the values of prohibition. He had a head start over most of the nation's racketeers, because state prohibition in Kansas long antedated that in the nation. But national prohibition brought with it a new and growing spirit of disrespect for law, and he took advantage of it.

He started his young men as booze runners, furnishing the cars. Two at a time usually made such a drive. Kansas City and Joplin were the chief sources of wet goods for Wichita, and Callahan's boys knew the back roads and how to avoid the towns, when transporting a cargo of liquor. It meant fast driving, and some risk, but Callahan paid them well.

The next lesson for the neophytes in crime was car theft, with all the refinements, such as alteration of appearance by paint jobs, removal of identification marks, and transportation to one or another of Callahan's distant connections, for sale probably in some other state.

Finally, his "star" pupils graduated into banditry. In his lengthy career the greasy old steerer of crimes developed a number of bandits who gained notoriety on a regional, even a national scale. Among them were the identical Poffenberger twins, Major and Minor; the three Majors brothers, Roy, Ray, and Dudley; and a deadly little man who went by the name of Eddie Adams.

His real name was W. J. Wallace, and he was born on a farm near Hutchinson, Kansas, in 1887. When he was a young boy his father died, and his mother remarried.

Disliking any form of hard labor, he learned the barber's trade when he began to shift for himself, and was for several years a barber in Wichita. There he became acquainted with John Callahan and went through that worthy's usual course of instruction—running and selling booze, petty crime, and finally banditry. For his criminal operations he adopted the alias of Eddie Adams.

It was a Jekyll and Hyde existence—the sober, law-abiding Wallace by day, becoming the evil crook, Eddie Adams, by night.

And as in the great Stevenson allegory, the evil nature finally was triumphant in him, so much so that at his death very few ever knew that he had started his career as Wallace, so firmly established was his identity as Adams.

Although he was roughly contemporary with Al Spencer, there were basic differences, of an ugly nature, which made Eddie Adams the worse criminal of the two. He did not like "hideouts" in remote fastnesses, belonging to a newer school of outlaws who believed that a city was easier to lose one's self in, besides offering accommodations and surroundings far more sybaritic.

Adams liked his liquor, his gambling, and his girls. For a time he even ran a gambling joint, but it landed him in jail. He had been married, but his wife left him when she discovered that he had many other women in whom he was interested, and more than that, was engaged in criminal practices. After that he allowed his fancy to roam where it pleased, and although he was not prepossessing, having an ugly look that was like a threat every minute, there seemed to be women enough who found a strange, unwholesome attraction in him. He liked to stay at Nellie Miles' place in Wichita, where he could indulge all his whims of pleasure. Whether or not he was a narcotics addict, I do not know, but he had one characteristic of the heroin fiend—he killed without any compunction or sign of moral awareness of murder.

John Callahan saw to it that Adams met the Majors brothers, and with them he began a desperate and bloody career. They robbed several banks together; but early in 1920 they made the mistake of holding up a gambling game in Tom Pendergast's town, Kansas City. The Kansas City gamblers were tough. In the shooting that followed, three dice players were hit, one fatally, while Roy and Ray Majors were wounded and captured, together with Eddie Adams. Dudley Majors escaped, to serve later a term in the Delaware state penitentiary.

The two Majorses were sentenced to five years each, and Roy died in the Missouri prison, while Ray later died in the Kansas penitentiary after subsequent arrests when he was released.

But Eddie Adams, who, as the actual slayer, was condemned to life imprisonment, served not one day of that sentence. While being shipped to prison he leaped from a moving train and escaped in the night.

Broke and desperate now, the evil little man beat his way back to Kansas, thumbing rides and asking for handouts. In spite of the wide publicity his escape had received in the newspapers, nobody seemed to suspect him, and surprisingly soon he was back in Wichita.

But bad luck seemed to follow him. He obtained a car and a gun—probably from that patron of the arts (of criminality), John Callahan—and held up a bank at Cullison, Kansas. Unhappily, for him, while hastening back toward Wichita he wrecked his car near Pratt, Kansas, and took refuge under a bridge. There he was found lying dejectedly on a timber, hoping that nobody would notice him. He surrendered quite peaceably, and presently found himself in the state penitentiary at Lansing, Kansas, under a sentence of thirty years.

There he met three other convicts, Frank Foster, George Weisberger, and D. C. Brown. With Foster he became very friendly, and told him his whole life story, perhaps with embellishments. He had, so he said, committed two singlehanded train robberies and a score of bank robberies, and killed a man in Kansas City. Always, he told Foster, he could hide out in Wichita, where he had an "understanding" with the authorities.

What Adams did not know was that in the period he was in the Kansas penitentiary conditions changed in Wichita. A new city administration cleaned up the police department, and a gray-eyed, courageous, incorruptible man named S. W. Zickefoose became chief of detectives. As his first act, Zickefoose "abrogated" the "treaty" with Callahan and his unfragrant friends, and began arresting on sight men with criminal records unless they could give perfect accounting for themselves.

Meantime Adams made an unholy alliance with Foster. He was hard to hold in any prison, and it was not very long before he made the authorities at the penitentiary look very foolish. On the night of August 13, 1921, he and his three friends grounded the current in the electric plant, blacking out the prison lights, and went over the high wall using a sectional ladder they had built in secret.

By the time the warden and his guards could turn on emergency lights it was too late to shoot the escapees. Outside waited a fast getaway car with the motor running, and the men were gone.

Later the car was found abandoned and Brown was recaptured. But the others were safely away. It was believed by police, who reconstructed the event sometime afterward, that the driver of the escape automobile was Billy Fintelman, a reckless young man who had made a brave record as a soldier in World War I, but turned bad.

It was after Eddie Adams slipped back into Wichita—by night—that he suffered the shock of learning that the pleasant "understanding" between the law and the lawless had ended. His career as an almost compulsive killer of the blood-chilling type began at this time.

For a while he hid at the house of Nellie Miles—whose husband, Clyde, was absent from the city, running dope up from Mexico. Nellie made Eddie most welcome, but there was no romance connected with it. He was interested in a girl who worked in a local photography shop, who had been most friendly with him before he became a convict.

But now the girl had turned cold. She preferred the company of A. L. Young, a policeman on a night beat.

Adams knew the answer to that, or thought he did. One night Young's dead body was found in an alley, with several bullets in it. Adams, unlike Bill Doolin, who would not shoot an officer in the back, had no such scruples. He ambushed Young, shot him down while he was unsuspectingly going about his duties, and left him. He now had two murders on his record.

But, incomprehensibly to him, the girl failed to respond to such a testimonial of regard on the bandit's part. Indeed, she refused to have anything whatever to do with him. She knew he had killed Young, although she did not go to the police, partly because of her former association with the outlaw, and partly because of her fear of him.

Adams must have considered that "women are kittle cattle," as some sage once remarked, but that did not salve his wounded pride. In sheer pique, perhaps, he went raging on a splurge of robberies, aided by his friends Foster and Weisberger.

They began by robbing two banks, at Haysville and Rose Hill, both near Wichita. In the Haysville holdup Adams showed the streak of brutality that was developing in him by hitting an old man, James Krievell, eighty-two years of age, a crashing blow over the head with his gun. He had no reason for that act. The old man was not resisting, and Adams was not angry with him. It was a causeless deed of pent-up homicidal fury. Old Mr. Krievell never fully recovered from the injury to his skull, and his death some time later was directly attributable to the bandit's irresponsible cruelty. If Eddie Adams did not murder him outright in the technical sense, he had his death to answer for.

But his conscience had atrophied to a point where nothing he did bothered him any more. With his thugs, Foster, Weisberger, and Fintelman, he left a trail of pillage across Missouri into Iowa, robbing a series of banks, including one at Osceola, Iowa, October 19, 1921.

They had been traveling almost day and night, and were tired. Perhaps they were overconfident. At any rate, after the Osceola holdup, Adams directed Fintelman, the driver of the bandit car, to turn off along a side road, not far from Murray, Iowa, to divide the loot and take a nap.

They anticipated no pursuit, nor would there have been any, had not C. W. Jones, a farmer near whose place they parked their car, thought their actions suspicious and telephoned Sheriff E. J. West, of Osceola. The bandits had halted within twelve miles of Osceola, and it did not take Sheriff West, with a hastily summoned posse, consisting of John Miller, Charley Eaton, and a couple of other men, long to reach farmer Jones' house.

Jones accompanied them to show where the outlaws were sleeping, and also to help in their capture.

It was Adams, alert as a cat, who awoke just in time. At his sudden shot, Jones, who had warned the officers of his presence, sank down, dying. There was a brief burst of firing by both sides. Miller, Eaton, and an unidentified posseman were wounded. Sheriff West escaped on foot, in spite of the lead which ripped the ground about him.

Not one of the outlaws was injured, but a bullet fired by one of the posse struck their car, shattering a vital part of the mechanism.

Left in possession of the bloody field, with a dead man and three wounded men lying about, they coolly appropriated the sheriff's car, which was standing not far away, and leaving the fallen where they lay, drove off, heading back for Kansas.

It was standard practice to abandon stolen cars, steal others, and leave them in exchange for still others, to baffle pursuit, and this pattern was now followed. At Mound City, Kansas, the sheriff's car was discovered a morning or so later. The bandits had disappeared with an automobile they had stolen at that town. There followed a wholesale looting of eleven stores at Muscotah, Kansas, a second car theft, and Eddie Adams and his murderous crew headed back for Wichita.

Near Newton, Kansas, in sheer effrontery, they paused long enough to hold up two deputy sheriffs, wreck and set fire to their vehicle, and then race on, taking with them the money and weapons of the officers, leaving the disconsolate deputies afoot and unarmed.

Back in Wichita, they spent a few days recuperating. But on November 5 they were in the headlines again with the robbery of a Santa Fe express train near Ottawa, from which they escaped with $35,000.

That was Eddie Adams' last big robbery.

For a time he hid once more in Nellie Miles' house. He made it a policy to stay closely hidden indoors by day, but his restlessness forced him to get out now and then at night.

It was on one such occasion, the night of November 20, that two carloads of Adams' friends took a pleasure ride. In one car rode Adams with Nellie Miles, Foster, and two girls, Wilma Fleming, eighteen years old, and Annie Jones, only fifteen. The driver of the car was George J. Macfarline, a local hoodlum. In the other car were Fintelman and his wife, Weisberger, P. D. Orcutt, and a couple of girls.

Two motorcycle patrolmen, Rudolph La Croix and Bob Fitzpatrick, noticed the automobiles. Orders had been issued by Chief Zickefoose to investigate all suspicious-looking cars after night, and on a routine investigation they overtook the Adams car and ordered it over to the curb.

A spurt of flame from the automobile, and Fitzpatrick fell dead.

Adams had fired the shot. "Step on it! Get out of here!" he yelled, and Macfarline gave the gas to the machine.

La Croix halted to attend his companion and did not pursue. He had recognized Nellie Miles in the car, but it was not until later that the identity of the murderer was learned. Why Adams did not kill him also is hard to explain, unless perhaps it was because of his eagerness to get out of town.

The outlaws threatened to kill the women if they said anything about the episode, and let them out of the car. Adams now had the deaths of five men on his hands, and two of them were Wichita police officers. He fled south into Cowley County, where Bill Doolin once had sought refuge, with Macfarline and Foster in the car with him.

In the night their car ran low on gas, and they stopped and aroused a farmer named George Oldham, to buy gas from him. Oldham did not know who they were and was willing to sell them gas, but when he saw Eddie Adams get into his own car and try to start it, he went over toward the bandit protesting.

Adams drew his automatic and coldly shot the farmer down.

For the first time, now, he seemed to lose his nerve. With the other two he ran across a field on foot. But presently he thought better of such a flight and with Foster returned to the Oldham place. After filling their car with gas they drove away.

Now occurred a bizarre episode. Macfarline had become separated from his companions and did not return with them to the farm. Instead he continued, alternately running and walking, for several miles until he reached the little station of Akron, Kansas. There he bought a railroad ticket for Gordon, Kansas, an oil town twenty miles farther north, where he perhaps thought he might steal a car.

Macfarline was weary from his long flight on foot and lack of sleep. It would be some time before his train arrived, and he began to nod as he half reclined in one of the waiting-room seats, and presently dozed off into slumber.

After a time the station agent heard him muttering in his sleep. A curious soul, the agent listened, and presently he realized with some alarm that the rambling words uttered by the sleeping man who was the solitary occupant of the waiting room, had to do with a murder—one of which he had read in the papers, the killing of Officer Fitzpatrick in Wichita.

Quickly he went to a telephone and called the police at Winfield, a few miles to the south. When he reported the matter to the officers and confirmed a description they gave him of Macfarline, the Winfield police made hurried arrangements with officials of the railroad to help in the capture of the outlaw.

The plan, which was followed, was to take Macfarline on the train as if everything was normal, but carry him through Gordon, to Augusta, a somewhat larger oil town, where officers would be waiting.

When the train failed to stop at Gordon, Macfarline protested. He was told the town was not a scheduled stop and relaxed. At Augusta, W. A. Marshal, chief of police of that city, boarded the train with a couple of other officers. Macfarline was not enough of a desperado to attempt resistance. He surrendered meekly.

No announcement was made of his capture. Chief Marshal quietly turned him over to Sergeant J. G. Yeager and Detectives Dan Carrier and Walter Rambo, of the Wichita police department, and the prisoner was spirited to that city.

It was an embarrassed Macfarline who was confronted not only by the fact that he had talked in his sleep but that he had mumbled out some highly interesting—and incriminating—information about the killing of Fitzpatrick. Under questioning he said that he and his wife had a house in the southern part of Wichita, told of the Oldham shooting, and from what the police sweated out of him, coupled with information furnished by La Croix, Zickefoose gained a very fair idea who were concerned with the murder of his police officer.

There is an axiom that a cop killer is himself to be killed.

To this end the Wichita police turned with angry determination.

One of Zickefoose's first orders was to have the Macfarline house searched and watched. Two motorcycle officers, Ray (Tommy) Casner and W. W. Wright, went on this assignment. They found the place empty, Mrs. Macfarline having taken refuge at Billy Fintelman's. So they prepared to wait.

The Macfarline house was an old-fashioned frame structure of two stories with a very narrow porch. Casner and Wright had been hiding in it for about five or six hours when a car drove up in front. At the wheel was Fintelman. He remained in the car, the motor running, as Eddie Adams got out and came up on the porch.

Wright ran up the stairs, leaving Casner alone to confront the killer.

According to Casner's report, made later, he was carrying a sawed-off shotgun, and when Adams opened the door, he leveled the weapon and said, "Come on in!"

For answer, Adams in almost crazed desperation, seized the gun by its barrels and tried to wrest them aside, meantime drawing his own automatic.

It would have been certain death for the outlaw—but Casner was using a weapon to which he was not accustomed. He pulled the trigger. The gun failed to fire. It was on safety!

Now it was Casner who was in deadly peril. He dropped the shotgun and leaped for the door, trying to draw his revolver. After him came Adams, to kill him.

The outlaw had forgotten the extreme narrowness of the porch. Just as he pulled his trigger, he stepped over the edge and fell. By virtue of that accident Casner, instead of dying, only received a wound in one of his buttocks.

The wound in no way impeded Casner's speed—in fact it seemed to give him added impetus. Adams picked himself up from the ground where he had fallen, sprinted to the car, and he and Fintelman drove away.

Later, Casner was taken to a hospital. The bullet was removed from his posterior, and save for the embarrassment of having a wound in such a place, he soon recovered.

When Casner reported the shooting, a police car containing Detective Frank Rogers, Guy Wertz, who was a city prosecutor, and Bliss Isely, a newspaper reporter, went to the Macfarline house. Inside they found Wright, sitting on a chair. He said he had been in the house all the time and would certainly have gotten Adams "if he had time."

"Who's in the house now?" demanded Rogers.

"I don't know," said Wright.

"Damn it, get your gun! We're searching the place!"

Nobody was in the house; but Isely, looking around, noticed lint, very much like house dust, on Wright's uniform. When they went upstairs the newspaper man glanced under a bed.

"Come here," he said to Detective Rogers, pointing.

Under the bed was a very clear outline where Wright had been lying, collecting that lint. For this evidence of somewhat less than lionhearted courage, Wright later was dismissed from the force.

Shortly after, Mrs. Macfarline, with Orcutt, returned to her home. The two were immediately arrested.

By this time police squad cars were all over Wichita. Billy Fintelman was picked up and so were the two girls, Wilma Fleming and Annie Jones, who were with Adams when Fitzpatrick was killed. From their frightened story Zickefoose was able to reconstruct the crime clearly. Another squad car brought Nellie Miles to the station, and Weisberger was found later and captured.

All told, in the next few hours, eighteen persons with police records of one kind or another were rounded up in Wichita. But though the entire city was in a hysteria of excitement and the police switchboard was almost continually jammed by calls from people who thought they had information to give, or who were asking information, no trace could be found of the men most wanted, Eddie Adams and Frank Foster. It was discovered later that they were hiding in a room in the very heart of the city, where they could see the cars cruising about hunting them through their windows at all hours.

Zickefoose took the precaution of notifying every garage and filling station in the city to report the appearance of any suspicious person. Full descriptions of the fugitives were given these places.

A day passed, and funeral services were held for Officer Bob Fitzpatrick. Most of the police force attended, but Chief Zickefoose, alert to every contingency, left some very watchful men on duty.

It was as he had expected. Eddie Adams chose the hour of the Fitzpatrick services for his getaway, reasoning that every officer who could possibly attend would be at the funeral. While the rites for the murdered officer were in progress, two men appeared at a drive-yourself garage in the center of the city, within two blocks of the police station itself. One of them was J. C. Burns, who lived next door to the garage. He introduced his companion, a short, harsh-faced little man, as a stranger in town who wanted to rent a car, and offered to vouch for him.

An attendant took the two to the rear of the place to make a choice of rental cars; but another, remembering the police warnings, slipped into a telephone booth and got word to the detective office that a "suspicious looking" stranger was in the place.

It took three detectives, Charles Hoffman, Ed Bowman, and D. C. Stuckey, less than two minutes to traverse the two blocks to the garage from their office. They arrived just as the stranger—Eddie Adams himself—was about to enter the car he had selected.

Adams recognized Hoffman.

"How are you, Mr. Hoffman?" he said. "Come here, I want to talk with you."

Hoffman approached. As he did so, Adams who had not yet entered the car, drew.

With a lunge the officer leaped forward and threw his arms about the killer, trying to pinion him and get control of the gun.

The snarling Adams pulled his trigger. At the report of the automatic, loud in the confined space of the garage, Hoffman reeled backward, falling to the floor but dragging Adams with him.

The bullet had mortally wounded the detective, and he died from it soon after.

Adams, deadly as a venomous snake, wriggled out of Hoffman's slackening grasp and rose, shooting again, this time at Bowman.

The bullet passed through the officer's belly, piercing both body walls; but as luck would have it, Bowman was a portly man and the lead slug missed any vital organs.

Backward staggered Bowman. At the same moment Stuckey, standing behind a concrete post which supported the floor above, held his revolver barrel against the post to steady his aim, and fired. The bullet took Adams in the mouth and brought him to the ground.

An instant later Bowman, who was still on his feet, fired also. It was his shot that actually killed the outlaw.

Bowman later recovered from his wound.

I was on the city desk of the Wichita *Beacon*, getting out the late edition, while these events were taking place, and I well remember the screaming "Extra" we rushed through the presses when the news came in of Eddie Adams' death and identification. Later I viewed his body at a morgue, along with hundreds of other persons. I had never seen him in life, although I was more than measurably familiar with him through his rogue's gallery pictures and the reign of terror he created, which kept headlines leaping in the newspapers. The undertakers had done a good job of repairing his shattered features, but even in death his face bore the grim and cruel lines of a remorseless killer.

The horror story of Eddie Adams was over. He had wielded his deadly gun with almost insane ferocity. Seven men, three of them police officers, died as victims of his merciless blood lust. Two other police officers were wounded by him, not counting any of the three in Iowa that might have fallen to his automatic. There was no good in him.

In the cleanup that followed, Burns, who introduced Adams to the garage people, was arrested and charged with being an accessory to crime. But he had no previous record of lawlessness and was released.

Frank Foster escaped from Wichita in a stolen car, but was arrested at St. Joseph, Missouri, with his brother-in-law, Robert Maddox, and a third man, Marion Cook. They were returned to Kansas, and Foster, Fintelman, Macfarline, and Weisberger, all were sent to the Kansas penitentiary, Foster for life.

After the roundup, when things had somewhat settled down, Zickefoose, in looking over the Nellie Miles place, noticed some fresh dirt in the back yard. He ordered it dug up. Buried there was found some of the loot taken from the Haysville and Rose Hill banks. Both of the Miles couple were later sent up on charges of smuggling and selling narcotics.

All the principal figures in Eddie Adams' malodorous entourage were accounted for—except for John Callahan.

12. *Public Enemy No. 1*

Some time around 1920 a youth from Sallisaw, deep in the Cookson Hills of Oklahoma, appeared in Wichita. His name was Charles Arthur Floyd, but he became known as Pretty Boy Floyd—a title hung on him humorously by his neighbors at home, because he was intensely vain of his appearance and wore his hair slicked back. To achieve this effect he used various pomades, but his unfeeling home-town associates maintained that he kept it in that gleaming condition with axle grease.

Floyd was born in Georgia, but as a child went to Sallisaw, living with his mother, his father having died. He grew up to be a muscular youth, medium of height, standing five feet seven and a half inches tall, with chestnut-brown hair and light-blue pin-pupiled eyes. His face was broad, and not bad-looking except for the flat stare of his heavy-lidded eyes and the rather full-lipped sensuous mouth. It is not overdrawing it to say that his face was interestingly reminiscent of that of William Clarke Quantrill, although there was no relationship of blood between them.

Perhaps because of the jocular attitude of his neighbors, young Floyd shook the dust of Sallisaw from his feet rather early and set out to find a place where he would be better appreciated. Briefly he worked as a roustabout in the Oklahoma oil fields. But a little of this was enough to convince him that it was both laborious and messy. Having his face and clothes smeared with grease and mud did not appeal to him any more than did aching muscles.

At this time he was only about fifteen or sixteen years old, but as tall as he would ever be, and already reckless as well as vain. His preoccupation with his own looks aroused his interest in barbering. In Wichita, at that period, were one or two rather well-known so-called "barber colleges" in which young men were trained in the trade. It was one of these institutes of tonsorial technique that brought Floyd to the city.

In Wichita he perhaps met another barber, Eddie Adams.[1] Whether or not he did so, it is certain that he met that professor of crime, John Callahan; and under Callahan's tutelage he was launched on the long line of outlawry we have been following. At first the raw youth was considered too young for important assignments. So he served as an apprentice to Callahan, running errands and doing odd jobs, and absorbing wisdom in the chancy art of law evasion. Very soon, however, a streak of hardihood was recognized in him, and he began running booze.

Pretty Boy Floyd's usual route was from Wichita to Joplin, Missouri. The country intervening is wooded, much cut up by ravines and streams, with numerous side roads. Knowing the terrain thoroughly, Floyd could transport a cargo of whisky from

[1] In a letter to me, Bliss Isely, a veteran newspaperman of Wichita, of unquestioned integrity, and now retired, expresses the belief that Floyd must have met Eddie Adams, in Wichita. It is a tempting theory, especially since Isely, who was covering the police at the period, is one of the best of all authorities on Floyd and Eddie Adams in their Wichita period. If Pretty Boy did meet Adams, however, it must have been at the very last of the older bandit's career, because Floyd apparently did not appear in Wichita before late 1920 or early 1921. The Adams influence on him seems to be revealed in some of his later holdups, and particularly in his escape from a train while being transported to prison in a manner very similar to that employed by Adams.

Joplin to Wichita without using a single main highway, except perhaps to cross one now and then. Traveling at night, he would deliver the liquor to one of Callahan's "warehouses"—the locations of which were constantly being changed because of police curiosity.

So well did he do his job that there is no record that he was ever arrested in Wichita. Police, however, knew of him as a Callahan "handy man." Captain W. O. Lyle told me on one occasion, "We considered him a no-good kid, but hardly worth bothering about."

Floyd, however, seems to have been warned that the law was beginning to be interested in him, for some time before he reached his majority he departed from Wichita. In the ensuing period, which is vague, he acquired a wife, Ruby, and there was a son, Charles Dempsey Floyd, usually called Jackie.

How his trail as a developing criminal continued is marked by police records. He went to Missouri, with which state he was familiar through his liquor running, and being out of funds, he one night relieved a citizen of Kansas City of his wallet at the point of a gun. On September 16, 1925, he was sentenced to the Missouri penitentiary for five years.

Paroled for good behavior after four years, he returned to Kansas City. But he found his welcome there less than cordial, although the city, as of that era, was characterized by Maurice M. Milligan, U.S. district attorney, as "the center station of the corridor of crime." The slick-haired youth had not won his spurs as a "big-time" criminal, and the Italian underworld, of which Johnny Lazia was then king, wanted no amateur outside crooks. So the police, first of Kansas City, Missouri, and then of Kansas City, Kansas, across the state line, picked him up for "investigation"—a way of warning an undesirable to go elsewhere.

As a matter of sober truth, Pretty Boy Floyd never was a city gangster, in Kansas City or anywhere else. The close-knit "mob" with its tentacles of criminal "business," its payoffs, its obedience to a "boss," its entire old-world paraphernalia of organization, crime, and deadliness inherited from the Mafia of Sicily, was too treacherous and complicated for him. Throughout his career he worked as a free lance.

The inhospitable attitude of the gendarmes of the two Kansas

Cities caused him to decide to make his fortune in the West. But in Pueblo, Colorado, he was arrested May 9, 1929, for a theft, and spent sixty dreary days in jail.

That made him well weary of Colorado. As soon as he was released he journeyed east to Ohio—and straight into the "big time" of major crime. Under the alias of Frank Mitchell, he was arrested March 8, 1930, for investigation in connection with the murder of an officer, but the evidence at that time did not point to him and he was released. Shortly afterward he committed his first important robbery—the holdup of a bank at Sylvania, Ohio.

Arrested at Toledo, Ohio, May 20, 1930, he showed at once the kind of strenuous criminal he was. First he escaped from jail. Recaptured, tried, and convicted, with his record against him including his violation of his Missouri parole, he was sentenced to the Ohio penitentiary for twenty-five years.

But Pretty Boy Floyd had no intention of serving time. While being transported to prison, he broke away from his guards, leaped from a moving train as Eddie Adams had done, and escaped. It was the last time he was in the custody of the law, although for four years and more he was an inveterate and later a nationally notorious outlaw.

In a stolen car he headed for the Cookson Hills, the home of his youth. There it was, in all probability, that he first met Adam Richetti, who was to be his constant partner and associate until his death.

Richetti, in spite of his Italian name, was not a big-city mobster. He was brought up in Oklahoma on a farm, and he had a brother who owned a garage in Bolivar, Missouri, a town in the Ozark Mountains a few miles northwest of Springfield, Missouri. This was old James and Younger territory. Not forty miles away were the Monegaw Springs, a favorite resort of the Younger brothers in their bandit days, and even closer was the little village of Roscoe, near which the Pinkerton detectives, Louis J. Lull and E. B. Daniels, and the outlaw John Younger lost their lives in the memorable shooting affray of 1874.

Richetti had committed a holdup at Crown Point, Indiana, for which he served time; and a bank robbery in Oklahoma. Arraigned for the latter crime, he jumped his bond and became an outlaw.

From the first he and Floyd, both highwaymen and bandits, both ex-convicts, both desperate and daring men, took to each other. They formed a partnership and thereafter were almost inseparable.

Whenever the two, thereafter, wanted to escape the "heat" after one of their crimes, they usually took refuge in the Cookson Hills. Other outlaws who became acquainted with them were introduced to the Hills and found them to their liking. Among these were men whose names bulked large in the reign of terror created by kidnapings, murders, and robberies that gripped America in the raucous '20s; such men as Harvey Bailey, Wilbur Underhill, Machine Gun Kelly, and Matt Kimes. Another top-flight criminal who already knew the Cookson Hills passing well was Frank Nash. The Hills had been part of Al Spencer's and Henry Starr's old stamping grounds.

At other times Floyd and Richetti found friends and hiding places in the sprawling Seminole oil fields, where Floyd, at least, had once worked. To this day, in the Cookson Hills and in the shanty oil towns, Pretty Boy Floyd remains a hero to some of the inhabitants. Legends are told, in which the old, almost outworn Robin Hood pattern appears, picturing him as one who robbed the rich to give to the poor.

That he committed many robberies there is no question—more than twenty bank and several train holdups are credited to him—but it is difficult to find where he ever gave anyone, poor or otherwise, much of anything. Wrote Anthony Gish, one of his chroniclers:

> Floyd was a good time man. He played around the resorts, frequently posing as a wealthy tourist from Kansas City. In his native Osage [*sic*] Hills, he had many hideouts. He and his faithful companion, Adam Richetti, would lie around, getting drunk and sending to town for women.

In Pretty Boy there was a large streak of exhibitionism, as there was in so many of his predecessors from Jesse James on down. Newspaper clippings were as important to him as they could be to any Hollywood starlet. There is no doubt that be believed he had a "public," which looked to him for daring exploits and excitement.

Frequently, when robbing a bank or a train, he would tell his victims, "You can say to your friends that you were robbed by Pretty Boy Floyd." Sometimes he would vary this with "I'm Pretty Boy Floyd. If you could get me it would be worth $10,000 to you in reward money."[2]

One of his bank robberies was staged in his own home town of Sallisaw, the bank which he held up standing within a few doors of the residence of his mother, Mrs. W. F. Floyd. Floyd and Richetti herded a number of townspeople into the bank lobby with automatic pistols.

When he recognized acquaintances among these, Pretty Boy called out to his fellow gunman: "Don't shoot any of my friends—if you can help it."

Nobody was shot, because nobody resisted. The robbery yielded only about $2500, no very large sum. But Floyd probably did not expect a big haul. The raid was rather in the nature of a "home appearance," to give the folks a thrill; much as a famous actor might stop off at the little place where he was born to let his former neighbors have a glimpse of his eminent self.

Floyd was reckless, even rash. Once, when officers waited for him at a funeral parlor in an Oklahoma town where the body of one of his friends lay in a coffin, Floyd surprised them, disarmed them, calmly viewed the body, and vanished with the weapons of the guards.

Said an Associated Press dispatch of the period:

> Floyd's methods have been ultra-modern. Eastern Oklahoma officers say they have fired at him point blank and that he only laughed and fled unscathed. They believe he habitually has worn a bullet proof vest and a steel skullcap. Submachine guns have been standard equipment in his bank raids, and usually he has kidnaped the cashier or bank president after scooping up his loot, releasing his hostage unharmed after pursuers were distanced.

The theory about the bulletproof vest and skullcap is, I believe,

[2] Some officers have theorized that a few of these "statements" were made by "less notorious thugs in an obvious attempt to impersonate Floyd for purposes of intimidation."

only a part of the Floyd legend. He had no such protection when he was killed.

Pretty Boy was ambitious, and jealous. The nation-wide attention focused on John Dillinger, who was given the title of Public Enemy No. 1 by the FBI, made Floyd exceedingly unhappy. He wanted to bear that title himself, and eventually he succeeded in doing so, after Dillinger fell before FBI guns in Chicago, July 22, 1934. Undoubtedly he was proud of that perilous designation when it was given him, even though it amounted to his death warrant.

I have a letter from J. Edgar Hoover, commenting on the outlaw, which reveals another facet of the character of the man:

> With regard to "Pretty Boy" Floyd, our records do not reflect that he was a close associate of either Alvin Karpis or John Dillinger. We do know, however, that Floyd, Karpis, and Dillinger had mutual friends, and it is very possible that their paths may have crossed.

That sentence, from the Director of the Federal Bureau of Investigation, is a terse observation not only on Floyd but on the other major outlaws of his era. Though he probably knew Dillinger, who bore the title of Public Enemy No. 1 before him, and certainly knew Al Karpis, who bore it after him, he did not work with either of these men. Each of the three archcriminals considered himself the star of the act, and not one of them wished to be associated with the others for fear of losing what the theatrical world calls "top billing."

When he emerged from the Cookson Hills with Richetti for new forays, after the excitement of his escape on the way to the Ohio penitentiary died down, Floyd became a killer. And what made him sinister was the fact that he was a killer with a streak of brutality in him, like Quantrill.

Some of his murders had no point to them; others were for trivial reasons. Some, of course, were to escape arrest.

In 1931 he murdered two brothers, William and Wallace Ash, in Kansas City, Kansas. He said they were "informers," but the truth was that he was infatuated with the wife of one of them, although he already had a wife and son, and thus tried to clear the way for himself with the woman. She, however, rejected him.

At Akron, Ohio, he shot down a traffic officer named Harold F. Manes, because the policeman tried to whistle him down for running a red light. Near Pacific, Oklahoma, he killed Irvin Kelly, who tried to ambush him before dawn, April 9, 1932. At Bowling Green, Ohio, he fatally shot Ralph Castner, a police officer, who tried to arrest him for robbing a bank in Mount Zion, Kentucky. During a liquor raid in Kansas City, Missouri, he murdered Curtis C. Burks, a federal prohibition agent; and a spectator, also killed in that affair, was another victim of Floyd's bullets.

It was a ghastly record, not equaled by any other individual outlaw of his time, and it would become still more ghastly.

Floyd and Richetti belonged to no gang, although they sometimes summoned subordinate criminals to assist them in certain holdups where numbers were necessary. They were, for the most part, sufficient unto themselves, operating always together, sharing secrets with nobody else. But there were gangs—not only the city racketeers but wide-ranging bandits who terrorized the country in the latter days of prohibition and the early years of the depression. Some of those still remembered are the following:

Alice Barker, called "Ma" by the underworld, was a female Fagin who taught crime to her fearful brood of sons. She dominated them absolutely, and she also ruled Al Karpis, the only outsider allowed to belong to this family gang. All but Karpis died violently: the eldest son, Herman, by suicide rather than be captured in 1927; Lloyd, killed by his own wife in 1939 after a term in the Leavenworth federal penitentiary; Arthur, killed in 1939 while trying to escape from Alcatraz prison; Ma Barker herself and her son Fred, slain in a machine-gun duel with FBI officers in Florida in 1935. Karpis was captured in New Orleans in 1936 and went to Alcatraz for life.

Another female bandit of the era was Bonnie Parker, as daring and murderous as her Texas hoodlum paramour, Clyde Barrow. Before they were both killed when they elected to shoot it out with officers in a road block near Arcadia, Louisiana, in 1934, they were charged with seven murders between them.

John Dillinger, the first to bear the title Public Enemy No. 1, after a career of extreme brutality, was killed by FBI officers in Chicago, July 22, 1934. There were others: Wilbur Underhill, Killer Burke, Machine Gun Kelly, Harvey Bailey, and the like.

None of these were identified with big-city gangs, but moved over large areas of the nation, like the old free-traveling outlaws. Yet sometimes they received protection and hiding places from the city underworlds, and sometimes they performed services for the underworld in return for such favors.

It was such a repayment that brought about the climactic crime that gave Pretty Boy Floyd the title of Public Enemy No. 1 after John Dillinger ceased to wear it by reason of death.

To go back in time, it will be remembered that Frank (Jelly) Nash, the Oklahoma bandit and chief lieutenant of Al Spencer, was captured after the death of his leader, and sent to Leavenworth penitentiary for twenty-five years, together with Earl Thayer, Grover Durrell, and others of that gang.

At the great federal penitentiary the Osage Bad Lands outlaw underwent a considerable metamorphosis. He spent his leisure time in study, reading law, finance, anything to do with law enforcement and prison methods. In short, he educated himself to become an expert in the wider fields and problems of criminality.

He also made contacts in the prison. His old pals Thayer and Durrell were there; but Nash sought the acquaintance of more "important" inmates like Jimmy Keating and Tom Holden, train robbers; Charley Harmon, another big "operator"; and George Kelly, later to become known as Machine Gun Kelly.

Keating and Holden escaped, using forged prison passes said to have been the work of Kelly and Harmon. It was Nash's turn next. He had been made a trusty, assigned to a deputy warden's home. On October 19, 1930, he walked out of that home—carrying a set of Shakespeare's works—and never returned.

It was a different Frank Nash who in this manner returned to the outlaw world. Before Leavenworth he knew local criminals only and had no connections outside of his own state, Oklahoma. But now he knew, or had recommendations to, "big shots" elsewhere.

One of his first acts was to have his big and homely nose operated on. At the same time he bought a wig to disguise his balding head. Then he busied himself making "worthwhile" contacts, among them being Fred Barker, Shotgun George Ziegler, and Harvey Bailey.

With these he formed a gang of his own, adding Keating and Holden, his old prison friends. Nash took the leadership because he was the most intelligent man among them. He could use a machine gun but preferred subtler methods. As a "cover" racket, he became an expert croupier for roulette wheels in night clubs, and after his nose operation and with his wig, hardly anyone would have recognized the polished, smooth-spoken man, who called himself Frank Harrison to all except his friends, as the weather-beaten rough-riding Oklahoma bandit of the Al Spencer days.

Under his shrewd guidance the gang robbed bank after bank, chiefly in the northern part of the country. The boss bandit frowned on train holdups: the Okesa affair had left him memories so unpleasant that he never forgot them. Some of the bank robberies, however, were memorable. From the Kraft State Bank of Menominee, Michigan, the bandits took $100,000. They also kidnaped a vice-president as a hostage. In the pursuit the hostage was killed, together with two members of the gang, Frank Weber and Charley Harmon. But the others made their escape with the loot. Another important haul came from the First American National Bank of Duluth, Minnesota. From this, big trouble came later.

Meantime Nash made the acquaintance of two persons who were to be climactic in his life. One was a slim, brunette night-club hostess named Frances Luce, whom he met at Fox Grove, near Chicago. She was a divorcee with a small daughter, and she and Nash began living together, without benefit of clergy.

The other was Verne C. Miller, who not only was a bandit but also was linked in the seamy, filthy type of underworld inhabited by the city racket gangs, thus forming a curious sort of liaison between the two worlds of crime.

By this time Frank Nash was acknowledgedly a "big shot"

criminal in his own right, associating with the "aristocrats" of lawlessness and disdaining "little shots."

One of the "little shots" whom he probably knew, and of whom he certainly had heard, was a brash, reckless young Oklahoman named Pretty Boy Floyd. Nash, now a master of crime, considered him a crude newcomer, not worthy to mingle in the select circles to which Nash himself belonged.

In the spring of 1932 he tried to engineer an escape of some of his pals in Leavenworth, including Durrell and Thayer, by smuggling into the penitentiary guns concealed in a barrel of shoe paste, together with forged passes.

Durrell, Thayer, and others escaped, kidnaping the warden. But they wrecked their car, abandoned the injured warden, and were themselves rounded up. Durrell and two others committed suicide rather than face capture, and Thayer surrendered and went back to the penitentiary.

Oddly, the Kansas City Union Station Massacre, capsheaf of Pretty Boy Floyd's criminal career, was the result of a series of coincidences rather than any plan. And it was committed almost perfunctorily, a sheer cold-blooded slaughter that was the more gruesome because it lacked any motives of personal loyalties or hatreds, human passions or emotions.

The first step, which triggered the apparently unrelated series of events leading up to the massacre, was a strange occurrence on a Kansas City golf course, in the second week of July 1932. A foursome of smartly dressed golfers, as they came in from a game, found FBI officers awaiting them in the clubhouse. Three of them were arrested. The fourth got away.

All four were criminals who had been traced to Kansas City by the patient G men through some bonds—those stolen from that robbery of the First National Bank of Duluth. One of the three was Harvey Bailey, later to go to Alcatraz for life with Machine Gun Kelly for the extortion-kidnaping of the oilman Charles F. Urschel in Oklahoma. The other two were Keating and Holden. The one who got away was Bernard Phillips, who owed his escape to the fact that he went to the men's washroom before he went to his locker, and thus was warned of what was happening before he encountered the officers. Phillips later was killed, presumably because it was thought he double-crossed the others.

They had been living in Kansas City for months in expensive apartments, unmolested by the police of that Pendergast-Lazia-bossed town, playing golf and otherwise amusing themselves. It was said by the newspapers, later, that they sometimes carried submachine guns in their golf bags, but on this occasion they were unarmed.

Frank Nash also was living in Kansas City, at the same time, with Frances Luce. Brought up in the rough bandit years in Oklahoma, he had never learned the game of golf, so he was not with his friends on the links. Instead, he read of their capture in a local newspaper while sitting in his apartment.

At once he and Frances left the city and went into hiding, visiting their friend Verne C. Miller at a resort in Wisconsin. Miller was a top-flight criminal with an unusual record. Born in South Dakota, he was a man of exceptional daring. His career started as a parachute jumper at county fairs. Afterward he became a prize fighter. During World War I, he was a machine gunner who was decorated for bravery. When he returned to his home after the war, his admiring neighbors elected him sheriff; but he showed the weakness of his character by embezzling some of the public funds, and was sent to prison.

After his release he went into outlawry, robbing banks and committing a murder or two. Even before joining Nash's gang, he became associated with underworld city mobs, particularly in Kansas City, Detroit, and Montreal—in the last of which he was heavily interested in lottery and gambling operations. As a home he preferred Kansas City, where he lived expensively under the name of Moore, dressed well, and maintained a very pretty blond mistress named Vivian Mathias.

This was the man, then on a fishing vacation at Lake Geneva, Wisconsin, whom Nash and Frances Luce visited. Miller later took them to New York and introduced them around to his important underworld friends there.

The second step leading to the massacre was a daring escape from the Kansas penitentiary at Lansing on Memorial Day 1933. On that day Warden Kirk Prather had scheduled a baseball game, within the walls, between two American Legion teams from Topeka and Leavenworth, for the benefit of the convicts.

Choosing a moment in the fourth inning, with the score tied two and two and the crowd of inmates and guards intensely interested, eleven men, acting by a preconcerted plan, kidnaped the warden and two guards, and using them as hostages, commandeered motor cars and were gone from the penitentiary. The escape was made possible because the convicts were armed—with guns smuggled in to them by Frank Nash, who had only recently returned from the East.

In the group were Harvey Bailey and Wilbur Underhill.

Five of the escapees were rounded up and the warden and his guards were rescued. But the others got away, and Bailey and Underhill—significantly—headed for the Cookson Hills to hide. During the flight the brutal Underhill wanted to kill Prather and the guards, but Bailey intervened for them and saved their lives.

Presently these two made contact with Frank Nash, and the crime wave in the Midwest at once soared. Venturing out from the Cookson Hills, between robberies, the outlaws began to appear at towns like Hot Springs, Arkansas, and Joplin, Missouri, always in the guise of peaceful citizens, living on a highly comfortable, not to say luxurious scale.

It was after the escape of his gang members—perhaps as a sort of celebration—that Nash made an honest woman of Frances Luce, marrying her under the name of Harrison. Later she said that she believed that was his real name, and thought he was a bootlegger, but nothing worse.

Living at Joplin was a man named Herbert Farmer, alias Deafy Farmer, alias Snyder, alias Herb Black, who had forsaken active crime to play "host" to persons with money who desired seclusion from the strains and stresses—and the police—of the world. Deafy Farmer and his wife did quite well, because his guests spent money freely for board, lodging, liquor, and other entertainment.

At Hot Springs was an establishment known as the White Front Pool Hall, owned by a man named Dick Galatas, where crooks of all kinds hung out, including the more eminent practitioners of their craft.

Both these places had been marked down by the FBI as

criminal resorts, the Hot Springs spot especially as one favored by Frank Nash. And Frank Nash was one man they very much wanted.

In the middle of June 1933 he was spotted in Hot Springs. To make doubly sure of him, the FBI sent for Otto Reed, chief of police at McAlester, Oklahoma, who knew Nash by sight, having become acquainted with him when he was serving time at the penitentiary there.

It thus happened that on June 16, Nash, while drinking a glass of beer in the White Front Pool Hall, was arrested by F. J. Lackey and Frank Smith, FBI agents, and Chief Reed, who positively identified him in spite of his wig and his remodeled nose.

The officers handcuffed their prisoner and put him in a car, intending to drive him to Kansas City, and perhaps on to Leavenworth. But a series of curious events made them decide to change their mode of proceeding. Police officers stopped them at Benton, Arkansas. A telephone call had been received from Hot Springs, they said, saying that a man had been kidnaped there and spirited off in a car. The FBI men showed their credentials and were allowed to proceed.

At Little Rock, Arkansas, the same thing happened, except that this time the local police, when assured of their legitimate errand, gave the FBI agents an escort out of the city. By the time the car with Nash reached Fort Smith, his captors were convinced that the underworld was delaying them, perhaps to ambush the car and "spring" their prisoner somewhere along the road.

They therefore transferred to a train for Kansas City and wired ahead for officers to meet them there.

Now came another coincidence in the amazingly complicated network of incidents. By pure chance, on the very day Nash was arrested, Pretty Boy Floyd and Adam Richetti, driving to Kansas City, stopped in Bolivar, Missouri, to have their car tuned up in the garage owned by Richetti's brother.

As they waited for the job to be done, Jack Killingsworth, sheriff of Polk County, of which Bolivar is the county seat, happened to walk into the garage.

No time to wait for the tune-up now! Floyd and Richetti drew guns on the astonished sheriff, entered another car in the garage, and carrying the officer with them as a hostage, sped out of the town.

A few miles out of Bolivar, near Osceola, Missouri, they abandoned the Bolivar machine, held up Walter Griffith, a traveling salesman, and forced him to drive them to Kansas City in his car. During this ride Richetti rode in the front seat with Griffith. He had a bottle of liquor, from which he imbibed frequently, used a good deal of profanity, threatened both the driver and the sheriff, and sometimes napped.

Floyd did not nap. He sat in the back seat with Killingsworth, his automatic in his hand ready to fire, and spent the time scolding the sheriff for the "meanness" of police officers in general, who "hounded" men into crime.

It was late that night when the car reached Kansas City. The bandits let Killingsworth and Griffith out in the stockyards district, without harming them, and drove off in Griffith's car to an apartment which they had used before as a hideout.

Meantime, telephone wires between Hot Springs, Joplin, and Kansas City had been hot as the crime world flashed back and forth messages concerning Nash. His wife, Frances, called "friends" in Chicago, and took a plane for Joplin, where she met the Farmers. Galatas telephoned Verne Miller in Kansas City. Miller had important connections in Kansas City. Under the name of Moore he lived with his "wife"—attractive Vivian Mathias, who was his mistress but never his wife—in a fine home and a good neighborhood. He liked golf and probably introduced the gentlemen who were arrested on the Kansas City links to those particular fairways. He also, through his connections in gangland, knew Johnny Lazia, head of Kansas City's underworld.

Miller made frantic efforts. He telephoned Chicago asking for gunmen, and a party of gangsters actually started for Kansas City but failed to arrive. He also telephoned St. Paul and tried to get in touch with the Barker-Karpis gang, but could not reach them.

Of course he called on Lazia, asking him to furnish "guns" to deliver Nash. But Lazia demurred. The Pendergast machine, of which he was an important member, was moving along smoothly on its harvest of gold from liquor, vice, and various rackets, and it would never do for any of the local "boys" to be mixed up in something that might attract undue attention.

But Miller was being besieged by calls from Frances Nash and the Farmers, as well as from Galatas. At length Lazia said, suavely, that if Miller really wanted Nash freed it could be accomplished by outsiders without compromising the Kansas City mob. And he happened to have learned that a couple of talented outsiders had just blown into town. With that he gave Miller the address where Pretty Boy Floyd and Adam Richetti were staying. He even went farther. He arranged for the two "visitors" to meet Miller, at his house, for an interview.

Just what was said at the interview is unknown, but it is certain that some beers were drunk by the guests—with important after results. It is not probable that money was discussed. Miller could hardly have paid the kind of money that Floyd and Richetti would have asked, if money was the object. It is more probable that the two outlaws agreed to do the job as an accommodation, much as one housewife might lend another her vacuum cleaner—Oh, don't mention it! It's nothing at all! Glad to be of service—I might want a small favor from you someday!

And so, next morning, June 17, 1933, as the Missouri Pacific train from Fort Smith slid into the Union Station at Kansas City, Pretty Boy Floyd, Adam Richetti, and Verne Miller formed a reception committee.

Police and FBI officers were at the Union Station also. As Lackey, Smith, and Reed escorted the manacled Frank Nash off the train, they were greeted by Raymond J. Caffrey and Reed E. Vetterli, of the FBI, and W. J. Grooms and Frank Hermanson, Kansas City police detectives. The group of men walked directly toward the exit of the station which led to the parking plaza.

As they reached the car which was waiting for them, Nash started to get into the back seat. Caffrey ordered him into the front seat. Chief Reed, Smith, and Lackey took the rear seat. Caffrey walked around the car to take his place at the wheel. The two city detectives and Vetterli were to follow in a second car.

A sharp voice suddenly shouted, "*Up, up!*"

The officers turned. Two men armed with submachine guns, and a third holding two automatic pistols, had their weapons trained on them.

Grooms, the city detective, was a brave man. Instead of raising his hands at the order, he drew a revolver and fired, wounding one of the trio of gunmen in the shoulder.

At the shot the wounded man yelled furiously, "Let 'em have it!"

With a rattling roar the machine guns and automatics punctured the car with holes and wilted the men outside to the pavement.

"Don't shoot me!" cried out the frightened Nash.

An instant later he sagged in his seat, riddled by several bullets, including one through his head, silenced forever.

By a strange twist of fate one branch of the outlaw succession, Nash, had been lopped off by another branch of that same succession, Floyd.

In the fusillade Caffrey, Grooms, Hermanson, and Reed were instantly killed. Vetterli was shot through an arm, and Lackey had two bullets in his spine and a third through his hips. Though he survived these wounds, he was so badly crippled that he had to retire. Smith, the other FBI man, who had taken the seat Nash intended to take, was miraculously unwounded, because he was shielded by the bodies of Reed and Lackey on either side of him.

As suddenly as they had appeared the three assailants were gone, leaping into a car and vanishing from sight.

There has always been a strong theory that Frank Nash's death was not accidental—that the underworld feared he would talk, perhaps, and felt it necessary to close his mouth. I do not believe so. Nash was too high a figure in the crime world, too well known for his reticence for such a fear. Furthermore, he was too close a friend of Verne Miller, one of the gunmen, for a deliberate murder to have been planned among the three.

Frank Nash was swept away with the others in the hot gush of Pretty Boy Floyd's aroused blood lust, a victim of the fury of a man he had once scorned, who went berserk when he was wounded.

Not immediately did the murderers leave Kansas City. Instead they went to Floyd's hideout apartment and sent for a doctor. Pretty Boy had lost considerable blood, and there was some question whether he could stand a trip out of the city. But he called for one of the submachine guns, swung it into firing position, and said:

"I'm O.K. I can shoot, and if I can shoot, I can travel."

After Floyd was treated and bandaged by the doctor, Miller went downtown and held an interview with Johnny Lazia. Local gangsters had not committed the murders, but Miller demanded that he and the others be given an escort out of the city, to some place of safety. Afterward, Mike LaCapra, a Kansas City hoodlum, told the FBI that Lazia agreed to furnish the escort because he wanted the "hot" trio out of his town.

Floyd and Richetti departed and disappeared. So did Miller.

As a crime, the Kansas City Union Station Massacre was a complete success. The killers were not apprehended at the time: indeed, at first there were no clues as to the identity of the murderers. And though Floyd nursed a wounded shoulder, he soon recovered.

Yet actually that callous machine gunning was the turning point in the long war against the outlaws, not only in the West but all over the nation.

It was after the massacre that J. Edgar Hoover had his men trained in the use of weapons by marine and army experts; and sent them out to run down not only "name" criminals but the whole scrofulous fringe of petty collaborators who surrounded them, with his famous order: "Take them alive if you can—*but protect yourselves.*"

As the result of the Kansas City killings and other crimes, there was at one time actual agitation in Congress to invoke martial law throughout the nation. This was opposed by Hoover, who insisted that, given proper powers, the Federal Bureau of Investigation could cope with any wave of outlawry.

The upshot was a series of new national crime bills, authored by Homer S. Cummings, attorney general of the United States, passed in May and June of 1934 by Congress, and immediately signed into laws by President Franklin D. Roosevelt.

The laws included the following measures:

1. To assault or kill a federal officer became a federal crime, punishable by federal courts and penalties.

2. To rob a national bank became a federal offense, which deprived bank robbers of the device of skipping over state lines and laughing at authority which could not follow them. Since most banks became affiliated with the federal banking system, this provided an almost universal avenue by which the FBI could, and did, move against bank robbers.

3. To flee from one state to another, across a state line to avoid prosecution or giving testimony in federal criminal cases, became a federal crime.

4. To carry stolen property worth $5000 or more across a state line was a federal offense.

5. To use interstate communications, such as the telegraph or telephone, in extortion attempts, was a matter for federal criminal prosecution.

6. The kidnap law was amended so that abductions across state lines became federal violations, even when ransom or reward was not the motive, which directly hit at certain gangland death-kidnapings, or the carrying off of hostages after bank robberies or escapes from prison.

7. FBI special agents were given full police powers, such as they had not had before, when in many cases they had to enlist the cooperation of local enforcement agencies in carrying out their missions.

8. Where before FBI agents had to have special authority on given occasions to carry weapons, Congress authorized them to be armed at all times in carrying out their duties.

It was this series of laws, which gave the Federal Bureau of Investigation authority to proceed in areas of crime and in ways where it had not possessed the authority before, that meant the downfall of the desperado gangs.

One by one the major outlaws were tracked down. Ma Barker and her brood, Jake Fleagle, Wilbur Underhill, Charley Harmon, Shotgun George Ziegler, John Dillinger, Baby Face Nelson

(Lester Gillis), Clyde Barrow, and Bonnie Parker all went to their deaths.

Others, including Al Karpis, Machine Gun Kelly, Harvey Bailey, Al Bates, Ralph Fleagle, Francis Keating, Tom Holden, Eddie Bentz, and Killer Burke went to prison, most of them for life terms.

But what about the perpetrators of the Kansas City Union Station Massacre?

At first the crime was believed to be the work of Underhill and Bailey, known to be pals of Nash. Shown photographs of those two men, persons who had seen, or claimed to have seen, the shooting "positively" identified them. Another suspect "indentified" was Robert Brady. These three were named in the first indictment returned by a grand jury in the case.

Only one person had named Pretty Boy Floyd. She was Mrs. Lottie West, a matron in charge of the Traveler's Aid Bureau at the Union Station. On the morning of the massacre Mrs. West noticed a young man with a "singularly cruel face" sitting on a bench not far from her. She even attempted to speak to him, wondering if the morose expression he wore was due to some trouble in which she could help him. He refused to answer her, but abruptly and rudely turned away. So she left him.

A little later she was one of the horrified witnesses who saw the machine gunning of the FBI car in the plaza. It was Mrs. West who ran for a policeman, Officer Fanning, who was in the station, and cried to him to come. Fanning arrived too late. He took a shot at the car in which the murderers were fleeing, but failed to hit it.

Afterward, when she was shown a number of photographs of known criminals, Mrs. West at once identified Pretty Boy Floyd as the young man she had seen in the station and later using his machine gun on the officers. At the time, however, her identification was received with skepticism because of the other "positive" identifications of Bailey, Underhill, and Brady. Those identifications were all wrong, as the FBI gradually learned, and that of Pretty Boy Floyd was not believed either.

Quite soon the G men learned that on the day Nash was

arrested, Dick Galatas and Nash's wife in Hot Springs, Arkansas, had done a lot of long-distance telephoning. Because Verne Miller, alias Moore, lived in Kansas City and was known to be a friend of both Nash and Galatas, the officers reasoned that some of those long-distance calls might have been to him, and on a hunch some FBI men and police visited his house. It was empty. Miller and Vivian Mathias were gone. The furniture had been taken away in a van.

A few empty beer bottles in the basement were all that remained. One of the FBI men in the investigating squad picked up one of the bottles and carried it away with him.

Questioning of local hoodlums, from Johnny Lazia on down, convinced both the Kansas City police and the FBI that the massacre at the Union Station was an "outside job," by killers who were migrant in the city. But Miller's record, his friendship with Nash and Galatas, and his sudden disappearance made the authorities almost sure he had some sort of a hand in it. For the present, however, there was no trace of Verne Miller, or of his girl friend.

For a time the FBI, though by no means forgetting the Kansas City machine gunning, became more than busy with other matters. On July 23, 1933, only a little more than a month after the Union Station Massacre, an Oklahoma City oilman named Charles F. Urschel was kidnaped and held for $200,000 ransom. The payoff was made in Kansas City, by the gang's dictation, and Urschel was freed, unharmed.

It took the rest of the summer to round up the kidnapers, chief of whom were Harvey Bailey and Machine Gun Kelly.

Then came the murder-mad career of John Dillinger and his gang of outlaws, during which ten men were killed by members of that mob, seven wounded, four banks robbed, three police arsenals plundered, and three jails raided to free prisoners in the nine months from September 1933 to July 1934.

Dillinger, cornered in an alley near a motion picture theater in Chicago, July 22, 1934, was killed in a gun battle with FBI men led by Melvin G. Purvis. The others of his gang were soon killed, or captured and sent to prison.

On May 23, 1934, after a career of banditries and murders,

Clyde Barrow and his pistol-packing mistress, Bonnie Parker, were killed in Louisiana. Other outlaw gangs went into hiding, or were on the run, and soon would be eliminated by the amazingly resourceful and courageous agents of the FBI, aided, of course, by the good work of local officers of the law.

Still, however, persisted the mystery of the Union Station Massacre.

One day someone thought of the old beer bottle picked up at the Verne Miller house, and had it gone over for fingerprints. It resulted in an intensely interesting discovery—on the bottle was a fingerprint clearly identifiable as belonging to Adam Richetti.

Since the close association between Richetti and Pretty Boy Floyd was known, it was at least a good surmise that if Richetti was in Kansas City, drinking beer at Miller's house, Floyd probably was there also. All at once the insistence by Mrs. West, the Traveler's Aid matron, that she had seen Floyd at the Union Station the morning of the crime became very important—and very pertinent.

With that a new, fierce incentive was given to the hunt. FBI agents invaded the Cookson Hills, a known Floyd hangout, but the clannish people of the Hills gave no information on the outlaw's whereabouts.

By now the FBI was grimly determined to find him and his friend Richetti, wherever they might be.

At last Pretty Boy Floyd won the title he had coveted: Public Enemy No. 1. Now that he had it, was he happy with it? That is a question only a psychiatric expert in sick minds could have answered.

Before this, however, Verne Miller's hideout in Chicago was located not long after the Union Station Massacre. In a running battle he escaped the police dragnet, but Vivian Mathias later was captured. She was given a prison sentence for harboring a fugitive from justice, but she refused to give any information, and the officers of the law were as much at sea as ever.

Suddenly a series of ghastly developments occurred. On November 26, 1933, the dead bodies of Eddie Fletcher and Abe Axler, Detroit mobsters, were found near Pontiac, Michigan, riddled with machine-gun bullets. Two days later, November 28, a third corpse, that of Walter Tylczak, a gunman, was discovered near Detroit, also punctured by many slugs from a machine gun. It was evident that some kind of a gangland war, or "elimination," was taking place. The police of Detroit cruised the streets in armed groups, seeking vainly for information of the killers.

The following night, November 29, a motorist reported to police that he had seen a strange heap in the beam of his headlights, near a road he was traveling. He did not stop to investigate, since the papers were full of the gang killings.

A squad car went to the place he described. Beside a drain under the road embankment, covered by cheap blankets and an auto robe, was the nude body of a man. He had been tied up and brutally killed by heavy blows that crushed his skull. After the murder he was cast out of a car and left beneath the ragged coverings that were thrown over him.

Every mark of identification had been removed except one. The fingerprints of the corpse were those of Verne Miller.

The criminal's slayers never have been discovered, but FBI agents believe that they were "executioners" of the Detroit Purple Mob. Perhaps Miller was involved in an internal feud of that gang, to which he belonged. Or perhaps his death was only by coincidence associated with the other gangsters killed in those four days.

It is not improbable that the underworld of Detroit, like that of Kansas City, wanted no part of the Union Station Massacre, and when Miller turned up in his old haunts there, they "took him for a ride" to be rid of him and close his mouth forever.

Soon after, Dick Galatas was arrested in Florida. He and Mrs. Frances Nash, who also was taken into custody, supplied enough details of the telephoning that took place after Frank Nash's arrest to prove beyond any doubt that Miller was one of the three killers. But where were the other two?

At midnight, July 9, 1934, Johnny Lazia, king of the Kansas City underworld, was killed by machine gunners as he was helping his wife out of his car before their fine home in an exclusive Kansas City residential district. Mrs. Lazia escaped the stream of bullets very narrowly. It took Lazia hours to die, and he kept saying,

"Why did they do this to me—Johnny Lazia, the friend of everyone?"

A highly interesting piece of information came out of this killing. Ballistics experts determined that the machine gun that killed Lazia was one of those which had been used in the Union Station Massacre. Therefore, even though the murders were committed by outsiders—Pretty Boy Floyd, Adam Richetti, and Verne Miller, as the FBI now had become sure—local gangdom must have supplied the weapons.

Michael James (Mike) LaCapra, alias Jimmy Needles, who had turned against Lazia and told of the gang boss's part in getting Verne Miller, Floyd, and Richetti together and later in furnishing them an escort out of town, was found dead, his body dumped from a car near Plattekill, New York.

Three Kansas City gangsters were believed to have been the slayers of Lazia. Two of them later were victims of gangland murders, and the third disappeared. A convenient method of disposing of a victim, if there was time, was to put him in a cylinder, pour cement around him until it was solid (and cement was cheap, since Tom Pendergast had a virtual monopoly on it in Kansas City), and then dump it into the river. The Missouri River is both deep and wide. A secret like that would probably never be given up by it.

And still, throughout all this tangled mesh of murders and treachery, Pretty Boy Floyd and Adam Richetti, the men most wanted, remained at large, their whereabouts unknown.

According to later disclosures, the outlaws reasoned that the FBI would comb the Cookson Hills for them—so they went in the *opposite* direction.

Buffalo, New York, is a city large enough for two men to lose themselves in, yet it was not noted as a center of crime. There they took an apartment—complete with a couple of charming though wayward girls, whose first names were Juanita and Rose—and stayed there for several months while the whole nation was being searched for them. The feminine companions later supplied the details concerning this period.

During that time Floyd and Richetti remained quiet and

secluded, dallying with the girls, only occasionally slipping out at night to see a motion picture show, reading the papers, and waiting for the "heat" to die down. But at length the inactivity was too much for them; at least it was too much for Floyd, whose whole nature craved excitement and action.

He wanted new scenery, and he induced Richetti and the two girls to go with him. The ladies were sent out to purchase a car. By this time it was October of 1934, and more than a year had passed since the deadly rattle of the machine guns echoed in the plaza of the Kansas City Union Station. Surely, Floyd reasoned, people must have forgotten the crime. There had been, since then, other crimes, some of them of the sensational variety. They must have diverted the attention of the public from the massacre.

What Pretty Boy did not take into full consideration was the newer FBI, the FBI that had arisen since he committed those murders, the FBI now geared into a fighting machine against gangland and crime on a nation-wide basis, and with the laws to authorize its operations.

No longer were state or county lines limitations to pursuit. The FBI crossed over all such barriers. The airplane, the radio, and all other modern means of travel or communication were at the disposal of the G men, and they were keen and trained, not only in the detection of crimes but in fighting criminals with their own weapons.

Furthermore, four officers of the law, including two agents of the FBI, had been killed in the Union Station plaza at Kansas City. The FBI would never relax until it had the murderers of those men.

Pretty Boy Floyd was to find that the Federal Bureau of Investigation had an enormously long memory, a memory reinforced by a vast and perfectly organized system of records, fingerprints, and directives burned into the minds, whetted to a razoredge in the war against crime, of its personnel. Behind all this sat J. Edgar Hoover, directing, prompting, stimulating. The head of the FBI had not forgotten the Union Station Massacre either.

As a result of all this, when Floyd and Richetti, with their two feminine friends, set out from Buffalo in the new car, to return by devious ways to the Cookson Hills of Oklahoma, they did not travel through a country lethargic and confused as in the past. It was now a country conspicuously alert, over which men watched with every device of criminological detection and communication, armed and expert with their arms, and above all, unafraid.

So well established had the FBI become in the public mind as the great spearhead of combat against the desperadoes, that everywhere it received immediate and willing co-operation, not only from local officers but from private individuals, when called upon.

Merely by appearing in a community, the G men gave to law-enforcement agencies there new confidence and new eagerness for battle with the thugs.

Nobody knows exactly what route Floyd and Richetti intended to take to the Cookson Hills after they got through the more populous areas of the Midwest. But first they headed southwest along Lake Erie, and then almost due south into Ohio. One of the men drove while the other held a machine gun.

Hardly had they progressed three hundred miles in their perilous hegira when fate overtook them. Nearing Wellsville, Ohio, the night of October 21, 1934, they found themselves in a heavy fog which made it almost impossible to see the road ahead.

The car skidded at some curve, and went off the road into a telephone post. Nobody was injured, but the automobile was damaged.

A conference was held and it was decided to send the two girls into the nearby town for a wrecker, while the two men stayed out of sight until the repairs were made. Floyd and Richetti accompanied Juanita and Rose into Wellsville, and waited for them in a wooded public park.

Local officers, making a routine investigation of the park, found two men lying on the ground. The men arose as they approached, but vagrants were suspect, so the police began to question them.

Suddenly one of the "vagrants" drew a gun. He fired, but fortunately one of the officers was near enough to leap on him and spoil his aim. With the help of the other policeman, the man was subdued and disarmed.

His companion, meantime, took to his heels, leaped into a car which happened to be parked near, and escaped.

Not dreaming of the caliber of their quarry, the Wellsville policemen took him to the police station. It was at this point that the first of the new methods came into play, whereby local police made a practice of co-operating with the FBI. When the prisoner's fingerprints were taken, the Wellsville police checked with the FBI giving the fingerprint classifications and a description of their man.

Back came astounding news—their prisoner was none other than Adam Richetti!

Into immediate action went the FBI headquarters at Washington and in Chicago. Where Richetti was, Pretty Boy Floyd almost surely was also.

By plane and car, G men swooped toward the Wellsville area. At their head was Melvin G. Purvis, who had been the nemesis of so many outlaws.

Every device was used to put the public on the alert. Floyd's picture was published in the newspapers, together with his description; and an appeal was made to citizens to call the nearest law-enforcement office if they saw anyone answering the description or resembling the picture.

Hours passed. Then the police of East Liverpool, Ohio, five miles east of Wellsville, up the Ohio River and almost on the Pennsylvania line, received a tip that Floyd had been seen north of the town.

Those must have been hours of desperation and despair for the outlaw. Hunted and harried, he knew the end was nearing. He did not even dare stop at a filling station for fear that his presence would immediately be communicated to the men who were on his trail.

When he stole the car in which he was riding, it was low on gas. Now its tank was almost empty. He turned north toward the little village of Clarkson, Ohio.

But the country was swarming with grim hunters. Someone telephoned that a car answering the description of the one Floyd was driving was seen on the road to Clarkson, and G men, reinforced by East Liverpool officers, headed in that direction as fast as speeding cars could take them. Their instructions from Purvis were substantially as follows:

> Gentlemen, you all know the character of the man we are after. If we locate him and he makes his escape, it will be a disgrace to our Bureau. It may be that he will be unarmed—yet, he probably will be armed. There will be an undetermined element of danger in taking him. It is hoped that he can be taken alive, if possible, and without injury to any agent. Yet, gentlemen, this is the opportunity we have all been waiting for and he must be taken. Do not unnecessarily endanger your own lives. It will be up to each of you to do whatever you think necessary to protect yourself in taking him.[3]

Still northward, on through Clarkson, Floyd drove desperately. But beyond Clarkson, before he reached Spruceville, the next small place, the fugitive's car at last ran out of gas, and came to a stop.

It was near a farmhouse, and Floyd ran into the farmyard.

"Give me your car!" he demanded of the farmer, drawing an automatic.

Before the startled householder could even answer, the roar of a fast-speeding automobile was heard coming from the south. Already it was too late for Pretty Boy.

Floyd cast a despairing glance around as the car with the G men whirled into the farmyard.

Then he drew himself behind a corncrib.

No refuge there.

A shot from back of the crib answered the demand that he come out.

Answering shots began to drill through the flimsy structure.

Suddenly Pretty Boy Floyd, savage as a cornered beast, emerged from behind the shed, his automatic pistol blazing in his last de-

[3] This is adapted from Purvis' instructions before Dillinger's finish, as quoted by Whitehead. He gave such directives before closing with most of the desperate men he hunted down.

fiance, his bitter hope to take at least one of them with him into the shades.

The FBI men were expert shots, too. A machine gun beat out its deadly tattoo and guns cracked from various places where officers had posted themselves.

Floyd staggered. "You've hit me—twice—" he cried as if in accusation.

Then he fell, his pistol dropping from his hands, paralyzed by oncoming death, his face fouled by dirt and blood.

Pretty Boy was not very pretty now.

"Who the hell tipped you?" he gasped as officers picked up his guns and stood over him.

Then, "Where is Eddie?" Those were his last words.

Eddie? It was an alias used by his friend Adam Richetti. Floyd's dying thought was of that companion of his crime career.[4]

Back in Sallisaw, in the Cookson Hills, which were turning yellow and red as the fall frosts changed the leaves of the trees, Mrs. W. F. Floyd learned of the death of her son.

"Charles was a good boy," she said, with a mother's refusal to accept the world's judgment on her offspring.

She sent for his body and buried him at Sallisaw.

For Pretty Boy Floyd it was the end. But did it mark the finish at long last of the fantastic and dreadful trail of outlawry of which he was the final link?

Only time and history can supply the answer to that; but the reasonable probabilities are that outlawry, of the type described in these pages, will not again assume the proportions it once reached. Sporadic outbreaks there may be, but they will be quickly snuffed out.

Urban crime is today's problem, but even in considering that it is well to remember that in bringing the careers of Floyd and others to an end, the FBI won a remorseless battle, and proved that it is a force with which every future criminal must henceforth contend.

[4] Richetti was executed October 7, 1938, in the gas chamber of the Missouri penitentiary, for his part in the Union Station Massacre.

Nor is the FBI the only agency that makes crime perilous to the criminal. J. Edgar Hoover, in a foreword to Whitehead's book *The FBI Story,* wrote in 1958:

> I wish to state emphatically that the FBI is not and never can be a national police organization as long as its development continues to be on cooperative lines. The most lasting contributions made by the FBI have been those which encourage cooperation with local, county and state law enforcement agencies. Through the FBI National Academy . . . more than 3,200 select representatives of the country's law enforcement agencies have been graduated. Today, more than a fourth of the graduates head their law enforcement agencies. Better police training and administration, with a growing recognition of civil rights, have been the result. There is never any doubt within the FBI that the home-town law enforcement agency must ever be in the forefront of crime control.

Crime and criminals have always been with us; and probably always will be with us. But such are the improvements in police methods everywhere, including training, equipment, and *esprit de corps,* that the would-be enemy of society must know the cards are stacked against him from the very first, and this, in itself, cannot help being a deterrent to crime.

As for those who foolishly and recklessly take the risk, the records show the losing game they play. Even in the days described herein, when at times the advantage actually seemed to be with the bandits, they always paid the bitter price in the end. Gang after gang ran its course, but at last every one of them came face to face with death or prison cells.

Looking back, over the perspective of years, those outlaws sometimes may appear picturesque. But in reality the lives they lived were sordid, beset often with hunger and suffering, full of hardships, lacking for even the best of them the compensation in money an honest job would have given, and endlessly shadowed by the terror of that final fate they knew they could not escape.

BIBLIOGRAPHY, EVALUATED

There is a considerable literature touching directly or indirectly upon the outlaws of the West. Following is a list of books and some of the other sources consulted in the preparation of the present work. Some are good, some bad. A few are magnificently written, others are almost illiterate. I have attempted in each case to give some critical estimate of their value.

Appler, Augustus C., *The Younger Brothers,* New York, 1955 (republication).

Written by a newspaperman, the editor of the Osceola, Missouri, *Weekly Democrat,* this is a personal account of the Youngers, whom he knew. Osceola is in St. Clair County, within ten miles of Monegaw Springs, a favorite Younger resort, and about the same distance from Roscoe, near which John Younger was killed and the Pinkerton men, Edward B. Daniels and L. J. Lull, slain in the gun battle with James and John Younger. Appler's work is largely a defense of the Youngers, and has much to do with the Civil War record of Cole and Jim as guerrillas. Until the Northfield robbery, Appler evidently did not believe the Youngers were involved in any crimes, but were being persecuted because of their former guerrilla service. But after Northfield he wrote an additional chapter for his book. For some reason the manuscript, which bears internal evidence of being written in the 1870s, before Northfield, did not find immediate publication. The first printing as a book was in 1892. It was revived and republished, with a foreword by Burton Rascoe, in 1955.

Arthur, George Clinton, *Bushwhacker*, Rolla, Mo., 1936.
A history of Bill Wilson, a guerrilla and bandit, chiefly interesting because of its descriptions and pictures of caves and other outlaw hideouts in Missouri.

Asbury, Herbert, *The Great Illusion,* New York, 1950.
The sorry record of prohibition, its rise and fall, including the terrifying growth of gangsterism and outlawry as the result of the enormous riches placed in the grasp of the underworld by the prohibition laws.

Ball, Max W., *This Fascinating Oil Business,* Indianapolis, 1940.
An account of the amazing mushrooming of the oil industry, which so changed the face of America and produced its own peculiar crime problems.

Barnard, Evan G., *A Rider of the Cherokee Strip,* Cambridge, Mass., 1936.
Written in a refreshing style by an old-time cowman, it contains some breezy recollections of Territorial days in Oklahoma and some of the bad men of the era. Contains much color and information of the sort too often neglected in reminiscent books.

Block, Eugene B., *Great Train Robberies of the West,* New York, 1959.
Mostly concerned with holdups in the Far West and Pacific coast, but contains an account of the Daltons and their California train robbery, though it is short on details, and fails to describe Grat Dalton's escape. Other robberies are better handled. In the chapter on the Jennings gang, it follows Al Jennings' personalized account, which, to say the best for it, frequently disagrees with the known records.

Breihan, Carl W., *Quantrill and His Civil War Guerrillas*, Denver, 1959.
A modern review of the activities of the band, valuable for its roster of followers of Quantrill. John Younger is listed as a member of the band, but John Younger was not old enough to belong to it. Some others, such as Wood and Clarence Hite and Dick Liddil, are not mentioned. Of the list at least twenty can be identified as being associated with the James-Younger outlaws at some time or other after the war.

Britton, Wiley, *Memoirs of the Rebellion on the Border*, Chicago, 1882.
This is the opposite side of the medal from the Trow memoirs. Britton, a lieutenant in the Sixth Kansas Cavalry, gives his version of the border fighting, including actions against Quantrill, from the Union viewpoint. This and J. P. Burch's book, *A True Story of Chas. W. Quantrell*, listed below, furnish interesting contrasts. Out of print and rare.

Buel, J. W., *The Border Outlaws*, St. Louis, 1882.
This may be the first of the books published about the James and Younger outlaws. Buel was a newspaper reporter, at first in Kansas City, and later in St. Louis. He personally covered for his papers many of the events he relates, including the controversial Kansas City Fair Grounds robbery—in which his facts rather straighten out that "controversy." As with Appler, a considerable part of the text is devoted to the guerrilla exploits of the men who later became outlaws, but unlike Appler, Buel had no illusions about them. He names names and quotes dates. At times he includes contemporary newspaper accounts. At others he cites correspondence from the outlaws themselves, to relatives or friends, and in some instances to himself. He is authority for the story of Jesse James' proposition to "end the sufferings" of Jim Younger, in order to facilitate the escape of the others, after Northfield. In this he does not name his source, except to say "an ex-guerrilla who has maintained relations, for many years, with the James and Younger boys." That man probably was George Shepherd, and the episode, if true, could account for Cole Younger's statement in a letter to Buel, while in prison at Stillwater, Minnesota, that he and Jesse James were "bitter enemies afterward" (after the Northfield affair). In the same letter Cole mentioned Buel's "seeing George Shepherd," which lends strength to the theory expressed above. When Buel

interviewed Cole at the prison and asked the question directly, the outlaw did not deny it, but simply refused to answer it. Had the incident not occurred, I believe Cole would have said so. The wartime episodes may be hearsay accounts, but Buel displays evidence of being close to the picture during the outlaw years. Long out of print and very rare.

Burch, J. P., *A True Story of Chas. W. Quantrell,* Vega, Tex., 1923.

The very title of this book is wrong, the name being William Clarke Quantrill. But it contains the recollections, when he was a very old man, of Harrison Trow, a member of the famous guerrilla band. The viewpoint of course is from the guerrilla side. Included are bloodcurdling accounts of the deeds of the James brothers and Cole Younger. There is a short chapter on the outlaws after the war, including an account, probably from the Samuels themselves, of the Pinkerton raid and "bombing." Trow identified the body of Jesse James after his assassination. The book is a defense of the guerrillas and outlaws, and while it is overdrawn in some instances, it provides much background material.

Connelley, William Elsey, *Quantrill and the Border Wars,* Cedar Rapids, 1909.

As secretary of the Kansas State Historical Society, Connelley had unparalleled materials and sources from which to write this book, to which he added voluminous correspondence and personal research. The result bears every evidence of thorough study, and forms a vertiable mountain of source material. Unfortunately, however, it bears the evidence of strong personal bias. Connelley did not write a fair and dispassionate history. He devotes every possible device to prove his major point—that Quantrill was a fiend incarnate, without one redeeming quality. So far does he lean in this direction that the book loses the merit of convincing the reader, because it makes the guerilla unbelievable. At times, also, Connelley embarks on furious outbursts against other writers who do not entirely agree with his viewpoints. Yet this curiously unbalanced and at times venomous book remains the best basis for information about the guerrillas, provided it is used with a due regard for the highly prejudiced attitude of the author. Connelley would have made a far better case if he had not been so intemperate.

Crittenden, H. H., *The Crittenden Memoirs*, New York, 1936.
Though disorganized, these memoirs of Missouri's governor, who offered the rewards for the James brothers and saw the gang broken up, contain much vital material, including newspaper articles of the time, his own versions of the surrender of Frank James and the killing of Jesse James, and an account of the Frank James trial, together with the bitter controversies that raged during the period.

Cunningham, Eugene, *Triggernometry*, Caldwell, Ida. 1941.
Not germane to the present book, but a very readable account of various gun fighters in the West. Some of it may be apocryphal. A number of modern armchair "experts" on the West have said so. But some of it also is authentic, and my opinion of the armchair expert is not sufficiently high to condemn this book merely on their word.

Dale, Edward Everett, *Cow Country*, Norman, Okla., 1942.
A professorial account of the cattle industry, chiefly in Oklahoma.

Edwards, John N., *Noted Guerrillas*, St. Louis, 1877.
Whatever you want to say about Major Edwards he did not fear to say what he thought, and he once fought a duel (bloodless) to prove it. This work, of which my copy is very old and lacking the covers, is exaggerated, and according to modern fashions overflorid in its writing, although the style was much admired in his day. The major leans about as far in one direction, to make Quantrill a hero, as Connelley leans in the other, to make the guerrilla leader a fiend. Extremely rare.

——, *Biography, Memoirs and Miscellaneous Writings*, Chicago, 1889.
Contains some of the old major's newspaper editorials, including those on Quantrill and the death of Jesse James—the latter a piece of undying Americana. Rare.

"Eye Witness," *The Dalton Brothers*, Chicago, 1892; republication, New York, 1954.
This is by every standard the best account of the Coffeyville fight, written by a man who preferred to remain anonymous, but who either was present when the fight took place or interviewed everyone who saw it immediately thereafter. Burton Rascoe believes he was a reporter on the Coffeyville

paper at the time. "Eye Witness" evidently talked to members of the family to obtain earlier history, and he gives the best account of the California robbery and Grat Dalton's remarkable escape, with so much corroborative detail that it must stand as the most accurate report of those events.

Foreman, Grant, *The Five Civilized Tribes*, Norman, Okla., 1934.
Useful as a study of the "Indian Nations," when the Cherokees, Choctaws, Creeks, Chickasaws, and Seminoles enjoyed autonomy as "independent governments." It contains material on Indian courts, the Starr-Ross feud among the Cherokees, mention of the Younger's Bend headquarters, and a description of Tom Starr and his activities.

Gard, Wayne, *Frontier Justice*, Norman, Okla., 1949.
An excellent study of lynch law, vigilantes, frontier officers, courts, and judges, including some mention of Judge Isaac Parker, Bill Tilghman, and the Oklahoma, Missouri, and Kansas outlaws.

Garwood, Darrell, *Crossroads of America*, New York, 1948.
Actually this is a history of Kansas City, but it includes a version of the border warfare, the James-Younger outlawry, and the Pendergast-Lazia underworld empire.

Giffen, Guy J., *Collections*.
Giffen, an antiquarian with Western interests, for years kept scrapbooks containing not only correspondence with persons who had figured in or knew something concerning the outlaw history of the West, but a great mass of clippings from newspapers and other periodicals which provide some highly interesting side lights. At his recent death I acquired the scrapbooks and have found them most valuable.

Gish, Anthony, *American Bandits*, Girard, Kas., 1938.
While this booklet is small and unpretentious, in its 101 pages it presents thumbnail biographies of many of America's most noted outlaws, in most cases surprisingly accurate. It is particularly handy as a quick reference concerning the bandits of the Floyd-Dillinger-Karpis era. Quite rare.

Harman, S. W., *Hell on the Border*, Fort Smith, Ark., 1898.
This is incomparably the greatest source on the history of

Judge Ike Parker and his Fort Smith tribunal. I have depended heavily upon it, as have all others in writing of the period and territory. Rascoe has pointed out that Harman was inaccurate in his summation of Belle Starr's career, and in this I agree, as he seems to have taken at face value the extravagant accounts of her doings in sensational periodicals and books of the times. But in general Harman, who was a newspaperman and a great admirer and friend of Judge Parker's, presents an admirable firsthand report of the "Hanging Judge" and the problems of law in the Territory. Out of print and rare.

Hines, Gordon, and E. D. Nix, *Oklahombres,* Chicago, 1929.
Although this book credits its authorship to E. D. Nix "as told to Gordon Hines," the man who really wrote it was Hines. Rascoe sneers at the book, but Gordon Hines had the enterprise and ability to put together an immensely valuable account of the campaigns of the great marshals of the Territory, as seen through the eyes of Nix, himself the first U.S. marshal of the Oklahoma Territory. I see no reason for belittling this book. In fact I highly recommend it to anyone desiring to read a spirited account of the years covered. There will always be disputes over minor details—even between men who personally took part in the events involved. Hines—and Nix—have a legitimate right to their views.

Horan, James D., *Desperate Men,* New York, 1949.
This book, the first half of which is devoted to the James-Younger outlaws, is one of the major contributions to the literature of that period, because not only is the author a careful researcher and fine writer but he had access to the archives of the Pinkerton National Detective Agency and thus obtained much new material. Its only defect is that it is devoted to trying to make a strong case for the Pinkertons; and the Pinkertons, in actuality, played a rather awkward role in their efforts to break up the James gang. Horan is accurate as to dates, places, and events, but his book is one-sided. The outlaws are too pitch-black, the Pinkertons too lily-white. Nevertheless, he is frank enough in making clear his position, and I like a partisan book in that it gives a viewpoint and makes for good reading. It is the author's privilege to write it

that way, particularly when he is honest about it, as Horan is, but in weighing the testimony this attitude should be taken into consideration.

Hough, Emerson, *The Story of the Outlaw,* New York, 1907.
One of the old-timers in the field, Hough gathered his material as near to the firsthand sources as possible, in many cases from actual actors in his recounted episodes. Included are sections devoted to the James-Younger and the Dalton gangs.

Hunter, J. Marvin, and Noah H. Rose, *The Album of Gunfighters,* Bandera, Tex., 1951.
A publication of the wonderful Rose collection of photographs of Western figures, both outlaws and lawmen, some of them ghastly picutres of lynchings and bandits laid out in death. With commentary, in most cases accurate.

Isely, Bliss, *Correspondence.*
Bliss Isely, a veteran newspaperman, whose work covered half a century in, both Kansas and Missouri, now retired, is one of the most highly respected members of his profession in the Midwest, his intelligence and integrity universally acknowledged by all who know him. Due to his keen observations and long service with the press, he obtained personal knowledge of the Wichita era of banditry. Supplementing his memory with references to the files of the Wichita *Beacon* and Wichita *Eagle,* the Topeka *Capital,* and the Kansas City *Star* and *Times,* his letters on the Callahan-Adams-Floyd period, of which I have many, are invaluable. When I had the idea for this book, twenty years ago, Captain W. O. Lyle, of the Wichita police force, undertook to help me in putting some of the scattered pieces together. Captain Lyle is now dead. Isely and he were contemporaries in Wichita. I owe a great debt to both of them.

Jennings, Al, *Through the Shadows with O. Henry,* New York, 1921.
This is the ex-outlaw's highly personalized account of his own bandit career, and his relationship with O. Henry before and after their imprisonment together. His stories in many cases differ strikingly from those of other men. The book appears to be an apology couched in boastful terms.

Jones, W. F., *The Experiences of a Deputy U.S. Marshal of the Indian Territory* (no date).

This strange little pamphlet, only forty pages long, was published, apparently, by the old deputy marshal himself, in 1937. It contains some reminiscences of Jones, including the pursuit and capture of the Jennings gang; and of Orrington (Red) Lucas, another deputy marshal, with his account of the Ingalls fight, in which, although he somewhat exaggerates his own importance, he provides some important information concerning the layout of the bandits' town, movements of the posse, and the escape of the outlaws. Very rare and out of print.

Kansas Historical Society, Publications.

I owe a debt of gratitude to the fine Kansas Historical Society with its rich archives and its long-continued annual, later quarterly publications. I availed myself of them for more than a score of years, and found them among the finest of all state historical collections, and the staff of the society more than glad to put forth any effort to assist the inquirer.

Kansas, A Guide to the Sunflower State, New York, 1939.

One of the American Guide Series, published under the auspices of the Works Progress Administration, it is better than some of the others.

Katcher, Leo, *The Big Bankroll,* New York, 1958.

In this biography of Arnold Rothstein, major racketeer, Katcher tells the amazing story of the gigantic financing of the city rackets, especially the liquor and narcotics trade, which was made possible by the situation created by prohibition.

Larkin, Lew, *Bingham, Fighting Artist,* Kansas City, 1954.

A thorough account of George Caleb Bingham's feud with General Thomas Ewing as a result of the latter's Order No. 11, issued during the Civil War.

MacDonald, A. B., *Hands Up!* Indianapolis, 1927.

Collected articles, with Fred E. Sutton, a former Western deputy marshal, as the central figure, written by MacDonald for *The Saturday Evening Post.* Rascoe says that the author drew the long bow in some instances. I worked with MacDonald on the Kansas City *Star*, and he was a great reporter, winner of a Pulitzer award, in fact.

Mechem, Kirke, *The Mythical Jayhawk*, Topeka, Kas., 1956.
A whimsical account by the editor of the Kansas State Historical Society's publications, of the genesis of the term. An old friend of mine, Mechem makes an amusing, pseudo-scientific study of the question, which received an accolade from H. L. Mencken and was widely reprinted, but makes no pretense to an actual solution of the problem as to where that nickname for Kansas ever came from.

Missouri, A Guide to the "Show Me" State, New York, 1941.
One of the American Guide Series, with much material about the state in general, including not a little history.

Newspapers
I have a considerable collection of newspaper articles, particularly from the Kansas City *Star*, Kansas City *Times*, Kansas City *Journal*, New York *Herald Tribune* (including a photostatic copy of the article in the old *Tribune*, April 4, 1882, telling of the killing of Jesse James), New York *Times*, Chicago *Tribune*, St. Louis *Post-Dispatch*, Topeka *Capital*, Wichita *Eagle*, Wichita *Beacon*, Oklahoma City *Daily Oklaman*, Tulsa *World*, Los Angeles *Times*, Denver *Post*, Fort Worth *Star-Telegram*, Associated Press dispatches, and others. Such articles, when contemporary with the events discussed, while frequently furnishing on-the-spot information, are also interesting in showing how far afield were the authorities and others, in many cases, in speculating on identities of the perpetrators of specific crimes, or the movements of the criminals, at the times when the crimes were committed or the criminals were being pursued. One priceless item in this collection is a yellowed page from the Ashland, Kas., *Clark County Clipper*, of March 9, 1944, telling of the death of Chris Madsen, and including a reprint of a letter more than 1000 words long, from Madsen to his friend Lon Ford, then sheriff of that county, in which the old marshal supplied some extremely relevant information on the Doolin gang and other outlaws with whom the Territorial marshals had to deal. The letter was written in 1942, two years before Madsen's death.

Oklahoma, A Guide to the Sooner State, Norman, Okla., 1941.

Similar to *Missouri, A Guide to the "Show Me" State* and under the same auspices, the Works Progress Administration. Some references to outlawry.

Parker, Emma, and Nellie May Cowan, *Fugitives, The Story of Clyde Barrow and Bonnie Parker,* Dallas, Tex., 1934.

The mother of Bonnie Parker and a sister of Clyde Barrow give an account of the criminal career of the pair. Though sympathetic to the outlaw couple, it is not an attempted vindication of them.

Rascoe, Burton, *Belle Starr, "The Bandit Queen,"* New York, 1941.

A literary critic by profession, Rascoe made a sort of side career of writing prefaces for books on the West. Unhappily, he appeared to look down on most of the authors of Western history, particularly those who were in the field before him. *Belle Starr* is an excellent contribution to the literature, but for a writer who is so toplofty about the errors of others, this effort of Rascoe's contains some remarkable pieces of careless misinformation. I have commented in the text about his statement concerning Temple Houston. Equally curious is his reference to Frank James in which he says, "You must remember that after Frank James got his release from prison (after serving twenty-one years) he had a tough time making a living. He was 60 years old and he had never worked a day in his life except when he was in the penitentiary, and about all he had done there was to sort gunny-sacks." The defect in this statement is that Frank James never served *one single day* in any penitentiary, sorting sacks or otherwise. There are other errors, and it is almost impossible to avoid mistakes, particularly when there are many versions of a given event; but the old adage about the throwing of stones by residents in glass houses holds true here as elsewhere.

Raine, William McLeod, *Famous Sheriffs and Western Outlaws,* New York, 1929.

Another veteran writer of the history of the West, primarily for magazines, Raine's accounts must be respected. An excellent chapter on the Oklahoma outlaws is contained in this book.

Rainey, George, *The Cherokee Strip,* Enid, Okla., 1933.

This is an unpretentious personal account of life in the Territory, especially the Cherokee Strip. Of interest are Rainey's recollections of outlaws of the period, and the long battle by settlers, led by David L. Payne, to have the Oklahoma Territory opened for "free land."

Reddig, William M., *Tom's Town,* Philadelphia, 1947.

An excellent history of Kansas City during the Pendergast regime, with an account of the Union Station Massacre, some interesting side lights on that affair, and the pursuit and final death of Pretty Boy Floyd.

Rister, Carl Coke, *Land Hunger,* Norman, Okla., 1942.

The story of the campaign of David L. Payne, the Oklahoma Land Boomer, against all authority, to have the Territory opened to white settlement, including his brush with the courts in the person of Judge Isaac Parker.

——, *No Man's Land,* Norman, Okla., 1948.

That long strip called the Oklahoma Panhandle, extending west from the rest of the state, at one time was called "No Man's Land," because no law existed there. Dr. Rister gives a history of the area. One of its more interesting passages tells of how Chris Madsen singlehandedly put down an incipient riot for the purpose of breaking up a sitting of the first court at Beaver City, merely by announcing his identity to the would-be rioters, who promptly slunk away when they found out whom they were confronting.

Robinson, Charles, *The Kansas Conflict,* Lawrence, Kas., 1892.

This book, by the first governor of Kansas under statehood and during the first two years of the Civil War, has been too little read. Governor Robinson was one of the great leaders in the Free State movement, risking his life more than once, but he also was an eminently fair observer. He was present at the Lawrence Massacre, and was sickened by it, but his reputation for just dealing was such that the guerrillas did not molest him. At the time he said that raid was prompted by Jim Lane's depredations across the border in Missouri, and his analysis of Lane's character is most unflattering. Connelley attacks Robinson bitterly in his book on Quantrill, but Connelley was not on the ground when the events of the border wars took place, and Robinson was in the thick of them. Quite rare and hard to find.

Shirley, Glenn, *Law West of Fort Smith*, New York, 1957.
Using Harman's book, *Hell on the Border*, as his basic material, the author adds a great deal of additional and pertinent facts to the proceedings of Judge Parker's court, and the activities of the marshals who attempted to enforce the law in the old Indian Territory.

Shoemaker, Floyd C., *Missouri and Missourians* (2 vols.), Chicago, 1943.
A history of the state, including the border and outlaw troubles, by the respected secretary-emeritus of the Historical Society of Missouri.

——, *Missouri Day by Day* (2 vols.), Jefferson City, Mo., 1943.
An interesting day-by-day calendar of significant events in the history of Missouri, together with brief biographies of eminent Missourians, arranged by dates throughout the year.

Smith, C. Alphonso, *O. Henry Biography*, New York, 1916.
Contains some material on O. Henry's experiences with Al Jennings in Latin America and later in prison.

Sondern, Frederic, Jr., *Brotherhood of Evil: the Mafia*, New York, 1959.
A shocking account of the operations of the Mafia, the sinister criminal secret society from Sicily, which gained its chief power through the riches it gathered in illicit liquor sales during prohibition. This book tells of how, with its financing in the millions secure, the Mafia has turned its attention to narcotics, poisoning the children of America and creating thousands of criminals with heroin. Its international scope, the extortion rackets it carries on, its murders and other crimes, and its arrogant defiance of the authority of the United States government, all are related, in connection with the long campaign of the FBI to combat it, climaxed by the Apalachin arrests and disclosures.

Tilghman, Zoe A., *Outlaw Days*, Oklahoma City, 1926.
The wife of Bill Tilghman, the great deputy marshal, who kept her own records of her husband's life, in this short paper-bound booklet provides some valuable information on

the operations of the men who fought to uphold the law in the Territory, including dates and personal details hard to find elsewhere. Rascoe suggests that the booklet may have been written by someone else, under her name. If so, Mrs. Tilghman furnished the information. Very rare.

Wallace, William H., *Speeches and Writings,* Kansas City, 1914.
In his autobiography, which forms the last section of this rare and interesting book, Judge Wallace tells his experiences as a boy during the border warfare and under Order No. 11, his reportorial newspaper work while the James-Younger gang was in full career, and his relentless fight against the outlaws when he became a public prosecutor, including his trials of Bill Ryan and Frank James. Judge Wallace's life many times was in danger.

Whitehead, Don, *The FBI Story,* New York, 1956.
A history of the Federal Bureau of Investigation spanning its entire existence, written by a man who twice won Pulitzer prizes for distinguished reporting. It has a preface by J. Edgar Hoover setting forth the aims and policies of the great organization. Of especial interest, in relation to this book, are the chapters and notes dealing with the sometimes spectacular, always efficient work of the FBI agents against the outlaws and the underworld.

INDEX

N

O

P